The Forty-Nine Percent Majority:

The Male Sex Role

The Forty-Nine Percent Majority:

The Male Sex Role

Edited by

Deborah S. David

Northeastern University

and

Robert Brannon
(Order of the editorship was determined randomly)

Brooklyn College, City University of New York

ADDISON-WESLEY PUBLISHING COMPANY

Reading, Massachusetts • Menlo Park, California
London • Amsterdam • Don Mills, Ontario • Sydney

ISBN 0-201-01448-3
EFGHIJKLMN-HC-7987

To the memory of our fathers

Preface

The past few years have seen a surge of interest in the topic of sex roles — an interest fueled mainly by the Women's Liberation Movement and the reactions to it. As women have begun to call for a reevaluation of their position in society, a number of analyses have been undertaken to determine exactly what is the position of women and what changes will be necessary to achieve the status they desire.

But for the most part the male sex role has been ignored, and for both instructors of and students in courses on sex roles this has proved to be a source of ongoing frustration. Although a small volume of work on the male role has begun to appear in both academic and journalistic sources, little of the published material is easily accessible to undergraduate students. Indeed, this reader grew out of the experience of one of the editors in teaching a course "Male and Female in American Society," where one found numerous books on women, but none on men — a situation which was both an embarrassment and a handicap. Furthermore, it was felt that a book which was interdisciplinary — drawing on the backgrounds of a sociologist and a psychologist, one female, one male — would offer a wider perspective on the male role than one by a single editor.

In selecting articles for this volume, we were confronted with the task of essentially defining a new area of study, and one that does not yet have a core of work that can be considered essential for inclusion. Many of the pieces that describe the male role are per-

viii   Preface

sonal accounts of one man's experience. While these are fascinating
to read and point to the problems facing American men, they lack
the rigor of more scholarly work. In reviewing the literature of the
social sciences, very little appears on the male role as such; there is,
however, material relevant to the male role in the more traditional
areas of these disciplines, e.g., social stratification, small group
dynamics, role theory, etc. The selections we have included reflect
these limitations while underscoring the need for more theory and
research in the area of the male role. We hope that in the next
several years more systematic study of the male role will be undertaken.

This collection is organized into three parts. The introduction
presents the conceptual model of the male role which we developed,
and it is this model that is used to organize the readings in Part I,
which form the core of the book. Part II presents selections illustrat-
ing the way in which men in America learn the role, while Part III is
designed to explore the changes occurring in the role today and the
possible directions for future change.

We would especially like to thank Joseph Pleck, our friend and
colleague, for the invaluable help he so generously gave us. We also
appreciate the assistance given us by our students Deborah Coultas,
Patti Geier, Diane Noble, Jessica Schein, and Marlene Steinberg
during the initial review of the literature.

The sociology editor would like to express appreciation to the
Department of Sociology and to its chairperson, Deborah Offen-
bacher, for facilitating the production of this book. A debt of
gratitude is owed to other friends and colleagues, Lucy Komisar,
Gregory Lehne, Judith Lorber, Constance Hammett Poster, and
Laurel Walum for both intellectual and personal contributions to this
volume. Finally, this manuscript would never have reached its final
phase without the secretarial assistance of Charlotte Fisher and
Josie Loos.

The psychology editor would like to express appreciation to the
following: Warren Farrell and Marc Feigen Fasteau for their contributions to the field of the male sex role, so helpful in the course of
this work; Sidney Miller, whose life and thought has proved inspirational; Suellen Ward, Joanne Brannon, Jim Harrison, Art Reber,
David Gangsei, Joan Breibart, Kathy Grady, and Susan Lee for
reading and criticizing various portions of the manuscript; Ray
Montemayor, Sheldon Feldman, Sandy Haber, Sylvia Miller,

Dorothy Tennov, Marianna Brannon, Nechama Liss-Levinson, Billy Levinson, Judith Rose Sanders, Shelley Edelman, Robert Gould, Rob White, Bob Clark, Jim Levine, Esther Rosenberg, and Phil Shaver for other useful and constructive suggestions; Peter Grams, Sharon Lord, Carol Tavris, Karl White, Nancy Henley, Mimi Keifer, Ursie Farrell, Al Krakow, Bernard Seidenberg, Alvin Snadowsky, Glen Hass, Judy Waters, Jo-Ann Evans Gardner, Paul Siudzinsky, Fredrika Clare, Robert Fein, Joyce Borkin, Tom Peele, David Sanders, Roberta Unger, Marti Fager, Shelley Juran, and Arthur Kurtz for discussions over the last few years which illuminated and clarified some of the issues explored here.

Brooklyn, New York
November 1975

D.S.D.
R.B.

Contents

**Part II
Learning the Role**

**Part III
Changing the Role**

The Male Sex Role:
Our Culture's Blueprint
of Manhood,
and What it's Done for us Lately

By the latest count there are approximately 2,439,028 books currently in print devoted largely or entirely to psychology, sociology, anthropology, and other social sciences.* Browsing in the New York Public Library I find whole aisles of books about racial prejudice, juvenile delinquency, personality theory, learning, attitude change, speech defects, sexual deviations. There's an impressive and scholarly book concerned with public attitudes toward the profession of dentistry; an account of cross-cousin speech among the Tikopia; a report on prisons and jails in the state of New Jersey.

But there are no books on the male sex role, no entries of: "Sex Role–Male" in the index of any textbook I pull from the shelves.† Between "Maladjustment" and "Management" — nothing. Apparently this topic I'm interested in is so obscure, unimportant, or self-evident that it merits no serious attention from the thousands of scholars and researchers busily engaged in the struggle to understand the deepest of all mysteries, human behavior.

The purpose of this essay, and indeed this book, is to present an argument which almost every reader will find incredible — at first. Yet I believe that it's true, and the more I think about it the surer I become. This idea is that human sex roles of male and female, and specifically the male role itself, have shaped and molded the social structure and social world we live in more deeply and extensively than any other single influence one could name.

---

* Office of Information, Library of Congress of The United States, Washington, D.C.
† Since this writing, I am glad to report, they have begun to appear.

To argue that a factor which most social scientists have never discussed or even thought about could be so enormously important, one needs a rather unusual explanation. I think there's a very simple one. There is an old folk saying that "The fish will be the last to discover the ocean." I believe that the male sex role has been able to elude scientific study — or even notice — because, rather than in spite of, its enormous and pervasive influence on the knowledge, thoughts, attitudes, and assumptions of every person who has grown up under its influence. Our culture has been dominated by males for as long as records exist, and every man and woman alive today has grown to maturity and developed styles of thought and stores of knowledge while as deeply immersed in the values, concerns, and emphases of the male sex role as fish in the depths of the ocean. The role's values permeate and affect what we notice and what we remember about people, what we know about the world, what we've heard about the past, what we think is "human nature," the questions we think to ask. Our recorded history is almost literally His-Story, full of male accomplishments, formal offices held, wars fought. Social scientists haven't actually studied the whole range of all human behavior, only the parts that somehow "seemed important." Veblen's famous book *The Theory of The Leisure Class* might have been called a theory of the male leisure class, since wives are briefly discussed along with servants, estates, possessions, and other symbols of prosperity. Robin Williams' famous volume, *American Society*, is largely an account of American male society; the examples are innumerable.

From these and a thousand other reports and studies we know a mountain of facts about American males. Yet with all that is known about the comings and goings of men, the deeper reasons for their actions often seem mysterious. As one scholar of war said, "We know everything about war — except why." The same might be said of competition, conspicuous waste, status striving, homophobia, and rape, to name just a few other issues which have perplexed thoughtful people. We have vast amounts of data about the good and bad things men do, but the deeper question of their motives has usually been answered, if at all, with "that just seems to be human nature."

Yet social scientists have continued to wonder about the "why," and in recent years the search for the origins of human behavior patterns has intensified. Scholars have speculated endlessly about the habits of prehistoric man, poked in the ashes of campfires dead a million years, peered through glass-bottomed boats at the movements of coral-reef fish, watched troops of grazing baboons through binoculars, and slaughtered countless thousands of white rats. They've examined the brains of dead luminaries, strained and tested the blood of convicts, embryos, and college students, and focused the most powerful microscopes ever built on the curiously unrevealing chromosomes of the human cell.

Yet I and many other young social scientists now believe that the most promising answer to most questions about human behavior lies not in our genes, or in our hormones, or in the faded drawings in some prehistoric cave. To borrow the metaphor of Yeats, we must learn "to tell the dancer from the dance." That life-long and compelling "dance," the invisible but almost irresistible social patterns of pressure which shape and direct the behavior of every man and every woman, is the subject of this book.

Ironically, social scientists "discovered" the male sex role only because a few years ago a small number of American women began to think about, and carefully study, the lives of women. A feminist consciousness had existed before, of course, both in this country and abroad, but around 1965 it suddenly flickered to life again, this time with a new intensity and urgency. The same things had happened to so many, many women — and though the personal details differed as endlessly and randomly as autumn leaves, there were themes which connected many lives, variations on simple patterns, stories which repeated again and again beneath the uniqueness of each woman's experience. Gradually some themes began to be seen: patterns of economic and emotional dependence on men; of cultivating the traits men valued and extinguishing others; of helping and nurturing but not achieving for oneself; of nagging self-doubt and, beneath the warm friendships, an isolation.* What they described all together was a loose sort of "blueprint" for what a woman was supposed to be, to want, to be good at, to be unsuited for. There was a collection of female stereotypes — Betty Crocker and Gracie Allen, Jayne Mansfield and Annabel Lee — which at first seemed laughably different, yet hung together in some deeper way: different paths which eventually led toward the same goals, the same needs.

---

* See for example the original works by Friedan, 1963; Freeman, 1970; Weisstein, 1970; Bird, 1968; Morgan, 1970; Bem and Bem, 1970; Millet, 1970; Salzman-Webb, 1970; Dixon, 1969.

All together, this cultural blueprint become known as the "female sex role," and in the late 1960's and early 1970's its outlines gradually emerged, first in and through women's consciousness-raising groups and underground feminist writers, then to the popular press and the mass media, and finally to the level of a general public awareness.

At some point along the way a few feminist writers began to wonder: Might there not also be a "male sex role"; a distinctly male, as opposed to general human, way of thinking and acting; a male blueprint composed of culturally encouraged goals, needs, and secret insecurities? To a limited extent the feminist movement had already discovered what was male by simple contrast with what was female. If women were *passive*, men must be *aggressive* in comparison. If women lacked confidence, men must therefore be confident. But something more than a mirror image was, and is, needed; surely there are dynamics and conflicts which are distinctly male, which cannot be inferred solely by looking at women.

If so, they certainly do not form a simple pattern. The unwritten guidelines for manhood must have been taking form even as the glaciers receded, and probably appeared first in simple nomadic hunting societies. They evolved and grew more specialized and complex as farms, cities, firearms, factories, corporations and computers successively appeared. It apparently still means something today to say of someone "Now there's a real man!" but what exactly does it mean? What threads of common image, accomplishment, or style somehow connect such diverse symbols as John Wayne, Humphrey Bogart, Malcolm X, Lou Gehrig, Mike Fink, John Mitchell, James Bond, Daniel Ellsberg, George Wallace, Paul Bunyan, Father Berrigan, Robert Taft, Marlon Brando, John F. Kennedy, George Patton, I. F. Stone, Billy the Kid, Sergeant Joe Friday, John Foster Dulles, Neal Cassidy, John Galt, and The Incredible Hulk? Does it make sense to speak of a "male sex role" if all of these represent "real men" in at least someone's eyes?

This is the major question I will grapple with in this essay, the underlying themes which define our culture's particular conception of masculinity. The answers I'll propose will not be totally satisfactory. It is difficult for fish to study the ocean, I've discovered, even when we know it's there. Its values and assumptions have so infiltrated our minds that we're almost blind to them; only gradually and imperfectly can we disentangle them and give them names.

In a sense this is also a personal story. I have gradually come to realize that I, with every other man I know, have been limited and diverted from whatever our real potential might have been by the prefabricated mold of the male sex role. I do not say "oppressed," for to do so would suggest to many people a complaint about "the burden of power." White adult males obviously possess enormous power and privilege in comparison with blacks, women, children, and other minorities in our society; in any fair accounting we are, and always have been, the oppressors of others. But such comparisons, true as they are, are not the only truths that matter. It is worth remembering that wounds are wounds, and that literally hundreds of millions of human beings who are male have been wounded — are wounding themselves — with the cruel demands we'll discuss in these pages. And there's another point. In the particular case of the male sex role, the "wounded list" includes virtually everyone who has ever lived in our male-dominated society. But before we get to these issues, we must briefly examine the basic concept of role behavior, which is the key to this whole book.

THE SCIENTIFIC CONCEPT OF ROLE

The term *role* was first borrowed by social scientists from the language of the theatre (from the French *role*, referring to the "roll" of paper containing an actor's part), and much of its scientific meaning is suggested by the theatrical analogy. The most basic point is that a role is not the same as the person who is performing it at the moment. The role of "Hamlet" has existed for over 350 years and the noble, moody prince has been played by countless actors long deceased; it will be played by others who are not yet born. Social roles are also different from the person who plays them at any given time, though the individual is rarely so conscious of the role playing as an actor with a script.

A role may be broadly defined as: *any pattern of behaviors which a given individual in a specified (set of) situation(s) is both: (1) expected and (2) encouraged and/or trained to perform*. Roles are closely related to the concept of "stereotype," but there is an important difference. Stereotypes are cultural expectancies for people in certain categories and situations, but without the element of active encouragement by others. (Expectations do sometimes become self-fulfilling, so the distinction is not always a sharp one.) There are social stereotypes about Cadillac owners, redheads, and

Frenchmen, but we don't normally try to encourage people in these categories to live up to the stereotype, and are often pleased if they don't.

The role concept applies with almost equal logic to very simple behavior patterns and to those which may span a lifetime. The roles of "parent" and "child" can last an indefinite time; they involve elaborate reciprocal patterns of rights and obligations. The role of "person standing in line" is a brief and simple one which we play automatically, yet even this role must be *learned*. One must stand more or less behind the last person already in line, not so close as to touch but not so far as to leave a large gap, wait until the line moves ahead, and be reasonably quiet.

Most social roles involve very few exact behaviors. More often they consist of clear but general guidelines as to how to conduct oneself. Most of us have a definite idea of how a "house guest" or a "playboy" is supposed to act, even if we can't state an exact list of requirements. There is a range of acceptable performances, just as a stage role may be "interpreted" differently by different actors.

Theatrical roles are written by playwrights and actors memorize them line by line; how do people learn social roles? Children learn the broad outlines of most roles through simple observation of adults. Books, movies and television convey still more information. Parents both unconsciously model and directly teach a wide variety of roles, sometimes giving specific instructions, like a director on a set: "Not like that, son, — like *this*." As individuals begin to play more elaborate social roles they learn more (especially the finer points) from others already in the role. The college sophomore notices how other students dress and speak; the new man on a construction job learns from older hands how hard to work, what to gripe about, even what to bring in his lunch box.

Roles are also learned from people who are playing "complementary" parts. Like the various roles in a theatrical drama, social roles are often interdependent; each has meaning only with respect to the complementary roles. There simply cannot be wives without husbands, teachers without students, leaders without followers. The opportunity for each to play their role depends on others playing theirs. Messages about how to act can come in many forms: compliments for "good" behavior, vocal admiration of others who are playing the role properly, rebukes and aloofness, and carefully proper performance of one's own role, which signals to the errant partner, "Now see, *this* is my part, the matching behavior is what I expect from you."

SEX AS A LEARNED SOCIAL ROLE

By far the most complex, demanding, and all-involving role that members of our culture must ever learn to play is that of male or female. "Casting" takes place immediately at birth, after a quick biological inspection, and the role of "female" or "male" is assigned. It is an assignment that will last one's entire lifetime and affect virtually everything one ever does. A large part of the next 20 years or so will be spent in gradually learning and perfecting one's assigned sex-role; slowly memorizing what a "young lady" should do and should not do, how a "little man" should react in each of a million frightening situations . . . practicing, practicing, playing house, playing cowboys, practicing, . . . and often crying in confusion and frustration at the baffling and seemingly endless task.

Children often confuse sex roles, and make "inappropriate" choices. When a little girl announces that she plans to be a fireman, adults merely smile. They know she doesn't yet have it right, but they're not worried. By the time it matters, she will have learned her sex role so thoroughly that it simply will never occur to her to be a fireman. In the meantime she has other things to learn: there are new dolls to play with and take care of, pretty clothes to try on, shiny black patent-leather shoes — and as a special reward she may help mommy with housework and stir the batter in the big white bowl. No one ever really tells her to be "domestic" or "esthetic" or "maternal" — *but she's learning*.

A little boy meanwhile is learning other things. Balls and bats have miraculously appeared to play with, realistic toy pistols, and trains, blocks, and marbles. The shoes he finds in his closet are sturdy enough to take a lot of wear, and just right for running. One day there is an old tire hanging by a rope from a tree in the back yard, just right for swinging. No one ever really tells him to be "active" or "aggressive" or "competitive" *but somehow, he's learning*.

The groundwork for proper sex-role behavior is laid during these childhood years, but there is still a certain tolerance for mis-

takes, and different levels of maturity. With the arrival of adolescence the game rather suddenly becomes real. Teenagers must begin
to perform sex roles (sometimes exaggerated caricatures of the adult
roles) correctly, or face a kind of cruelty and ridicule from each
other which has few human counterparts — and which most adults
have mercifully forgotten. How one *dresses, speaks, looks, walks,
eats, relaxes — everything suddenly matters*. "Look at how Sam
throws a ball! Hey, throw it here, Samantha!" "Watch how Betty
walks; she looks like a horse!" Cruel, cutting remarks, hurts that
may last for a lifetime . . . and nowhere to hide. The teenager can
retreat to home and parents but not for long; tomorrow, the same
snickering, judging schoolmates must be faced.

Little wonder that detailed sex-role learning takes place fast in
adolescence, and remarkably uncritically. Exactly why is it that girls
eat in small bites? Why do boys not like poetry? *Who cares*, just get
it right! Why is it that boys "like sex" and girls don't? Never mind.
Just get it right, or else! Why do girls wear make-up? Boys hold
doors? Girls wait to be called? Boys drive the car? We are too busy
learning these never-ending rules to question them. The crucial
practicing of sex-role behaviors takes place during these anxiety-
filled years, and personalities emerge and begin to harden around
habits and styles adopted by teenagers wanting desperately to fit in,
to be liked and accepted by their equally anxious classmates. The
deeper cultural images of maleness and femaleness are seldom ar-
ticulated. Their assumptions are implicit however, for they hold
together and make whatever sense there is to the welter of specific
rules and customs. Males are strong, females are weak; males are
aggressive, females are passive; males are coarse, and direct,
females sweet, and emotional. In time the exaggerated rigidity of
teenage sex roles will soften and mellow, but these basic role-
concepts remain embedded in the knowledge and assumptions of
virtually every member of our culture. Men are just "naturally" one
way, and women another; how could it be otherwise?

It comes as a surprise to most Americans to learn that in other
societies what we so automatically assume is "male" may not be
viewed as male at all. In a study of three societies in New Guinea,
anthropologist Margaret Mead (1935) described three patterns of
sex-appropriate behavior and personality which are in striking contrast to those assumed by Americans. Among the mountain-dwelling

people known as the Arapesh, both sexes aspire to a pattern which strongly resembles the personality associated with the female role in our culture. Both male and female Arapesh tend to be passive, cooperative, peaceful, and greatly concerned with nourishing and growing living things. The father as well as the mother is said to "bear a child"; it is believed that only the continual caring and participation of the father can make a child grow in the mother's womb or continue to healthy adulthood. Sexual interest is relatively low, and the preferred sexual style is passive for both sexes. The role of authority figure is repugnant to both women and men. Leaders are selected during childhood and specifically trained to be more assertive; otherwise there might be no takers for leadership positions in the tribe.

Less than 80 miles from the Arapesh dwell the Mundugumor, who present a remarkable contrast in temperament and behavior. For both males and females the ideal is an aggressive and belligerent style which almost parodies our own male sex role. "Both men and women," the anthropologist discovered, "are expected to be violent, competitive, aggressively sexed, jealous, and ready to see and avenge insult, delighting in display, in action, in fighting" (Mead, 1968, p. 213). Hostility and aggressiveness are omnipresent and pervade the whole social order, giving it a constantly competitive and violent atmosphere. The mother spends little time with her offspring, nursing them as seldom as possible, weaning them early and abruptly.

A third tribe in this area of New Guinea is the Tchambuli, who have preferred traits which differ sharply for the sexes, but along lines essentially *opposite* to our own. Males are expected to be sensitive, artistic, nervous, gossipy, fond of adornment, and emotionally dependent. The Tchambuli male, with "his delicately arranged curls," his "flying fox skin highly ornamented with shells, his mincing step and self-conscious mein" lives mainly for art and sees the world as an audience for his flute-playing, dancing, carving, and skill at creating costumes.

Tchambuli females must be competent, dominating, practical, and efficient; they actually run almost all of the important domestic and economic institutions. Females are also the sexual aggressors; the male is less interested in sex, and more passive: ". . . he holds his breath and hopes" (*Ibid.*, p. 241).

When we add to these three societies the case of our own, in which males are expected to be aggressive and dominant, and females sensitive and passive, it becomes clear that every major combination of roles is represented in human cultures. Mead's provocative conclusion was that:

Many, if not all, of the personality traits which we have called masculine or feminine are as lightly linked to sex as are the clothing, the manners, and the form of head-dress that a society at a given period assigns to either sex . . . the evidence is overwhelmingly in favor of social conditioning.

(*Ibid.*, p. 260)

The discovery that most of what we associate with being male or female is actually a learned social role does not mean that biology is totally irrelevant. Prior to acquiring the appropriate role there may be innate differences among individuals which make learning a certain role more difficult for some than others. The culture acts, however, to encourage some human potentials and suppress others, and most human beings seem to be flexible enough to learn whatever the culture dictates, at least reasonably well. The Tchambuli male who finds himself inclined to be calm, practical, and unartistic will have doubts about his "manliness," and try to cultivate the more masculine traits of nervousness and esthetic appreciation. The American male who is naturally shy or passive will often realize that these qualities are not considered manly and try to either change or compensate for them. Both are likely to succeed, for whatever the sex-role profile of a given culture, most people are able to approximate it by the time they reach adulthood.

A strong indication of the predominant power of social role-learning over natural and biological factors may be found in the cases of occasional individuals who were mistakenly identified at birth due to physical abnormalities and raised in the sex-role category opposite to that of their primary biological make-up. Money and Ehrhardt (1972) studied a number of these individuals and concluded that sex-role identification and satisfaction were not correlated with chromosomal, gonadal, hormonal, or external genital characteristics, but were very strongly related to being *raised* as a member of one or the other sexual classifications. In such cases they report that surgery to alter the biological sex features is more successful than trying to change the effects of socialization.

DIMENSIONS OF THE MALE SEX ROLE

Now let's return to the specifics of the male sex role in our own culture. We already know some of the broad outlines, but there are seeming inconsistencies in the common-sense view of masculinity. One senses that there is not one ideal image of the "real man" in our society but several. Consider for example the following male stereotypes, each of which in one way or another strikes us as distinctively masculine:

- The football player; big, tough, and rugged, though not precisely a towering intellect;
- The jet-set playboy; usually sighted in expensive restaurants or fast convertibles, accompanied by a beautiful woman (whom he's ignoring);
- The blue-collar brawler; a quick temper with fists to match; nobody better try to push *him* around;
- The big-shot businessman; the Babbitt traveling salesman Rotary Club booster type of expansive back-slapper;
- The Don Juan; he's smooth, smoldering, and totally irresistible to women; a super-stud on the prowl;
- The strong, simple working man; he's honest, solid, direct, and hard-working;
- The Truly Great Man; a statesman, prophet, scientist, deep-thinker, awesome genius.

They don't look, act, or sound very much alike, but somehow these images all seem distinctively masculine to at least some of us. Does this mean that the male role is so infinitely flexible that anything a man does can seem "manly"? No; most male images and examples are by no means as masculine as these selected examples. The image of the "average guy," the man-in-the-street, is not especially masculine; many successful, familiar, and popular male personalities seem anything but manly.

The answer is that the male role is demanding but, except on a few points, not very specific. There seem to be several basic routes, and many specific variations, to fulfilling the minimum demands of the role. A man can in some sense choose what to "specialize" in — how to project a viable masculine image, choosing from among the options the role provides. In choosing, he is likely to be influenced by his age, class, ethnic subgroup, and physique, as well as individual talents and capacities. There are many acceptable combinations and certain styles become "fads" after they're popularized by movie stars or public personalities. As with other cultural fashions, there are changes over time. Beneath all the permutations, however, are a small number of basic themes which pervade and ultimately define the male sex role. I believe that there are four such general themes, or dimensions, which underlie the male sex role we see in our culture. Each has subparts and complexities and at some points they overlap, but the following four themes seem to comprise the core requirements of the role:

1. No Sissy Stuff: The stigma of all stereotyped feminine characteristics and qualities, including openness and vulnerability.

2. The Big Wheel: Success, status, and the need to be looked up to.

3. The Sturdy Oak: A manly air of toughness, confidence, and self-reliance.

4. Give 'Em Hell!: The aura of aggression, violence, and daring.

There may seem to be a mechanistic quality to such an inflexible listing, and a model which proposes to examine sex roles in terms of four (or any other number of) components. Obviously such a model overstates what is definitely known about sex roles. Remember also that there are many human traits and characteristics (e.g. generosity, loyalty), which are not strongly associated with either male or female sex roles. Some widely admired male images — *Zorba The Greek*, or Sam-the-Lion in *The Last Picture Show* are good examples — combine masculine qualities with unmasculine ones in a very appealing way. But our focus here is on the pure case, the purely masculine part of a man's image. This discussion is focused primarily on the male role in the present day United States. Much of it is relevant to other areas of Western culture, but there are also national variations which we won't be able to consider here.

Finally, a note about the kinds of evidence we shall consider. As a behavioral scientist I look for and prefer experimental data where it's available. Only a controlled experiment can definitively prove causal relationships between variables (Cronbach, 1957; Campbell & Stanley, 1963). However, such evidence is necessarily limited to factors which can be manipulated by the experimenter. Observational and correlational studies are less conclusive, but have greater scope, for nature has been experimenting since the dawn of time on a far grander scale than man can contemplate. By carefully studying covariations among events social scientists can extend the scope of science far beyond the controlled certainty of the laboratory.

Writers and novelists have no "controls" at all, but sometimes they show enormous powers of analysis. It has often been observed that novelists are among the greatest psychologists. Freud acknowledged the genius of those writers who can draw "from the whirlpool of their emotions the deepest truths, to which we others have to force our way"; "they draw on sources not yet accessible to science" (quoted in Stone and Stone, 1966). Men and masculinity have provided the subject matter for countless great writers in all ages. So to explore this familiar but strangely uncharted domain of masculinity, we'll consider material and insights from all these sources.

1. No Sissy Stuff: the Stigma of Anything Vaguely Feminine.

The earliest lesson: Don't be like girls, kid, be like . . . like . . . well, not like girls.   Children of both sexes initially identify most strongly with their mothers, the usual caretakers of infants and children (Hartley, 1959; Lynn, 1969; Schaffer and Emerson, 1964). As a child gradually becomes aware that there are two adult sexes, one of which he or she will grow up to be, the first major difference in the psychological development of males and females takes place. While the young female may continue to identify with her mother, the boy must gradually switch to a new source of identification, a process often made difficult by the absence of the father during daytime hours:

The girl has her same-sex parental model for identification with her more hours per day than the boy has his same-sex model with him. Even when home, the father does not usually participate in as many intimate activities with the child as does the mother, e.g., preparation for bed and toileting . . . Despite the shortage of male models for direct imitation, a somewhat stereotyped and conventional masculine role is spelled out for the boy, often by his mother, women teachers, and peers in the absence of his father and male models . . . Consequently, males tend to identify with a culturally defined masculine role, whereas females tend to identify with their mothers.

(Lynn, 1969, pp. 24–26)

Since boys must learn to perform a masculine role for which there are few models in their immediate environment, one might expect that adults would be relatively tolerant of early mistakes. The reality is that parents are substantially more concerned that boys conform to the male role than girls to the female; both parents, but especially fathers, express substantial displeasure when boys display "feminine" qualities (Lansky, 1967; Goodenough, 1957). Summarizing a number of studies of preschool children, Hartley concludes:

Demands that boys conform to social notions of what is manly come much earlier and are enforced with much more vigor than similar attitudes with respect to girls . . . and at an early age, when they are least able to understand either the reasons for or the nature of the demands. Moreover, these demands are frequently enforced harshly, impressing the small boy with the danger of deviating from them, while he does not quite understand what they are.

(Hartley, 1959, p. 458)

Surrounded by adult females, offered few positive images of what he is expected to be, but chastised and sometimes shamed for being a "sissy" if he emulates girls and women, the young male child is likely to feel:

. . . an anxiety which frequently expresses itself in over-straining to be masculine, in virtual panic at being caught doing anything traditionally defined as feminine, and in hostility toward anything even hinting at "femininity," including females themselves.

(*Ibid.,* p. 458)

This terror of being a sissy, at an age when the child can hardly understand the meaning of that accusation, let alone ignore it, apparently leaves a deep wound in the psyche of many males. It has a clear embodiment in the adult male sex role:

A "real man" must never, never resemble women, or display strongly stereotyped feminine characteristics. This simple rule is applied to almost every aspect of life and explains a great deal about what is and isn't considered masculine. Women are smaller, have less hair and higher-pitched voices, so boys lucky enough to be big, hairy, and deep-voiced start off with an advantage. People automatically describe such males as more masculine (Gilkinson, 1937). "Develop a deep, manly voice," advises the Charles Atlas home improvement course, "and watch your confidence improve."

Women are thought to be neat and tidy, so a man who seems too fastidious will draw wise-cracks. Will Rogers' mother tried scolding and begging her defiant youngster to keep his shirt tail in, all to no avail. Finally she found a sure-fire method: she simply sewed a patch of frilly white lace to the tail of every shirt he owned.

Women wear cosmetics and sweet-smelling toilet waters too, so no two-fisted man would be caught dead in that junk. "Men are actually hungry to buy scents and cosmetics," one product-researcher confided, "But the product has to have a name like Command, Tackle, Brut, Bullwhip, or Hai Karate, and have FOR MEN stamped all over the goddam bottle." (One favorite men's scent was originally a women's cologne — until it was renamed *English Leather*.) When teen-agers first began to wear their hair longer in the late 1960's, most older men were incredulous, sometimes outraged. This was no harmless fad . . . those kids look like . . . like . . . well, like women!

The stigma of femaleness applies to almost everything: vocabulary, food, hobbies, and even choice of a profession. Pastimes such as knitting, flower arranging, and needlepoint are so strongly regarded as feminine that it made the news when a professional football player (a linesman, at that) revealed his hobby of *needlepoint*. "Aren't you afraid people will think you're a sissy?" an incredulous reporter asked the 230-pound giant. Art, poetry, music, and virtually all "fine arts" are seen as somewhat feminine pursuits; men who enjoy, create, or even write about these things are widely assumed to be less manly than men who ignore them. Male ballet dancers train harder and are actually in better physical shape than the average professional football player (Chass, 1974), yet their masculinity is highly suspect to most American males. Sports writers, coaches, truck drivers, engineers, and military men, in contrast, are automatically seen as masculine regardless of their physical condition. Their professions place them safely in a man's world — far away from anything that might interest a woman. The threat to this masculine isolation probably explains more of the opposition to women's attempts to enter professional sports than the economic competition reasons usually cited.

If everything associated with females is so potentially stigmatizing, it's not hard to guess how much real intimacy with women themselves a manly man is expected to want. Writing about the social life of men in the typical Western adventure movie, Manville concludes:

Girls are nice to take your hat off to on Sunday morning when you meet one of them on her way to church, and there's another kind of lady with whom you enjoy a drink in the saloon on a Saturday night when you're ready for fun . . . But a woman as a friend, or deeply moving lover, or equal-partner wife? Never!

(Manville, 1969)

Men who are most intensely concerned with their own masculinity seldom desire close contact with women. "A highly intelligent man should take a primitive woman," wrote another hard-driving bully-boy, Adolph Hitler; "Imagine if on top of everything else I had a woman who interfered with my work." (cf. Spiegelman and Schneider, 1974)

Openness and Vulnerability Women are permitted and even expected to be "emotional;" they're allowed to show when they're feeling anxious, depressed, frightened, happy, loving, and so forth. This kind of openness about feelings, especially ones which cast the feeler in a weak or "unfavorable" light, is strongly prohibited for men. It's not that men can never show *any* emotions. Open displays of anger, contempt, impatience, hostility or cynicism, are not difficult for most men. But emotions suggesting vulnerability, and even extremely positive feeling such as love, tenderness, and trust are almost never acceptable.

Try to imagine two rugged he-men standing eye to eye and saying: "I've been so upset since we had that argument I could hardly sleep last night. Are you sure you're really not mad at me?" "Heck, Jim, you mean so much to me, I get so much from our friendship . . . I was just afraid that you'd hold a grudge against me." Men do have these emotions and feelings, but we try like hell never to show them. When a male friend does start to say something like that, there are husky cries of "Get a grip on yourself," "Pull yourself together, man," or "Stiff upper lip, old boy."

Some men become so skilled at hiding feelings that their wives and closest friends don't know when they're scared, anxious, depressed, or in pain. They didn't get to be that way accidentally though. Marc Fasteau remembers consciously practicing the style while in college:

I tried to maintain a flat, even tone in conversation. I discussed only issues, the larger the better. I worried about every instance of doubt, of self-consciousness, of emotion, of not being in control of groups I was in. The men I admired seemed to feel none of these things. Since I did, how could I play the game?

(Fasteau, 1974, p. 125)

Probably no action is more stereotypically feminine or humiliating for a man than crying. One businessman who had an outstanding performance record with his company learned at an executive meeting that a project he had spent a year developing was being taken over by someone else, for fairly arbitrary reasons; he broke down and cried. He was told later that he was totally discredited with his colleagues, had no future with the company, and should look for another job. (Fasteau, 1974, p. 123)

Jourard (1971) has developed an index of how much personal information people reveal to others with whom they interact. He finds that men reveal far less than women, no matter who the audience, and that both sexes reveal less to men than to women. Revealing yourself to a man can be dangerous.

Once as a freshman in college I found myself sitting with a stranger in the college cafeteria. I had been undergoing a lot of changes in my thinking about religion that year, and I guess I was in a talkative mood, because I told him all about it: what I'd believed until recently, and the changes I was going through. "Very interesting," he said, puffing on his cigarette with a bored, distant look; not one word about his own religious doubts, or convictions. I felt like such a damn fool it was all I could do to get through the meal and leave the table.

Years later, in a men's consciousness-raising group, I met a man who was incredibly open about his feelings. He could and did say that he loved our group, and what it had meant in his life, and even — get this! — how much he *cared* about another man, right to his face! We had a lot of other things in common and I was enormously drawn to him — but hell! Didn't he know how "uncool" that was? When he would reveal himself in that way, I would involuntarily look at the floor and squirm in embarrassment. I'd like to say I don't react that way to men any more — but I can't.

Male Friendship and the (Gulp!) Unspoken Fear   When men want to express affection to one another, their means are rather limited. In the place of directness, we've developed ritualized gestures which are safer, and a lot more ambiguous; often in fact they parody hostility and aggression. Two old friends will celebrate their reunion by slugging each other on the arm. Instead of "I hope you make a good impression today," we say "Give 'em hell."

The unspoken fear which bedevils friendships between men is, of course, the fear of being seen as a homosexual. Surveys have shown that a majority of all men have been worried about being latent homosexuals at some point in their lives. Almost 40% told Kinsey they had actually had what they thought was a homosexual experience since adolescence, yet their descriptions of these events sounded more friendly than erotic (Kinsey, Pomeroy, and Martin, 1948). Fears of being a latent homosexual are many times more common among men than among women (Hoffman, 1969). Why?

The answer is that the male role so totally prohibits tenderness and affection toward members of the same sex that few men can live a normal lifetime without experiencing supposedly forbidden feelings. Many men inevitably find that they care deeply for — and even love — another man, but believe these warm feelings abnormal and unnatural. Thus the secret, gnawing fear that "I must be one of *those* . . ."

Like the majority of men (as I was greatly relieved to find out later!), I secretly feared at one time in my life that I was a "latent homosexual." In college the affection and caring I felt for my three roommates worried me, because I could sense that it wasn't really *all that* different from the affection I felt for the girlfriends I knew best and liked most. If the truth be known, I cared more genuinely for my male friends at this time than for any female I knew. What's worse, when we were sprawled out somewhere watching T.V. or reading, and our legs or arms would touch comfortably, it was . . . well, pleasant! Once one of my roommates and I were lying on our old sofa, talking and drinking beer. For some reason — as I recall there wasn't much room — he put his head in my lap with some wisecrack about getting comfortable. We continued talking. But I felt a closeness, a sort of emotional bond that hadn't been there before. And . . . after a while, I felt a very real desire to lightly stroke his hair, the way I would have done had he been a woman. Finally, I said something brilliant, like "Get off me you lazy sonofabitch, you're gettin' heavy."

That seems pretty stupid now, but I don't think my fears were unusual, or my caution unjustified. Men do not take "mistakes" of this sort lightly.

2. The Big Wheel: Success, Status, and the Need to be Looked Up to.

A man can't go out the way he came in, Ben; a man has got to add up to something!

(Willie Loman in *Death of a Salesman*, Miller, 1971)

One of the most basic routes to manhood in our society is to be a success: to command respect and be looked up to for what one can do or has achieved. There are several basic ways to accomplish this, but by definition this kind of status is a limited commodity which not every man can achieve.

Wealth and Fame The most visible and sought-after source of status in our society is what we loosely refer to as "being a success." Success is usually defined in terms of occupational prestige and achievement, wealth, fame, power, and visible positions of leadership. These things usually tend to be correlated; however, *extremely* high standing on any one of them seems to have a very special status quality. The tycoon, the congressman, the movie star, and the sports hero enjoy an automatic kind of status, and will often be viewed as masculine role-models on this basis alone. There's something ineffably masculine about the word "millionaire," or even "the richest man in town." It's also quite helpful to be President of the United States, author of a best-selling novel, or even conductor of a symphony orchestra. Really massive doses of success at almost *anything*, in fact, seem so inherently manly that the "World's Greatest" artist, pianist, chef, hair-dresser, or tiddlywink player is to some extent protected from the taint of unmasculine activity which surrounds less successful members of his profession. Intellectual prominence is also valuable in the right circles, but for most people nothing succeeds quite so well as money. "If Karl, instead of writing a lot about capital, had made a lot of it," said Anna Marx about her famous son, "it would have been much better." (Spiegelman and Schneider, 1974, p. 49)

The Symbols of Success Simply being a doctor, lawyer, or moderately successful businessman is enough to qualify as success in most social circles. A man who has launched a successful career and is earning an impressive salary can usually enjoy the respect of his family, friends, relatives, co-workers, employees — everyone who is *aware* of his accomplishments. Unfortunately though, neighbors, casual visitors, passing motorists, and the waiter at The Ritz may not happen to know who's Vice President For Local Sales at Crump Amalgamated — to them he's just a middle-aged schlepper with thinning hair and a pot belly. The answer is simple: a $300 hand-made suit, glove-leather Gucci shoes, and a hand-made attache case of unborn calf.

These symbols are wasteful of course, but in another more psychological way, they make sense. Quadraphonic stereos playing dusty old Lawrence Welk albums; hosts serving Chivas Regal to business friends who couldn't tell it from Old Overshoe; we may chuckle at what seem to be foolish excesses, but the rewards are not what they seem. What's a little wasted money compared with the precious feeling of Being A Man?

What about men to whom real financial success is out of reach, temporarily or permanently, for reasons of age, social class, or race? Many hunger for it anyway, and seize on its smallest symbols in a parody of material success, for even the fleeting feeling of "being a man" can be precious. Kenneth Clark (1965) has described young black men with menial jobs, who carry empty briefcases to and from work. One such youngster wore a white shirt and tie downtown each day to what he said was his "management trainee" job in a large department store; in reality he was a stock-boy.

Other Routes to Status Men who haven't "made it" by the standards of the mainstream often find other battlegrounds to fight on, other routes to status before smaller but highly appreciative audiences. A neighborhood bar may have a champion dart thrower, with a standing bet to lick any man in the house. A mailroom may have its fastest sorter, a men's club its stalwart whose record for beer drinking has never been equaled. In truth almost anything pursued seriously can become a source of status. Specialized sub-groups often develop their own status ranking systems, sometimes very different from or even opposite to the mainstream male role. Aggressive violence plays a minor part in the general cultural male role, as we'll see later, but in certain juvenile street gangs it serves as the major "currency" on which reputations are based. Miller (1967) reports that lower-status gang members committed four to six times as many violent, illegal crimes as the high-status members, who had already "made it." Once the low-status men have acquired reputations for bloodthirsty recklessness, they too can "retire" to the relative ease (and safety) of senior status.

One of the most interesting examples of subgroup status is found in the encounter-group, clinically-oriented "human potential" movement. In the mainstream male role, showing tender or fearful emotions is distasteful and embarrassing, while being "sensitive" to other people's emotions is fairly irrelevant. In the clinical counter-culture, sensitivity and being "in touch with one's emotions" have been redefined as extremely good. Naturally, the subgroup leaders who are most awesomely in touch with every emotion and can "sense" things in other people that no one else can are . . . men! At such gatherings as Humanistic Psychology and Orthopsychiatry conventions, these super-sensitive Gurus glide around like whacked-out birds of paradise in beads and Indian gowns, followed by their retinues of admirers.

Being "Competent"   "Ask any man a factual question and you'll get an answer," says a single woman I know. "He may not know a damn thing about it, but he'll make up something rather than say he doesn't know." Men feel a strong need to seem knowledgable, on top of things, and generally equal to any situation that arises. When a husband and wife are driving in a car and get lost, it's almost always the woman who suggests stopping to ask directions of some-one. When a car won't start, men gather around like flies to peer intently at the mysterious innards. "She's probably flooded," somebody grunts knowledgably.

The act of lovemaking was once considered a natural function, and the male's prerogative at that. With the widespread discussion of female orgasm, not to mention multiple orgasm, and the appear-ance of hundreds of sex manuals telling men how to bring any woman to the brink of ecstasy in 35 easy steps, a whole new proving ground for male competence (and status) has appeared. "And I didn't have to consult my sex manual even once!'' crowed Woody Allen after his night of debauchery in *Play It Again Sam*. "My husband has studied those things so much," said one med student's wife, "I can tell when he's flipping from page forty-one to forty-two."

The Breadwinner Role   Most men seek and long for at least part of their lives in which they feel like a "big wheel." Status of course is a relative thing: A man whose wife looks up to him can feel like a "real man" in relation to her, but not necessarily to anyone else. A shopkeeper who is feared and respected by his employees may feel sublimely masculine at work — but he doesn't look or feel manly when he's asking for a loan at the bank or being ignored by the maitre d' in a fancy restaurant. The famous "fragile male ego" that marriage manuals warn women to be so careful of is one symptom of the status vulnerability most average men must endure. ("Better to let him win a few games of checkers than to put up with a sullen, humiliated man for the rest of the evening," one such guide cautions young women.) For many men the need to feel important is most usually met in role-dictated dominance/submission interactions with women, or with traditional labor divisions in the family.

In the traditional nuclear family the male is the only paid worker, the Breadwinner, the Sole Provider. Even if his job is dull and routine, he leaves the home, labors, and returns with "food for the table" — a computerized paycheck with federal, state, and local withholdings, perhaps — but a direct descendant of Neanderthal's haunch of bison. This bastion of status within the family is traditionally available to virtually every male, a haven in which one basic demand of the male role can be satisfied. When unemployment occurs on a wide scale, such as when the chief industry in a small community fails, the psychological consequences to men are often as severe as the economic.

Despite the importance of having a job, an astounding proportion of men do not especially like what they do for a living, the way they spend approximately two-thirds of their waking hours for the better part of their lives. In a series of interviews I conducted to pretest a questionnaire on masculinity, men's answers about their jobs were notably unenthusiastic. "Well, it's a living," said a restaurant manager. "I guess I like it — I been doing it 15 years," said a window dresser. "Hell, I gotta eat," said a car salesman.

These are all men who are far from the pinnacle of success (as are most of us), so perhaps it's not surprising they don't see their jobs as heaven on earth. But a member of my men's consciousness-raising group had a different problem with his job. He's an executive with one of the largest corporations in America, in his early forties, and was making over $50,000 a year in an assignment he actually enjoyed and was good at. *His* problem was an impending promotion. Having proven his competence at this level of the company hierarchy, he was expected to move on to the next level. It meant more money but a substantially different kind of work, which he was fairly sure he wouldn't like as well, and he'd have to commute a lot further. It made sense to stay where he was . . . but he couldn't. For one thing that would label him as a "quitter" in the company, and his chances of ever being promoted later would evaporate. For another he really couldn't resist the urge to move upward, or live with a reputation as a guy who was headed nowhere. He accepted the promotion, and, as predicted, hated his new assignment.

To the blue-collar worker struggling to make ends meet, such executives are a privileged class of rich mandarins, and obviously, in a way, they are. But based on some close observations I'd say there's another fact that's relevant. They're not very happy.

3. The Sturdy Oak: A Manly Air of Toughness, Confidence, and Self-Reliance

If you can keep your head when all about you
Are losing theirs and blaming it on you,
If you can trust yourself when all men doubt you,
But make allowance for their doubting too; . . .

If you can force your heart and nerve and sinew
To serve your turn long after they are gone,
And so hold on when there is nothing in you
Except the Will which says to them: "Hold on!" . . .

If you can fill the unforgiving minute
With sixty seconds' worth of distance run,
Yours is the Earth and everything that's in it,
And – which is more – you'll be a Man, my son!

(From "If," by Rudyard Kipling)

You had to have some quality that was hard to pin down, a certain kind of confidence, a little swagger but not in a boastful way, an easiness, a style, an air of casual good nature, of leadership that wasn't sought but seemed to come natural. You couldn't pin it down, but you could see it in a person.

(Wakefield, 1970, p.195)

There's another basic theme in our culture's positive prescription for masculinity which has little to do with success or traditional measures of social status, and has seldom been noticed or mentioned by social science. Some of the most widely admired figures in American motion pictures are men who conspicuously *lack* social status: William Holden in *Stalag 17,* Bogart in *The African Queen,* Paul Newman in *Cool Hand Luke,* Marlon Brando in *Streetcar Named Desire,* John Wayne in *True Grit,* and many more. What they have is harder to identify, for it seems more a matter of style than tangible achievement, and its ingredients are variable. There's a distinct sense of strong manliness however, not usually belligerent or looking for trouble, but tough and self-possessed, which some-how emerges from the variable combination of quiet confidence, self-reliance, determination, indifference to opposition, courage, and seriousness. Most of all, there's a sense of mental and physical toughness — the big and little signs which signal that "here is a man," a force to be reckoned with, not a straw that blows with the changing wind. It doesn't matter so much *what* he's doing, whether holding "the system" together, like Marshall Dillon of *Gunsmoke,* or striking at its very foundation, like John Galt of *Atlas Shrugged;* what matters is *how* he's doing it. There's a self-confidence and seriousness in all these figures which demands respect even in de-feat.

There is something rather unreal about this formidable creature that every one of us is supposed to be — something illogical, impos-sible, and for most of us, deeply thrilling. Growing up in America as life became increasingly civilized, urban, and complex, we sat in darkened movie theatres and watched these unreal men, fashioned as much by a collective cultural demand as by some Hollywood script writer, larger and far more compelling than our real lives. We watched Gary Cooper standing all alone on that long, dusty street, in *High Noon,* watched by the town that would not stand beside him:

ready to die, but not to run. Usually the man we longed to be was big and fast on the draw like that, but sometimes it was a seemingly ordinary guy who showed real strength when the chips were down. Montgomery Clift's unforgettable Corporal Prewitt, in *From Here to Eternity,* couldn't be broken by anything a whole army could dish out, and he showed us that "real men" come in all sizes. The moving *Nothing But A Man* showed us that they come in all colors too; the film's battered hero finally turns on his Uncle-Tom father-in-law, who is berating him to accept white supremacy, and delivers the punch line of a powerful film: "You been bendin' down so long, you don't know how to stand up straight; you ain't a man at all."

A man can not always win in this world, but he can always stand his ground win or lose . . . *stand up straight,** something in that metaphor of standing captures the image of nonbelligerent strength we so admire. A joke about an old German Jew and a young Nazi illustrates it well: A Nazi soldier is watching an old Jew hobble by. As the man passes, he shouts: "Swine!" The old Jew slowly turns and replies: "Cohen, Pleased to meet you." Even in desperate circumstances, a man can stand up and be a *mensch.*

Another of these Sturdy Oak qualities is self-reliance — the idea that a man should always be "his own man," should think for himself. One of the most popular motion pictures in recent years was *A Man For All Seasons* (Best Picture of 1966), the story of Sir Thomas More's fight to the death against Henry VIII. Few of the modern viewers so enthralled by this 16th century story could have had much enthusiasm for More's position — that divorce was immoral. What was so majestic was the spectacle of one man's personal conviction arrayed against the might of imperial England, refusing to accept any compromise which would save his life.

Strong and independent in action, the *style* of such a man is calm and composed, unimpressed by pain or danger. "Of course it hurts," smiled Peter O'Toole as *Lawrence of Arabia,* as a match burned into his fingertips; "The trick, you see, is not to *care* that it hurts." It goes far beyond the mere avoidance of "feminine" emotionality; it's the cultivation of a stoic, imperturbable persona, just this side of catatonia. A "real man" never worries about death or loses his manly "cool."

---

* As the Everly Brothers would wail in a popular song called *Cathy's Clown:* "A man can't crawl, he's got to stand tall, or he's not a man at all."

"To hell with the handkerchief," said Walter Mitty scornfully. He took one last drag on his cigarette and snapped it away. Then, with that faint, fleeting smile playing about his lips, he faced the firing squad; erect and motionless, proud and disdainful, Walter Mitty the Undefeated, inscrutable to the last.

("The Secret Life of Walter Mitty," James Thurber, 1964)

Physical Strength, Athletic Prowess For adults, athletic skill by itself is not strongly related to the appearance of masculine toughness. Famous sports figures such as Tom Seaver, Bob Cousey, Sandy Koufax, and Rod Laver are obviously skillful, but they don't have an exceptionally tough, or masculine, public image. Their reputations as celebrities are based as much on status and public exposure as on being sports figures *per se*. Professional athletes who do have a strong image of manliness aren't always the most successful, but they usually embody one of the traits we'll examine in the next section. They have a reputation for being unnecessarily violent (e.g. Ty Cobb, Derek Sanderson, Marlin McKeever) or they're famous for their off-the-field hell-raising (Paul Hornung, Babe Ruth, Billy Kilmer, Joe Kapp).

Physical size and strength are more directly relevant to the Sturdy Oak image. A physically big man is usually able to stand up to physical intimidation more easily than a small one, so he may be called on less often to prove himself. But when a big man loses to a smaller man, or appears to have no "guts" in the crunch, he becomes an object of scorn, the butt of innumerable jokes and stories. *The Harder They Fall* was a popular Bogart film about a titanic boxer from South America who bowls over his seemingly terrified opponents — in fixed fights. He really can't take a punch, you see, but nobody knows that. When he finally faces an honest fighter he crumbles, and his total disgrace is symbolized by a bout of crying. The hard-bitten sports writer (Bogart), at a fraction of the giant's body weight, is obviously much more of a Man.

The Sturdy Oak and the Average Guy The need to be seen as a tough customer operates on Park Avenue as well as the gridiron. In executive jobs in which effectiveness can't be gauged directly, promotions often go to a man who has built the best reputation for toughness. In one company it's fairly common practice for a new regional manager to fire 15 of his 60 branch managers, without regard to competence, just to show his superiors he's tough enough to handle the new job. At another large corporation it was once arranged for someone to rise from the audience during a presentation by a new manager, walk up to the charts he was using and throw them to the floor, stomp on them, and return to his seat. If the speaker kept his cool while this happened, and then continued his presentation without appearing upset, he had passed the test (Fasteau, 1974, p. 123).

The kind of confidence and toughness required by a test like this, and portrayed so often in popular fiction, is an idealized image, not an accurate picture of the way flesh-and-blood males usually behave. Yet this deeply socialized ideal can exert a powerful strain on men's attitudes, values, and judgments; it can kindle a sudden longing in the mildest of men to appear tough and decisive, whether or not the situation calls for it. A businessman may cling to a losing investment rather than concede that he miscalculated. A father may decide on a stern punishment for his son and stick to it, when understanding and support are what's needed. A husband may insist on lifting heavy objects or fighting a fire in the attic by himself. Women sometimes reinforce this need, for reasons related to their own sex role and the desire to feel sheltered and protected. As one young woman candidly put it "I want a real man, someone I can lean on, depend on." But the man's inner response is often: "Oh God! How can I be that? I don't know the answers; I'm scared as she is." Like Willie Loman in Arthur Miller's *Death of a Salesman,* we often respond with bluster and braggadocio that fools almost no one; how many women must privately say, like Willie's wife "He's only a little boat looking for a harbor."

4. Give 'em Hell: The Aura of Aggression, Violence, and Daring

There is nothing inherently or necessarily bad about being a success, earning respect, or having confidence and determination. It can be oppressive to *have to be* these things, but the qualities themselves are not inherently undesirable by usual standards.

There is another deep and rich vein in the male sex role that also smacks of strength and toughness but is *not* fundamentally wholesome, constructive, or benign. It is the need to hurt, to conquer, to embarrass, to humble, to outwit, to punish, to defeat, or most basically, in Horney's useful phrase, "to move against people."

Like the other deep themes in the male role, this behavior takes many forms, some more disguised than others. But whereas what we have called the Sturdy Oak qualities encompass essentially defensive resources, the underlying theme here is one of attack.

This male penchant for moving against people is not always directed at the strong and powerful, however. There is a disturbing experiment by Titley and Viney (1969) in which aggression (in the form of electric shocks) toward a helpless victim was studied. Women tended to deliver less intense shocks to a victim who appeared to be physically disabled than they did to a normal victim. Men did exactly the opposite.

The Meanings of Aggressiveness   When a particular man is described as "aggressive" (presumably meaning more so than average for a man) it usually seems to be meant as a compliment. "Aggressive businessman," "aggressive thinker," "aggressive ballplayer" are all relatively favorable images in our culture (as opposed for example to a "passive businessman," "unaggressive ballplayer," etc.). Help-wanted ads refer to great opportunities for "hard-working, aggressive" young men. Businessmen speak admiringly of ruthless executives who fire 50 men at a shot and impose their wills on subordinates at a moment's whim. A *Playboy* cartoon shows a smartly-dressed young man ripping the clothes off a startled receptionist, while announcing to her grinning boss: "I think your firm can use a man like me sir! I'm young, aggressive, and won't take 'No' for an answer!" ("He's got the idea all right" chuckle the magazine's readers, "if he can just redirect it a little!")

As these examples suggest there is considerable ambiguity about just what constitutes aggressiveness, and where the line is drawn between approved and frowned-upon male behavior. The dictionary provides two meanings of the word "aggressive": (1) *tending to aggress, making the first attack;* and (2) *energetic, vigorous.* It's no accident that two such basically different meanings are served by the same word, for our society has a deeply ambivalent attitude toward aggression and its less savory first cousin, violence.

Violence   Violence, of course, is officially condemned and certified "bad" by our civilized society. It is denounced in sermons, speeches at the U.N., and Presidential addresses, and we have a prestigious National Commission on the Causes and Prevention of Violence. Yet violence holds a deep fascination for us, which does not appear to be totally a matter of viewing with alarm. Our favorite entertainments — movies, novels, and television — are literally packed with violence: eight serious violent incidents per hour in prime-time television, according to a recent study (Gerbner, 1971). The largest paid audience in the history of mankind was recently assembled, via satellite telecast and rented theatres around the world, to watch a heavyweight boxing championship, and the largest audience prior to that was for another boxing match.

Fathers do not openly condone "violence" to their sons in so many words, but they don't totally condemn and abhor it either. The message is more often "This world is full of dangerous bullies, son, and that's too bad, but you'd better know how to handle them or you're going to have a rough time." "Never *start* fights, boys," one of my friend's father told us out in his garage one afternoon, "but always *finish* them!" My own father gave me this advice about how to handle a bully: "When you see that a guy is planning to give you a hard time, you just wait for an opening, like maybe he shoves you or something. Then you just rare back and knock his head off, that first time, and you won't ever have any more trouble with him." The message behind all this is that a real man never asks for trouble but he can sure handle it when it comes along. Innumerable Hollywood movies (*Straw Dogs, Deliverance, The Quiet Man*) have been built on exactly this theme — a mild-mannered "civilized" man is pushed beyond his limit, and explodes in a blast of awe-inspiring violence.

Yet the line between self-defense and violence for the sheer fun of it is narrow in theory and often ignored in practice, especially among adolescent boys out of sight of adults, where the rule that "might makes right" usually rules supreme. For their fathers, the allure of violence must take other, more disguised forms, such as "contact sports." Take our most popular American sport, football, for example. There is a widespread conviction that football "builds character" in young men, and there are rules against "unnecessary roughness" in the game. No real football player or fan is fooled by this window dressing. College coaches tell their players they want men who "like to hit" (Shaw, 1972), and in the pros a great lineman must "enjoy hurting" and "love to hit" (Meggyesy, 1971). Sensitive microphones on telescoping booms are placed along the sidelines backed by the latest in electronic devices and circuitry, so that we can hear the crash of huge bodies colliding. The admiring exclamations of the sportscasters leave little doubt that these gladiators are the real he-men of our pallid age, the ultimate masculinity symbols.

Violence is to some extent a Southern and Western ideal more than Northeastern, and more typically working class than middle class, but it has deep roots in the general American experience. Support for the social use of violence (e.g. police using clubs and guns to stop student demonstrations) are highest in the South and Border States, lowest in the Middle Atlantic and New England States; highest among the least educated, and lowest for those with graduate degrees; highest among Fundamentalist Protestants, and lowest among Jews (Blumenthal *et al.*, 1972, pp. 45–51). Yet 58% of *all* American males currently agree that a man has a perfect right to kill a person "to defend his house," and fully 46% think that "hurting people" is no worse an offense than stealing or damaging property (Blumenthal, 1972, pp. 29, 108).

Adventure and Daring   In another variation of the impulse to "Give 'Em Hell," men sometimes direct their defiance more toward life in general than at a specific target. The result is a glamorous idealizing of reckless adventure, daring exploits, and bold excesses of all kinds. William Faulkner recounts the tale of young Sartoris who with Jeb Stuart galloped 40 harrowing miles behind Union lines to get a pot of coffee. After routing a Union General to the woods in his night shirt and capturing half the Yankee staff, Sartoris tossed his life away on a whim by returning to get — a tin of anchovies. In generations to come,

The tale itself grew richer and richer, taking on a mellow splendor like wine: until what had been a hare-brained prank of two heedless and reckless boys wild with their own youth had become a gallant and finely tragical focal point to which the history of the race had been raised from out the old misasmic swamps of spiritual sloth by two angels valiantly fallen and strayed, altering the course of human events and purging the souls of men.

(Faulkner, 1953, p. 33)

Decades later, another generation thrilled to Keroac's *On The Road*, the unforgettable saga of Dean Moriarity and his friends careening stark naked through the desert in a '47 Hudson at 110 flat across a sleeping and sodden continent and plunging through experimental sex, drugs, jazz, scenes, America! in a wildman's search for *life* and *kicks* and *meaning*. Largely ignored by social scientists, the impetuous, wild-blooded male figure gallops through American literature like the headless horseman, as magnificent in disaster as in victory.

Aggressiveness, Violence, and Sex   One of the vivid images of a certain kind of powerful masculinity is Marlon Brando's role of Stanley Kowalski in Williams' famous play and movie, *A Streetcar Named Desire*. As a coarse, robust, and totally sexual blue-collar man, Kowalski stirs strong emotions in every audience, and has come to virtually symbolize the working class brute. Stella's relationship with Stanley is deeply and powerfully sexual, with the explosions of violence serving as foreplay to "making those colored lights flash." For the genteel sister Blanche, Stanley's appeal to her sister is at first unfathomable, but the lady doth protest too much; we finally learn that she too is a rider on that streetcar named Desire and understands all too well her sister's view that: "There are things that happen between a man and a woman in the dark . . . that sort of make everything else seem unimportant."

Both men and women grow up in our culture thinking of male aggressiveness as natural and normal, and of men as the sexual aggressors; by adulthood our private experiences of eroticism and aggression/submission are often so deeply intertwined that we cannot easily untangle them. Even among men and women in consciousness-raising groups, actively working to overcome sex roles, erotic fantasies are often embarrassingly traditional, with man as the ruthless aggressor, woman the helpless submittor. We've grown up whispering such euphemisms for making love as "having," "taking," "getting it"; they pose man as the aggressor and often still convey a deep thrill, however irrational it may be to mutually consenting adults. We watched Rhett Butler lift Scarlet O'Hara, kicking and screaming, and sweep her up that spiral staircase into the velvety darkness of the boudoir. Our parents may have watched Rudolph Valentino as *The Sheik*, bear the swooning heroine off to his desert tent with equal fascination.

Some would call this mock conquest "the dance of love," while others consider it a demeaning and ridiculous charade that subverts real intimacy and communication. If it stopped here, at the level of mutual role-play, it would be relatively harmless — but it does not.

The marriage of sex and aggression has spawned in many men something far more sinister and serious: a sadistic eroticism which thrives on inflicting pain as an end in itself, widely seen in our culture as erotic rather than sado-masochistic. A forcible rape is committed every 14 minutes in the United States, or rather reported; experts believe that from three to ten times more rapes are committed than reported. Here, a man who raped thirty-three women fondly recalls his first:

It was a good clean fuck with no bullshit about it . . . Broads really want to cut the bullshit too, but society won't let them tell a guy they meet for the first time, 'Hey, let's make it,' so they get repressed and it comes out in rape fantasies . . . a good eight or ten of the broads I connected with had orgasms – that's a better percentage than among married women.

(Youree, 1970, p. 57)

Others are more candid, or insightful, about their own motivations:

The main reason why I do the things I do is that I find rape enormously stimulating and very exciting. It's fun.

(Csida and Csida, 1974, pp. 32–33)

Despite the prevailing notion that rapists are sick, deranged perverts, the most extensive study of rapists (Amir, 1971) could find few differences between them and "average" males. Seemingly average men, with regular sexual partners, apparently rape women when opportunities arise. One 22 year old woman was raped in a public park, and left bleeding and weeping. She screamed to the first man passing by: "Mister, I've been raped, please help me." That man raped her too (*Ibid.*, p. 16). A woman gave a man a ride and he asked her to stop at a pool hall. When she stepped inside, the proprietor locked the door and six customers raped her. Meanwhile the proprietor made some phone calls, and ten more arrived and all raped her; she was hospitalized for three months (*Ibid.*, p. 16). The most compelling fact of all is that many, perhaps most, men do not regard rape as an especially serious abuse. On a T.V. documentary on KNXT in Los Angeles in 1973, one construction worker paused on his job and explained, "Hell, I think it's one way of getting sex without having to go out and socialize for it." Another told the reporter: "Rape's not really a serious crime . . . uh . . . other than, no more than beatin' up a girl or something like that."

Average Men and the Aura of Violence   Most men are not really dangerous brutes, tough customers, or knife-wielding bullies. We fullfill the male role in other, less dangerous ways, and know better than to get into fights with strangers.

Real violence scares the hell out of most of us. But men are brought up with the idea that there ought *to be some part of them, under control until released by necessity, that thrives on it.*

(Fasteau, 1974)

We sense that if a man is *too* civilized and predictable and well-mannered, too completely the practical husband and dutiful provider, his image loses much of its "sex appeal." There's no spike in the punch, no hint of danger of excitement; just good old predictable George, not *exactly* a sissy, but thoroughly domesticated and a little . . . well, dull.

To be seen as a "real man" then, there should be at least a hint of untamed, primitive force beneath a civilized exterior. We often strive for this effect in superficial ways, and merchandisers play on this strategy. These props can collapse in an instant when reality intrudes: a drunk blocks one's path and demands "spare change," a construction worker shouts an obscene remark at your date. It is a rare male who doesn't feel humiliated and diminished as a man when he wisely (did I say, *"cowardly"?*) lets it pass (did I say, *"runs away"?*).

Somewhere in me a voice was still saying, even though I haven't been in a fight since high school, "If you were a real man, if you had any guts, you'd get out and knock him on his ass, instead of trading insults from the safety of the car."

(Fasteau, 1974)

As I sit writing these words in a Northern university, I am thinking back to the region where I was raised, and how deeply the image of masculinity I learned there has affected me, and affects me still. I grew up in the Bible Belt of the Deep South, where Men were Men, or so it always seemed to me. My grandfather was a rough-and-ready frontiersman who killed several "lawbreakers" in his youth and to this day carries a loaded gun in his car, occasionally using it to break up traffic jams on pleasant Sunday afternoons. My father was a powerfully built man, a football star and later a lumberman, who believed a good fistfight was the best way to solve life's little problems. And the inheritor of this proud tradition of rugged manhood was me, an absent-minded 90-pound weakling, with a fondness for far-fetched science projects. I devoted an enormous portion of my teen-age years to becoming a man in ways for which I had little talent, and finally achieved a painfully won mediocrity. I played on a city-league football team at a level which matched my physique (we were the Class YYYY Ruby-Throated Hummingbirds, I think) and there on the gridiron, armored in shoulder pads, pants, and helmet, I received the humiliating nickname "birdlegs." But I tackled with such abandon that I broke my leg in the final game, and was named to the league All Star team. I lifted weights . . . (light ones, as my workout buddies constantly pointed out). I spent hours practicing my wildly erratic jump-shot in a backyard basketball court. By my senior year in high school I was the star of an inter-club basketball game played before the whole student body — the zenith of my athletic greatness. My friends and I would take rifles and drive out to the gravel quarry and blaze away at bottles and beer cans or any bird that was foolish enough to fly into that din (we never hit any).

But still at 120 pounds I wasn't exactly what you'd call the violent type, and I backed down from more challenges to fight than I can remember. Once I hid from a boy named Bobby who had promised to bash my head in if I showed up at the bus stop after school. I walked all the way home rather than find out if he could do it, and I felt like crying but couldn't. I doubt if Bobby could remember that incident now for a million dollars (or my name, perhaps), but two decades later I can shut my eyes and see the sidewalk on that miserable walk home, remember the shirt I was wearing.

My experience was wounding because I had been a coward, I had run away from a little violence (I wouldn't really have been killed, after all). I had really just failed to be a man. It always seemed worse in these cases because my own father was such a stupendously powerful and violent man. *My Father, God!* When he got angry he could be terrifying. He had a way of stomping in rage on the floor of our jerry-built ranch house that would make the rafters shake and the china rattle. But even this awesome superman (or so I saw him) was not immune to occasional failures to live up to the male role.

When I was around 15 we had as neighbors a pair of newlyweds we all called Dick and Birdie. One evening after a loud quarrel Dick left in a huff, and when he returned home hours later, he found both the front and back doors locked. He pounded and pounded, to no avail. By now in a blind rage he raced over to our house, seized my boy scout axe, and proceeded to chop his own front door to splinters. The newlyweds apparently settled their differences that night (like Stanley Kowalski and Stella), for the next morning he was cheerfully repairing the mayhem, while the domestic aroma of eggs and bacon drifted across our fence.

Several years later my father attended a poker game with "the boys," not quite like the scene from *Streetcar Named Desire*, but I guess there were drinks, and good times. He had promised to be home by one, but finally stumbled back in the wee hours of the morning — to discover that my mother had locked him out! After knocking and banging around for awhile my father left in disgust, probably feeling a little guilty about breaking his promise, and spent the night somewhere else. The misunderstanding was settled the next day, and presumably forgotten. But in the midst of an argument some years later, I heard my mother say to my father: "Well, I'll say this: if you were a *real man*, you'd have chopped down my front door that night I locked you out, the way Dick next door did to Birdie!"

No one less than Attila the Hun could have lived up to that role all the time; we were all losers. But we believed in the values and norms that made us losers, we reinforced them, and we imposed them on others. My father actually felt ashamed, after that conversation, that he hadn't chopped or knocked the door down like a "real man," just as I feel ashamed that I ran away from Bobby. It's hard to believe, and I could claim otherwise, but I still feel ashamed.

PUTTING IT ALL TOGETHER: HOW MEN RESPOND TO THE FOUR-PART ROLE

All together and in its purest form, the male sex role depicts a rather remarkable creature. This hypothetical man never feels anxious, depressed, or vulnerable, has never known the taste of tears, is devoid of any trace or hint of femininity. He is looked up to by all

who know him, is a tower of strength both physically and emotionally, and exudes an unshakable confidence and determination that
sets him apart from lesser beings. He's also aggressive, forceful, and
daring, a barely controlled volcano of primal force.

While this description summarizes the total male role in pure
form, it's obviously unrealistic and unbelievable. We would be hard
pressed to think of one such man, even a fictional stereotype who fits
all these demands. If a character in a novel were described in this
manner, adult readers would complain that he was completely implausible and that the writing lacked authenticity. (Someone once
said of a compulsively straight-laced lady in one of Thackeray's
novels "She drank, but Thackeray didn't know it.") One of the
most significant facts about sex roles, then, is that *real people do not
and cannot fulfill the idealized cultural prescriptions in every respect, and are not expected to.*

In the extreme case there are probably a few men who aren't
affected by the male role at all. Some, for one reason or another, had
unusually sheltered backgrounds, and were never exposed to it.
(Members of cohesive religious and ethnic subgroups are often isolated from the mainstream American version of the male role, but
usually have a very distinctive sex role prescriptions of their own —
an issue we can't explore in detail here*). Some others were exposed
to the mainstream male role while growing up but find it so impossible to fulfill that they simply give up, resigning themselves to living
with the burden of being considered a "hopeless case" in the realm
of masculinity. And some — increasingly in recent years — have
found some totally different drummer and embarked on another
course, largely oblivious to how masculine or successful they appear
in the eyes of the world. But most men "hang in there" and try to
somehow make it, even when they don't have much to work with.
We might call this the "Woody Allen syndrome" after the comedian
who has virtually made a career of portraying a likable loser who
desperately wants to be seen as A Man. Some men are obsessed with
the male role and some think about it very seldom, but very few men
are totally unaffected by it. Before looking at the adult case, however, let's briefly examine the dynamics of the male sex role as it
first appears to adolescent males.

---

* See Yorburg, 1974, for brief descriptions of Black, Jewish, Japanese, and Chicano
variations of sex role patterns.

The Early Version of the Male Role: High Stakes and Few Options

In childhood and early adolescence, boys acquire a picture of masculinity which is far narrower than the adult model, but enforced
with more severity. We saw earlier that due to lack of contact with
adult men during most of the daytime hours, boys often show considerable uncertainty about what men are supposed to be like, but at
the same time receive rather harsh criticism when they act like
"sissies." The result is that maleness is often understood in negative
terms, with a deep unease and discomfort at doing anything vaguely
feminine.

In the absence of adult male models, boys turn to each other
and to older boys for guidance as to how a man should act. Peer
groups thus have enormous importance for boys.

Unfortunately the conception shared by many boys is distorted,
drawn largely from Hollywood movies, adventure stories, and their
own collective anxieties. The peer group's image of manhood is
likely to be, as Hartley describes it:

> . . . a picture drawn in black and white, with little or no modulation,
> [and] including only a few of the many elements that go to make up
> the role of the mature male. Thus we find overemphasis on physical
> strength and athletic skills, with almost a complete omission of
> tender feelings or acceptance of responsibility toward those who are
> weaker. It is, after all, a picture drawn by children, and it is not
> enough.

(Hartley, 1959, p. 459)

While Dimension One, "No Sissy Stuff," is at its zenith of
influence in childhood and adolescence, Dimension Two, "Success
and Status," remains relatively underdeveloped. It's not lacking
altogether, but at this age it's simply impractical to base very much
on objective achievements or possessions. There are hints of status
games to come: the boy who owns the football getting to play
quarterback, the status of the guy with the best collection of baseball
cards. These early symbols give way to more important ones: the
teenager with a new sports car is truly in a powerful status position.
But the status currency of adolescence *par excellence* is success at
sports.

The physically gifted youngster finds the world a friendly and
approving place, while the small boy, the weak boy, the sickly or

uncoordinated boy must be content to watch and cheer. Studies show that in adolescence physique bears a strong relationship to positive self-concept (Mussen and Jones, 1957; Washburn, 1962). There is also evidence that some small and skinny boys try to compensate by adopting even more "masculine" values and interests than more muscular boys (Biller and Liebman, 1971).

Adults usually distinguish between the nonaggressive Sturdy Oak qualities in Dimension Three and the threat of aggression and violence in Dimension Four. In childhood and to some extent also in adolescence, these two themes are fused and merged into a general admiration for size, strength, and toughness. There is some scorn for bullies, and admiration for "spunk," but as a rule the boy who gets beaten to a pulp wins few points from his peers. Presumably it takes time and experience to determine that magic line between starting fights and finishing them, between handling violence that arises and seeking it for its own sake. In contact "sports" as we've already seen, the difference is merely theoretical.

Thus in youth and adolescence sports can provide a royal road to satisfying all four dimensions of the male role. As the almost exclusive domain of males, sports easily establish that a young man is not a sissy; they also carry the aura of physical toughness, excitement, and violent activity which seems so uniquely masculine. Most of all, they're the best available source of social status and success for the teenager. Sports thus play a critical role in this period which they will never play again. Almost every small town in America it seems has its story of the high school big shot who now works at the gas station and sometimes wonders at how his fortune has changed — the human result of what sociologists rather dryly call "a discontinuity in the socialization of males." (Knox and Kupferer, 1971).

Dynamics of the Adult Role

With the dawning of adulthood the stage broadens and new options appear, and with them, greater flexibility. Probably the major new element is the necessity to "earn a living," a simple phrase that will preoccupy the young male for most of the remaining years of his life. But with this incalculable burden comes a whole new approach to being a man. Now the money one earns and the things it will buy become the surest and safest route to status and respect, and the second dimension of the role comes into its own. For most men the status of athletic prowess suddenly shrivels from all-encompassing to a virtually negligible sliver of male interest. A few will make their careers as athletes or coaches, but these are exceptions; for most men the whole issue can now be buried without regret. True, spectator sports are a way to relive the old days of schoolboy athletics; in each man's fantasy life, this time it is he who spins and weaves down the sidelines for that crucial touchdown, who cracks that fastball over the fence with two on in the ninth. But sports fantasies are largely optional for the adult male, a poking in the ashes of an old fire. The pigskin has given way to the greenback, the letter-jacket to the Brooks Brothers suit, for the man who achieves financial success can now afford to laugh, if he chooses, at children's games with leather-covered balls.

In big-city, middle class, and "modern" circles, the Success and Status dimension is clearly the basic route to acceptance as a man. In rural, small-town, working class, and "traditional" circles, the Sturdy Oak virtues of toughness and manly demeanor are closer to what's usually thought of as manliness. To get a top score in either setting, however, it seems necessary to have some credits on both dimensions. Neither the anxious and uncertain millionaire nor the tough-as-nails failure is a completely satisfying manly image. Our culture seems to long for both toughness and success in one awe-inspiring package. One of Hollywood's favorite themes (*Death Wish, Straw Dogs, Z, The Man Who Knew Too Much, North by Northwest, Bridge on the River Kwai,* etc.) is the successful businessman/politician/general who's made it to the top of the heap but hasn't lost the two-fisted grit that got him there, as he gladly proves to anyone who tries to push him around.

Dimension Four, "Aggression and Violence," is somewhat less basic to the male role in the present-day United States. Few people would consider someone a "real man" solely on the basis of aggressiveness and violence. These qualities are very useful, however, in bolstering a male image that doesn't quite make the grade on other dimensions. Journalists are not usually considered especially masculine, but the ones that argue for capital punishment and stiff jail sentences for criminals, men like William Buckley, Robert Ruark, or Westbrook Pegler, usually seem more masculine than liberals like Max Lerner, Drew Pearson, or Walter Lippman. "Hawks" on the issue of war are often viewed as more masculine than "doves;" when Senator Goodell changed his position from supporter of

Vietnam to critic, Spiro Agnew christened him "the Christine
Jorgensen of the Republican Party."

The *adult* male role, then, is basically a set of alternatives, some
portion of which must be met to qualify one as a "real man," but
with many possibilities for choice and compensation. It has considerably more flexibility than the rigid, harsh, and demanding adolescent conception of manliness. But one rule has not changed appreci-
ably: the old first commandment of *No Sissy Stuff!* remains intact,
with almost the force it possessed in the testing period of adolescence. Small transgressions are somewhat more tolerated than before; a taste for classical music and a love of neatness don't add to a
masculine image, but they're not fatal either. Any real minuses here
though, and nothing else counts at all. One of the greatest stars in
professional football was showered with contempt when he admitted
to a sexual deviation. The heavyweight boxing champion of the
world became an object of derision overnight when he defied the
draft. A U.S. Senator, and the leading candidate for President of the
United States, became the butt of crude jokes after he cried in
public. And no matter how rich, famous, talented, or athletic he is,
no man who admits to being gay will be considered a "real man" by
other American males.

CONCLUSION

Why do men — not people in general, but human males — act so
consistently and predictably in patterns as irrational as they are
self-defeating? Why deny normal human emotions, and strive for an
unreal and unobtainable indifference? Why hide deep affection for
other people, especially other men? Why amass money long after
any real need for more money has passed? . . . accept promotions
one doesn't want? . . . resort to physical violence at small provoca-
tions, or feel humiliated for walking away? Until quite recently these
questions never interested social science. We have been accustomed
to thinking of women, children, teenagers, minorities, etc., as special categories of humanity with unique psychological problems and
conflicts. Men have been the implicit standard, the norm against
which all others were judged. The idea of a sociology or psychology
of masculinity seems novel, if not distinctly odd.

Troubled by certain distinctively male social problems, chiefly
social violence and crime — and beyond that, the madness of wars

— researchers have in recent years intensified the search for the deeper roots of "human nature." They have searched first and hardest for physical, biological causes. They have analyzed the blood of violent criminals and prominent businessmen, searched in vain for a chemical clue to the mysteries of human life choices. They have trained gigantic microscopes on the mysterious genetic specks within the human cell. They've run rats and watched monkeys and searched the ashes of ancient campfires for shards of pottery, anything that might tell us where we came from, why we do what we do.

In the past decade a new and different approach has begun to emerge: the sex-role concept. The results are not all in, but already this concept has shown remarkable success in accounting for what we know of human behavior. Perhaps ironically, its first discoveries and major impetus came not from the ranks of social science but from the self-searching reflections and insights of the American feminist movement. The best explanation for vast areas of human behavior, feminists have realized, is not in our stars, or our genes, or our hormones (the same hormones that flow in the peaceful, nurturing Arapesh male, and the artistic, temperamental Tchambuli male), but in the major social roles that human beings play.

The perceptive Southern novelist Lillian Smith once described another major role system, the division of people according to race in the old South, as " . . . the dance that cripples the human spirit" — a complex lifelong dance practiced every day from childhood until it became an automatic reflex for both races. That haunting metaphor describes equally well the two great roles which have choreographed our lives according to sex. We have practiced their confining and crippling steps, day by day and year by year, all our lives. When we danced them awkwardly we were laughed at and felt miserable; when we danced them well we were popular and happy. Now, as adults, we know their curious steps and complex cadence by heart — but find, if we try, that we cannot walk without them.

Many social scientists, I believe, have been scrutinizing the dancer but ignoring the music; failing to see that most of the motion is part of a larger dance which is far more cultural than individual in origin, whatever choices and nuances the individual may add.

When we begin to realize the almost incalculable influence that sex roles have had on people's lives and on our social system as a whole, it seems almost incredible that for hundreds of years social science has said so little about them. But that too is part of the pattern we are now discovering. Like fish who are not aware of the ocean that envelops and permeates them, social scientists, like everyone else, have been living and thinking inside the system of sex roles. We academics too, like the insecure politicians who decided to "hang tough" in Vietnam, like the ulcer-driven executives in their paneled offices, like the strutting youth-gang leaders, the young G.I.'s at My Lai, the ambitious counter-culture gurus, the casual and unfeeling rapists, and the silent Walter Mitty's who only dream . . . we each have been dancing the crippling steps, *are dancing them still.* Only recently have we begun to discover the invisible cords which have moved us for so long, to feel their silent tugs at our fantasies, judgments, and fears. One can only dimly imagine what the world would be like if we could somehow turn the music off, cut the cords of sex roles, and discover ourselves.

REFERENCES

Bem, S. L., and D. J. Bem. Training the woman to know her place: The power of a nonconscious ideology. In M. H. Garskof (ed.), *Roles women play: readings toward women's liberation.* Belmont, Calif.: Brooks/Cole, 1971.

Biller, H. B., and D. A. Liebman. Body build, sex-role preference, and sex-role adoption in junior high school boys. *The journal of genetic psychology,* 1971, **118,** 81–86.

Bird, C. *Born female: the high cost of keeping women down.* New York: David McKay, 1968.

Blumenthal, M. D., R. L. Kahn, F. M. Andrews, and K. B. Head. *Justifying violence: attitudes of American men.* Ann Arbor, Mich.: Institute for Social Research, 1972.

Brown, R. *Social psychology.* New York: Free Press, 1965.

Campbell, D. T., and J. C. Stanley. *Experimental and quasi-experimental designs for research.* Chicago: Rand McNally, 1963.

Chass, M. A gut issue: who shapes up best, athletes or dancers? *New York Times,* August 18, 1974, Section 2, pp. 1, 25.

Clark, K. *Dark ghetto.* New York: Harper, 1965.

Clinch, N. G. *The Kennedy neurosis.* New York: Grosset & Dunlap, 1973.

Crandall, V. C. Sex differences in expectancy of intellectual and academic reinforcement. In C. P. Smith (ed.), *Achievement related motives in children.* New York: Russell Sage Foundation, 1969.

Cronbach, L. J. The two disciplines of scientific psychology. *American psychologist,* 1957, **12,** 671–684.

Csida, J. B., and J. Csida. *Rape: how to avoid it and what to do about it if you can't.* Chatsworth, Calif. : Books for Better Living, 1974.

Dixon, M. The rise of women's liberation. *Ramparts,* December 1969, **8,** 57–64.

Farrell, W. *The liberated man — beyond masculinity: freeing men and their relationships with women.* New York: Random House, 1974.

Fasteau, M. F. *The male machine.* New York: McGraw-Hill, 1974.

Faulkner, W. *Sartoris.* New York: Signet, 1953. Originally published in 1929.

Freeman, J. The social construction of the second sex. In M. H. Garskof (ed.), *Roles women play: readings toward women's liberation.* Belmont, Calif.: Brooks/Cole, 1971.

Freidan, B. *The feminine mystique.* New York: Norton, 1963.

Gerbner, G. Violence in television drama: trends and symbolic functions. In G. Comstock and E. Rubinstein (eds.), *Television and social behavior.* Vol. 1. *Content and control.* Washington, D.C.: Government Printing Office, 1971.

Gilkinson, H. Masculine temperament and secondary sex characteristics: a study of the relationship between psychological and physical measure of masculinity. *Genetic psychology monographs,* 1937, **19,** 105–154.

Goodenough, E. W. Interest in persons as an aspect of sex difference in the early years. *Genetic psychology monographs,* 1957, **55,** 287–323.

Gunther, M. *Virility 8: a celebration of the American male.* Chicago: Playboy Press, 1975.

Hacker, H. M. The new burdens of masculinity. *Marriage and family living,* 1957, **3,** 227–233.

Hartley, R. E. Sex-role pressures and the socialization of the male child. *Psychological Reports,* 1959, **5,** 457–468.

Hoffman, M. *The gay world,* New York: Bantam, 1969. Originally published in 1968.

Jourard, S. *The transparent self.* New York: Van Nostrand Reinhold, 1971.

Kerouac, J. *On the road.* New York: Viking, 1955. Signet reprint.

Kinsey, A., W. Pomeroy, and C. Martin. *Sexual behavior in the human male.* Philadelphia: Saunders, 1948.

Knox, W. E., and H. J. Kupferer. A discontinuity in the socialization of males in the United States. *Merrill-Palmer Quarterly,* 1971, **17,** 251–261.

Korda, M. *Male chauvinism! How it works and how to get free of it.* New York: Berkeley, 1974. Originally published in 1972.

Lansky, L. M. The family structure also affects the model: sex-role attitudes in parents of preschool children. *Merrill-Palmer quarterly,* 1967, **13,** 139–150.

Lynn, D. B. *Parental and sex-role identification: a theoretical formulation.* Berkeley: McCutchan, 1969.

Maccoby, E. E., and C. N. Jacklin. *The psychology of sex differences.* Stanford: Stanford University Press, 1974.

Manville, W. H. The locker-room boys. *Cosmopolitan,* November 1969, 110–115.

Mead, M. *Sex and temperament in three primitive societies.* New York: Dell, 1968; first published 1935.

Meggyesy, D. *Out of their league.* New York: Ramparts, 1971.

Miller, A. Death of a salesman. In Clurman (ed.), *The portable Arthur Miller.* New York: Viking, 1971.

Miller, W. B. Violent crimes in city gangs. In T. Dye (ed.), *Politics in the metropolis.* Columbus: Charles Merrill Books, 1967.

Millett, K. *Sexual politics.* Garden City, New York: Doubleday, 1970.

Money, J., and A. A. Ehrhardt. *Man and woman, boy and girl.* Baltimore, Johns Hopkins University Press, 1972.

Morgan, R. (ed.), *Sisterhood is powerful; an anthology of writings from the women's movement.* New York: Vintage, 1970.

Mussen, P., and M. C. Jones. The behavior inferred motivation of late and early maturing boys. *Child development,* 1957, **28,** 243–256.

Nadel, S. F. *The theory of social structure.* New York: Free Press, 1957.

Pleck, J. H., and J. Sawyer. *Men and masculinity.* Englewood Cliffs, N.J.: Prentice-Hall, 1974.

Rubin, Z. *Liking and loving: an introduction to social psychology.* New York: Holt, Rinehart & Winston, 1973.

Salzman-Webb, M. Woman as secretary, sexpot, spender, sow, civic actor, sickie. In M. H. Garskof (ed.), *Roles women play: readings toward women's liberation.* Belmont, Calif.: Brooks/Cole, 1971.

Shaw, G. *Meat on the hoof.* St. Martin's Press, 1972.

Spiegelman, A., and B. Schneider. *Whole Grains: a book of quotations.* New York: Douglas Links, 1974.

Steinmann, A., and D. Fox. *The male dilemma.* New York: Jason Aronson, 1974.

Stone, A. A., and S. S. Stone. *The abnormal personality through literature*. Englewood Cliffs, N.J.: Prentice-Hall, 1966.

Thurber, J. The secret life of Walter Mitty. In *The Thurber carnival*. New York: Delta, 1964.

Titley, R. W., and W. Viney. Expression of aggression toward the physically handicapped. *Perceptual and motor skills,* 1969, **29,** 51–56.

Tumin, M. Social stratification: the forms and functions of inequality. Englewood Cliffs, New Jersey: Prentice-Hall, 1967.

Veblen, T. *The theory of the leisure class*. New York: Mentor, 1953.

Wakefield, D. *Going all the way*. New York: Delacorte Press, 1970.

Washburn, W. C. The effects of physique and intrafamily tensions on self-concept in adolescent males. *Journal of consulting psychology,* 1962, **26,** 460–466.

Weisstein, N. Psychology constructs the female, or the fantasy life of the male psychologist. In M. H. Garskof (ed.), *Roles women play: readings toward women's liberation*. Belmont, Calif.: Brooks/Cole, 1971.

Williams, R. M. *American society*. (3rd ed., rev.) New York: Knopf, 1970.

Williams, T. *A streetcar named Desire*. New York: New Directions, 1947. Signet reprint.

Yorburg, B. *Sexual identity: sex roles and social change*. New York: Wiley, 1974.

Youree, G. Jack the raper. *Avant-Garde,* May 1970, 54–61.

Part I

Dimensions of the Male Sex Role

Chapter 1

No "Sissy Stuff": The Stigma of Anything Vaguely Feminine

One of the first things an American male learns is to hide his emotions; indeed the one proscriptive element of the male role concerns the injunction against being warm, open, tender, emotional, and vulnerable. "That's all right for women, but *men* are not like that."

We suggest that development of the ability to hide these feelings is the first hurdle confronting men in our society. If they clear it successfully, men can go on to compete with other men for the rewards society has to offer. If they do show a more expressive side, they are deemed not to be men, and they no longer are taken seriously by other men. It therefore becomes imperative that men learn this part of their role well — or else they will not have a place in adult male society.

Public displays of emotion — other than anger, of course, which is appropriate for a strong, aggressive male — lead to a rapid decline in prestige. By showing such emotionality, a man demonstrates his lack of masculinity, and therefore does not have to be accorded the same status as before. He is, after all, no "better" than a woman. The only time when an outburst, such as tears, will be accepted by others, is after a man has achieved something extremely prestigious; for example, winning an election. Then, having just triumphed over others, which is a confirmation of his masculinity, a man is permitted some emotional expression. The loser, needless to say, is not entitled to the same public demonstration.

It is difficult to have one personality in public and another one in private, and inexpressiveness becomes a way of behaving in intimate relationships as well as in more impersonal ones. Men do not confide many of their innermost thoughts to their wives; to show doubts and insecurities would reveal men to be "less than" they have claimed to be. Once the inexpressive image is created, it becomes increasingly difficult for a man to open up and to confide that he does indeed have "feminine" feelings.

Men suffer in their relationships with children too. These relationships, already attenuated because of the father's involvement with work, have little closeness and intimacy. Since a man deals with everyone else in a rational, unemotional manner, it requires a lot of effort to learn to relate to children in an emotional way — an effort that many men are not willing to make.

In the long run, however, it is in men's relationships with each other that the proscription against having "feminine" feelings is most costly, because it precludes having a deeply intimate involvement with someone who might share similar problems. In our society, where sex and affection are closely intertwined, if one gets too close to other men there is a fear that this affection will be seen as sexual, and homosexuality is the antithesis of masculinity. Furthermore, it would be difficult indeed to be supportive toward those persons with whom one is competing. This ban on emotionality does not necessarily apply to other cultures where men are allowed more latitude in expressiveness; in many European cultures men are allowed to embrace each other without compromising their masculinity.

Much of the need to reject the more emotional aspects of a man's personality stems from the view that men and women are polar opposites, and that men must eschew any traits belonging to the opposite, and far less prestigious, group. Men thus reject half their personalities.

THE POLITICS OF VULNERABILITY

WARREN FARRELL

Little boys are told not to cry, but the injunction is far more crucial for "big boys." As Farrell notes, men can gain power by hiding their feelings and emotions — and they must often pay a price for lapses into honesty and openness.

What do George Romney, Edmund Muskie and Thomas Eagleton have in common? Each had a political career severely damaged or totally ruined after an admission of weakness. George Romney admitted to being brainwashed; Edmund Muskie allowed tears to escape his eyes; Thomas Eagleton admitted to having had electric shock treatments. American society responded to each confession of vulnerability as its own shock treatment, thoroughly willing to castrate each of them. In the 1968 primary campaign Romney's admission that he was brainwashed by White House briefings about the war in Vietnam supposedly made him "unfit for the Presidency," where presumably he could be brainwashed by anybody. The public's reaction was not "Here is a man big enough to recognize when he is wrong and admit it in the middle of a primary," not "Too bad Lyndon Johnson, Dean Rusk, and Clark Clifford could not admit their mistakes while they were in office." Instead, it was a nationwide torrent of criticism exacerbated by the press, which forced Romney to withdraw from the primary race against a man less willing to admit vulnerability, Richard Nixon.*

In the next primary campaign it happened again. During his 1972 campaigning in New Hampshire Edmund Muskie learned the price of crying when he broke into tears while countering a slur on his wife. The crying generated much speculation about Muskie's emotional stability, not only in New Hampshire but throughout the

---

* In late 1972, as a Secretary of Housing and Urban Development, Romney became one of the rare American politicians to suggest that the programs over which he presided were largely unsuccessful, request their dismantling and withdraw from his post.

country. *The New York Times* reported that Muskie "showed himself here, in the view of many politicians, to be a man who tires
easily and tends toward emotional outbursts under pressure."[1]
There were no headlines saying "Muskie not emotionally constipated."

If the cases of Romney and Muskie are important, the disaster
befalling Thomas Eagleton is the perfect example of the male
eunuch. Eagleton, the first vice-presidential candidate in the history
of the United States who was forced to resign, admitted he had
received shock treatments, the last of which were six years prior to
his candidacy. Despite no recent evidence of depression, his admission of vulnerability, *of seeking help to solve a problem* (rather than
projecting his problems into public policy), indicted him to a much
greater extent than if he had refused to admit that he had suffered
through periods of depression or had sought help. To internalize
weakness — to keep it to oneself and consequently to allow it to
remain within oneself — is the American public's method of castrat-
ing its leaders and itself; the weakness that remains within the leader
is his ultimate defeat and often the nation's defeat as well.

The masculine mystique in all of us prevents us from electing
leaders who can admit to being brainwashed or admit fault in
Vietnam. It is that mystique which allows us to accept a Watergate
— even after the wire-tappers are found guilty and directly connected to the Office of the President. Nixon's genius politically was
recognizing that the American people would accept erased tapes,
ignored subpoenas and a blaming of the incidents on Haldemans —
but not an admission he was wrong or brainwashed. Rather than cry,
he "toughed it out," "kept a stiff upper lip," associated the pressure
for him to quit with a national weakness, saying "we are not a nation
of quitters." He not only refused to examine himself but refused to
give others the tools for that examination. He knew the American
people well enough to know that wrongdoing clothed in weakness
would be met with rejection, but that mistakes clothed in strength
would be met with cynical acceptance ("that's just politics"). We
can accept scandal with cynicism — cynicism is an emotion we
know how to express. No wonder Watergate is virtually a male soap
opera. The masculine mystique is the masculine mistake.

Working-class men are also afraid of self-examination[2] and
the vulnerability it breeds. Police departments, for example, are
strongly opposed to real self-examination or even civilian review

boards. Although its job is to pry into the affairs of others, its members do not want to expose themselves to examination by others. The police are also conservative as a group,[3] a fact which is highly correlated with authoritarianism[4] and with opposition to women's liberation,[5] all characteristics of the "masculine" man.

Males in bureaucracies reinforce each other's tendency toward specialization and protect each other's safe bastion of expertise. As they specialize and protect, their personalities adapt. Max Weber's description of the development of bureaucracy is striking for its similarity to the male personality: "Its specific nature . . . develops the more perfectly the more bureaucracy is 'dehumanized,' the more completely it succeeds in eliminating from official business, love, hatred, and all purely personal, unrational and emotional elements which escape calculation."[6] In this atmosphere, men cannot help but be either emotionally incompetent (unable to handle emotions expressed by others) or emotionally constipated (unable to express their own emotions) or both.[7] His emotional constipation leaves no outlet for his stomach but ulcers. One wonders if there is such a thing as a liberated top executive, or does the trip through the bureaucracy maim them all?

When a man does question the criteria for success or the reflexive need for a schedule of achievement, he often does it in the form of a socially accepted cocktail cynicism: "Anyone who wants my job can have it!" Cynicism is a man's emotional diarrhea. Real emotions are stuck in his system. He does not have the strength to carry out the logical conclusion of his cynicism — open protest. His defense is the same as an unliberated woman's — "the risks are too great." They are both insecure.

If the emotionally constipated man acknowledges that he has emotions, he certainly cannot *show* them. A cardinal tenet of the masculine mystique is that a man must not cry. When confronted with this edict, many men say, "If a man wants to express himself crying or what have you, no one's stopping him." It is not easy to find a man who has tested this proposition in public. The overt liberalism expressed toward crying is like the overt liberalism once expressed by northern whites toward integration: People were free to do it until they did it.

A friend explained to me that he broke down and cried in front of a colleague at the office after some personal tragedies and office frustrations. He explained, "The news of my crying was all over the

office in an hour. At first no one said anything. They just sort of
looked. They couldn't handle the situation by talking about it. Before this only girls had cried. One of the guys did joke, 'Hear you
and Sally been crying lately, eh?' I guess that was a jibe at my
masculinity, but the 'knowing silence' of the others indicated the
same doubts. What really hurt was that two years later, when I was
doing very well and being considered for a promotion, it was brought
up again. My manager was looking over my evaluations, read a
paragraph to himself and said, 'What do you think about that crying
incident?' You can bet that was the last time I let myself cry. . . .''

Denial of dependency and emotions leads to silence and the
creation of a male mystique. Silence seems to contradict the description of the male as a striver and dominant interrupter, but men
employ silence in special situations — those requiring the expression
of emotional and dependency needs. Silence is an obvious by-
product of the striver's need to maintain an image of success, om-
niscience and invulnerability. This silence can also affect women, as
Nicholas von Hoffman, an insightful male journalist, notes:

*We master women by exuding a male knowableness. Men yuk about
women being mysterious, but it's usually the other way around.
Women lay themselves open to men who stay silent: many, many
women build their lives around their men, derive their identity from
them. They often sacrifice their friendship with other women in
doing so, while the men hide large patches of their lives and living
processes. Such an imbalance gives men great power over women,
and we use it.* [8]

Men can use this mystique of silence about their fears and
emotions to inhibit women. They know that women will try to
understand a man's unverbalized fears and not trample on them.
Steinmann and Fox find that 66 percent of women believe men will
not like it if they are promoted to a better job than their husbands.
Only 29 percent of the women, however, felt the men would express
these feelings. They felt, in fact, that the men would verbalize
surface approval of their promotion while thinking negatively about
it. More than a third (38 percent) of the women believed that holding
a better job would pose a threat to the husband's masculinity; but
only 4 percent thought their husbands would say so. They men did
not agree that their masculinity would be threatened, but they
agreed a man would not admit it if it were. [9]

References

1. *The New York Times*, March 9, 1972, p. 32.

2. T. W. Adorno, Else Frenkel-Brunswik, Daniel J. Levinson and R. Nevitt Sandford, *The Authoritarian Personality*. New York: Harper and Brothers, 1950, p. 235.

3. See Jerome P. Skolnick, *Justice Without Trial: Law Enforcement in Democratic Society*. New York: John Wiley and Sons, 1966, p. 61, cited in Arthur Niederhoffer, *Behind the Shield: The Police in Urban Society*. Garden City, N.Y.: Doubleday, 1967, p. 117.

4. See Niederhoffer, *op. cit.*, pp. 116–117.

5. See Chapter 11, "Highlights of Experiments on Changing Men's Attitudes," in Farrell, Warren, *The Liberated Man*. New York: Random House, 1974.

6. Max Weber, *Essays in Sociology*, translated by H. H. Gerth and C. W. Mills. New York: Oxford University Press, 1946, p. 214.

7. See Louis J. Cutrona, Jr., "What Goes on Inside a Men's Liberation Rap Group." *Glamour*, August 1971.

8. Nicholas von Hoffman, "Misogyny in Everyday Life." Washington *Post*, August 14, 1970.

9. Anne Steinmann and David J. Fox, *The Male Dilemma*. New York: Jason Aronson, 1973.

THE INEXPRESSIVE MALE: A TRAGEDY OF AMERICAN SOCIETY

JACK O. BALSWICK AND CHARLES W. PEEK

The following selections suggest an inevitable consequence of men's fear of revealing emotions. The ritual of courtship, as defined by the male role, inhibits openness and vulnerability among single men. And, the boyfriend who can't say "I'm afraid" may become the husband who can't say "I love you."

In learning to be a man, the boy in American society comes to value expressions of masculinity and devalue expressions of femininity. Masculinity is expressed largely through physical courage, toughness, competitiveness, and aggressiveness, whereas femininity is, in contrast, expressed largely through gentleness, expressiveness, and responsiveness. When a young boy begins to express his emotions through crying, his parents are quick to assert, "You're a big boy and big boys don't cry." Parents often use the term, "he's all boy," in reference to their son, and by this term usually refer to behavior which is an expression of aggressiveness, getting into mischief, getting dirty, etc., but never use the term to denote behavior which is an expression of affection, tenderness, or emotion. What parents are really telling their son is that a real man does not show his emotions and if he is a real man he will not allow his emotions to be expressed. These outward expressions of emotion are viewed as a sign of femininity, and undesirable for a male.

Is it any wonder, then, that during the most emotional peak of a play or movie, when many in the audience have lumps in their throats and tears in their eyes, that the adolescent boy guffaws loudly or quickly suppresses any tears which may be threatening to emerge, thus demonstrating to the world that he is above such emotional feeling?

At least two basic types of inexpressive male seem to result from this socialization process: the cowboy and the playboy. Manville (1969) has referred to the *cowboy type* in terms of a "John Wayne Neurosis" which stresses the strong, silent, and two-fisted male as the 100 percent American he-man. . . .

Alfred Auerback, a psychiatrist, has commented more directly (1970) on the cowboy type. He describes the American male's inexpressiveness with women as part of the "cowboy syndrome." He quite rightly states that "the cowboy in moving pictures has conveyed the image of the rugged 'he-man,' strong, resilient, resourceful, capable of coping with overwhelming odds. His attitude toward women is courteous but reserved." As the cowboy equally loved his girlfriend and his horse, so the present-day American male loves his car or motorcycle and his girlfriend. Basic to both these descriptions is the notion that the cowboy does have feelings toward women but does not express them, since ironically such expression would conflict with his image of what a male is.

The *playboy type* has recently been epitomized in *Playboy* magazine and by James Bond. As with the cowboy type, he is resourceful and shrewd, and interacts with his girlfriend with a certain detachment which is expressed as "playing it cool." While Bond's relationship with women is more in terms of a Don Juan, he still treats women with an air of emotional detachment and independence similar to that of the cowboy. The playboy departs from the cowboy, however, in that he is also "non-feeling." Bond and the playboy he caricatures are in a sense "dead" inside. They have no emotional feelings toward women, while Wayne, although unwilling and perhaps unable to express them, does have such feelings. Bond rejects women as women, treating them as consumer commodities; Wayne puts women on a pedestal. . . .

The playboy, then, in part is the old cowboy in modern dress. Instead of the crude mannerisms of John Wayne, the playboy is a skilled manipulator of women, knowing when to turn the lights down, what music to play on the stereo, which drinks to serve, and what topics of conversation to pursue. The playboy, however, is not a perfect likeness; for unlike the cowboy, he does not seem to care for the women from whom he withholds his emotions. Thus, the inexpressive male as a single man comes in two types: the inexpressive feeling man (the cowboy) and the inexpressive non-feeling man (the playboy).

References

Auerback, Alfred. "The Cowboy Syndrome." Summary of research contained in a personal letter from the author, 1970.

Cox, Harvey. "Playboy's Doctrine of Male." In *Witness to a Generation: Significant Writings from Christianity and Crisis (1941–1966)*. Wayne H. Cowan (ed.), New York: Bobbs-Merrill Company, 1966.

Manville, W. H. "The Locker Room Boys," *Cosmopolitan*, **166** (1969), no. 11, pp. 110–115.

Popplestone, John. "The Horseless Cowboys." *Transaction*, **3** (1966), pp. 25–27.

WHY HUSBANDS CAN'T SAY "I LOVE YOU."

JACK O. BALSWICK WITH JAMES LINCOLN COLLIER

In the United States we have long admired what I call the "John Wayne" type — the man who kisses his horse instead of his girl — as a symbol of masculinity. He likes girls, of course, but he finds it easier to conquer a new frontier than to talk with a woman. His way of expressing affection for a brother or an old friend is to punch him on the shoulder or slap him on the back. Strong and capable in the world of men, he's shy in his dealings with the people he loves.

Back when marriages were judged on how well the partners produced — the husband as provider, the wife as manager and mother — the John Wayne type was an ideal to strive for. But today we have a different ideal. We believe that partners in a marriage — all members of a family, in fact — ought to be companions and friends. We no longer have houses full of relatives — aunts, uncles, cousins, grandparents — to fill the gap if one member of the family is uncommunicative.

Today's families are not only smaller than in the past, they move frequently, leaving friends and relatives behind. We have become increasingly dependent on members of the family for affection, communication, friendship. Husbands and wives often have nobody else with whom to share their joys and sorrows — a situation that magnifies the tragedy of the man who is unable to express his feelings.

Some things have not changed, however. Despite a growing effort by the women's movement to eliminate the old-fashioned stereotypes in child-rearing, most boys growing up in America still learn very early that a "real man" doesn't vent his feelings. When his sister cries, she is comforted; when he cries, he is told, "Big boys don't cry." If he talks about his feelings — about being unhappy or worried or scared — his friends look at him askance. If he gives up his baseball game to take his little sister to the beach, they taunt him; if he cries, they jeer. In the movies and on television he sees male heroes brawling and shooting each other; rarely does he find a hero who is tender toward a friend or loved one.

From *Woman's Day Magazine,* April 1974. Excerpts reprinted by permission of Woman's Day Magazine, a Fawcett publication, and John Cushman Associates, Inc. Copyright © 1974 by Jack O. Balswick and James Lincoln Collier.

The most influential hero in a boy's life, however, is his father. If he never hears his father say "I love you." if he never feels his father's arm around his shoulder hugging him, if he never sees his father cry, it confirms his impression that these are things men don't do. Inevitably, by the time he reaches manhood, he has learned not to show his feelings — regardless of how deeply he may (and often does) care about his family and friends.

This male inexpressiveness is no laughing matter; it's a real tragedy for the man's wife, his children, and most especially for himself. Think of the wife who, year after year, never hears the words "I love you." Consider the child who is never told, "Fine work, I'm proud of you." And think of the tragedy of the man himself, crippled by an inability to let out the best part of a human being — his warm and tender feelings for other people.

I know what this is all about because I grew up as a typical inexpressive male myself. Fortunately I happened to meet and marry a warm, responsive woman who was willing to draw me out. She began pointing out that I wasn't very expressive. "Why don't you talk about your feelings more?" she asked. "Everybody has them, but you don't ever admit yours to anybody." It finally began to dawn on me that I was missing a lot by keeping my feelings bottled up. And being a sociologist, I was better prepared than most men to understand how I got that way.

My personal experience has convinced me that men who have trouble expressing their deeper feelings *can* change — if they really want to. I see more and more evidence of it every day — particularly among the younger generation that participates in sensitivity training and encounter groups. As part of their rebellion against exaggerated distinctions between the sexes, they are becoming more in touch with their emotions and more confortable in expressing them.

While the inexpressive males contribute to the rising number of divorces, those who manage to break out of the pattern often develop very strong marriages. Although some are able to show their emotions only within the confines of marriage, they do learn to express their feelings toward their wives and this can lead to stronger emotional bonds and greater fidelity.

MEN AS PARENTS

MARC FEIGEN FASTEAU

Men often have difficulty developing warm and spontaneous relations with their children, perhaps not so much
through a lack of real love and affection as through
difficulty in experiencing and expressing their own emotions. In this sensitive passage from *The Male Machine,*
Fasteau observes that "rational" discussions, stereotyped
activities, and sarcastic kidding are no substitute for genuine emotional relationships with children.

Being a father, in the sense of having sired and having children, is
part of the masculine image; but fathering, the actual care of children, is not. Men who spend a lot of time taking care of their
children — washing, dressing, feeding, teaching, comforting, and
playing with them — aren't doing quite what they should be. A truck
driver who spent an hour with his four-year-old son and his
classmates at nursery school, after being coaxed into it by a teacher,
and enjoyed himself immensely asked with a pained look as he was
leaving, "What'll I tell the guys at work about this?" [1] The image of a
lawyer, businessman, or even a professor wheeling a baby carriage
around in public is still jarring. Part of the feeling that care of
children is inappropriate as a strong commitment for men comes
from the fact that it is a diversion from men's "real" work, the
building of a successful career. Any man who not only says that he
wishes he could spend more time with his children, but actually does
so is suspected by his associates of not being properly ambitious.
One young lawyer with a large New York firm told me that he very
much wanted to see more of his eighteen-month-old son but was
afraid he wouldn't be made a partner unless he worked evenings and
Saturdays.

Even if, despite all this, a man should want to play an active
part in the rearing of his children, he is generally ill-prepared for it.
Men have little opportunity to learn how to care for young children.

Boys who have younger friends are viewed as strange in many neighborhoods ("how come he's not with kids his own age?"), whereas it is "natural" that girls are attracted to young children. Men who play with children they have not fathered (not their "own"), and who may not even be fathers at all, are viewed with suspicion by some ("what's he doing with that kid?"), while it is assumed and demanded that women like and be comfortable with children.[2]

At even younger ages, boys are discouraged from playing with dolls, the first, imaginative trying out of parental role.*

Moreover, the role traditionally assigned to fathers and most compatible with the masculine ideal — the benevolent but authoritarian rule maker and naysayer — is no longer viable in our permissive culture. Still called in primarily to intervene in moments of high crisis or to punish, the father is today regarded as a genuine authority by neither himself nor his children. Only Draconian measures, which he no longer believes in, will extract compliance, and these fail, too, as children grow older. Except in the limited field of "doing things with" and being a "pal" to his children (mainly the boys) there are very few models for mutually rewarding relationships between men and their children. The counterpart to the motherhood myth in popular culture is the image of fathers as bumbling outsiders in the household, men without a significant role vis-à-vis children.

For every newsnote published or broadcast that highlights a caring experience between a man and a child, the media still trot out five situation comedies or horror stories that show men who are tyrants, or incompetent, or plain uninterested in nurturing young children. . . . Ads for Pampers show a man carrying a puppy greeting two women holding infants. Women care for babies, is the message, men take care of dogs. . . .[3]

For individual fathers, apart from the amount of time spent on the job or career, the most serious obstacle to developing rewarding and useful relationships with their children is an inflexibly masculine personality. Small children cannot be dealt with on the basis of reason alone. They don't have the ability to understand or the emotional control of adults. One has to confront and deal with their

---

* One available antidote is a song called "William's Doll" included in the nonsexist children's record *Free to Be . . . You and Me.*

feelings. But to understand and accept another person's feelings one must be able to put oneself in his or her place, to experience a little of the feeling oneself. For men who are uncomfortable with and repress their own emotions, especially weak, dependent, "childlike" emotions, this is difficult.

One male nursery school teacher found himself angry at little boys who cried when they felt hurt or sad. His anger was so upsetting to him that he withdrew whenever little boys needed consolation or support. Under the careful and supportive probing of the head teacher in the school, who sensed his conflict, he exclaimed that "I never was allowed to cry when I was little and they shouldn't cry either." [4]

Men tend to camouflage their tender feelings toward children, to express them in roughhousing: a mock punch instead of a hug; telling a six-year-old boy on his way to a birthday party to "give 'em hell" when that isn't what is meant at all. The scene in old westerns of two friends expressing their pleasure at meeting after a long separation by slugging each other in the arm is not far from the truth in many father-son relationships. The more they like each other, the harder they hit. Sarcasm is another camouflage men use, especially in their relationships with boys. According to Tilla Vahanian, a psychologist with broad experience in family counseling, it is often a kind of self-protection against a more direct and affectionate way of speaking. But, she says, "children find it unbearable, because they don't understand that it is not all ill-tempered. They don't know how to respond. And the father doesn't realize what he's doing because it's so much a part of his growing up." [5] Until they reach puberty, men find it somewhat easier to be affectionate with their daughters. Then, uncomfortable with the sexual overtones of physical contact, they back off. Some decrease in the level of intimacy is certainly appropriate as children grow up, but much of this discomfort seems misplaced, the result of viewing all pleasurable physical contact as a prelude to sex and thus off limits when the child reaches sexual maturity.

Men's insensitivity to the inner lives of their children makes them feel that they must earn their love and respect in a mechanical way. Children respond best to whoever performs the mundane tasks of childrearing — feeding them, helping them clean up their messes, taking them to buy shoes, putting them to bed — with love and respect for their thoughts and concerns. But men tend to believe that their children's love must be coerced by more unusual and necessarily sporadic acts — buying presents, doing things with kids that they are supposed to like. And when these things fail, as they must if used as a substitute for day-to-day contact and more personal exchange, they are bewildered and hurt: "I gave him (or her) everything, and I get nothing, not even gratitude, in return."

Children know when adults are angry or unhappy, although they often don't know why, and they tend to blame themselves. Sometimes they ask about it directly and sometimes they are too afraid or confused to ask. In either situation, the adults involved can relieve their children's anxiety effectively only if they are aware of the feelings they are communicating and able to acknowledge and accept them. A father who refuses to admit to himself that he is upset and angry over a flap at the office is not only likely to take it out on his kids along with everybody else, but to be unable to explain to them that they are not the cause of his anger.

The rewards of caring for a child are real, but essentially personal, hard to measure or hang on to. This is not the kind of experience men are taught to value. It does not lead to power, wealth, or high status. As we have seen, the male stereotype pushes men into seeking their sense of self-esteem almost exclusively in achievement measured by objective, usually competitive standards. Fathers apply these criteria to their children, taking pride in their being advanced in school or good at sports "for their age;" in fact, teaching these skills is the parental task that most holds their interest. But this is only a part, and when children are young a small part, of being a parent. And all too often the father's emphasis in the teaching will shift, without his being aware of it, from the child to the task or skill itself. Instead of focusing on the child's learning, pleasure, and feelings, with the shared effort as the vehicle, he concentrates, as men are taught to do, exclusively on getting the job done. Sometimes this means impatiently taking a tool away from a child who is working slowly but with concentration and contentment on a project and finishing it himself. Sometimes, particularly in sports, it means pushing a child, especially a boy, beyond his interest or ability, creating anxiety by making him feel that his father's love and esteem depend on his reaching an arbitrary level of competence.

The masculine mania for competition also comes between fathers and their children, again especially boys. According to Vahanian, fathers often convey contradictory and tension-creating messages about competition to their children. First, the way to earn my love and approval is by being a good competitor; but, second, you'd better not beat me:

Father gets down on his knees and he asks the kid to punch him. He says, in effect, "Come on, hit me, and the harder you hit me, the better I like it. But don't hit me too hard, because then I'll hit you back." . . .They do the same thing with games, and mothers often get terribly concerned. "Why is my husband competing with a six-year-old in checkers?" The father is not just playing easy, to teach the child; he gets involved, and he has to win, and the poor kid doesn't stand a chance.[6]

The impulse runs very deep, Vahanian observes:

I know a man, for example, who really loved having children. He talks about the years when his children were small as the greatest years of his life. He especially enjoyed playing with them. But when you listen to the kids, all you hear about is the competitive games that they always played, how even at the dinner table, one was pitted against the other to see who could win out. And this father is one of the kindest men I can imagine.[7]

Many fathers have to win every time, not only in games but in their other dealings with their children. There is no doubt that the traditional manifestations of patriarchy, harsh discipline and absolute, unquestioned authority, have eroded over the last several decades, but the sense of hierarchy and the need to control on which it was based is still very much alive. Under its influence, regardless of their intellectual beliefs about child rearing, fathers often require a stultifying deference from their children. The most common complaint Dr. Vahanian hears from children about their fathers is that they can't talk to him:

What they mean is "He's always up there, and I'm always down here." The fathers find it impossible to drop that air of authority, of talking to the kid from a distance, and telling him what to do. It doesn't have to do necessarily with the authoritarian spirit in the sense of being a Puritan or being rigidly arbitrary. It's just that the consciousness of status is so strong that there is rarely any give on the father's side, no respect for the integrity of the child's personality. The father doesn't reveal the human side of himself, he can never admit he's wrong, for example. You can't suddenly go up to a kid and say "Let's have a heart-to heart talk." There's got to be a kind of back and forth that goes on every day. The child has to feel free to say what's on his mind without feeling he's going to be put down for it.

When fathers are challenged by their kids, they tend to lose all perspective. For example, if a boy told his parents to shut up, they would both be justifiably angry. But there would be a difference. The father would probably blow sky-high: "How dare you talk to me like that you little bastard." The mother is less likely to feel personally threatened because her self-image doesn't depend so much on her status. She can see the incident better from the kid's point of view, of his getting to the point where he feels he has no other way out. She's more likely to say: "Don't talk to me that way, I don't like it. Come back later when you can talk to me politely." And then it's over.[8]

Nevertheless, most fathers want very much to be close to their children, even if their conception of what this means is vague and inchoate, and the estrangement which their actual behavior creates is a painful disappointment.

References

1. Robert A. Fein, "Men and Young Children" (unpublished paper, July 1973).
2. *Ibid.*
3. *Ibid.*
4. Fein, *op. cit.*
5. Interview, December 27, 1973.
6. *Ibid.*
7. *Ibid.*
8. *Ibid.*

HOMOPHOBIA AMONG MEN

GREGORY K. LEHNE

In this analysis, here published for the first time, Lehne describes the powerful connection between the male sex role and homophobia, or as he aptly labels it, "homosexism." From childhood on, American males are told not to be like women, so that the accusation of not being a man is a very potent one, and is often translated into being called a homosexual. This fear plays a major part in maintaining the sex roles in our culture.

Summer days are great for swims. The thrill of swimming is greatest in those prohibited areas where adolescent boys gather on hot days. Although these swimming holes may be outside the laws of society, they still exist in the world of social norms. Splashing around develops into competetive daring games; as surely as boys will become men, swimming will become a game of follow the leader, test your skill and courage, prove yourself to be a man. Perilous leaps from rocks and trees become tests of masculinity. The encouraging taunt: "I done it three times. Come on, fellas. *What are you, a fag? Jump!"*

Homophobia is the irrational fear or intolerance of homosexuality. Although both men and women can be homophobic, homophobia is generally associated with the fear of male homosexuality. Homophobia is not currently classified as a "mental illness" (neither is homosexuality), although psychiatrists like Dr. George Weinberg (1972) have stated, "I would never consider a patient healthy unless he had overcome his prejudice against homosexuality." Homophobia is the threat implicit in *"What are you, a fag?"* If male homosexuality were no more threatening than being left-handed, or athletic, homophobia would not exist: *"What are you, a jock?"* implies no equivalent threat for most men. In many ways, and in all but extreme cases, homophobia is a socially determined prejudice much like sexism or racism, rather than a medically recognized phobia.

A more appropriate name for the general phenomena is perhaps *homosexism*, which implies sexism between individuals of the same sex (although they may differ in sexual orientation). Homosexism is similar to sexism between the sexes, although it refers to maintenance of sex roles by individuals of the same sex and therefore lacks the power differential inherent in sexism between males and females. I believe that it is useful to distinguish between the general phenomena of homosexism and an underlying motivation in maintaining the male sex role, which I refer to as homophobia. Homophobia, as I will show, does not exist in most cases as an isolated trait or prejudice; it is characteristic of individuals who are generally rigid and sexist. Homosexism, however, can exist in homosexuals and others not personally afraid of homosexuality. In these cases it is related to homophobia only in so far as homophobia is a social norm.

Homosexism and homophobia, I believe, must be eliminated for fundamental changes to occur in male and female roles. To support this thesis, I will discuss first whether homophobia reflects an accurate perception and understanding of homosexuality or is an irrational fear. Then I will examine the social aspects of homophobia and personal characteristics of people who are highly homophobic. Finally, I will explore the functions of homosexism and homophobia in society, the viability of homophobia as a useful technique of social control, and its effects on society and the individual.

Is Homophobia Irrational?   Homophobia is irrational because it generally embodies misconceptions and false stereotypes of male homosexuality. These belief systems, or prejudices, are rationalizations supporting homophobia, not causes of homophobia. Levitt and Klassen's 1973 Kinsey Institute study of 3,000 American adults found the following beliefs about homosexuality to be widespread: homosexuals are afraid of the opposite sex (56% of the sample believed this); homosexuals act like the opposite sex (69%); only certain occupations are appropriate for homosexuals (for example, 86% thought a homosexual could be a florist, while 76% thought a homosexual should not be a school teacher). The beliefs that homosexuals molest children (71%) and that homosexuality was unnatural were extremely common in this representative sample of Americans.

First, let's consider the mistaken belief that homosexual men do not like women. Since relations with women (especially sexual) are considered one of the proving grounds of masculinity, homosexual men who do not treat women as sex objects are regarded as suspect and unmanly in our male-oriented culture. While these attitudes toward women are not laudable, research does not support the belief that homosexual males are afraid of women. About 20% of men who consider themselves homosexuals have been, or currently are, married. Around 75% of homosexual males have engaged in heterosexual kissing and necking, and about 50% have participated in heterosexual intercourse in their youth, with a frequency and success rate highly similar to that of heterosexual males (Saghir and Robins, 1973). About 50% of the homosexual men in this comprehensive study reported to have at some time established a relationship with a woman, lasting more than one year and including sexual relations. While homosexual males were not adequately satisfied with their heterosexual experiences, they generally did not have negative reactions toward women or heterosexual activities. This should not be suprising since homosexual males are raised in ways highly similar to heterosexual males, and often tend to share with most men in our culture these attitudes toward women. Thus, participation in the heterosexual dating and mating game does not significantly differentiate homosexual and heterosexual men during adolescence and early adulthood. As homosexual men get older they are characterized by a lack of sexual relationships with women, but not a fear of women.

Another popular stereotype is that homosexual men are similar to women, in appearance and psychological functioning. Studies reported by Freedman (1971) as well as Saghir and Robins (1973) suggest that only about 15% of male homosexuals appear effeminate. Effeminacy, unfortunately, is highly stigmatized in the homosexual subculture. Weinberg and Williams (1974) estimate that not more than 20% of male homosexuals are suspected of being gay by the people they come in contact with, although Levitt and Klassen (1973) recport that 37% of the American public believes that "it is easy to tell homosexuals by how they look." Psychological testing of homosexual men reported in these studies indicates that they cannot be differentiated from heterosexual males, and that they are not highly similar to women psychologically. Freedman, and Weinberg and Williams, report that the psychological adjustment of homosexuals who have accepted their sexual orientation is superior in many cases to most heterosexual males in terms of openness and self-disclosure, self-actualization, and lack of neurotic tendencies.

Levitt and Klassen (1973) found that many people (the percentages given in parentheses below) stereotyped some professions as appropriate for homosexuals and others as inappropriate. For example, the "unmasculine" careers of artist (83%), beautician (70%), florist (86%), and musician (84%) were believed appropriate for homosexual men. But the "masculine" careers of medical doctors (66%), government officials (66%), judges (76%), teachers (76%) and ministers (75%) were considered inappropriate for homosexuals. In the real world of work, however, there is no evidence that homosexual men tend to avoid characteristically "masculine" or professional occupations. Ironically it may be true that heterosexual men avoid certain stereotyped "homosexual" occupations, resulting in a higher proportion of homosexuals in those fields. For example, it is my impression that many male dancers in the U.S. may be homosexuals, while this does not seem to be the case abroad where dance is a respectable "male" occupation in countries having a strong male folk-dancing tradition.

Many studies of homosexual males have found that they tend to be disproportionately concentrated in higher status occupations, especially those requiring professional training (Saghir and Robins, 1973; Weinberg and Williams, 1974). This trend is often dismissed as "sampling bias," or it is suggested that homosexuals tend to come proportionately more often from higher social classes, or that homosexuals in higher status occupations are more likely to "come out." However, a careful study of this trend in Germany suggests that homosexual males tend to be more upwardly mobile than comparable heterosexuals (Dannecker and Reiche, 1974). This carefully conducted study of a large group of homosexuals found that the social class of the families of homosexual men was representative of the general population, while the social status of the homosexual men themselves was higher than would be predicted from their family backgrounds even when the mobility trends of the entire population were taken into account. This suggests that in spite of the prejudice which homosexuals encounter in work, they are still highly successful in fields outside the low status occupations which the general public seems to feel are appropriate for homosexuals.

While the belief that homosexuals often molest children is widespread, I have been unable to locate any demographic research supporting it. A pedophile, an adult who seeks sex with young children, generally does not have sexual relationships with other adults and thus could not appropriately be considered either heterosexual or homosexual. Many of these individuals have sex with children of either gender. Pedophilia is a rare disturbance. Heterosexual rape, involving adolescents or adults, is much more common than homosexual rape, according to court records and sexual experience surveys. The fear that homosexuals molest children (or rape adolescents) is grossly exaggerated, and ultimately is based on the confusion of pedophilia with homosexuality.

The final misconception relevant to homophobia which I will consider is the idea that homosexuality is "unnatural." Evidence reviewed by Ford and Beach (1951) indicates that homosexual activities occur in most species of animals. Some porpoises, for example, form lifelong, monogamous homosexual relationships. Homosexual relations are important in establishing dominance among monkeys and canines. Lorenz (1974) has discussed homosexual coupling among geese and other birds, concluding that it is often very adaptive.

Homosexual activities are as "natural" in human society as in the animal world. In 49 of the 77 societies for which we have adequate anthropological data, homosexual activities are socially sanctioned for certain individuals, or in specified situations; in some situations they are virtually compulsory (Churchill, 1967). Ancient Greek and Roman societies are most widely cited in this regard, although most of the societies condoning specified homosexual activities would be considered "primitive" (see Symonds, 1901; Licht, 1932; and Eglington, 1971, for discussions of Greek and Roman homosexuality). In most of Europe and many other parts of the world, homosexual relations are legal, although they may not be socially sanctioned or encouraged. The "unnatural" rationalization supporting homophobia receives further disconfirmation from the experiences of the 37% of the American male population who Kinsey et al. (1948) reported had homosexual experiences to orgasm after adolescence. Homosexual activities are also widespread in many predominantly male situations such as prisons, boy's schools and camps, and the military.

These facts about homosexuality suggest an interesting dilemma. If the stereotypes about homosexuality were accurate (I have tried to show that they are not), then why should homosexuality be threatening to males who presumably do not fit these stereotypes? If these stereotypes are not valid, then how and why are the rationalizations of homophobia maintained?

Since sexual orientation, unlike race or sex, is rarely known for certain in everyday interactions, it is relatively easy to maintain false stereotypes of the invisible minority of homosexuals. Men who appear to exhibit parts of the stereotypes are labeled homosexual, and the rest are presumed to be heterosexual. Thus as long as most homosexuals conceal their sexual preference, homophobia is easily maintained, because heterosexuals are rarely aware of homosexuals who do not reflect their stereotypes of homosexuality.

However, by showing that the prejudiced stereotypes of homosexuals are not characteristic of most homosexuals, it becomes clear that these stereotypes are not learned from experiences with homosexuals. Homophobia is socially transmitted. It precedes and encourages the development of stereotypes of homosexuals in a world where most homosexuals are not known. The presence of homophobia among some homosexuals, whose experiences disconfirm stereotypes of homosexuality, suggests that homophobia must be derived from other sources which are equally relevant to men of all sexual orientations.

Homophobia is theoretically applicable to fears about female homosexuality. That it is primarily directed against male homosexuals is another indication that the roots of homophobia and its social effects relate to the general male role in society, not to any specific characteristics of homosexuality. If the rationalizations used to justify homophobia were in fact valid, then homophobia would not exist as a threatening motivation for males. If you can tell a homosexual when you see one, and if they exhibit the characteristics of the stereotype, then why would heterosexual men be afraid that someone might mistakenly think they were homosexuals? For homophobia to exist as a threat it is necessary that the associated stereotypes of homosexuality be false, otherwise the taunt *"What are you, a fag?"* would be so patently untrue that it would not be threatening.

Homophobia and Social Beliefs   Although there is no rational basis
for the negative stereotypes of homosexuals, and thus for
homophobia, nevertheless homophobia is widespread. It is characteristic of societies as well as individuals. The bases for homophobic
social attitudes are generally related to (1) religious beliefs that
homosexuality is "morally wrong," (2) "scientific" theories of
homosexuality as an illness or deviance, and (3) social beliefs that
homosexuality is damaging to society.

Religious prohibitions are generally considered to be the source
of homophobia (Symonds, 1896; Churchill, 1967; G. Weinberg,
1973; M. Weinberg and Williams, 1974). The United States, as a
result of its puritan heritage, is generally considered one of the most
homophobic (and erotophobic) cultures in the world. In 1969 a
Daniel Yankelovich survey of American college students found that
42% of the students felt that homosexuality was morally wrong. In
1974 this percentage had declined to 25%; the rapid change suggests
that deep-seated religious feelings are probably not the general cause
of homophobia.

There are clear biblical injunctions against homosexuality.
However, as Benson (1965) argues, there are also clear biblical
statements condemning a wide variety of behaviors which are commonly accepted in modern times. Thus, while the Bible may provide
moral support for homophobic individuals, the salient issue is why
these individuals choose to maintain a belief in the immorality of
homosexuality while selectively ignoring other biblical injunctions.
The most reasonable interpretation is that while people may support
their homophobia with biblical quotations, the Bible itself is not the
ultimate source of this homophobia. This reasoning avoids the con-
troversies of theological scholarship (see Bailey, 1955) and religious
reinterpretation (such as Pittenger, 1970), although this thinking has
resulted in more positive statements on homosexuality from a wide
range of religious denominations (see Heron, 1963, for example).

Science seems to have replaced religion as a source of justifications of homophobia for many people. The social sciences are frequently criticized for providing pseudo-scientific justifications of
public morality and the status quo. While there is no scientific
evidence that homosexuality is a mental illness, it was only recently
that the American Psychiatric Association removed the classification
of homosexuality from its official list of mental illnesses. The belief
among many psychiatrists that homosexuality was a mental illness,

in spite of the lack of scientific evidence, is probably a result of their uncritical acceptance of common stereotypes of homosexuals (see Fort *et al.*, 1971; Davison and Wilson, 1973), and the fact that they overgeneralized from homosexuals who were possibly mentally ill, and sought treatment, to the entire homosexual population. Nevertheless the psychologically untenable conceptualization of homosexuality *per se* as a mental illness, which can be "cured," is believed by 62% of the American adult population, according to Levitt and Klassen (1973).

Certain psychological theories, such as Freud's, posit that while homosexuality is not an illness, it is nevertheless not "normal." Freud viewed it as a form of arrested psychosexual development, related to aspects of the parent/child relationship. Although committed psychoanalysists like Bieber *et al.* (1962) have selectively analyzed cases of homosexuals from their clinical practice which they interpret as supporting Freud's theory, Bieber's conclusions have not been supported in other studies sampling a cross section of homosexuals (Saghir and Robins, 1973).

Freud further believed that homophobia, and also paranoia, is related to "latent homosexuality," which is present in nearly everyone since he conceived of people being born ambisexual and learning to become heterosexual. Freud's belief in latent homosexuality has received general acceptance in our culture, both among heterosexuals and homosexuals. Latency, by definition, implies the existence of no behavioral evidence. Therefore if anyone may be a latent homosexual, it becomes extremely difficult for a person to prove beyond a doubt that he is not a homosexual. Thus the concept of latent homosexuality contributes in a major way to homophobia, for it allows the possibility that anyone might be a "secret" homosexual even though the person does not exhibit any of the stereotypes, or behaviors, of homosexuals.

Sociological studies of homosexuality provide other popular scientific justifications of homophobia since they tend to view homosexuality as deviant. While it is certainly true that exclusive homosexuality is deviant in all societies, the term deviant has taken on moral connotations not in keeping with its scientific meaning of "not majority." (See Scarpitti and McFarlane, 1975, for further discussion of this point.) Of course, it can be argued that in our society, with its emphasis on conformity, to be "deviant" is to be "bad." This type of reasoning, however, has not been extended to

other areas such as high intelligence or attractive physical characteristics. When Simmons (1965) asked a cross-section of Americans
to list the people who they considered deviant, the most common
response was homosexuals (49%). The morally suspect occupation
of prostitution was also seen as highly deviant, while other less
common professions did not occur. The equation of deviance with
bad or immoral, while it may be indicative of popular thinking, is not
inherent in sound sociological research.

The most common source of homophobia is probably the belief
that homosexuality is damaging to society. An Opinion Research
Center poll in 1966 showed that more than 67% of the people con-
tacted viewed homosexuality as "detrimental to society." The Harris Survey has been asking large cross-sections of American households whether they feel homosexuals (and other groups) do more
harm than good for the country. In 1965 homosexuals were placed
third (behind Communists and atheists), with 82% of the males, and
58% of the females, thinking they were primarily a danger to the
country. In 1973 about 50% of the respondents still felt that
homosexuals did more harm than good. Levitt and Klassen (1973)
similarly found that 49% of their sample agreed that "homosexuality
is a social corruption which can cause the downfall of a civilization."

These studies do not make it clear why homosexuality is perceived as such a social menace, especially by men. That private
sexual activities commonly engaged in by homosexuals (as well as
by many heterosexuals) are illegal in 42 states perhaps attests to the
fear that homosexuality might damage society, although the moralistic language of many of these laws suggests explanations based more
on religious beliefs than on social concern. It is common for
societies which place great importance on increasing their population to act punitively toward homosexuals, but this would not seem
to be a significant factor in the United States, where overpopulation
is a more important issue.

Two arguments have been frequently advanced against legalization of homosexuality in states which are considering legal reform.
Occupational groups such as firemen and policemen argue that if
homosexuality is legalized, then homosexuals will "sexually cor-
rupt" their fellow workers (a belief of 38% of Americans, according
to Levitt and Klassen, 1973). The fact is that homosexual men have
little interest in having sexual relationships with unwilling

heterosexual colleagues (the same does not necessarily seem to be true of heterosexual men at work, as many working women will attest).

The most influential argument advanced against decriminalizing homosexuality is that it would allow homosexuals to molest or "convert" children. We have discussed the distinction between pedophiles and homosexuals and the mistaken stereotype that homosexuals molest children. The children's issue is a red herring because in no state has legalization of sex acts between adults and children, or rape, been proposed. Homosexuals are not seduced or converted into homosexuality. In a study by Lehne (1974) only 4% of the male homosexuals reported that they were somewhat seduced into their first homosexual act, and in no case was force involved. By comparison, Sorensen (1973) reports that the first sexual experience of 6% of nonvirgin adolescent girls was heterosexual rape. Lehne's study also found that most of the homosexual men reported that they were aware of their sexual orientation (because of their sexual fantasies) about four to five years before their first homosexual experience. The notion that homosexuals, legally or illegally, will seduce, rape, or convert others into homosexuality is not supported by any substantial data. There seems to be no reason to believe that homosexuals act any less morally than most Americans of different sexual orientations, or that they in fact pose a threat to society.

Homophobia and the Individual   Although homophobia is still widespread in American society (and reflected in the laws of most states), it is increasingly a fear of only a minority of people. There have been several studies of homophobic individuals which suggest that homophobia is not an isolated prejudice or fear of homosexuality; this might further indicate that homophobia is a dynamic in homosexism rather than a cause of homosexism.

Using a sample of 93 college students, Smith (1971) identified a high- and low-homophobic group with questions like:

Homosexuals should be locked up to protect society.

I would not want to be a member of an organization which had any homosexuals in its membership.

It would be upsetting for me to find out I was alone with a homosexual.

Smith found that the high-homophobic group was significantly more *status conscious,* more *authoritarian,* and more *sexually inflexible* than individuals scoring low on homophobia. Homophobes tended to agree with statements like:

> Although I don't always like to admit it, I would like friends to see me with a big house and a fine car after I graduate.
>
> My country right or wrong.
>
> Sexual fidelity is vital to a love relationship.

They tended to disagree with statements like:

> A belief in God is not important to the maintenance of morality.
>
> There is nothing wrong with a man being passive when he feels like it.

Smith's questionaire study was interpreted in terms of its face validity, but his general findings have been supported by other researchers using more sophisticated research techniques.

Lack of support for equality between the sexes was found to correlate very highly with homophobia in several extensive and sophisticated research studies. Work by MacDonald (1973, 1974a,b) found that support for the double standard in sex-role behavior correlated with homophobia as did conservative standards of sexual morality. Sherrill's (1974) analysis of data collected from more than 1,500 Americans by the National Opinion Research Center found that homophobes are "politically pathological;" highly homophobic individuals are generally politically intolerant. He found a "strong relationship between the desire to repress sexual behavior and the willingness to engage in political repression."

These and other (Schur, 1973; Dunbar *et al.,* 1973a,b) studies of homophobia have all found similar characteristics among individuals who are most prejudiced against homosexuals: they strongly support traditional sex roles and the double standard, and they are authoritarian and conservative in their social attitudes (which must be distinguished from politically conservative, with an emphasis on individual liberties). People who are homophobic generally do not support broad civil rights for women, blacks, or other minorities. Thus homophobia would seem to be part of a constellation of general social-political attitudes, rather than an individualistic fear of homosexuality.

It is a consideration of the results of these studies which led me to define the term *homosexism*. There is no general evidence that "homophobia" is a personal phobia. Phobias are usually compartmentalized; they do not correlate highly with social beliefs. Homosexist individuals, however, share a belief in the importance of rigid roles for the continuation of society, and they believe in the acceptability of authoritarian techniques to enforce their social beliefs. The question remains of why these individuals are homophobic. It is not surprising that people who are sexist are also racist and intolerant of individuals of differing political beliefs. Changes in the roles of women and blacks, or changes in the system of government and society, all clearly pose threats to many men who presently enjoy the advantages of power and exploitation in society. But there is little reason to expect that a change in the treatment of homosexuals in society would directly affect the lives of homosexist individuals.

Homosexism: the Social Functions of Homophobia   Homophobia is part of a constellation of general attitudes which are socially transmitted. Homophobia is used as a technique of social control by homosexist individuals to enforce the norms of male sex-role behavior. This is why individuals whose lives are generally unaffected by homosexuality are homophobic; homosexuality is not the real threat, the real threat is change in the male sex-role. Since sexist and racist individuals are usually homophobic, an example of the changing roles of women and blacks can illustrate the dynamic of homosexism. In the past, it was to the great advantage of many men to keep blacks and women in relatively oppressed roles. This oppression was sanctioned by society, and was to the economic and personal advantage of many men. Because blacks and women are easily identified and discrimination against them was socially sanctioned, it was easy for many to support this discrimination with arguments about their inferiority, and it was easy for men to enforce this discrimination because they tended to control power. However, when blacks and women began to challenge their inferior position in society, various sexual arguments were advanced. These arguments, while not logically defensible, carried great emotional power: Give blacks equal rights, and they'll go around raping and marrying white women; Liberate women and they'll emasculate men. But what social supports are there to maintain the male sex-role, except for men's collusion in oppressing others, and the many benefits derived from the power of a role of male superiority? If men are in a position of power in society, and power is usually used to define social roles, who was there with more power to help maintain male roles?

The male role is predominantly maintained by men themselves. Men devalue homosexuality, then use this norm of homophobia to control other men in their male roles. Since any male could potentially (latently) be a homosexual, and since there are certain social sanctions which can be directed against homosexuals, the fear of being labeled a homosexual can be used to ensure that males maintain appropriate male behavior. Homophobia is only incidentially directed against homosexuals — its more common use is against the 49% of the population which is male. This explains why homophobia is closely related to beliefs about sex-role rigidity, but not to personal experience with homosexuals or any realistic assessment of homosexuality itself. Homophobia is a threat used by homosexist individuals to enforce social conformity in the male role, and maintain social control. The taunt *"What are you, a fag?"* is used in many ways to encourage certain types of male behavior and to define the limits of "acceptable" masculinity.

Since homosexuals in general constitute an invisible minority which is not distinguishable from the 49% male majority in most ways except for sexual preference, any male can be accused of being a homosexual, or "latent" homosexual. Homosexuality, therefore, can be "the crime of those to whom no crime could be imputed" (Gibbon, *Decline and Fall of the Roman Empire*, Ch. XLIV). There is ample historical evidence for this use of homophobia from Roman times to the present. For example, homosexual fantasies were made illegal in Germany in 1935, and later Hitler sent more than 220,000 "homosexuals" to concentration camps (Lauritsen and Thorstad, 1974). It is probable that many of these men actually were not homosexuals. But since there was no satisfactory way for individuals to prove that they were not homosexuals (and for this offense in Germany, accusation was equivalent to conviction), imputed homosexuality was the easiest way to deal with undesirable individuals. Homosexuality was likewise an accusation during the American McCarthy hearings in the 1950s where evidence of Communism was lacking. The strong association of homophobia with authoritarianism means that the potential for this exploitation of homophobia is very real during times of stress and "strong-arm" governments. This is no accident, but is in fact the explanation for the maintenance of homophobia. Homophobia exists as a device of social control, directed specifically against men to maintain male behavior appropriate to the social situation. Since male behavior involves much more than sexual preference, homophobia is used to control all men, not just male homosexuals.

Of course, homophobia is not generally used so overtly to eliminate dissent and enforce social norms. It is generally used in a more subversive, pervasive way in everyday interactions where men are continuously proving their masculinity. Given the nature of homosexuality, the proof of "manhood" must be continuous; no diploma, or marriage license, is possible to demonstrate once and for all that a man is not a latent homosexual. I am not claiming that homophobia is the most important factor enforcing social norms for males: economic sanctions, for example, are probably more wide-spread and effective, although they are difficult to enforce *specifically* against males.

The areas of employment where most Americans feel homosexuals should not be allowed to work (medicine, law, politics and the judiciary, higher education, the ministry) are the same fields which have generally excluded blacks and women. In most states homosexuals are excluded *by law* from obtaining state certificates necessary to practice medicine or law or to teach; women and blacks have been *de facto* excluded from these fields by the admission standards of professional training schools. Homosexuals, blacks, or women have not been excluded from these fields because they congenitally lack the necessary abilities, or because there is an uncontrolled opportunity for sexual exploitation in these jobs. Beauticians have about as much personal contact with clients as doctors; performing artists can be as influential as role models or heroes as politicians. But clearly a doctor has more power over his patients than a beautician; a politician has more power to control social reality than a performing artist. Since males control power in our society, and use this power for their own benefit, people who may not support the dominant male role are excluded from positions of power because of the possibility that they will not use this power to further male interests. By definition (although not necessarily in reality) homosexuals, as well as blacks and women, do not have a vested interest in the male role, and thus pose a threat to the continuation of male power. In reality, homosexuals who support male power are not excluded from positions of power, but wielding this power is conditional on the fact that their sexual orientation is not known; this is the proof that they have accepted the male role.

Homophobia is used directly to enforce social stereotypes of appropriate sex-role behavior for women. Men define and enforce women's roles, and men who do not participate in this process may be suspected of being homosexuals. The use of homophobia to maintain female roles is necessary only in extreme cases, since male power is pervasive. Perhaps it might be alleged that women who do not defer to men, or who do not marry, are lesbians (this accusation is most often directed against liberated women who advocate changes in female roles). But in general, men help maintain male roles through the use of homophobia, and they directly define and maintain women's roles. There are, of course, other factors besides homophobia which maintain sex roles in society, such as early learning and habit. I am arguing not that the elimination of homophobia will bring about a change in sex roles, but that homophobia must be eliminated before a change in sex roles can be brought about.

Homophobia also exists as a motivating force for homosexuals, making it an especially effective instrument of social control. Homosexuals may feel that they have to work twice as hard as heterosexual men to avoid the accusation that they are homosexuals, and suffer the discrimination directed against known homosexuals. Homosexual men may aggressively defend traditional male roles, and female roles, to avoid suspicion about their sexual orientation. However, for men who are known to be homosexuals, homophobia does not seem to be an effective motivating force.

Further social control occurs in that most societies attempt to "civilize" the sex drive, either to control individuals or to use sexual energy for work. Sex, a powerful human drive, is used to bind a couple together. Once the bond is formed, the man must work to support his family, and a man with such obligations is easily controlled: revolutions are started by people who feel that they have nothing to lose. Sex is restricted to marriage so that promiscuous sex, or sexual attraction, does not become a distraction from work. The association of homosexuality with promiscuity threatens the social control of the sex drive. Ironically, most homosexual men desire to form stable relationships, and it is the homophobic laws and attitudes of society which make this difficult, thus contributing to homosexual promiscuity (Lehne, 1974). According to social norms, participating in sexual activity with a woman carries with it an obligation to financially support the woman. If these social norms were rigorously enforced, no male would be allowed to have sexual contact with a woman unless he agreed to support her: men who did not support women would not be allowed to have sex. Reality, fortunately, differs from the theory, but I hope that this hypothetical example of legal sexuality illustrates how regulation of the sex drive contributes to the support of sex roles. The marriage contract is an agreement of financial support which also regulates sexuality. It is not necessary to marry another person in order to love them; however it is generally required that two people must be married to legally have a sexual relationship. Institutionalized homophobia is not related to the fact that the person whom a male homosexual loves is male, since heterosexual women also love males. Homophobia is related to the fact that the sexual orientation of homosexuals does not fit into a system where men are supposed to support women, thus defining the roles of men and women and the social structure of society. What is threatening to society is that homosexual males generally do not financially support women, while the sex-role structure of our society has been based on men working to support women and their families.

How you evaluate the use of homophobia as a technique of social control depends on your opinion about the validity of the norms which homophobia supports: the male role, the female role, the nature of work. Homophobia is inevitably used to support the status quo; it is an effective technique regardless of the nature of the status quo which it supports as long as women and homosexuals are considered to be inferior and devalued. Homophobia must be evaluated independently of whatever personal feelings you may have about homosexuality, because the main social function of homophobia is not primarily directed toward homosexuals (although it certainly affects them). If homosexuals could be granted civil rights, including the right to marry, their lives would improve. Little would be gained by most men and women, however, unless the prejudice against homosexuality were also eliminated.

The Personal Pain of Homosexism   In addition to deciding whether you agree with the norms which homophobia supports, you must also decide whether homosexism is worth the personal cost. Women have decided in substantial numbers that they are not willing to pay

the price of sexism; it is mainly up to men to decide whether they
wish to bear the pains of homosexism.

It is commonly thought that homosexuals suffer most of the
effects of homophobia, since they are brought up and live in a
society which does not recognize the validity of their lifestyle. Many
homosexuals do suffer from guilt and discrimination because of their
sexual orientation. In the process of accepting the validity of a
homosexual identity, homosexual males must make their own separate peace with homophobia. They are forced to recognize the
falsity of homophobic beliefs, and to question many of the other
common assumptions of our society, to facilitate successful adjustment to a homosexual lifestyle. This task is difficult, but data from
Weinberg and Williams (1974) show that most homosexuals are quite
capable of coping. In many cases they go beyond coping to utilize
the knowledge they have gained in rejecting sex-role stereotypes to
critically examine other aspects of society, and thus become less
homosexist. Perhaps the critical acumen which some homosexuals
acquire in coming to terms with their homosexuality is the source of
the creative accomplishments of prominent homosexuals in many
fields (Rosenfels, 1971).

The pain which heterosexual males bear as a consequence of
homophobia and homosexism is so chronic and pervasive that they
probably do not notice that they are in pain, or the possible source of
their discomfort. Homophobia is especially damaging to their personal relationships. Homophobia encourages men to compete. Since
competition is not a drive easily turned on and off at will, there is
probably a tendency for homophobic men to compete with others in
their personal lives as well as work. Only certain types of relationships are possible between competitors. Love and close friendship
are difficult to maintain in a competitive environment because to
expose your weaknesses and admit your problems is to be less than
a man, and gives your competitor an advantage.

The allied sexism of homophobic men must make relationships
with many women difficult, since a close relationship usually implies
some type of equality. Homophobia and homosexism also limit the
types of relationships which these men can have with other men.
Sexual-type attractions between men (not necessarily homosexual,
since the sexual drive involves affection as well as sex) contribute to
powerful male bonds. Lionel Tiger's book *Men in Groups* is a
careful, although controversial, study of this phenomena from a

wide range of perspectives. Tiger believes that the bonds between men are just as powerful as heterosexual bonds.

When men realize the intensity of their bonds with other men, homosexuality can be very threatening to the homophobe, and might lead to a limiting of otherwise fulfilling relationships. On the basis of a suggestion from Lester Kirkendall, I've asked men to describe their relationships with their best male friends. Many offer descriptions which are so filled with positive emotion and satisfaction that you might think they were talking about their spouses (and some will admit that they value their close male friendships more than their relationship with their wife, "although they're really different, not the same at all"). However, if I suggest that it sounds like they are describing a person whom they love, these men become flustered. They hem and haw, and finally say, "Well, I don't think I would like to call it love, we're just best friends. I can relate to him in ways I can't with anyone else. But, I mean, we're not homosexuals or anything like that." Homosexual love, like heterosexual love, does not imply participation in sex, although many people associate love with sex. The social stigma of homosexual love denies these close relationships the validity of love in our society. This potential loss of love is a pain of homophobia which many men suffer from because it delimits their relationships with other men.

Because men are unwilling to admit the presence of love in their male friendships, these relationships may be limited or kept in careful check. If male love is recognized, these men may be threatened because they may mistakenly believe this indicates they are homosexuals. Male friendships offer an excellent opportunity to explore ways in which individuals can relate as equals, the type of relationship which is increasingly demanded by liberated women. Most men have learned to relate to some other men as equals, but because they deny to themselves the validity of these relationships they respond to women out of fear or frustration that they don't know how to deal with this "new" type of relationship. Loving male relationships are part of the experiences of many men which are rarely thought about or discussed because of homophobia. As a consequence, many men are unable to transfer what they have learned in these male relationships to their relationships with women. They may also deny to themselves the real importance of their relationships with other men. Male love is so pervasive that it is virtually invisible.

Homophobia, as a chronic affliction of some heterosexual males, can impair their sex life as much as their love life. We indicated earlier how very homophobic men were more likely to experience frustration and guilt over sex than men who were not so prejudiced against homosexuals. The two most widespread sexual problems of men, which affect most men at some time during their lives, are premature ejaculation and impotence. These problems are rarely discussed among men because to let other men suspect that you might have these troubles is to admit that you are less than a man. The inability to have successful sex with a woman is part of the common (although false) stereotype of homosexuals. Homophobia demands that sex be discussed among men mainly as a tale of exploitation and supreme pleasure, with no hint of failure or dissatisfaction. Thus, if occasional sexual difficulties are experienced, a man might become anxious about his sexual abilities, especially if he thinks he is among a very small group of men (including many homosexuals) who have such a problem. Anxiety is the enemy of good sex. If the homophobic taboos were lowered, men could more frankly and realistically discuss sex and sexual problems. I expect that the result of this would not be a loss of masculinity, but an open and appreciative understanding of anxiety-free sexuality which more men could enjoy. Homophobia thus affects even this most intimate area of interaction between men and women.

Homophobia also circumscribes and limits areas of male interest. Homophobic men do not participate in sissy, womanly, "homosexual" activities or interests. Maintenance of the male sex role as a result of homosexism is as limiting for men as female sex roles are for women. An appreciation of many aspects of life, although felt by most men at different times in their lives, cannot be genuinely and openly enjoyed by men who must defend their masculinity through compulsively male-stereotyped pursuits. Fear of being thought a homosexual thus keeps some men from pursuing areas of interest, or occupations, considered more appropriate for women or homosexuals.

The open expression of emotion and affection by men is limited by homophobia. Only athletes and women are allowed to touch and hug each other in our culture; athletes are only allowed this because presumably their masculinity is beyond doubt. As children we all learned the pleasure of an affectionate touch. But as some of us became men in our culture, we learned that such contact with men was no longer permissible, that only homosexuals enjoy touching other men, or that touching is only a prelude to sex. In a similar way men learn to curb many of their emotions. They learn not to react emotionally to situations where, although they may feel the emotion, it would be unmasculine to express it. Homosexuals, homophobes claim, are known to be emotional. Once men have learned not to express some of their emotions, they may find it difficult to react any other way, and may even stop feeling these emotions. Men are openly allowed to express anger and hostility, but not sensitivity and sympathy. Perhaps this is why men fight wars and build concentration camps. But the strain of suppressing emotions until they are no longer felt is certainly great for many men.

A Fairy Tale?   Is a society without homosexism merely a fairy tale? We have seen that homophobia is not rational, although it may be pervasive in societies with rigid sex-role stratification. Homophobia is not related to widespread characteristics of homosexuals. It perhaps has its origins in certain religious beliefs and social needs which have been preserved into modern times with the imprimatur of science. However, homophobia was best explained by its relation to certain characteristics of individuals, mainly their conservative support for the status quo, authoritarianism, and rigidity of sex roles. Thus homophobia was seen to be one dynamic of the more general phenomena of homosexism. Homosexism refers to the general maintenance by men of a society where men control power through regulating sex roles. We saw that homophobia serves several functions in society which are of dubious value in modern times: it defines and enforces sex-role distinctions and the associated distribution of power, it facilitates social control, and is part of the regulation of sexuality and work. We also saw that the price paid for homosexism is great among many men, especially in terms of their personal relationships with men and women, and the delimitation of legitimate male interests, activities, and emotions. We discussed the relation of the concept of "latency" with homophobia, which showed that homophobia has great potential for abuse as an instrument of social control. Is a society without homophobia, and homosexism, a fairy tale, or will it become a reality? Only when men begin to make a serious attempt to deal with their prejudice against homosexuality can we look forward to living in a world which is not stratified by rigid sex-role distinctions.

References

Bailey, D. *Homosexuality and the Western Christian Tradition*. London: Longmans, Green, 1955.

Benson, R. *What Every Homosexual Knows*. New York: Julian Press, 1965.

Bieber, I. *et al. Homosexuality: A Psychoanalytic Study of Male Homosexuals*. New York: Basic Books, 1965.

Churchill, W. *Homosexual Behavior Among Males: A Cross-Cultural and Cross Species Investigation*. Englewood Cliffs, N.J.: Prentice-Hall, 1967.

Dannecker, M., and R. Reiche. *Ger gewoehnliche Homosexuelle*. Frankfurt am Main, Germany: S. Fischer, 1974.

Davison, G., and T. Wilson. "Attitudes of behavior therapists toward homosexuality." *Behavior Therapy*, 1973, 4(5), pp. 686–696.

Dunbar, J., M. Brown, and D. Amoroso. "Some correlates of attitudes toward homosexuality." *Journal of Social Psychology*, 1973, **89,** pp. 271–279.

Dunbar, J., M. Brown, and S. Vourinen. "Attitudes toward homosexuality among Brazilian and Canadian college students." *Journal of Social Psychology*, 1973, **90,** pp. 173–183.

Eglington, J. *Greek Love*. London: Spearman, 1971.

Ford, C., and F. Beach. *Patterns of Sexual Behavior*. New York: Harper & Row, 1951.

Fort, J., C. Steiner, and F. Conrad. "Attitudes of mental health professionals toward homosexuality and its treatment." *Psychological Reports*, 1971, **29,** pp. 347–350.

Freedman, M. *Homosexuality and Psychological Functioning*. Belmont, Calif.: Brooks/Cole, 1971.

Heron, A. (ed.) *Towards a Quaker View of Sex*. London: Friends Home Service Committee, 1963.

Hood, R. "Dogmatism and opinions about mental illness." *Psychological Reports*, 1973, **32,** pp. 1283–1290.

Kinsey, A., W. Pomeroy, and C. Martin. *Sexual Behavior in the Human Male*. Philadelphia: Saunders, 1948.

Knowles, J. *A Separate Peace*. New York: Macmillan, 1960.

Lauritsen, J., and D. Thorstad. *The Early Homosexual Rights Movement (1864–1935)*. New York: Times Change Press, 1974.

Lehne, G. "Gay male fantasies and realities." Paper presented at the

Groves Conference on Marriage and the Family, 1974. In preparation for publication in H. Feldman (ed.), *Man's Place in a Human World*.

Levitt, E., and A. Klassen. "Public attitudes toward sexual behavior: The latest investigation of the Institute for Sex Research." Paper presented at the annual convention of the American Orthopsychiatric Assoc., 1973.

Levitt, E., and A. Klassen. "Public attitudes toward homosexuality: Part of the 1970 National Survey by the Institute for Sex Research." *Journal of Homosexuality*, 1974, **1**, pp. 29–43.

Licht, H. *Sexual Life in Ancient Greece*. London: Abbey, 1932.

Lorenz, K. Interviewed by R. Evans in *Psychology Today*, Nov. 1974, pp. 82–93.

Mac Donald, A., J. Huggins, S. Young, and R. Swanson. "Attitudes toward homosexuality: Preservation of sex morality or the double standard?" *Journal of Counseling and Clinical Psychology*, 1973, **40**, p. 161. Extended report available from the author (1972).

MacDonald, A., and R. Games. "Some characteristics of those who hold positive and negative attitudes toward homosexuals." *Journal of Homosexuality*, 1974, **1**, pp. 9–27. (a)

MacDonald, A. "The importance of sex-role to gay liberation." *Homosexual Counseling Journal*, 1974, **1**, pp. 169–180. (b)

Morin, S. "Traditional values, sexism, and homophobia." Unpublished paper, 1973.

Pittenger, N. *Time for Consent: A Christian's Approach to Homosexuality*. London: S.C.M. Press, 1970.

Rosenfels, P. *Homosexuality: The Psychology of the Creative Process*. New York: Libra, 1971.

Saghir, M., and E. Robins, *Male and Female Homosexuality: A Comprehensive Investigation*. Baltimore: Williams & Wilkins, 1973.

Scarpitti, F., and P. McFarlane (eds.). *Deviance: Action, Reaction, Interaction*. Reading, Mass.: Addison-Wesley, 1975.

Schur, R. "Survey of sexual experience and homophobia." Unpublished paper, 1973.

Sherrill, K. "Homophobia: Illness or disease." Paper presented at the annual meeting of the American Political Science Associaton, 1974.

Simmons, J. "Public stereotypes of deviants." *Social Problems*, 1965, **13**, pp. 223–232.

Smith, K. "Homophobia: A tentative personality profile." *Psychological Reports*, 1971, **29**, pp. 1091–1094.

Sorensen, R. *Adolescent Sexuality in Contemporary America*. New York: World, 1973.

Symonds, J. *A Problem in Modern Ethics*. London: 1896.

Symonds, J. *A Problem in Greek Ethics*. London: 1901.

Tiger, L. *Men in Groups*. London: Panther, 1971.

Weinberg, G. *Society and the Healthy Homosexual*. New York: Doubleday, 1972.

Weinberg, M., and C. Williams. *Male Homosexuals*. New York: Oxford University Press, 1974.

Chapter 2

The Big Wheel
Success, Status, and the Need to be Looked Up to

Next to proving that one is not at all feminine, success and status are the bedrock elements of the male sex role, and no man in America escapes from the injunction to succeed. Success historically has been one of the key values in America, and it was seen as possible for any man who was industrious. Coupled with the strong Protestant ethic, which states that work is good in and of itself, the pressure to work hard and succeed became a major theme in our culture.

This pressure was applied selectively, however; women were exempt, and the norm pertained only to the males in the society. Women could, of course, be successful, but their status was measured in terms of the status of the man they married. Status in American society depended on a man's worth; despite the ideal of a classless society, social classes did (and do) exist, and the ideal of open mobility is less true in reality than many people would like to believe. But the belief in its possibility meant that most men were enjoined to succeed — with the difficulty in doing so frequently discounted — so that many men found themselves involved in a continual struggle to be successful.

Mainstream Success   Success in America has most frequently been measured in terms of a man's work, because this is often the easiest way of seeing how much money or how much power a man has. Of course, many factors go into calculating a man's social status, but because of the ubiquity of occupational status, this is usually the first one examined.

Occupational success must, however, be translated into visible and socially acceptable symbols — money, possessions, power. Clearly not every man has the opportunity to acquire these badges of status; if it weren't for the scarcity of such symbols, they wouldn't be used to denote success. Acquiring something that every other man has would not mean much; it is only in their scarcity that such rewards come to be coveted. Status indicators such as salary, title, number of subordinates, etc., all denote the relative position of workers. The appearance of a man's office is yet another indicator for gauging relative status. It has also been noted by some astute observers of the status game that executives who receive a promotion with an accompanying change of title will get new business cards printed, but if their address is changed they merely cross out the old one and write in the new one.

We have not discussed two frequently mentioned aspects of the male role — work and achievement — as separate dimensions of the role because we do not believe that the male role today values these things in and of themselves. Instead, working and achieving are seen as means to the goal of status and success. Little value is placed on what is called "mastery" — the ability to learn and accomplish something because it adds to a person's repertoire of skills. The question, "What will it get me?" is generally the more important one. For most men work is used to acquire the success symbols; if they actually enjoy or learn from what they are doing, that is an unexpected bonus, but it is not necessary to their measure of status.

But if work is one area where the need for status is played out, the more pervasive status-seeking is shown by consumption patterns. Of course it is nice to have luxuries and to make life as pleasant as possible, but that is irrelevant to achieving status by stockpiling possessions. Rather, the objects acquired are supposed to tell the world just how successful one is relative to other men. Cars, houses, clothing, leisure activities are all used to inform the world as to the level of status one has achieved. So too with women — the best man can acquire the most desirable woman, and maintain her as one of his possessions.

Other Routes to Success   If few men can "make it" in the eyes of society, then what happens to the large majority of men who, for various reasons, cannot get these rewards? Since they, too, have internalized the norm of success, we believe that they turn to other arenas and enact the same drama, but on a smaller scale. For example, the college professor who, by the standards of the larger society, is not blessed with many of the more tangible rewards, turns to "oneupmanship" within the university to gain status. The criterion of success can be as subtle as the question of the relative prestige of the journal in which one's articles appear, not just the total score of publications. Athletic prowess and sexual performance are two other major areas where men can gain status if they have not been able to earn the more obvious rewards. For those who are succeeding in the more traditional manner, these status symbols may seem trivial; but in the absence of any others, they take on an overwhelming importance.

Anything Can Be Done Competitively Competition is the basic process by which men in America try to achieve the goal of status and success. This rests on the assumption that the man who is the winner has the most status. While to most of us this seems "natural," it does not have to be so. In other societies it is possible to be a success as a result of a collective effort, rather than of an individual one. But with the push to succeed, and the belief that it is possible for any man to do so, and the emphasis American society places on the individual, competition as the mode of interaction between men almost becomes inevitable.

It would be hard to find an American man who is completely devoid of the competitive spirit. Even if a man is relatively noncompetitive with regard to others, he will frequently compete against himself (i.e., can he do it faster/better/etc. than he did it last time?). While this may have the positive effect of increasing the level of achievement, in many cases it can be turned against oneself, since one's own record was not broken.

But usually more aggressive measures are used, such as those which try to make the opponent lose his "cool." During the famed Bobby Fisher–Borris Spassky chess match several years ago, Fisher engaged in a prolonged campaign to rattle his opponent. While this was not technically illegal, it has nothing to do with the playing of chess, but was designed to unnerve Spassky so that he would make errors in his playing.

The economic history of the United States in the 1800's is dominated by the exploits of the robber-barons, who engaged in violent measures in order to eliminate their competition. And while such ruthless behavior may have been illegal, the successes of these men were often seen as justification for the means, since status and success, however achieved, are vital for defining American men as masculine.

━━━━━━━━━━━━━━━━━━━━━━━━━━━━━━━━━━━━

THE BREADWINNER

MYRON BRENTON

> Working to earn a living is usually considered a necessity, an obligation. But when work becomes the primary source of status and identity for men, Brenton argues, it begins to occupy so large a place in their lives that other things — and people — are excluded.

When sociologist Helena Lopata of Roosevelt University queried more than 600 women in the Chicago area to find out how they viewed their roles in life, in order of importance, she discovered that they considered themselves mothers first of all. When she asked them to do the same for their husbands, their replies were an even greater revelation. Did these women — suburban wives in their thirties, with a family income between $6,000 and $10,000; urban wives with a median age of forty-nine and a family income from $5,000 to more than $16,000 — see their mates primarily as husbands? As fathers? Or as breadwinners? The answer, startling though it is, isn't difficult to guess. Nearly 65 percent of the wives in both groups stated unequivocally that the most important role of the man of the family is, in their eyes, his breadwinning one. Father came second; husband, a poor third.[1]

These statistics lend themselves to a very plausible explanation. Since the American male bases his masculine identity so narrowly on the breadwinning role, since it occupies — both psychically and physically — the central position in his life, his wife naturally is inclined to see him in the same utilitarian way. If one leaves aside the implications this has for the emotional relationship between husband and wife, the fact is that by depending so heavily on his breadwinning role to validate his sense of himself as a man, instead of also letting his roles as husband, father, and citizen of the community count as validating sources, the American male treads on psychically dangerous ground. It's always dangerous to put all of one's psychic eggs into one basket.

This is not to deny the meaning and importance of work in a person's life. Ideally, work is an outlet for creative energy, a way of channeling aggression, a tie with reality, and what Erik H. Erikson has called the backbone of identity formation. What is suggested here is this: (1) The other roles a man plays in life may also be very valuable in these respects; (2) present-day working conditions do not permit fulfillment of the traditional psychological aims of work to any significant degree; and (3) a narrow concentration of work in terms of his identity does not allow the male enough scope and flexibility to deal with the complexities of the times.

In a bureaucratic, technological society with its insistence on rote and specialization the psychological meaning of work undergoes considerable reduction. With roughly 80 percent of the working population of the United States employed by someone else, most breadwinners are to some extent alienated from their work. Sociologist Robert Blauner defines alienation along four principal lines:

1. The breadwinner feels a sense of *powerlessness* because he has no say over the end result of his efforts, no control over his actions, is at the mercy of the machine or the front-office brass.

2. The breadwinner feels a sense of *meaninglessness* because all he knows are his specialized little tasks, which he can't relate to the various other departments, to the organization as a whole.

3. The breadwinner feels a sense of *isolation* because he can't really identify with the firm or its goals.

4. The breadwinner feels a sense of *self-estrangement* because there's little or no integration between his work and other aspects of his life.[2]

Although Blauner was referring principally to industrial workers, it's clear that his definitions are — to a greater or lesser degree — applicable at all levels of the working world. There aren't too many men who have the autonomy or the freedom to make decisions that is the hallmark of individual initiative. Nor are there many people — whether in business, industry, or even the professions — who can fully escape the feeling that they are cogs in some impersonal machine. Furthermore, the more work is fragmented, the less able a man is to relate to people not in his immediate speciality. To be sure, many breadwinners are interested in their work, but on a comparatively narrow level. For the most part, what challenges there are lack real dimension. Truly creative jobs — those in which the individual feels a sense of autonomy, a call for his best efforts, a solid sense of accomplishment, a real recognition of his particular services, *and* a knowledge that what he's doing is truly a worthwhile contribution to the world — are relatively few in number. On the whole, men are more acceptant of their jobs than actually caught up in them. Thus, for the tremendous ego investment a man makes in his job, the great emphasis he places on it in terms of his masculinity, the work he does will not, generally speaking, reward him commensurately. And he shows it. The growing problems of pilferage, restriction of output, malingering, "putting something over" on the company, expense-account cheating, and heavy drinking at lunch or after work — all are, in part at least, manifestitations of job alienation. It may well be that in some instances strikes are also a manifestation of the psychic distancing between a man and his job.[3]

Actually, these days it is not the task itself that the majority of American males are primarily involved with when it comes to their breadwinning role. The *fruits* of work are what the male considers more meaningful to him in terms of his manliness: the pay he gets, the prestige the job has, the status it gives him in the community, the possessions it allows him to buy, and the better life it enables him to give his family. His wife views his breadwinning role the same way; many wives have little comprehension of what their mates actually do for a living. . . .

One of the most important things a democracy has to offer is the freedom for a man to choose his own line of work. Economics, lack of training, or other factors of this kind limit his choice, of course; often he has to take the first thing that comes along. But at least there's no government agency to tell him what he must do or where — no one shipping him off to pick crops in California, say, or putting him to work on space projects in Houston when the need arises. Yet the masculine stereotypes themselves serve to delimit job choice.

This is especially the case with occupations having a feminine or an artistic connotation. When masculinity is closely bound up with job status, as is so very much the case today, there's even more constriction of job choice. A study of middle-class fathers and sons shows that such fathers usually say that their sons are free to take any jobs they want, although further probing elicits the fact that what they really mean is that their boys are free to take any jobs that are safely middle-class. So many a middle-class boy who loves to get his hands dirty working on cars and who would make a skilled mechanic winds up in the pristine surroundings of an office, working at a job really not much to his liking. This also works in reverse: Some blue-collar workers who would otherwise enjoy their jobs can't allow themselves to do so because these jobs don't have middle-class status.

The rating of jobs in terms of prestige is probably inevitable; it occurs in all industrial nations. But its built-in hazards are intensified when the society is very competitive. It isn't the job that really goes on the rating scale; it's the man who holds it. This automatically creates a lot of losers. By definition, any rating scale can only accommodate X number of prestige positions; this means that about 80 percent of the working population is more or less disqualified. Dr. Marvin Bressler, professor of sociology at Princeton University, pointed out that when there's a hierarchical system in which the bulk of the population holds positions which aren't highly esteemed "the occupational structure itself systematically generates a sense of failure in many men. A janitor who does his work with skill and fidelity nevertheless remains a janitor and he may convert the low prestige attached to his job into a generalized estimate of his own self-worth. Men are peculiarly vulnerable to this process. Women may escape harsh self-judgment by invoking the durable symbols of feminine virtue — wife and mother — that by public and private consent still redeem their lives. The alternative of shrinking the universe to family size is not now a viable male option."

Even if the job carries a goodly measure of prestige — or, at any rate, enough to satisfy the man who has it — he isn't off the hook. The trouble is that prestige isn't a stable element. Once achieved, it has to be maintained, leaving the man who banks on it at the mercy of all kinds of competitive pressure and changing circumstances. For instance, Walter Buckingham, a specialist in automation, makes the point that in the past workers were dirty while managers were clean. This gave managers a prestige that automation has done away with, and they don't like it. He tells of a U.S. Bureau of Labor Statistics survey of an insurance company that was in the process of installing computers — machines that would displace many of the white-collar workers. The survey showed that it wasn't the workers who objected. Dissent came from the vice-presidents, who felt their own status would be diminished.[4] On every level of the executive pyramid in the larger corporations there has evolved what Vance Packard calls the "intense preoccupation" with "symbols of status." He quotes the comment of a Cleveland corporation president that "often the little privileges that go with an office are more important to an executive than a raise. You'd expect executives to be more mature, but they frequently aren't."[5] In effect, competition these days doesn't necessarily mean climbing up the ladder of success. It can also mean making one's particular rung as safe and plush and comfortable as possible.

The American male looks to his breadwinning role to confirm his manliness, but work itself is fraught with dehumanizing — *i.e.*, unmanning — influences. With the growing impact of automation, they're bound to increase. The very fact that leisure time is already becoming a social problem in America, a problem getting a great deal of expert scrutiny (several major universities have centers for the study of leisure, and the American Psychiatric Association has a standing committee on leisure), is a manifestation of how an over-emphasis on work in terms of identity has a boomeranging effect. Most factory workers don't want more free time; this is reflected in the fact that the majority of unions have stopped bargaining for a shorter workweek. It's the threat of being displaced, however, that makes automation a major threat for most people. That threat is felt not only by low-level workers but also by white-collar workers and junior executives. A contributor to *Mass Society in Crisis* observes in discussing the new computers:

[They] combine high technical competence with just enough of an I.Q. to keep them tractable. They do precisely the kind of work to which junior executives and semi-skilled workers are usually assigned. . . . Many middle management people in automated companies now report that they are awaiting the ax, or if more fortunate, retirement.[6]

Scientists themselves are becoming obsolete in terms of their present skills. Many scientists — especially those in government defense work — are overtrained in one specialty. As their jobs are being eliminated, these Ph.D.'s and technicians face serious adjustment problems, for circumstances require them to retrain so as to put their expertise to work in a new field.

Eventually, automation is expected to make some profound changes in the work role. Depending on which expert you talk to and which crystal ball he uses, everybody will work, but only a few hours a day or week; or most people will only be occupied in research and services; or every person will acquire several different skills and jobs in his lifetime; or one-third of the population will always be in school; or the definition of work itself will undergo radical changes, encompassing some of the activities we now call leisure-time activities. Such changes, however, won't come about in the very near future. As for now, the man who invests his entire identity in the work role is rendered extremely vulnerable. Dr. Bressler summed it up this way:

Many people invest too much of their psyches in work. A wide variety of circumstances – limited native capacity, skills that become obsolescent, impersonal socio-economic forces, capricious judgments by superiors – make the prediction and control of occupational success very hazardous. Accordingly, a prudent man would do well to develop other sources of ego-gratification.

References

1. Marya Mannes, "I, Mary, Take Thee, John, as . . . What?" *The New York Times Magazine* (November 14, 1965).

2. Robert Blauner, *Alienation and Freedom* (Chicago: University of Chicago Press, 1964), Ch. 2.

3. See, for instance, C. Wright Mills, *White Collar* (New York: Oxford University Press, 1953); Fred H. Blum, *Toward a Democratic Work Process* (New York: Harper & Bros., 1953); and Daniel Bell, *Work and Its Discontents* (Boston: Beacon Press, 1956). With job mobility becoming the mode for increasing numbers of Americans, even the emotional value of working with other men and of becoming a member of the team is lessened in contemporary times.

4. Walter Buckingham, *Automation* (New York: Harper & Row, 1961), Mentor Executive Library edition, p. 63.

5. Vance Packard, *The Status Seekers* (New York: David McKay Co., Inc., 1959), Ch. 8.

6. Ben B. Seligman, "Man, Work, and the Automated Feast," *Mass Society in Crisis,* Rosenberg, Gerver, and Howton, editors (New York: The Macmillan Co., 1964), pp. 468 ff.

BLUE-COLLAR WORK

ARTHUR B. SHOSTAK

The status rewards of work are less obvious for blue-collar workers than for men in prestigious occupations, but they are no less important. In the absence of obvious status symbols, blue-collar men value certain "manly" features of their jobs enormously, and they may fight belligerently for what seem to the observer to be meaningless tokens.

Blue-collarites begin and end the workday with the knowledge that their employ could hardly have less status. Manual workers occupy the bottommost rungs on the occupational status ladder. What is worse, their status may have even declined further with time. With regard to the five components of occupational status level (money, power, prestige, nature of the work, and amount of prerequisites, like education), blue-collar work clearly earns a low ranking in the judgment of the general public.[1]

Blue-collarites are sensitive to their low status. They are especially resentful of the debasing stereotypes that frequently accompany it: Longshoremen, for example, are commonly thought "craggy, tough, suspicious, close-mouthed, uncompromising, often one step ahead of the law, ready to strike at the drop of a baling hook." A New York longshoreman challenged this image of his occupation in a recent discussion with a newspaper journalist:

The longshoreman always gets the blame whenever anything happens on the waterfront. We built up this industry with our backs and brawn, but we never get the credit, only the blame. I don't know

*what kind of people they think work down here . . . . Everybody is
right some of the time, but we're never right.*[2]

Other reactions of workers toward the public include accenting
selected aspects of the job, as with janitors who seek status in their
boast that the safety of the building's inhabitants depends on them,
or accenting the upgrading of job titles (waitresses become "food
service specialists"; garbagemen become "sanitation aides").

Business often supports the process of enhancing blue-collar
status: Typical is the copy of a new series of ads sponsored in 1967
on behalf of the American trucking industry. The ads praised the
safety-conscious heroism of the blue-collar teamsters, men who
have "earned their title, 'knights of the road,'" and concluded:
"The American Trucking Industry is proud of its drivers." Similarly, a number of vocational schools seek to raise the image of the
trades they prepare men for. A prominent school for truck drivers
recently took nationwide ads urging readers to "put yourself in the
'Commander's Cockpit' ":

Earn as much as $10,000 yearly and more! *Enjoy the excitement,
adventure, and prestige that can be yours as a pilot of giant over-
the-highway transport rigs! Join the exclusive corps of keen-eyed,
quick-thinking, professional men who help maintain America's life-
line.*[3]

The imagery speaks to issues of manliness, responsibility, elitism,
professionalism, and patriotic contribution — a handsome list of
alleged occupational attributes, all of a marked status-enhancing
character.

Within the work group itself, blue-collarites seek status increments from variations in seniority, work skills, "pull" with management or with the local union, knowledge of baseball statistics,
and the like. Many gain respect for an ability to mediate between the
rigid specifications insisted upon by customers or supervisors and
their own knowledge that much looser specifications will do. The
informal association of workers enters in here, assigning in-plant
status to "wise-old gray-hairs" and others valued in the work group.
The informal association also operates to assign low status to whole
categories of coworkers, such as Negro or women workers, who
thereafter constitute a negative reference group. Blue-collarites
spared membership in the disparaged reference group gain much
in-plant status from this fact alone, and the gradations here, however

"invisible" to casual visitors to the workplace, can be very significant to the status-hungry men involved..

With all of this, the discomforts of low status remain serious. The situation is further compounded by the rising level of educational attainment of many younger workers, the rising standard of living of all workers, and the rising level of material expectations of many workers. As a significant increase in job status can lag far behind these other developments, blue-collarites may suffer the additional discomfort of status inconsistency: They may earn enough to "command respect," but the low blue-collar origins of their high earnings may undermine both their self-esteem and the respect they command from others. . . .[4]

Work Meaning

To further compound the situation of the worker, his blue-collar work may also be in the process of losing its once-distinct and always precious ability to affirm manhood. Men especially rely on their work to confirm their sex role identity: Both in their own minds and in the judgment of others this constitutes an increasingly troublesome issue for blue-collarites.[5]

Work can affirm manhood, sociologist Robert Blauner explains, when it entails responsibility, control over tools and machinery, certified skill, initiative and self-assertion, the use of some intelligence, and the securement of the relatively high wages that symbolize masculine adequacy within the family and the larger society.[6] Craft jobs in particular encompass these characteristics. Moreover, they generally take place in an all-male setting and rely on a long apprenticeship that "separates the men from the boys." Little wonder then that being on a craft job in the first place more or less affirms masculine identity.

The situation is very different for the vast majority of blue-collarites who are semiskilled men working at machine-tending tasks (as in textile mills) or on assembly lines (as in auto, meat-packing, or rubber plants). Here the subdivision of labor has often permitted women to enter the labor force, and their presence as peers can threaten the firm sense of maleness of certain blue-collar men. The simplification of job tasks also means that not only women but "mere boys" are now capable of doing the work. Close supervision further implies the worker himself is still a child and is not yet mature enough to responsibly use freedom and autonomy. Finally, mechanization threatens the distinction men desire to preserve between themselves and their own machines (á la Chaplin in *Modern Times*). To the extent to which mechanization lessens the worker's control over technology and cuts down on the responsibility and mind-reliance of the job, the blue-collarite may find new meaning on the job hard to confront.

As if in desperation, workers earnestly play out the drama of manliness in work settings. Blue-collarites infuse their language with obscene oaths of Anglo-Saxon origin, stockpile impressive collections of off-color jokes, and traffic in pornography — all in an attempt to make the workplace "feel" more like a gathering place of men.[7] Others react to the encroachments of technology by inventing unofficial means of reasserting some degree of personal control (such as working out of sequence). The defense pattern here consists of rationalizations (work has no meaning for anyone), denial (reluctance to identify with the job), projection (the work force includes others still worse off), aggression (verbal and mitigated hostility toward the work process, the work, and the supervisors), withdrawal (horseplay, daydreams, fantasies of leaving to set up a small business), and compensation (emphasis on discussions of offwork sources of meaning, including sex relations, family life, and leisure activities). Most of the blue-collarites involved eventually adjust their identity to the erosion of work meaning (acquire an "occupational personality") or shift out of work roles that excessively punish them.

Blue-collarites, in short, may find the meaning of work as often as not a negation rather than an affirmation of a basic sense of worthiness. Certain blue-collar work may and often does reduce manhood potentials, the vast majority of workers adopting a stance of indifference as a form of self-protection. If blue-collarites appear preoccupied with "playing it cool" at work, they may be so animated by the paucity of meaning of other possible responses. The typical worker appears lightly committed to his work, and his work appears to grow ever lighter in meaning for him.

Work Satisfaction

Research data, especially that collected and interpreted by psychologist Frederick Herzberg and his associates, suggest the novel conclusion that blue-collarites may know little of either dissatisfaction or satisfaction from their work.[8]

There are apparently three states of being where job-related sentiments are involved: Workers can be dissatisfied, or they can be satisfied, or they can be neither. Satisfaction is viewed as resulting primarily from the challenge of the job itself, through such factors as achievement, responsibility, growth, advancement, and earned recognition. Dissatisfaction more often springs from workplace factors peripheral to the task, such as conditions of work, character of supervision, level of pay, and others.

All of these workplace items conjoin with important external variables, including the worker's frame of reference (a steadily employed worker thinks himself well off in a depressed area), to form a complicated calculus of job sentiment. This calculus is further conditioned by the worker's history (for example, former rural dwellers find change in blue-collar work more unsettling than do comparatively inured urbanites), the comparative performance of "significant others" (usually the worker's male relatives of the same age cohort), and the worker's estimation of available or future realistic alternatives to his present job.[9]

Taking all this into account, the research of Herzberg and associates suggests blue-collarites by and large are neither dissatisfied or satisfied, but are instead uneasily in-between. They "make do." Such men often tell researchers work is not a "central life interest" for them; they are working only to insure an after-work pursuit of happiness.[10] Many such men remain vaguely aware and uneasy about the possibilities for job satisfaction that they never totally experience. In their situation satisfaction at the job has apparently become less significant (for being less attainable) than satisfaction from consumption, and success at one's job has become less important than success in one's after-work style of life.

Worker Relationships

So significant is the need for positive association with fellow workers, for communication with others who can be counted upon to understand, that men regularly rank this need very near the top of their list of significant situational items at work. This is not to suggest that things are always rewarding when blue-collarites are in continuous contact with one another. On the contrary, a number of tradition-bound animosities divide blue-collarites in many work situations, animosities by no means as characteristic of white-collarites.

Typical here is the strain that sets men and women against one another in the workplace. Constant wrangling characterizes situations where women give orders to status-anxious blue-collar men. Male kitchen help, for example, resent taking orders from female waitresses. The men demand social insulation and insist that orders be written down rather than shouted loudly about the place.[11] More generally, blue-collar men resent the possibility that working women might be displacing other men from gainful employ. A woman's place, they believe, is in the home with her kids, away from the competitive labor market. Her presence as a workplace peer is thought to jeopardize the physical and emotional health of her children, undermine the self-esteem of her husband, and provide industry with a competitive menace it will use to depress wages, dilute skills, and remove men from their "natural" work roles. Women who want to remain in the plant are condemned for "trying to get ahead of the Joneses." Married women are thought to stay in the shop because they "spend indiscriminately, consume conspicuously, and overextend household income in their nervous desire for social status."[12] Working women, of course, deny and resent these allegations, the battle of the sexes raging both on and below the surface in many a blue-collar setting.

Race differences also set blue-collarites against one another and, as with sex antagonisms, appear more characteristic of blue- than of white-collar relationships. This is probably related less to relative degrees of sex or race prejudice than it is to the fact that there are more women either originating orders for men or working as peers in blue-collar settings than in white-collar workplaces; similarly, there are far more Negro manual than Negro white-collar workers. . . .

Many blue-collarites are critical and disdainful of the white-collar men they refer to as "desk jockeys" and "pencil pushers." (Sociologist Robert Blauner suggests that the traditional distrust and mutual feeling of distance here is probably as old as the division between the literate and nonliterate strata that emerged with the invention of writing.)[13] Blue-collarites frequently "write off" office workers as men who have sold out their masculine heritage for the dubious merits of a white shirt and higher social status. At the same

time, however, blue-collar derision of white-collarites does not pre-
clude many from selecting the white-collar post as an appropriate
occupational target for their sons. Indeed, blue-collarites seriously
differ among themselves in the character of their jealousy of white-
collarites. In the last analysis, many would rather have their sons
follow the white-collarite into a technical, professional, administrative, or even clerical post than follow the "old man" into the plant.
(One wonders at what price to family solidarity and father-son
relations comes the presence of the father as a negative reference
model, a man who insists his career is not to be emulated, but is to
be avoided?)

Sex, race, and class tensions only begin to suggest the kind and
quality of divisions where blue-collarites are concerned. Other divisive items include age, educational attainment, religion, region of
origin, marital status, political opinions, leisure preferences, and
occupational aspirations.[14] Informal relationships, of course, cut
across these demarcations, linking younger, better-educated men
regardless of race, or older deep-sea fishing enthusiasts regardless of
religion, marital status, or political opinion. The divisive items are
even-present, however, and remain both a challenge to local union
solidarity and a drain on affable relationships among shoulder-
rubbing manual workers.

References

1. National Opinion Research Center, "Jobs and Occupations: A Popular
   Evaluation," reprinted in Reinhard Bendix and Seymour M. Lipset
   (eds.), *Class, Status and Power* (Glencoe, Ill.: Free Press, 1963). See
   also Albert J. Reiss, Jr., *et al., Occupations and Social Status* (Glen-
   coe, Ill.: Free Press, 1961); Robert W. Hodge, *et al.*, Occupational
   Prestige in the United States, 1925–1963," *American Journal of Sociol-
   ogy* (November 1964), pp. 286–302: A. P. Garbin and F. L. Bates,
   "Occupational Prestige and Its Correlates: A Re-Examination," *Social
   Forces* (March 1966), pp. 296–302. A useful beginning for a new
   perspective is available in Richard T. Morris and Raymond J. Murphy,
   "The Situs Dimension in Occupational Structure," *American
   Sociological Review* (April 1959), pp. 231–239.

2. All quotations in the paragraph are from Frank Sugrue, "Longshoremen's Beef: Image Muddied Up," *World Journal Tribune,* March 26,
   1967, pp. 1, 24.

3. See, for example, the Bostrom Corporation ad, in *Business Week,* March 25, 1967, p. 26. See also the March 1967 ads of the National Professional Truck Driver Training School, Philadelphia, Pa., and the July 1967 *Saturday Evening Post* ads of the Whirlpool Corporation on their factory-trained repairmen.

4. For discussion, see Charles B. Nam and Mary G. Powers, "Variations in Socioeconomic Structure by Race, Residence, and the Life Cycle," *American Sociological Review* (February 1965), pp. 97–103. See also Elton F. Jackson, "Status Consistency and Symptoms of Stress," *American Sociological Review* (August 1962), pp. 469–480.

5. See in this connection, Ely Chinoy, "Manning the Machines — The Assembly-Line Worker" in Peter L. Berger (ed.), *The Human Shape of Work* (New York: Macmillan, 1964), pp. 75–80. See also David L. Miller, "The Individual as a 'Cog' in a Machine or in a System," *The Southwestern Social Science Quarterly* (Fall 1966), pp. 297–308: Lewis Mumford, *Technics and Civilization* (New York: Harcourt, Brace & World, 1934).

6. Robert Blauner, "Work, Self, and Manhood: Some Reflections on Technology and Identity," a paper presented to the 1964 Meeting of the American Sociological Association, Montreal, Canada. See also "The Themes of Work and Play in the Structure of Freud's Thought" in David Riesman, *Individualism Reconsidered and Other Essays* (Glencoe, Ill.: Free Press, 1954), pp. 301–333; "The Role of Work" in Sol W. Ginsburg, *A Psychiatrist's Views on Social Issues* (New York: Columbia University Press, 1963), pp. 162–177; Braude, *op cit.;* Arthur B. Shostak, "The Impact of Business on the Meaning of Work," in Ivar Berg (ed.), *The Impact of Business on American Life* (New York: Harcourt, Brace & World, 1968), pp. 338–360.

7. Lalia Phipps Boone, "Patterns of Innovation in the Language of the Oil Fields," *American Speech* (February 1949), pp. 26–35. "Amongst workers such words have . . . everyday use which almost empties them of derogatory significance" (p. 31).

8. Frederick Herzberg, *Work and the Nature of Man* (Cleveland: World, 1966). See also Alex Carey, "The Hawthorne Studies: A Radical Criticism," *American Sociological Review* (June 1967), pp. 403–416; F. Herzberg, *et al., The Motivation to Work* (New York: Wiley, 1959). Cf. "Work and Its Satisfactions" in Ginsburg, *op. cit.:* G. P. Fournet, *et al.,* "Job Satisfaction: Issues and Problems," *Personal Psychology* (Summer 1966), pp. 165–183; Frank Friedlander, "Motivations to Work and Organizational Performance," *Journal of Applied Psychology* (Spring 1966), 143–152.

9. Charles L. Hulin, "Effects on Community Characteristics on Measures

of Job Satisfaction," *Journal of Applied Psychology* (1966), pp. 185–192; William A. Faunce, "Social Stratification and Attitude Toward Change in Job Content," *Social Forces* (December 1960), pp. 140–148.

10. Robert Dubin, "Industrial Workers' Worlds: A Study of the Central Life Interests of Industrial Workers," *Social Problems* (1956), pp. 131–142; Robert Dubin, *The World of Work* (Englewood Cliffs, N.J.: Prentice Hall, 1958).

11. See in this connection, "From Kitchen to Customer," in W. F. Whyte, *Men at Work* (Homewood, Ill.: Dorsey Press, 1961), pp. 125–135.

12. See in this connection, "A Woman's Place Is with Her Kids" in Sidney M. Peck, *The Rank-and-File Leader* (New Haven: College and University Press, 1965), pp. 180–208. "Practically every suggested remedy [made by the white male union stewards] resolves to eliminate women from industry" (p. 205).

13. Robert Blauner, *Alienation and Freedom: The Factory Worker and His Industry* (Chicago: University of Chicago Press, 1964), p. 179. See also E. P. Thompson, *The Making of the English Working Class* (New York: Random House, 1963).

14. For rare comment on the division engendered by fears of homosexuality among anxious, overcompensating blue-collarites, see Gerald W. Haslam, "The Language of the Oil Fields," *Etc.* (June 1967), p. 197, *passim*.

ACHIEVEMENT AND SUCCESS

ROBERT M. WILLIAMS, JR.

Achievement has always been an important value in American society, but it is frequently replaced by the success ethic. In this selection, Williams discusses the differences between the two values and how the emphasis on economic success becomes central to American men.

First, American culture is marked by a central stress upon personal achievement, especially secular occupational achievement.[1] The

From *American Society: A Sociological Interpretation,* Third Edition, by Robin M. Williams, Jr. Copyright © 1951, 1960, 1970 by Alfred A. Knopf, Inc. Reprinted by permission of the publisher.

"success story" and the respect accorded to the self-made man are distinctly American, if anything is. Our society has been highly competitive — a society in which ascribed status in the form of fixed, hereditary social stratification has been minimized. It has endorsed Horatio Alger and has glorified the rail splitter who becomes President:

Periodic public opinion polls are not needed to justify the selection of Abe Lincoln as the culture hero who most fully embodies the cardinal American virtures. . . . Even the inevitable schoolboy knows that Lincoln was thrifty, hard-working, eager for knowledge, ambitious, devoted to the rights of the average man, and eminently successful, in climbing the ladder of opportunity from the lowermost rung of laborer to the respectable heights of merchant and lawyer. [2]

Emphasis upon achievement must be distinguished from the broader valuation of personal excellence. All societies have standards of character and proficiency, and accord rewards to those best meeting whatever standards are most highly appraised, whether of military prowess, ritual knowledge, asceticism, piety, or whatnot. The comparatively striking feature of American culture is its tendency to identify standards of personal excellence with competitive occupational achievement.[3] In the pure type, the value attached to achievement does not comprehend the person as a whole but only his accomplishments, emphasizing the objective results of his activity. Because of the preoccupation with business, the most conspicuous achievements have been those centered in business enterprise. We can say, with Harold Laski and many others, that the "values of the businessman" dominate and permeate national life. Yet achievement has never been completely identified with sheer business success; for example, such an assumption does not account for the respect and privilege accorded to the professions. Seen in the context of other major value themes,[4] business success seems to be a dominant focus, but not the dominant value-pattern, in American society. Increasingly, its position has to be shared with professional, political, military, artistic, and other types of achievement.

However, as already noted, economic success has been so heavily stressed in certain parts of our society as to impose a widespread and persistent strain upon institutional regulation of means used to attain this goal. At the extreme, only questions of technical effectiveness enter into the choice of means — thus, the

"Robber Barons," "business is business," and much organized crime, vice, and racketeering. Perhaps the apogee of large unrestrained economic acquisition was reached in the period of "business baroque" from about 1890 to 1912, when the leaders of business "exulted openly in power and riches, won by national centralization."[5]

Research evidence is not fully adequate for an accurate appraisal of the extent to which success rather than achievement has moved to the center of the values of our culture. Although we shall argue below that achievement is still a major value — a central criterion of desirability — there is a considerable amount of evidence indicating that explicit emphasis upon achievement has been declining during recent decades.[6] Whereas achievement refers to valued accomplishments, success lays the emphasis upon rewards. Amoral success striving may not have gone to the lengths suggested by some observers, but the important point is that once success goals are divorced from the ultimate values of society, the way is opened for a corrosion of regulative norms.[7] In the United States, the available evidence suggests that, even though success is often regarded as an end in itself and sometimes there is almost no positive relation between success and moral virtue, yet the success pattern is still linked to achievement, achievement is still associated with work, and work is still invested with an almost organic complex of ethical values. Thus, success is still not a primary criterion of value in its own right but rather a derivative reward *for* active, instrumental performance. There is growing evidence that performance in consumption is partly replacing performance in work: how one spends his income, rather than what he did to earn it appears increasingly to be a mark of "achievement."[8] Nevertheless, as Dixon Wecter has suggested, the American heroes are not merely successful — they must be successful within a certain ethical framework: they must be, or appear to be, "self-respecting, decent, honorable, with a sense of fair play; no Machiavelli nor Mussolini need apply."[9] The belief that virtue will be rewarded and that success attends upon effort dies hard; and in our culture failure is still more likely to be charged to defect of character than to blind fate, capricious accident, or impersonalized social and economic forces; and the wealthy and powerful still either desire or find it expedient to justify their position in the name of "service" and "stewardship." One need not be immediately persuaded by the intellectually fashionable cynicism which holds that all such defensive rationalizations are simply false. Achievement in valued activities may be alternatively formulated as contribution to societal welfare, if one can prove that the valued activities do contribute to a common good. This hypothesis obviously is not always defensible, for it is clear that some achievements may benefit small portions of the population while having a strongly negative effect upon others. Nevertheless, it is likely that an accurate accounting, could it be made, would show that many valued achievements do represent net increments to welfare — although, of course, there need be no one-to-one relation between degree of achievement and contribution to a common good, no matter how defined.

The dimensions of success values may perhaps be clarified by an examination of the place of wealth and its attainment in the culture. Many foreign and native observers have viewed American society as grossly acquisitive and materialistic, as naively impressed by bigness, speed, wealth, and power. Such a view is entirely too simple. For one thing, the theme of achievement unlimited is not limited to economic prowess or acquisition. In hundreds of complex forms it is pervasive in American *expressive* culture, where emphasis on the vision of the future produces impatience with the imperfect present and striving toward a salvation yet to be attained.[10] Furthermore, it is not self-evident that "materialism" is the essential component even in Americans' attitudes toward money.

We may begin by eliminating any interpretation such as "of course money is wanted because it is the universal agency for satisfying any desires that can be met by purchasable goods."[11] For many profitable activities are socially condemned and not widely carried on; and people strive intensely for wealth long after their basic physical needs have been met or even after thay have achieved nearly every conceivable means for satisfying their desires. Santayana's insight has more accurately indicated the central historic function of money in the American value system: "It is the symbol and measure he (the American) has at hand for success, intelligence, and power; but as to money itself he makes, loses, spends and gives it away with a very light heart."[12] In a society of relatively high social mobility, in which position in the scale of social stratification basically depends upon occupational achievement, wealth is one of the few obvious signs of one's place in the hierarchy. Achievement is difficult to index, in a highly complex society of diverse occupations, because of the great differences in abilities and effort required for success in various fields. At the same time, the central type of achievement is in business, manufacturing, commerce, finance; and since traditionalized social hierarchies, fixed estates, and established symbols of hereditary rank have had only a rudimentary development, there is a strong tendency to use money as a symbol of success. Money comes to be valued not only for itself and for the goods it will buy, but as symbolic evidence of success and, thereby, of personal worth.

Much of the same type of analysis applies to the so-called American love of bigness. It is said that Americans are impressed by size qua size; "bigger and better" is a childish love of quantity as such. Actually the important thing is that "better" is presumed to be *implied* by "bigger." Things are good not so much because they are big, but because goodness is assumed and bigness therefore means more of something already considered valuable. Again Santayana has well expressed the essential point: "Respect for quantity is accordingly more than the childish joy and wonder at bigness; it is the fisherman's joy in a big haul, the good uses of which he can take for granted."[13] Unquestionably, we are dealing here with a culture that values action and the mastery of the physical world;[14] and its whole history has been, in the main, an experience of expansionism and mastery: increasing population, increasing territory, increased levels of living, and so on. Given the definition of such things as good, respect for quantity directly follows.

It is obvious that one may hold achievement as a value without having a high level of motivation to achieve; for example, many persons who acknowledge high occupational achievement as a desirable state are not effectively motivated to do the things required for such achievement. Nevertheless, a rather high positive correlation exists. It is accordingly relevant that a number of studies report especially strong achievement motivation among executives and managers,[15] persons in both managerial and professional occupations more often than persons in other occupations give high ratings to the importance of achievement and accomplishment in their jobs.[16]

References

1. Earlier insights and hypotheses in this matter were developed and given imaginative research expression by David C. McClelland, *The Achieving Society* (New York: Van Nostrand, 1961). McClelland suggests, on the basis of historical data, that a protracted rise in "need for achievement" *precedes* periods of sustained economic growth and that long-term declines in need for achievement precede lengthy periods of economic stagnation or decline. Summaries and interpretations of research on achievement motivation contain much material relevant to achievement values; see, for example, Bernard Rosen, *et al.* (eds.), *Achievement in American Society* (Cambridge, Mass.: Schenkman, 1967); Brown, *op. cit.*, Chap. 9. See also Michael McGiffert (ed.), *The Character of Americans* (Homewood, Ill.: Dorsey Press, 1964), Chaps. V and VI.

2. Robert K. Merton, "The Self-Fulfilling Prophecy," *The Antioch Review* (Summer 1948), p. 199.

3. For other cross-cultural perspectives, see Don Martindale (ed.), "National Character in the Perspective of the Social Sciences," *The Annals,* **370** (March 1967), pp. 1–163; Robert M. Marsh, *Comparative Sociology* (New York: Harcourt, Brace & World, 1967).

4. The so-called success philosophy attains its full cultural meaning only along with a particular kind of moral individualism. See John F. Cuber and Robert A. Harper, *Problems of American Society* (New York: Holt, Rinehart & Winston, 1951), p. 356: "The basic premise of this philosophy is that individuals, not classes, are the real competing units. A man is said to reap his reward by his 'own' efforts, skills, and perseverance."

5. Miriam Beard: *A History of the Business Man* (New York: Macmillan, 1938), p. 641. For a similar period in the ancient world see Gilbert Murray, *Five Stages of Greek Religion* (New York: Columbia University Press, 1925).

6. This general idea had been persuasively presented by David Riesman, with Ruel Denney and Nathan Glazer, *The Lonely Crowd* (New Haven, Conn.: Yale University Press, 1950) and then by William H. Whyte, *The Organization Man* (New York: Anchor Books, 1956). For examples of the later scattered but often ingenious studies see: Richard DeCharms and Gerald H. Moeller, "Values Expressed in American Children's Readers: 1800–1950," *Journal of Abnormal and Social Psychology,* **64** (February 1962), pp. 136–142; Murray A. Straus and Lawrence J. Houghton, "Achievement, Affiliation, and Cooperation Values as Clues to Trends in American Rural Society, 1924–1958," *Rural*

Sociology, **25,** 4 (December 1960), pp. 394–403; S. M. Dornbusch and L. C. Hickman, "Other-Directedness in Consumer-Goods Advertising: A Test of Riesman's Historical Theory," *Social Forces,* **38,** 2 (December 1959), pp. 99–102.

7. A pioneering exploration pointing to some of the more important personality strains engendered by high levels of aspiration in a competitive order was the work of Karen Horney; see, for example, *The Neurotic Personality of Our Time* (New York: Norton, 1937). We already have reviewed the general problem of deviant behavior.

8. See, for example: Eli Chinoy, *Automobile Workers and the American Dream* (Garden City, N.Y.: Doubleday, 1955); David Riesman, "The Suburban Sadness," in William M. Dobriner (ed.), *The Suburban Community* (New York: Putnam, 1958).

9. Dixon Wecter, *The Hero in America* (New York: Scribner, 1941), p. 482. (This comment has to be qualified to take into account a Huey Long and an Al Capone, as well as the hero worship of the movie stars or television favorites who are presented as living in opulent success as the result of luck or "personality" — unrelated to traditional moral virtues.)

10. Robert N. Wilson, "Fitzgerald at Icarus," *Antioch Review* (Winter 1958); see this theme in a newer mode in Norman Podhoretz, *Making It* (New York: Random House, 1967).

11. The American sociologist Charles Horton Cooley pointed out as long ago as the turn of the century that "wealth as an object of ambition and a measure of success owes its ascendency to its social implications, and the pursuit of it is by no means a proof of materialism or sensuality. . . . The fact that a man desires it, throws little or no light upon the real object of his ambition." *Sociological Theory and Social Research* (New York: Holt, Rinehart & Winston, 1930), p. 222; the quotation is from the essay "Personal Competition," which first appeared as an article in 1899.

12. George Santayana, *Character and Opinion in the United States* (New York: Scribner, 1920), p. 185. Cf. Geoffrey Gorer, *The American People* (New York: Norton, 1948), p. 177: "It can be said that, as a general rule, the acquisition of money is very important to Americans, but its retention relatively unimportant."

13. Santayana, *op. cit.,* p. 182.

14. Cf. Harold J. Laski, *The American Democracy* (New York: Viking, 1948), p. 42: "No attempt to grasp the nature of the American spirit can be complete which does not emphasize the degree to which action is of its essence."

15. Victor H. Vroom, *Motivation in Management* (New York: American Foundation for Management Research, 1965), pp. 15–20.

16. Nancy C. Morse and R. S. Weiss, "The Function and Meaning of Work and the Job," *American Sociological Review*, **20**, 2 (April 1955), pp. 191–198.

MEASURING MASCULINITY BY THE SIZE OF A PAYCHECK

ROBERT GOULD, M.D.

The fastest way to measure a man's success is by external factors, and income is the most easily standardized indicator of status. Gould discusses how money becomes equated with masculinity in America, so that lack of the former implies lack of the latter.

Is Bobby Murcer a $100,000 ballplayer? Did Tom Seaver earn a raise above his $120,000 off his 21–12 record? How much is rookie Jon Matlack worth on the open market?

Lead paragraph from New York Post news story,
January 10, 1973.

In our culture money equals success. Does it also equal masculinity? Yes — to the extent that a man is too often measured by his money, by what he is "worth." Not by his worth as a human being, but by what he is able to earn, how much he can command on the "open market."

In my psychiatric practice I have seen a number of male patients through the years, of all ages, who have equated moneymaking with a sense of masculinity. Peter G., for example. He was 23 years old, very inhibited, and socially inept. Raised in a strict, religious home, he had had very little contact with girls and virtually no dating experience until his second year of college. He was sure that no woman would find him attractive unless he was making good

From *Ms*. **1**, no. 12, June 1973. Reprinted by permission.

money. In analysis it became evident that he was painfully insecure and unsure of his abilities in *any* area. Money was his "cover": if he flashed a roll of bills, no one would see how little else there was to him. He needed expensive clothes, a big sporty car, and a thick wallet; all these were extensions of his penis. Money would show women he could give them what they needed, and thereby get him what he thought he needed, "a beautiful girl with big boobs." His idea that women were essentially passive and looking to be taken care of by a big, strong male demanded that he "make" good money before he could "make" the woman of his dreams.

This kind of thinking is often reinforced by both men and women who have bought the myth that endows a moneymaking man with sexiness and virility, and is based on man's dominance, strength, and ability to provide for and care for "his" woman. We have many cultural models of this unrealistic and frequently self-defeating image of masculinity. Hollywood has gone a long way to reflect and glorify it in such figures as the John Wayne-style cowboy, the private eye, war hero, foreign correspondent, lone adventurer — all "he-men" (a phrase that in its redundancy seems to "protest too much") who use physical strength, courage, and masculine wiles to conquer their worlds, their villainous rivals, and their women. *Money* rarely has anything to do with it.

But in real life in the 1970s, few women have much concern about men like that. After all, there are few frontiers to conquer, or international spy rings to crack, or glorious wars to wage. All that is left for the real-life, middle-class man is the battle for the bulging wallet.

This measure of one's "masculinity quotient" becomes a convenient fall-back to those who have a weak sense of self and who doubt their innate ability to attract women. Because it is hard for these men to face their inadequacies and the anxieties that would follow, they strive for money as a panacea for all their personal ills.

For them, money alone separates the men from the boys. I have even seen youngsters drop out of school to make money, just to prove their manhood.

For their part, women have been taught that men who achieve success are the best "catches" in the marriage market. Women have also been taught that the right motives for marriage are love and sexual attraction. Thus, if a woman wants to marry a man with money, she has to believe she loves him; that he is sexually appealing — even if the real appeal is his money. She has to convince herself — and him — that it's the man behind the money that turns her on. Many women *learn* to make this emotional jump: to feel genuinely attracted to the man who makes it big, and to accept the equation of moneymaking power with sexual power.

There are many phenomenally wealthy men in the public eye who are physically unattractive by traditional criteria; yet they are surrounded by beautiful women and an aura of sexiness and virility. A woman in the same financial position loses in attractiveness (at least if she is *earning* the money rather than spending an inheritance); she poses a threat to a man's sense of masculinity. As I once heard a sociologist say: men are unsexed by failure, women by success.

Yet why is it that many men who have met the moneymaking standards are still not sure of their masculinity? Quite simply because money is — and always was — a pretty insecure peg on which to hang a masculine image.

Take Jerry L., a stockbroker. He lost most of his money three years ago during a very bad spell in the market. Distraught as he was over the financial loss, he was devastated over the sexual impotence which followed in its wake. This direct one-to-one relationship may seem awfully pat, but its validity can be attested to by many men (and "their" women) who have gone through serious financial setbacks. Even a temporary inability to provide properly for his family and to justify himself with his checkbook makes such a man feel totally "worthless."

When Jerry L. recouped most of his losses in the course of the next two years, he did *not* regain his previous sexual potency. The experience had made it impossible for him ever again to rely *solely* on money as proof of his masculinity.

The most extreme and dramatic reaction to personal financial loss is suicide. I have seen several men to whom great losses of money represented such a great loss of self, of ego, and ultimately of masculine image, that life no longer seemed worth living.

The situation becomes even more complicated when "the head of the house" is competing against his wife's paycheck as well as his own expectations. Recently, economic realities have made the two-paycheck family respectable. This is tolerable to Jack as long as he can provide for his family and Jill only earns enough to make all the "little extras" possible.

Given current salary inequities, it is unlikely that she will threaten his place as number-one breadwinner. But if she does, if she can make *real money,* she is co-opting the man's passport to masculinity (thus the stereotype of the successful woman being too masculine, too competitive, too unfeminine), and he is effectively castrated.

Thus it is vital that the woman be "kept in her place," which is classically "in the home," so that her second-class status assures him of his first place. Many divorces and breakups that are blamed on "conflict of careers" often mean nothing more than a wife who would not give up her career (and earning ability) in deference to her husband's.

I know plenty of men who are sufficiently "enlightened" intellectually to accept the idea that a woman has as much right (and power) to make money as a man does. But in practice emotionally — when it comes to *their* wives — these men often feel threatened and emasculated. Because he is unable to see this in himself, such a man expresses his anxiety by forcing a "conflict" with the woman in some other area of their relationship, like dealing with in-laws or running the house, where there is, in fact, no conflict. In this way he deflects attention from his problem but also precludes adequate resolution of it in their relationship.

There is one other common male defense against the income-producing woman. No matter how much she makes, he still maintains she doesn't "understand" money, calling upon the stereotyped image of the cute little wife who can't balance the checkbook. He doesn't have to look further for reassurance than the insurance company, for example, that appeals to a husband's protector-provider definition of himself with pictures of helpless widows and children, and the caption "What will happen to them after you're gone?"

Marty B. was caught in this bind. A successful doctor, he divided his time between research, which he found enjoyable but not very rewarding financially, and the practice of internal medicine, which was more lucrative but not so enjoyable. Marty felt it a strain to deal with many diverse people; he was more comfortable with animal research, which also fulfilled his creative talents and led to his writing a number of solid scientific papers. So far, so good. But then Marty's wife, Janet, an actress who had only middling success, became an actors' agent and clicked right away.

Soon, Janet began to earn more money than Marty. At first he joked about it with her and even with close friends, but, as it turned out later, the joking was uneasy, and laden with anxiety. Marty decided to increase his patient practice at the expense of his research. He forced himself to make more money — when he actually needed less, thanks to Janet's high income.

They began quarreling about many small things — arguments without resolutions because they had nothing to do with the real issue: that her new money-making powers were a threat to his masculinity.

Marty and Janet came to see me because they were considering separating after eight years of a happy marriage. After a number of sessions, it became clear that Marty felt that Janet's success meant she didn't need him any more; that he had been diminished as "the man of the house." This was not easy for Marty to admit; he had always claimed he was happy to see Janet doing what she wanted to professionally. But this was the first time he had to face her actually succeeding at it. Marty agreed, with some ambivalence, to go into psychoanalytic therapy. As therapy evolved, his problem with "masculinity" emerged even more clearly. He had never felt comfortable competing with men; this was a contributing factor to his going into animal research. He really received very little gratification from his medical practice, but he needed to make a lot of money to feel competent as a man. He resented Janet's success but since he was not aware that his manhood was threatened, he found "other" things to complain and argue about. After three years of therapy and six months of a trial separation, Marty worked through his problems. Their marriage and Janet's success both survived.

There are many marriages with similar tension that don't survive. Often neither husband nor wife is aware of how profoundly money and masculinity are equated, or of how much a husband's financial security may depend on having a dependent wife.

But are the old rules working as they once did? Increasing numbers of men making good money are not feeling the strong sense of masculinity it used to provide. A man can buy an expensive car and still get stalled in traffic; how powerful does he feel then? Money seems in danger of losing its omnipotence. In a complicated world, the formerly "almighty" dollar has all too few magical properties.

As a result, we may have to begin dealing with the fact that money has been an artificial symbol of masculinity all along, that we invested it with power and that, like brute strength, it can no longer get us where we want to go.

I suspect we will have to give up the whole idea of "masculinity" and start trying to find out about the real male person. We may find that masculinity has more to do with a man's sensitivity, with the nature of his emotional capacity to respond to others, than it has to do with dominance, strength, or ability to "provide for" a woman materially — especially if she isn't pretending to be helpless any more.

Some day soon virility may be the measure of how well a man relates to a woman as an equal, and masculinity will be equated not with moneymaking prowess but with a man's power to feel, express, and give love. That might just possibly be worth much more than money.

CONSPICUOUS CONSUMPTION

THORSTEIN VEBLEN

Money is useful only when it can be used to accumulate other symbols of success. Much of today's advertising plays on men's need to show this success by encouraging them to buy the most expensive and hence the most prestigious items. In this excerpt from *The Theory of the Leisure Class,* Veblen shows how men translate their monetary success into these other, more visible status symbols.

The quasi-peaceable gentleman of leisure, then, not only consumes of the staff of life beyond the minimum required for subsistence and physical efficiency, but his consumption also undergoes a specialisation as regards the quality of the goods consumed. He consumes freely and of the best, in food, drink, narcotics, shelter, services, ornaments, apparel, weapons and accoutrements, amusements, amulets, and idols or divinities. . . . Since the consumption of these more excellent goods is an evidence of wealth, it becomes honorific;

and conversely, the failure to consume in due quantity and quality becomes a mark of inferiority and demerit.

This growth of punctilious discrimination as to qualitative excellence in eating, drinking, etc., presently affects not only the manner of life, but also the training and intellectual activity of the gentleman of leisure. He is no longer simply the successful, aggressive male, — the man of strength, resource, and intrepidity. In order to avoid stultification he must also cultivate his tastes, for it now becomes incumbent on him to discriminate with some nicety between the noble and the ignoble in consumable goods. He becomes a connoisseur in creditable viands of various degrees of merit, in manly beverages and trinkets, in seemly apparel and architecture, in weapons, games, dancers, and the narcotics. This cultivation of the aesthetic faculty requires time and application, and the demands made upon the gentleman in this direction therefore tend to change his life of leisure into a more or less arduous application to the business of learning how to live a life of ostensible leisure in a becoming way. Closely related to the requirement that the gentleman must consume freely and of the right kind of goods, there is the requirement that he must know how to consume them in a seemly manner. His life of leisure must be conducted in due form. Hence arise good manners. . . . High-bred manners and ways of living are items of conformity to the norm of conspicuous leisure and conspicuous consumption.

Conspicuous consumption of valuable goods is a means of reputability to the gentleman of leisure. As wealth accumulates on his hands, his own unaided effort will not avail to sufficiently put his opulence in evidence by this method. The aid of friends and competitors is therefore brought in by resorting to the giving of valuable presents and expensive feasts and entertainments. Presents and feasts had probably another origin than that of naive ostentation, but they acquired their utility for this purpose very early, and they have retained that character to the present; so that their utility in this respect has now long been the substantial ground on which these usages rest. Costly entertainments, such as the potlatch or the ball, are peculiarly adapted to serve this end. The competitor with whom the entertainer wishes to institute a comparison is, by this method, made to serve as a means to the end. He consumes vicariously for his host at the same time that he is a witness to the consumption of that excess of good things which his host is unable to dispose of single-handed, and he is also made to witness his host's facility in etiquette. . . .

As wealth accumulates, the leisure class develops further in function and structure, and there arises a differentiation within the class. There is a more or less elaborate system of rank and grades. This differentiation is furthered by the inheritance of wealth and the consequent inheritance of gentility. With the inheritance of gentility goes the inheritance of obligatory leisure; and gentility of a sufficient potency to entail a life of leisure may be inherited without the complement of wealth required to maintain a dignified leisure. Gentle blood may be transmitted without goods enough to afford a reputably free consumption at one's ease. Hence results a class of impecunious gentlemen of leisure, incidentally referred to already. These half-caste gentlemen of leisure fall into a system of hierarchical gradations. Those who stand near the higher and the highest grades of the wealthy leisure class, in point of birth, or in point of wealth, or both, outrank the remoter-born and the pecuniarily weaker. These lower grades, especially the impecunious, or marginal, gentlemen of leisure, affiliate themselves by a system of dependence or fealty to the great ones; by so doing they gain an increment of repute, or of the means with which to lead a life of leisure, from their patron. They become his courtiers or retainers, servants; and being fed and countenanced by their patron they are indices of his rank and vicarious consumers of his superfluous wealth. . . .

Throughout this graduated scheme of vicarious leisure and vicarious consumption the rules holds that these offices must be performed in some such manner, or under some such circumstance or insignia, as shall point plainly to the master to whom this leisure or consumption pertains, and to whom therefore the resulting increment of good repute of right inures. The consumption and leisure executed by these persons for their master or patron represents an investment on his part with a view to an increase of good fame. As regards feasts and largesses this is obvious enough, and the imputation of repute to the host or patron here takes place immediately, on the ground of common notoriety. Where leisure and consumption is performed vicariously by henchmen and retainers, imputation of the resulting repute to the patron is effected by their residing near his person so that it may be plain to all men from what source they draw. As the group whose good esteem is to be secured in this way grows larger, more patent means are required to indicate the imputation of merit for the leisure performed, and to this end uniforms, badges, and liveries come into vogue. The wearing of uniforms or liveries implies a considerable degree of dependence, and may even be said to be a mark of servitude, real or ostensible. . . .

So, these offices which are by right the proper employment of the leisure class are noble; such are government, fighting, hunting, the care of arms and accoutrements, and the like — in short, those which may be classed as ostensibly predatory employments. On the other hand, those employments which properly fall to the industrious class are ignoble; such as handicraft or other productive labour, menial services, and the like. But a base service performed for a person of very high degree may become a very honorific office; as for instance the office of a Maid of Honour or of a Lady in Waiting to the Queen, or the King's Master of the Horse or his Keeper of the Hounds. The two offices last named suggest a principle of some general bearing. Whenever, as in these cases, the menial service in question has to do directly with the primary leisure employments of fighting and hunting, it easily acquires a reflected honorific character. In this way great honour may come to attach to an employment which in its own nature belongs to the baser sort. . . .

The dependent who was first delegated for these duties was the wife, or the chief wife; and, as would be expected, in the later development of the institution, when the number of persons by whom these duties are customarily performed gradually narrows, the wife remains the last. In the higher grades of society a large volume of both these kinds of service is required; and here the wife is of course still assisted in the work by a more or less numerous corps of menials. But as we descend the social scale, the point is presently reached where the duties of vicarious leisure and consumption devolve upon the wife alone. In the communities of the Western culture, this point is at present found among the lower middle class.

And here occurs a curious inversion. It is a fact of common observation that in this lower middle class there is no pretence of leisure on the part of the head of the household. Through force of circumstances it has fallen into disuse. But the middle-class wife still carries on the business of vicarious leisure, for the good name of the household and its master. In descending the social scale in any modern industrial community, the primary fact — the conspicuous leisure of the master of the household — disappears at a relatively high point. The head of the middle-class household has been reduced by economic circumstances to turn his hand to gaining a livelihood by occupations which often partake largely of the character of industry, as in the case of the ordinary business man of to-day. But the derivative fact — the vicarious leisure and consumption rendered by the wife, and the auxiliary vicarious performance of leisure by menials — remains in vogue as a conventionality which the demands of reputability will not suffer to be slighted. It is by no means an uncommon spectacle to find a man applying himself to work with the utmost assiduity, in order that his wife may in due form render for him that degree of vicarious leisure which the common sense of the time demands. . . .

From the foregoing survey of the growth of conspicuous leisure and consumption, it appears that the utility of both alike for the purposes of reputability lies in the element of waste that is common to both. In the one case it is a waste of time and effort, in the other it is a waste of goods. Both are methods of demonstrating the possession of wealth, and the two are conventionally accepted as equivalents.

HONOR OR CHAUVINISM?: TEST YOURSELF
MICHAEL KORDA

A woman is sometimes viewed as one of a man's possessions, with a man assuming the right to protect his property when it is trespassed upon. In such cases, defending a woman may have less to do with her safety than with a man's ego, as Korda has discovered.

As men, we don't see the way our behavior is *oppressive*, can't imagine what it's like to be alternately flattered and abused, to be a successful woman of 50 who can't go into restaurants alone because the headwaiter will often refuse to give her a table, to be a woman of 40 both of whose daughters have been molested and who herself now carries around in her handbag a container of Mace. The sense of danger, the inexplicable insult, the sudden obscenity, the feeling that one hasn't been understood and isn't going to be — how can men feel what it's like? How do we begin to treat women as equals?

Reprinted by permission of International Famous Agency. Copyright © 1973 by New York Magazine.

I *think* of my wife, C., as an equal — no question about it in my mind as we dine with a mutual friend in London. I try not to make decisions for C., try to ask what she wants to do, try not to impose, but the old urge to dominate, the simple crass desire to have my own way, still marks the male chauvinist's power erection, so linked to the sexual one that it is sometimes hard to separate sex from power.

Across from us, at a banquette, a group of noisy gentlemen on the verge of drunkenness are staring at us — at C., to be exact, who is beautiful and tanned and has her back turned to them. I, on the other hand, am facing them. Ponderously and inaccurately, they toss a few pieces of bread in C.'s direction to attract her attention. She ignores them. A few minutes later the waiter appears with a silver platter bearing a card, accompanied by the expectant giggles of our neighbors. Before C. can reach it, I pick it up and turn it over. It is one of those thick printed cards you can buy at fun fairs or in novelty shops: **I want to sleep with you! Tick off your favorite love position from the list below, and return this card with your telephone number.**

I tear the card up. Then, suddenly transfixed by the stupid, sniggering stare of the man who sent the card, I pick up the ashtray from our table and hurl it straight at his face. Instant scene: the crash of breaking glass, both of us on our feet, the headwaiter and my two companions pulling me away, the old instincts lurking there as strong as ever. "*Kill* the bastard. . . ."

Well, it's a scene — we've lived through them before — but outside on the street I find C. in tears, as furious as she is miserable. What did I expect? That she'd be *grateful?* That she'd thank me for defending her honor? I had made her into an object, *my* object. I wasn't avenging an insult to C., I was avenging an insult to *me*. Make a pass at C., and you have insulted me: man, possessor, enjoyer of her sexual favors, protector of her person. C. lashes out at me in the rainy street: "If you ever do that again, I'll leave you! Do you think I couldn't have handled that, or *ignored* it? Did I ask you to come to my defense against some poor, stupid drunk? You didn't even *think,* you just reacted like a male chauvinist. You leapt up to defend *your* woman, *your* honor, you made me seem cheap and foolish and powerless, you didn't even give me a chance to be a person, to make a decision about *my* situation. Make a remark to *my* woman and I'll kill you! In a restaurant, sure. I don't notice you defending me from Con Ed workers who make obscene remarks on Second Avenue! But in a restaurant it's a social situation, your sense of honor and propriety is involved, they've insulted you by staring at the woman you're with. In the street I'm on my own. The Con Ed workers insult *me,* not your honor, so you don't mind. God Almighty, can't you *see* it was none of your business? Can't you understand how it makes me feel? I don't mind being hassled by some drunk, I can take that, but to be treated like a chattel, to be robbed of any right to decide for myself whether I'd been insulted, or how badly, to have you react for me because I'm *your* woman — 'Hands off her, or I'll kill you' — that's really *sickening,* it's like being a *slave.''*

A slave? No. A man doesn't involve his honor, his *macho,* his masculinity with a slave. But yes, there it is, the essential male chauvinist reaction. C. is right, *my* woman. It's not that I care about the insult to her — later one can pretend that was the motive — it's that my possession of her was threatened, challenged, mocked, that *my* pride was involved.

C. and I cease glaring at one another, get into the car where our friend is waiting, make for home. Are my feelings about her merely an extension of my ego? I don't think so, but the possibility hovers between us, separating us momentarily in the night. After all, what stopped me from asking her what, if anything, she wanted me to do, or from letting *her* handle the situation? Was I not simply seeing her as an extension of myself? Yes, and don't we all, reducing woman to Adam's Rib, a part of ourselves once removed, but still somehow belonging to men by divine right?

ACADEMIC GAMESMANSHIP

PIERRE VAN DEN BERGHE

Beneath the mild, scholarly facade of the college professor dwells a competitive and status-conscious male animal — a trained jungle fighter in the swamps of Academe. Having safely clawed his way to full-professorship and tenure, van den Berghe now "tells all," in what may (or may not) be a caricature of academic life.

There remain three basic commodities over which most men spend most of their lives fighting: power, wealth, and prestige. Academics fight over all three, but most of all over the last. Universities and colleges are, first and foremost, institutions in which positions are gained or improved by patting your colleagues' backs, or by depreciating their efforts, or by a judicious combination of both techniques.

This is not to say that professors are indifferent to power and wealth, but the scope for invidious distinctions on these two dimensions is not very great. The salary ratio of a full professor to a beginning assistant professor is only about two to one. How unsatisfying for a Nobel Prize winner in Physics to think of himself as only twice as good as the young Ph.D. from Kansas State who may never get anything worthwhile published. (By comparison, the head of a corporation can regard himself as twenty or thirty times as valuable as a junior executive or production engineer.)

Power also does not differentiate well enough among professors. The basic power of professors is to flunk students, and hence to affect adversely their life chances. This power is jealously guarded and shared equally by all teachers, from the most junior assistant professor to the most senile full professor. Under the guise of protecting academic freedom and professional autonomy, every teacher has despotic power over students. . . .

The trouble with this power, however, is that, since it is equally shared by all professors, it cannot serve as a basis for making invidious distinctions among them. . . .

Luckily, there remains prestige as a basis of differentiation among professors. Here the possibilities are limitless, and professors have developed a pecking order of such scope, complexity, and subtlety as to deserve admiration. Vanity, a trait ascribed to certain male birds of bright plumage and to females of the human species who display varying portions of their epidermis on the screen or stage, is likewise the dominant characteristic of college and university teachers. . . .

Universities and colleges, as even laymen know, are ordered in a hierarchy of prestige. The layman's hierarchy does not necessarily correspond to the academic person's evaluations. Thus, it may be socially prestigious to go to an "elite" liberal arts college tucked away in the hills of New Hampshire or Connecticut, but such places do not rank high in the preference of most academics, except for a

few snobs and eccentrics who genuinely enjoy teaching. With a
remarkable degree of consensus, professors rank institutions of
higher learning into a number of pyramidal categories. At the top,
there are ten or twelve great universities, with the twin giants of
Harvard and Berkeley among them; then one finds a further fifteen
or so distinguished institutions trembling on the edge of greatness
but lacking the aura of the great ones. Following is roughly a score
of highly respectable schools, which however begin to show certain
weaknesses especially in graduate training and facilities; then come
some fifty to seventy-five colleges that do a decent job of educating
undergraduates and to whose staff one can belong without having to
apologize or explain where the school is located; a further 200 to 250
schools might still perhaps be described as on the right side of
academic respectability, but one would rather not be there if one had
a choice. Finally there is the great dismal mass of the 2000-odd
institutions that are of "higher learning" only by the most charitable
of definitions. . . .*

On the whole, however, in conformity with Veblen's theory of
conspicuous leisure, a top prestige symbol in academia is how little
one teaches. The higher one's rank and the more exalted one's
reputation, the fewer defiling "contact hours" one has with students, and the more senior the students. Lecturers and assistant
professors typically spend nine to twelve hours a week with
freshmen and sophomores; full and associate professors spend six or
fewer hours with seniors and graduate students. And a few prima
donnas manage to get research professorships that entail no teaching
at all beyond an occasional graduate seminar.

Academic title (instructor, lecturer, assistant professor, associate professor, etc.) is perhaps the most visible determinant of
prestige within the university. To each rank belong certain rights
and privileges. Tenure usually comes with promotion to an associate
professorship; salary and power increase with rank though not very
steeply, while work load decreases. Office space, especially where
scarcity forces some "doubling up," is generally proportional to
rank, and so is access to secretarial assistance. In short, the less one

---

* This last category has been termed "academic Siberia," a designation unfair to
Siberia, whose institutions of higher learning are undoubtedly of better quality.
Perhaps one should speak of academic Alaska instead. The reader should excuse my
refusal to name any schools (beyond the reference to Harvard and Berkeley), as doing
so might adversely affect the sale of this book.

has to do, the better the facilities one has to do it, and the more one gets paid for it. . . .

So much for the main factors making for prestige competition within the university. Let us now turn to the external prestige system — the prestige determined by the recognition of colleagues in your discipline. The overwhelming majority of them are attached to other institutions and are thinly spread all over the world. Each discipline thus constitutes a vast network of people isolated from each other except during the brief ritual of the annual convention when scholars converge on some large city's Hilton Hotel for three or four days of inebriated gossip, frantic job-hunting, and unashamed prestige-mongering. The national, indeed the international, nature of this prestige system, as well as the imputed expertness of the judgments passed makes the body of fellow specialists the ultimate measure of a scholar's worth. Unless your work is known and discussed by other experts in your field, you are a strictly local figure. It is immaterial that most criticisms be adverse, as they most typically are; the important thing is that you be spoken and written about, preferably by people you have never met.

One of the surest indices of academic prestige is the frequency with which your name is cited in colleagues' publications. As important as frequency is the context in which you are quoted. It may range from an incidental footnote, to a critical paragraph, an entire article, or even a doctoral thesis or a biography. . . .

Apart from printed evidence of scholarly status, the annual convention or meeting of the professional association is the greatest prestige show in the academic world. Conventions mean many things to many people. Ostensibly, they are a forum for the exchange of ideas and the presentation of papers on the latest advances in the discipline. In fact, this is little more than a pretext to justify the university's paying your travel expenses. To graduate students, conventions are a slave market for academic employment. More senior academics have a chance to peddle their manuscripts to publishers' representatives. Old classmates exchange gossip over cocktails. Various committees transact business. Foundation and government agents are solicited for support. All these varied and useful functions are overshadowed, however, by the fact that the annual meetings are first and foremost rituals of prestige competition. Professors strut around on the soft carpets of hotel lobbies with the assiduousness of birds of paradise in their display dances, but without even the excuse of a tangible reward such as the favors of females.

Unknown young scholars attend conventions to court the favor of the nationally known ones, and the latter in order to receive the homage of the nonentities, to bask in the sunshine of their glory, and to defend their territory against challengers. Regular attendance at conventions can actually be a substitute for publishing as a method for achieving a reputation. If the people who matter have seen you often enough, your name will be bandied about and suggested for editorial boards, offices in your professional society, and the like. After a decade of diligent attendance and proper courting of the mighty, you may find yourself an established star of a magnitude quite disproportional to your scholarly accomplishment. You will then be one of these people about whose accomplishments colleagues are understandably hazy, but whose name will nevertheless appear on a great many committees and boards. You will in fact have become the recipient of an unearned academic reputation, but as relatively few people can tell the difference between that and the *bona fide* article, the sources of your recognition are of little consequence.

Meetings are excellent barometers of professional standing. You know that you are leaving the drab herd of mere teachers of undergraduates when the following things begin to happen with increasing frequency:

1. People whom you cannot remember having ever seen claim to have met you at such and such a place.

2. Important colleagues recognize you on sight without having to cast a furtive glance at the name tag on your lapel.

3. Colleagues who have never met you read your name tag and exclaim: "Oh! I have long wanted to meet you," or "I am using your book in my class," or "I have just read your article in such-and-such journal."

4. People whom you only know slightly approach you and say: "The grapevine has it that you are unhappy at X. Would you be interested in coming to Y?"

5. Graduate students deferentially approach you as the authority on the subject on which they are writing their thesis, and ask for advice or for clarification on a fine point in your thinking.

6. You accidentally overhear your name mentioned in colleagues' conversations.

7. Your name is formally cited by colleagues reading papers. (It doesn't matter whether their comments are positive or negative.)

8. Rumors and anecdotes circulate about you. (Their nature is unimportant.)

9. Publishers' agents ask you: "Won't you write a textbook for us?"

10. Your feuds with colleagues become notorious.

11. A slight expectant hush follows your appearance in a group.

12. People approach you with greater frequency than you approach others.

13. Your own former classmates become openly envious.

If these flattering things do not begin to occur between five and ten years after getting your Ph.D., they will probably never happen. You might as well stop attending professional meetings and withdraw to the security of your college, where you can at least cut something of a figure at the faculty club and make students laugh at your jokes.

These two academic prestige systems — the one rooted in the local university and the other based on national recognition in the professional association — are intricately interconnected. Thus, in order to gain the respect of your professional peers, you must be affiliated with a respectable institution. If you are located at Apache Creek Junior College,* you have obviously fallen by the wayside, and no self-respecting school will condescend to pull you out of the hole. Conversely, tenure and promotion at the better universities depend in good part on publication and on some test of professional recognition outside the home campus.

The principal ground on which these two forces meet is, of course, the academic department. And, since the national system is paramount, day-to-day prestige competition between members of a department consists mostly in impressing upon others how much better known than your colleagues you are outside the home univer-

---

* The name is meant to be fictitious, but such a place probably does exist, in which case I proffer my apologies in advance.

sity. There are several ways to do this, such as discreetly attracting your colleagues' attention to quotations from your work in the publications of others. You may even resort to some such ruse as asking your secretary to drop into a departmental meeting to let you know that you have a person-to-person call from the Under-Secretary of Defense or the Chancellor of the University of Chicago.

By far the most effective way of establishing prestige is to be frequently away from the campus on long-distance trips. The top dogs in any department are the ones who are constantly attending international conferences, giving lectures at other universities, or consulting with government or industrial firms — in short, the professorial jet set. The jet-propelled professor does almost everything except that for which he draws his salary. His undergraduates have to be content with lecture notes hastily scribbled on the back of airline menus between the martini and the crab cocktail; the university that pays his way to give a prestigious public lecture will have to be satisfied with a few associations of ideas hastily thrown together between planes to the accompaniment of saccharine music at O'Hare airport. Some professors even keep a mental note of their annual air mileages. The truly big-league log at least 100,000 miles (about fifteen transcontinental round-trips). Meanwhile, the graduate teaching assistants get valuable experience, and the undergraduates get what is known in polite society as the short end of the stick but what in student culture goes by a more vivid (but alas, unprintable) simile. The airborne professor is no longer simply absent-minded, he is also absent-bodied, a fleeting shadow that can occasionally be sighted picking up his mail in the departmental mail room.

Short of being physically absent from campus, prestige competition calls for at least being inaccessible, ostensibly in order to engage in prestigious work, namely research or writing. The device of the secretary to answer the phone and screen visitors is of course widely used inside and outside of academia. But only a few of the more senior professors who are departmental chairmen or have large research grants have private secretaries. So professors have devised other ways of making themselves unavailable, especially to students. They can stay at home where they can keep a nice little tax-deductible study. More ingeniously, they can have unnamed office doors where only the initiated can find them. Or else they can get lost between their multiple offices. Thus a professor can belong to both an institute and a department and have an office in each; or he can abscond to the entrails of the library where he has a cozy cubicle and cannot even be reached by telephone.

WHY GANGS FIGHT

JAMES F. SHORT, JR. AND FRED L. STRODTBECK

Cut off from the mainstream status system by reason of age, class, or race, gangs of young men find other grounds on which to base reputations and command respect. Most of the groups described by Short and Strodtbeck base their status on public aggressiveness and their willingness to fight. But among the "retreatist" gangs that shun violence, another distinctly different value system confers status within the group.

Big Jake, leader of the Potentates, had been "cooling it" over the fall and winter. However Guy, leader of the Vice Kings, with whom the Potentates were often at war, warned: "Better watch Big Jake — he has to do something." Why? "He's got to build that rep again. He's been gone — now he's got to show everybody he's back!"

Report from a director of detached workers with juvenile gangs

Like Big Jake, Duke, of the King Rattlers, had also been in jail. Before his internment he had been known for his self-possession — for being a "cool" leader. Although a capable and active fighter when he thought it necessary, he never lost his head and was very effective in negotiation, conciliation, and control. When he came out of jail his leadership and his personal future were threatened and uncertain, and he became belligerent, aggressive, and apparently reckless — with the approval of his gang. Once things settled down for him, however, he reverted to the cool behavior that had made him such an effective leader.

As with leaders of nations, the qualities that raise boys to the

Published by permission of Transaction, Inc., from *Transaction*, **1**, no. 6. Copyright © 1964 by Transaction, Inc.

tops of the juvenile gangs are not necessarily those that best qualify them to stay there, or to rule. "A good suitor may not make a good husband, or a good campaigner a good president." Moreover gangs, though they may admire the fighting campaigner, are often more difficult to control than nations; members who feel abused can sometimes simply drop out, as citizens cannot.

On To Glory

These restrictions, however, do not limit fighting between gangs. Here a leader can work off his aggressions, show off his fighting prowess, and win prestige and popularity with his gang, making his position more secure. As with nations, tyrannizing outsiders is always more acceptable. A despot is someone who abuses his own people; if he attacks and tyrannizes other groups, he is a great and victorious leader, leading enthusiastic followers on to glory.

Juvenile gang leaders invest a great deal in their fighting reputations. Leadership and delinquency must therefore go together. In nearly all gangs we studied, over a three year period, we found that skill in fighting was highly valued, whether or not the gang itself had a fighting "rep." A fight often occurred because a gang, or its leaders, simply could not tolerate a real or implied threat to whatever reputation they had.

Some gangs are definitely "conflict oriented." Fighting is a major and necessary activity for them and a means of acquiring respect, admiration, and prestige within them. They must and do fight often. They have a heavy investment in — and therefore motivation toward — combat. Their leadership, reputation, and status are under constant challenge — anytime they falter some other gang will try to make them fall. They must be prepared for defense — indeed, they believe they must attack from time to time before others attack them, and to remind possible enemies to beware. "We are the mighty Vice Kings!" a leader will shout in challenge — much as Beowulf, using other names, might have done. The very titles and roles they create for themselves reflect the warlike stance — "war counselor," "armorer." These offices need not be clearly or formally defined or even performed; but they are recognized and given deference, and competition for them is fierce.

"Conflict" of course need not always involve major war — the primary purpose of battle is to prove oneself, not to capture anything. The kind of guerilla combat such gangs engage in was well illustrated in the following abstract of a detached worker's incident report:

"I was sitting talking to the Knights, re-emphasizing my stand on guns, because they told me they had collected quite a few and were waiting for the Vice Kings to start trouble. I told them flatly that it was better that I got the gun than the police. They repeated that they were tired of running from the Vice Kings and that if they gave them trouble they were fighting back.

"I looked out of the car and noticed two Vice Kings and two girls walking down the street. William then turned around and made the observation that there were about fifteen or twenty Vice Kings across the street in the alley, wandering up the street in ones or twos.

"The Vice Kings encountered Commando (the leader) Jones, and a couple of other Knights coming around the corner. The Vice Kings yelled across to Commando and his boys, and Commando yelled back. I got out to cool Commando down, since he was halfway across the street daring them to do something. I grabbed him and began to pull him back.

"But the Vice Kings were in a rage, and three came across the street yelling that they were mighty Vice Kings. At this point, along came Henry Brown with a revolver, shooting. Everybody ducked and the Vice Kings ran. I began to throw Knights into my car because I knew that the area was 'hot.'

"In the car the boys were extremely elated. 'Baby, did you see the way I swung on that kid?' 'Man, did we tell them off?' 'Did you see them take off when I leveled my gun?' 'You were great, baby . . .'

"The tension was relieved. They had performed well and could be proud . . . ."

Nobody Loses?

No doubt the Vice Kings too felt the thrill of having faced conflict and come off well. They had met great danger bravely, and had a good alibi for not having won unquestioned victory — the enemy had a gun. The Knights, on their part also had an alibi — the worker had intervened. Both sides therefore won, and could mutually share satisfaction and enhanced reputation. Gang combat is not necessarily a winner-take-all game. No one need be defeated. The two gangs had "played the game" according to the standards of their "community"; they had been rewarded, and law and order were now restored. The larger society too profits from a no-loser game. Of course, results are not always so harmless. Boys and gangs are often beaten and people and property often injured in this "game."

Threats to the status of a leader can result in violence to whole gangs; but the process is more complicated than it seems. Threat to leadership is merely a special case of "status management," which involves all gang boys. How can high status best be achieved and maintained in the continuing and risky give and take of gang life?

Humbug

Several kinds of threats to status are covered by the broad conception of status management. They are well illustrated in the elements involved in a "humbug" — a general brawl — that our workers witnessed and recorded.

Jim, the detached worker, had taken his gang, the North Side Vice Kings, to a professional basketball game at the Chicago Amphitheater. The boys were in good spirits, but restless and volatile. Duke, the strongest leader, had been drinking. He sat near a younger group, the Junior Chiefs. He was friendly to them but obnoxious to venders and others, and was generally putting on a show for the younger boys.

Duke announced that he was going to buy some beer — he had recently turned twenty-one. The worker told him that beer was out when they were on an officially sponsored activity. Duke bought it anyway, and after an argument in which Duke kept mentioning his age, Jim took the beer from him. Duke became abusive to the worker and other spectators; and the other Vice Kings also acted up. Jim then announced that the entire group had to leave immediately.

On the way out they met another group, the South Side Rattlers. As they passed, Duke "fatmouthed" one of them and blows were exchanged. The Rattlers, at first confused, retaliated and the humbug was on, while their workers, caught off guard, tried vainly to separate them.

A third group, the Cherokees, now happened on the scene. Having a grudge against the Vice Kings, they waited for no further invitation. "No one stopped to get an explanation of what was going on. The fellows just looked up, saw the fighting, and joined in.'' The Rattlers, apparently frightened by a couple of knives and a pistol, had started to run, and the fighting might have died had the Cherokees stayed out.

The police partially broke up the battle, but a new round of insults started it again. A fourth group, the Midget Vice Kings arrived; hearing challenge and counter-challenge, they too gave battle, siding with the Vice Kings.

After the combat, the detached workers reported that all three major groups involved talked about going home to get their "stuff" (weapons) and preparing to fight. The Rattlers, having been forced to retreat, were especially disturbed and made many threats. However, when the police came up and escorted them to their car, eliminating all possibility of further humbugs, they acted relieved and happy. On the way home they teased each other about running.

One group — the Junior Chiefs — had not been challenged, or otherwise received any "status threats." Not very surprisingly, they did not fight, and stayed and watched the basketball game.

Status and Manhood

The other gangs, however, did feel their reputations and "manhood" threatened. Elements of threat included:

- The worker publicly ignored and down-graded Duke's newly achieved adulthood.

- Following this, he degraded him in the eyes of his special, younger, audience, the Junior Chiefs — and of his own gang, of which he was supposed to be a leader.

- He publicly humiliated and degraded all the rest of the Vice Kings by ordering them to leave, like a bunch of kids who could not be trusted to behave in public. This too he did before the Junior Chiefs — an act which immediately downgraded them in the gang world — and before adults, who could immediately identify them as "kids."

- Searching for an outlet for rage and frustration, and for a means to rebuild their shattered "reps," the Vice Kings encountered the Rattlers. They attacked them. Now the reputations of the Rattlers (and later of the Cherokees) were threatened, and *they* counter retaliated.

Yet, for all the ferocity, the fights were short-lived. Every group except the Vice Kings, who had been most threatened, were brought under control fairly quickly and stayed to see the basketball game — only the Vice Kings missed it. Moreover, despite talk of retaliation, the humbug was self-contained; in the following months there was no more humbugging between these groups. The fight served the usual purpose of upholding reputations and preserving the images of street warriors ready for combat. . . .

"Kicks," Not Blows

This article is concerned primarily with juvenile gangs whose status is built around conflict. But it must be emphasized that, despite prevalent stereotypes, juvenile gangs are not all conflict oriented, and value systems may vary among them as among other human groupings. A "retreatist" gang, which built its value system around the effect of dope, provides a dramatic contrast.

Although criticized and ridiculed repeatedly by other gangs for their cowardice and lack of manhood, the retreatists seldom responded to taunts, and always retreated from combat. They did not worry about their reputations as fighters — they had none — and did not think them important — in fact, they thought the conflict oriented gangs to be "square." Directly challenged to join other white gangs in repelling Negro "wade-in" demonstrators on a beach in Chicago, they got "high" on pills and unconcernedly played cards during the entire incident.

The basis of camaraderie — what was important — to the drug users was "kicks." Past and present exploits — their legends of valor — continually recounted, concerned "high" experiences and "crazy" behavior rather than bravery or toughness. "You get the feeling," a member of the team of research observers said, "that whatever the activity of the moment, the guys will talk about it in relation to dope — how taking dope affects their participation in the activity. . . ."

Not all gangs value combat. But each will protect what it does value. When the retreatists find what they value threatened, they withdraw, protectively. When a conflict oriented gang feels its status threatened, it fights.

"Status threat" is a special case of the general status thesis — that people will tend to do what gives them standing and respect in society. But with adolescent boys in a gang "what gives them standing and respect" is contained in the limited compass of the face-to-face relationships within the gang, not — except indirectly — with the social class structure of society at large. . . . A boy can acquire "rep" by defiance of police, by vandalism of a neighborhood institution, or by showing "heart" in a gang fight. Whether or not the threat originated inside or outside the group, recognizing the existence of the gang and its internal dynamics is crucial to understanding how gang boys maintain status. The larger society is remote and abstract; even the neighborhood had indirect contact; the gang provides the face-to-face audience, the most direct and meaningful rewards and punishments.

"COOL HAND LUKE" GETS HIS NAME

DONN PEARCE

In the barren environment of a southern prison camp, all the usual standards of status are stripped away. As this selection by Pearce reveals, men can go to extraordinary lengths to create a status hierarchy, and *anything* can be done competitively.

But as time went on Luke gained a reputation of being not only one of the best poker players in Camp but also one of the biggest eaters. He could put away an incredible pile of beans and corn bread. And when Rabbit took up a Store Order Luke would buy all sorts of Free World groceries with his poker winnings — apples, bananas and cookies, raw carrots and sardines. Every day he bought a quart of milk. He'd spread his jacket on the ground, lay down on his back, open the container and drink the whole quart at once, gulping it down in one long, bubbling draught.

He was a natural. But in addition to his native aptitude he was given valuable lessons in technique from Curly. Recognizing Luke as a talented challenger to his position as the camp's biggest eater,

Curly taught him all sorts of esoteric tricks of the trade. It was Curly who gave him the extra-large tablespoon that he carried, digging it out of his locker where he had it stashed away as a spare, giving it to Luke with a big grin.

Here, Luke. Use this. That little toy you got there ain't big enough to keep a man alive.

Curly could eat. But he could work too. This is what kept him out of the Box in the old days when he would eat so much supper that the count was held up when the men checked into the Building for the night. Carr and the Wicker Man stood outside on the porch. The guards sat on the gun platforms. The captain was rocking and spitting in front of his Office. The cooks and trustees stood by in the kitchen. The Walking Boss sat in the Messhall, standing guard over Curly who sat there all alone — eating.

That was how he won the unique distinction of having the legal right to get in at the head of the chow line, this privilege granted by personal orders of the Captain himself.

It was inevitable that the day should come. It was hot and the Bull Gang had spent all day in a drainage ditch in water up to their waists, cutting out the dense undergrowth of briars and willows and palmettos with bush axes. Luke had worked like a fiend, slashing away at twice the speed of anyone else, lopping off the fronds and branches with forehand and backhand strokes of ferocity. But because of the temperature and because we weren't very far from Camp, the Bull Gang was the first squad to check in from the road.

Luke was the first man to reach the Messhall door, limping and staggering, his pants and shoes soaking wet with mud and slime. Everyone waited for the other squads to come in. Finally the Patch Squad arrived and then Curly came up, stepping right in front of Luke with a grin.

Everybody made jokes and wisecracks. The two double-gut giants stood by the screen door, grinding their teeth and stomping their feet, their spoons held in their hands at the ready, glittering in the sunset.

Boss Higgins was the Walking Boss in charge of the Messhall that night. He went inside. Taking his position by the kitchen door, he gave the signal.

Curly and Luke each grabbed a plate and leaped to the line of pots where one trustee was serving the scrap of fatback and another the catheads. On this particular night the Dog Boy ladled up the main dish, a concoction of stewed potatoes. It was a soft, over-cooked mess but not really bad at all. But for the big eaters it was a pure blessing. Ordinarily they always chewed a mouthful of food just twice and then swallowed. But on this night they didn't have to chew at all.

Before the sixth man had filed inside Curly and Luke were standing by the door, their empty plates dangling in bored, innocent hands. They ignored our grins, scowls and insulting whispers, calmly waiting there for the end of the line to come through so they could get seconds.

Then again they leaped to their places with overheaped plates, their spoons scooping in a whipped blur as they slopped, slurped and swallowed and jumped up neck and neck to go back for more. This time the Dog Boy stacked up their plates with a mountainous heap, never believing they could finish it and getting a vicious thrill out of the Heat he imagined they were bringing down upon themselves from the Free Man.

But they polished off that serving in less than sixty seconds and returned once again. And then we knew. For the first time in over three years, Curly's title was being seriously challenged.

The whole drama was acted out in silent pantomime. We couldn't cheer, shout or make bets. But we expressed our glee and our befuddlement with our eyes, our nods, fingers and smiles.

Reluctantly we finished up our own pitifully small portions. One by one we got up and stepped outside to wash off our spoons under the faucet, to take off our shoes and empty our pockets to allow the Floorwalker to shake us down. Inside the Messhall, a few brave ones were still dawdling, risking the wrath of the Free Man in order to witness at first hand this incredible contest.

Four plates and then five. The Dog Boy's remarks became louder and more cutting. Being a trustee he had the right to speak aloud in the Messhall. And being a Judas whose job was to train the bloodhounds and to chase escaping convicts, and being a natural son of a bitch besides, he tried his very best to put the Heat on the gulping, swelling duet.

Damn. Ain't never seen such gluttons. Keep on and the State's liable to go broke feedin' 'em. Here boy! Soooooeeeee! You want some more slops? Soooeeeee!

But the Free Man simply observed the proceedings from his chair in the corner, clutching his ulcered stomach with his fingers. Then he growled out impatiently.

Them two are the best Rollers in Camp. Boss Godfrey says Luke's able to do more work than any man in the Bull Gang. A man sure as hell cain't work if he don't eat right. Ah only wish ah could eat like that. Ah'd give anything.

And that shut up the Dog Boy who had come dangerously close to putting the Finger on himself.

After six plates of stewed potatoes each, the pot was empty. With a sigh of regret, Curly started to rise. But then Jabo the Cook came out with two aluminum bowls of stewed prunes that were left over from the guards' table at breakfast. He offered them to Curly and Luke and then sat down on the bench opposite them, holding his chin in his hand and watching. Babalugats was the last Gunman left in the Messhall. But then he could tarry no longer and came out to break the news to the rest of us who were clinging to the bars and wire of the windows, waiting for some word.

They both spit out the last pit at the same time to set the metal bowls ringing in an affirmative major chord. Sardonically the Cook offered to get them still another bowl but Curly was too cunning. He realized that if they ran the thing into the ground there was a serious risk of getting into trouble. They had had their fun. But they didn't want to become Wise Guys.

They left the Messhall, waddling with short, stiff-legged steps, their bellies swollen painfully. Then Curly stopped and twisted his big torso on his hips, letting go with a truly magnificent fart. Luke grinned, raised his right leg and answered the call, trumpeting far over the distant groves dim with the shadows of dusk.

It was a draw.

But to have eaten Curly to a draw was such an outstanding accomplishment that Luke's fame was immediately established. Shortly afterwards, Curly was made a trustee. No longer working under the gun, his appetite fell off considerably and although he had retired undefeated, Luke became the new Intestinal Champion.

And then one night while playing poker he managed to bluff his way into stealing a pot of a dollar and sixty-five cents. Everyone else had thrown in his hand except Bullshit Bill who was holding a pair of aces. But when Luke raised the last bet a dollar he refused to call the raise. After dragging in the nickels, dimes and quarters, Luke showed his hand to Bullshit Bill. He had a pair of nothing. Smiling, he murmured softly.

Just remember, man. Wherever you go and whatever you do. Always play a real cool hand.

And from that night on he always answered to the name of Cool Hand Luke.

SEX AT THE OFFICE

MICHAEL KORDA

In the high-rise jungles of the corporate business world, no potential status symbol is overlooked. And Korda, a top New York executive, is in a position to know. But illicit sex as a status symbol. . . .

In principle, there is something very attractive about the idea of sex in the office, a sense in which sexuality heightens one's pleasure in one's work, a complicity of shared concerns that in itself contains a certain excitement. Indeed, so exciting is the idea of sex at work that one of the major office games is pretending that it's taking place when it fact it isn't. On a basic male chauvinist level an office affair is a badge of status, always provided that it's handled well; that is, with the minimal amount of emotional disturbance and with its course and direction firmly controlled (or thought to be firmly controlled) by the male partner. Any display of emotion on the part of the man, or the suggestion that the woman either initiated the affair or decides when and how it will end, loses the man his status in his peer group. One of the most enduring traditions of business is the summer affair when the wife and the children have been safely set up in some beach house, to be visited, like expensive prisoners, on the weekends. The summer months are open season, the time for putting into practice the fantasies of the winter, and nobody who controls expense accounts can fail to notice a certain unexpected rise in expenditures in July and August, along with the repetitive mention

From *Male Chauvinism: How it Works,* by Michael Korda. Copyright © 1972, 1973 by Michael Korda. Reprinted by permission of Random House, Inc.

of those small, dark bars and restaurants on the Upper West Side
and around York Avenue, where the nightly attempt to find a domestic substitute for the dog days of summer take place, sometimes
successfully, more often not. Lust is very often less a factor than the
understanding unwillingness to be alone four nights a week in the big
city, not to speak of the sensual quality of those airless, hot evenings
that otherwise offer only eating alone with a copy of the evening
newspaper propped up before them. Sex, of course, does take place,
but even when it does not, most men are obliged to pretend that it
has. An executive invites a woman to have dinner with him, drops
her home and goes back to feed the cat. The next day, if questioned,
he is likely to answer with a smile of complicity, unwilling to admit
that there was never the slightest suggestion of sex on either side,
but thus changing the status of his dinner companion in everyone's
eyes, and making her relationship with other men in the office
(including those who decide her salary and her chances of promotion) that much more difficult and complex. Many men cultivate
meaningful reticence, broadly hinting that they have "something
going" outside the office. While early-morning conferences in the
summer months produce a kind of obligatory sexual recitation, the
equivalent of campfire fishing stories:

"I don't know, last year was terrific, but it's already July and I
haven't got anything going yet . . . ."

"You're lucky. I'm exhausted. There's this magazine re-
searcher I met at a party, and she's only twenty, and I'm using
muscles I never even knew I had, it's like the Kama Sutra."

"Hey, Steve, didn't I see you leaving last night with Nancy?
That girl has a great-looking ass on her."

"Mmmm. What's on the agenda this morning?"

Clearly, the last man is ahead on points, on the grounds that he
who says least means most, though he may very well have bought
Nancy a drink then gone home to read *Playboy* . . . .

Thus play-acting plays a large part in office sexuality, and
indeed the more obvious an office "affair" is, the less likely it is to
have been consummated. I have seen respectable men in their late
forties allow themselves to be interrupted in the middle of a meeting
by young women to be told that it was time to go home, or that they
were tired of waiting, and the only response was the sly smile of a
man caught out in domestic *contretemps*. A friend of mine used to
take his rather glamorous secretary to conventions, giving rise to

rumors that he did nothing to discourage. He was thought of by his colleagues as a very real *mensch* indeed, except that during an evening of heavy drinking, his companion revealed that they had separate rooms and kept to them. "Of course I'm not sleeping with him," she said. "I mean he's never even suggested it, if he *did* I might, who knows? But we just traveled down together, you know, and he talks a lot about himself and about his wife, and I think if I turned up in his room and took off my clothes, he'd *panic*.

Needless to say, his loss of status was irremediable, and shortly after he fired her, he left himself to take another job. There was simply no way his colleagues could take him seriously any more. It is better by far to be caught out *in flagrante delicto* on your office couch than to have your sexual *machismo* revealed as a fraud. Some men, in fact, are partisans of the public sexual encounter, building up their reputation by a series of open (and often drunken) seductions which have the advantage of establishing their sexual aggressiveness once and for all in the minds of their colleagues, leaving them free to get on with their work for several months or years afterward, secure in status.

In the age of sexual freedom, sex *is* status, and it is for this reason that men are reluctant to let it be known that they have dropped out of the sexual competition.

THE COMPETITIVE WORLD OF THE PURE SCIENTIST

F. REIF

To the layman, the world of pure science may seem a sheltered and peaceable kingdom, in which idealistic scholars pursue the search for knowledge with selfless devotion. But things aren't quite so simple, as Reif reveals from an "insider's" view of the science establishment. Ironically, many students are originally attracted to science by precisely this image of noncompetitive sharing, only to find a few years later that they are in a system not unlike the competitive world of business they once disdained.

From *Science*, **134**, December 15, 1961. Copyright © 1961 by the American Association for the Advancement of Science. Reprinted by permission.

The "pure scientist" is likely to be pictured as a person who devotes himself to the study of natural phenomena without regard to their possible practical or technological applications. Motivated by intellectual curiosity and immersed in his abstract work, he tends to be oblivious of the more mundane concerns of ordinary men. Although a few older scientists have become active in public affairs in recent years, the large majority who remain at work in their university laboratories lead peaceful lives, aloof from the competitive business practices or political manipulations of the outside world.

Stereotype Versus Reality

There is some truth in this stereotyped portrait. But if a young student took its apparent serenity too seriously, he would be forced to revise his perspective very early in his scientific career. The work situation of the scientist is not just a quiet haven for scholarly activity, ideally suited to those of introverted temperament. The pure scientist, like the businessman or lawyer, works in a social setting, and like them, he is subject to appreciable social and competitive pressures. The institutional framework within which he functions is distinctive: it is basically the university system. Furthermore his competition does not revolve primarily around money; there is no very direct relationship between the quality of the scientist's professional performance and the economic rewards he receives. But competition need not be confined to the acquisition of wealth or political power. It is, therefore, of particular interest to discover how intense competition can become in an area as remote as pure science. In recent years rapid expansion has occurred in many branches of science. More scientists are active in many fields, more laboratories (including some in industry and government) engage in pure research activities, and more dollars are spent on such research. While this expansion has given the scientist a more prominent social role, it has also intensified the competitive pressures under which he works.

A few examples will illustrate how such competition can manifest itself. I shall take these illustrations from the field of physics, because physics is a well-developed pure science and because this is the field with which I am most familiar. In this country research work in physics has traditionally been published in a bimonthly journal called the *Physical Review*. In addition to full-length research reports, this journal used to publish "Letters to the editor," short notes whereby scientists could briefly communicate important new developments. The time elapsed between submission of a manuscript and its appearance in print was approximately 5 months for a regular paper and 2 or 3 months for a "letter." But in a period of rapid growth and development the pressure to publish fast and to establish priority claims became sufficiently great to make the *Physical Review* appear an inordinately slow medium of communication. Three years ago, therefore, its editors decided to eliminate the "Letters" section and to found a separate bimonthly journal, the *Physical Review Letters,* devoted entirely to the fastest possible publication of short notes on important discoveries. The time between submission of a manuscript and its appearance in print has been reduced to as little as 4 weeks! Not only is the existence of such a journal a significant phenomenon in itself; it has also necessitated the formulation of new editorial policies. As a result, although editorials in scientific periodicals are ordinarily very rare, some illuminating examples have found their way into issues of the *Physical Review Letters.*

In one of these[1] the editor comments that a large number of manuscripts are submitted whose importance and meagre content are not adequate to justify publication in the *Letters.* He goes on to say: "When a 'hot' subject breaks there is a deluge of follow-up contributions. . . . With the rapid exploitation of new ideas, priority questions become serious problems. Possibly important technical applications often lurk in the background. . . ." After explaining that he feels compelled to reject as unworthy of publication more than 40 percent of the manuscripts received, he concludes: "We do not take kindly to attempts to pressure us into accepting letters by misrepresentation, gamesmanship, and jungle tactics, which we have experienced to some (fortunately small) extent."

From the foregoing comments it is apparent that scientists seem most eager to see their work appear in print as soon as practicable. But to achieve that purpose, even the *Letters* can appear unduly slow. Certainly, the daily press is even faster; and though it may be less suitable for erudite publication, it is more effective for publicity and no less effective for establishing priority. Consequently, there have been several instances in recent years when important discoveries in physics were first announced in the New York *Times.* This procedure is not, by traditional values of the scientific community, considered to be very ethical. Nor is it, as the *Letters* editor points out in another editorial, an activity to be confused with the well-developed public information and publicity activities carried out by his own office and by such agencies as the American Institute of Physics. The editor expresses himself quite forcefully:[2] "As a matter of courtesy to fellow physicists, it is customary for authors to see to it that releases to the public do not occur before the article appears in the scientific journal. Scientific discoveries are not the proper subject for newspaper scoops, and all media of mass communication should have equal opportunity for simultaneous access to the information. In the future, we may reject papers whose main content has been published previously in the daily press."

In the passages quoted, the editor of the official journal of American physicists makes some revealing comments about the behavior of his fellow scientists. What are some of the factors responsible for such behavior? Why should there be this exorbitant desire to publish and to do so ahead of others? The following discussion will focus attention on some of these questions in an attempt to clarify the conditions of modern science which contribute to this behavior . . .

Prestige and Success

The scientist is not different from others in his desire to be successful, but his definition of "success" has some distinctive features. The work of the pure scientist is abstract; it consists essentially only in gathering new data and formulating new concepts. To constitute scientific knowledge, these must be verifiable by other scientists and usable by them as the basis for further exploration. Thus, the very nature of scientific activity implies the need for recognition of the value of one's work by others in the field. Furthermore, success in such activities is not readily measurable in quantitative terms recognized by all. It does not revolve around tangible things such as amount of money earned or number of factories owned. Only other scientists in his field can understand the scientist's work and judge its merits. Indeed, throughout his life the scientist is dependent on the good opinion of significant other scientists for practically everything he does or hopes to attain. A review of the scientist's professional career will illustrate the truth of this statement.

While still in high school, the scientist-to-be becomes aware that competition and prestige will affect his future success. He must strive for good grades in order to be admitted to college and later to graduate school. He realizes the importance of attending a college of high reputation, not only because it will provide him with a better education but also because it will facilitate his later admission to a good graduate school. Finally, he must earn the good opinion of his teachers to secure the letters of recommendation which will help him enter college and gain scholarship grants or prizes.

After the student obtains his Ph.D. degree, his dependence on the good opinion of others is by no means ended. His first task is to find a suitable position. Characteristically, jobs in the better universities or in top industrial research laboratories are practically never advertised but are handled by personal communication between well-established scientists, who inquire informally whether their colleagues happen to know of some candidates for a given position or have an opening in their organization for a particular candidate. The job-seeking scientist is clearly in a more advantageous situation if he comes from a well-known institution and has been associated with a scientist of reputation. Invariably it is essential to him that there should be prominent scientists in the world who are willing to comment favorably upon the quality of his work. In most cases, before an appointment is decided upon, the hiring institution formally requests letters of recommendation concerning the candidate from several such prominent scientists. It is thus very important for the scientist to create, either through personal contact or through published work, a favorable impression among as many key scientists as possible.

Professional mobility of the scientist depends, therefore, in an essential way on the reputation he has acquired among prominent people in his field. This is true when he is securing his first job and true in his subsequent moves from one position to another. (In this connection it may be remarked that to move from an institution of high prestige to one of lower prestige is significantly easier than to move in the reverse direction.) Promotion to higher academic rank is subject to similar criteria. Again the university requests letters of recommendation from outside scientists and in some cases may appoint reviewing committees before deciding to promote someone to a tenure position. Even when the scientist has obtained a full professorship he has not reached the end of possible advancement based on his reputation. Within the academic hierarchy there

are still some "name" professorships, or ultimately some administrative posts such as dean or university president. In these days of
increasing importance of science in world affairs there are also
potential opportunities in government — for example, advisory positions to the President or appointments to some such agency as the
Atomic Energy Commission. Industrial organizations, as well, may
offer key positions, such as the directorship of a research laboratory. Needless to say, the academic promotions which the scientist
achieves carry with them increased financial rewards and, at the
higher ranks, the security of a permanent position. . . .

At times the scientist may be interested in obtaining a fellowship
or grant — for example, a Guggenheim or National Science Foundation senior postdoctoral fellowship. Grants of this nature permit him
to travel abroad for a year: or spend some time at a different
university, where he can learn new techniques; or gain temporary
relief from teaching duties to devote himself full time to his research.
In applying for such a fellowship, the scientist will again be judged
by some select prominent scientists, and once more his reputation
among these scientists determines whether the award will be made
to him.

The prestige acquired by the scientist very directly influences
the likelihood of his nomination by fellow scientists for special
honors or distinctions. Examples are the award of a Nobel prize or
selection to membership in the National Academy of Sciences.
Selection to serve as an officer of the national scientific organization
is another recognition of distinction. The scientist's prestige may
also lead to special invitations to attend scientific conferences as
guest speaker or to join another university as visiting professor;
finally, it may result in offers of remunerative consultantships in
industry.

I think it is worth while, before leaving this discussion of the
prestige system, to remark on a few of its peculiarities. One of these
is the "positive feedback" involved — the fact that the possession of
prestige tends to facilitate the acquisition of further prestige. For
example, a person of prestige is likely to be affiliated with one of the
better-known institutions, likely to obtain more funds to do effective
research, and likely to attract better students — all of which circumstances, of course, tend to enhance his prestige even further. There
is a similar relation between the prestige of individuals and the
prestige of institutions. Institutions of good reputation can attract

individuals of distinctions whose presence, in turn, lends increased prestige to the institution.

Another feature of interest concerns the people who set the standards against which the individual scientist appraises himself and whose opinion determines his general reputation in the field. It is mainly the well-established scientists in the major universities of the world who set these standards. Since the institution with which the individual scientist is affiliated tends to evaluate him chiefly on the basis of his reputation, it becomes of greater concern to the individual to seek the good opinion of people on the national or international scene than to strive for accomplishments which attract only local attention. The scientist thus tends to have stronger loyalty to his field than the specific institution of which he is a member. This is particularly true in the present days of expansion, when there is great mobility between different positions. The trend, in the major universities of this country, to minimize the importance attached to the teaching functions of the faculty reflects the situation. Teaching undergraduates is a local activity which may be appreciated by the students but does not serve to enhance the scientist's international prestige, on the basis of which the university will decide whether he is worthy of promotion. "Research and the training of graduate students are valued highly by the faculty: teaching, by contrast, is second-class. . . . It is a more usual, and probably a more realistic, view that time taken for teaching is time stolen from research, and that the road to academic heaven is paved with publications. . . ."[3]

Publishing "Fustest and Mostest"

Because the social context within which the scientist receives his training and does his research is one where the possession of prestige is highly rewarded, competition among scientists is largely directed toward the acquisition of prestige. The particular forms assumed by this competition are determined by the nature of the scientific discipline and the character of the institution where the scientist carries out his work. A scientist strives to do research which he considers important. But intrinsic satisfaction and interest are not his only reasons. This becomes apparent when one observes what happens if the scientist discovers that someone else has just published a conclusion which he was about to reach as a result of his own research. Almost invariably he feels upset by this occurrence, although the intrinsic interest of his work has certainly not been affected. The scientist wants his work to be not only interesting to himself but also important to others. He wants it to attract the maximum attention from other people, and in this quest priority is a crucial factor. An important discovery becomes intimately associated with the name of the scientist responsible for it. If somebody else makes this same discovery at about the same time, several names become attached to it and the contribution to his own prestige is correspondingly diluted. The chances of receiving a Nobel prize or a promotion are similarly decreased. Finally, if someone else succeeds in making this discovery a few months or weeks before he does, almost all of the scientist's efforts on the problem have come to naught. He may not even be able to publish his own results, since they may then represent only uninteresting duplication of work already in the scientific literature. Under the circumstances, it is not surprising if the scientist sometimes works at feverish speed under constant fear that he may be "scooped." Even a couple of weeks' delay can sometimes make a difference!

Being the first to make an important scientific contribution is, of course, only one way of obtaining recognition. For a scientist to be on the verge of making some discovery of far-reaching implications is relatively rare. Most of the time he is engaged in the less spectacular task of doing useful work leading gradually to increased knowledge. In this situation the most effective way to attract the continuing attention of other scientists is to publish as many papers as possible, to attend numerous scientific meetings, and to give many talks on one's research. The great emphasis on publishing copiously is exemplified by a motto familiar to all young faculty members — "publish or perish" — a phrase that well illustrates how the young scientist feels about the competitive pressures to which he is subject. Under the "up-or-out" rule, common in large universities, instructors and assistant professors are allowed only a fixed maximum number of years within their academic rank. If they are not promoted before the end of this time, then dismissal from the university is automatic. Whether or not an individual is promoted depends, of course, on the reputation he has achieved as a result of his publications.

Some of these competitive pressures have been familiar features of academic life for a long time. The expansion of scientific activity since World War II has, however, significantly changed the

conditions under which the scientist does his work. One consequence has been the emergence of new and intensified patterns of
competition as the number of scientists at work in many areas has
multiplied. Not only are more universities engaged in active research; more industry and government laboratories are also carrying
out pure research of a type nearly undistinguishable from its
academic counterpart. Many people in different institutions are thus
likely to be working along fairly similar lines. Furthermore, the time
lag between advances in basic science and the associated technological developments has become increasingly small. Sometimes new
ideas or techniques arising in the work of the pure scientist may be
such as to warrant patenting without further exploration. Even when
potential technological applications are not immediately apparent,
there are well-equipped industrial laboratories constantly poised to
exploit all possible consequences of a basic advance. In addition,
research has become an activity which involves the expenditure of
large sums of money and which has come to attract attention even
from the general public. Under these circumstances it is easy to
understand why the scientist finds increasing difficulty in carrying
out his work immune from outside pressures.

Rapid publication of results and questions of priority assume,
therefore, great importance; nor is the need for a journal such as
Physical Review Letters too surprising. No longer does a scientist
study a topic at some length before publishing his findings in a paper
or monograph. Instead, he tries to publish a note on a subject as
soon as he obtains any result worth mentioning — and occasionally
even before. The threat of someone else's getting there first is too
great. At times a scientist may publish just a proposal for an experiment, merely pointing out that such an experiment might be interesting and feasible. To obtain preliminary experimental results before
publishing anything may take too much time — time during which
the scientist might "get scooped" by someone else. For similar
reasons scientists may be led to engage in various practices which
the editor of *Physical Review Letters* finds reasons to discuss. In his
words,[4] there is the "author who uses the *Letters* merely to an-
nounce a later paper and whose Letter is incomprehensible by
itself"; the "author who submits many Letters hoping that statistics
rather than quality will cause one to be accepted"; or the "author
who tries to sneak a Letter in to 'scoop' a competitor who has
already submitted an Article. . . ."

Conflicting Values

In order to make his reputation with a steady stream of publications, it is safer for the scientist to work along more conventional and familiar lines, where he has greater assurance of obtaining results. Young scientists are in a particularly vulnerable situation. Since they must establish their reputation in a relatively short period of time to achieve a permanent academic position, undertaking risky projects during this period is dangerous. Interesting in this connection are instances where a fundamental discovery is made by someone in a small laboratory in an out-of-the-way place. As soon as the result is published, many big laboratories employ their superior facilities to exploit the consequences of the discovery so effectively that the scientist originally responsible for it finds it difficult to compete with them. People in big laboratories had available, of course, all the resources necessary to make the original discovery themselves, but they used them less imaginatively. Organizations well adapted to the exploitation of a field in which the direction of approach has become clear are not necessarily the best for stimulating exploration of the genuinely unknown.

A further conflict, which may lead to slipshod work when competitive pressures are pronounced, is that of careful versus fast work. Another *Letters* editorial describes the dilemma succinctly.[5] "One of our most ticklish problems concerns the large number of contributions that pour into our office when a 'hot' subject breaks and many groups initiate related work. . . . Because of the rapid development, and the intense competition, we have found it necessary to relax our standards and accept some papers that present new ideas without full analysis, relatively crude experiments that indicate how one can obtain valuable results by more careful and complete work, etc. — in short, papers which under less hot conditions would be returned to authors with the recommendation that further work be done before publication . . . Such incomplete papers have been accepted reluctantly since we realize that thereby we penalize some physicists who, working along the same lines, want to do a more complete job before publishing."

Another conflict is that of communication versus secrecy. It is intrinsic in scientific activity that knowledge and ideas are common property, to be shared and used by all scientists. But if scientist *A* has an interesting idea and describes it to scientist *B*, the latter may exploit it before scientist A himself can do so. It may then be better for A not to disclose his ideas before they are published and before his claim to priority is safely established. Closely related to this conflict is that of cooperation versus rivalry. Should scientist A tell scientist B about some new technique he has developed if B may use it in his own work to compete more effectively against A? Lack of full communication can, of course, slow down scientific progress. A significant amount of energy is diverted from struggling with the subject matter of science to fighting other people in the field. . . .

References

1. S. Pasternack, *Phys. Rev. Letters* **4,** p. 109 (1960).
2. S. A. Goudsmit, *ibid.* **4,** p. 1 (1960).
3. *Science* **134,** p. 159 (1961).
4. S. A. Goudsmit, *Phys. Rev. Letters* **6,** p. 587 (1961).
5. ———, *ibid.* **4,** p. 395 (1960).

LOVE DUEL AT CRYSTAL SPRINGS

JERRY FARBER

Supposedly the counter-culture is immune to the concerns of the establishment, especially in competing for status. Yet, as Farber shows in the following satire, these concerns are still very much present. If "keeping up with the Joneses" is what most men strive for, the anti-establishment men reverse this process, and gain status by having *less* than a competitor.

(Note: Let my anti-hippie readers take no comfort from this satire. That whole scene was beautiful, and, *at worst*, funny, while so many other scenes are ludicrous at best.)

Much of L.A.'s vast underground community is still not hip to
an unusual and significant tribal gathering that took place in the
Crystal Springs area of Griffith Park last Saturday. Two of our very
groovy local tribes met there at dawn in a sort of unpublicized
love-in to celebrate and arrange a tribal merger.

Like everyone who attended I was so flipped out behind all of it
that I have since had trouble describing what happened. But I want
to try just the same because anything as groovy, as mythic, as loving
and as Traditional as this just has to be shared.

First, can you dig the scene? Before dawn — when the two
groups were to meet — Lord Fairfax's tribe was encamped on the
flat grassy area near the road and Marco's people were spread out on
the slopes just beyond. Until it began to get light, all you could see
were a couple of small fires and, around them, moving here and
there in the dark, the glowing tips of joints and incense sticks. There
were also a number of flickering perfumed tapers, which both Marco
and Lord Fairfax used to sanctify various pre-dawn tribal cere-
monies. Marco performed several marriages as well as a briss and a
divorce. Lord Fairfax did two marriages, granted one temporary
restraining order and accepted a plea of nolo contendere on a matter
carried over from the previous Sunday's love-in.

All of this took place before the sun came up. When the light
finally did appear, both tribes greeted it with the Hare Krishna
mantra, of which Allen Ginsberg says, "It brings a state of ecstasy!"
After the mantra, Elliot Mintz read a telegram in which Allen expressed his regret at not being able to be present but sent his best
vibrations. Elliot also introduced the persons who made the tribal
gathering possible, and up front made a plea for everyone to help
pick up trash before going home in the evening.

By the time this holy morning raga ended it was light enough to
trip out on the beautiful scene. Marco's tribe had come down from
the slopes and was standing in a body facing Lord Fairfax's people
on the flat grassy area. They looked a lot like two small armies ready
for battle — and indeed they were, but these were armies of the
future, baby, carrying no weapons but love and beauty (In fact when
the uptight materialistic white world of fear-ridden brown-shoes,
power-trip politicians and hate-filled police blows itself up in an
orgasmic Armageddon and at last pays for its crimes against the
Traditional American Indian, then it will be just such love armies of
gentle seed-carrying hippies with their black and red flower brothers

who will wander triumphantly across the earth like freaked-out
nonviolent Mongol hordes).

Now in order for you to dig what was going down, I have to
explain the merger ritual. You see, each tribe before the merger had
its own spiritual leader; Marco was one and Lord Fairfax was the
other. But after the merger they would be one tribe, and it was
generally agreed that any single tribe with two spiritual leaders
would be sent on a bummer. "Too many yogin," as Marco put it,
"spoil the pirogen." So part of the merger ritual — in fact the main
part — was sort of an elimination thingy to cut down on spiritual
leaders, leaving just one, with the other becoming you know like a
sidekick. Now the square uptight way of solving this kind of problem
would be some kind of armed combat or at best some viciously
competitive civil service exam. But the two tribes chose to let it
happen lovingly and let their gurus compete — if you want to use the
word "compete" at all — in love. You dig? Marco and Lord Fairfax,
two of the most beautiful cats in Southern California, in an eyeball-
to-eyeball love duel.

So there, in the cool incense-fragrant dawn, were these two
tribes, facing each other across the still damp grassy field, getting
ready, turning on in an aura of gentle pagan sound: flute, drum and
tambourine. There was about a 15-yard stretch of ground between
the tribes, who were beaming love at each other through the pat-
terned psychedelic air. It was an earth thing, an ancient mythic
thing. Mr. Jones, take a good look! Here were the New Americans!
Sterling silver roach holders dangled from intricately beaded Traditional American Indian-style belts. Custom-made knee length
rawhide boots with fringed tops alternated with massive and ornate
all-leather sandals. Everyone had his button collection on. Everyone
wore bright short dresses with colorful tights or multi-colored
striped shirts and pants or bright long robes. Everyone carried toys
to look at or look through or play with. Every single person wore
handcrafted jewelry and bead necklaces supporting glittering gems
or emblems in metal or wood. It was Groovy New America giving
the lie to Materialistic Conformist Old America.

Then the two rock bands began to do their thing. Marco's band,
The Warren Commission, took turns with Lord Fairfax's group,
The Cherokee Omelet. In preparation for and as a symbol of the
coming merger, they had figured out a way to wire up both sets of
amplifiers so that their maximum volume was doubled. Are you

ready for that? Doubled? It was pure McLuhan, baby. When The
Warren Commission did their thing, they transformed Griffith Park,
Silverlake, Echo Park, Glendale, Eagle Rock and Burbank into a
tribal village right on the spot. And when The Cherokee Omelet took
over, it was a mind-blower you wouldn't believe. They just had to be
laying down the genetic code, man. The two-billion-year-old genetic
code itself. It couldn't have been anything else. I haven't checked
this out but I've heard that when The Cherokee Omelet played their
first number, three soldiers stationed at a Nike missile base in the
Hollywood Hills took off their uniforms, burned them and walked
off the job naked with flowers in their hair. If anyone has more
information on this, I'd appreciate hearing from him.

So the rock groups played and everybody freaked out dancing.
Imagine: It's like seven in the morning — still pretty cold and gray.
The musicians are laying down more sound in five minutes than the
average career artilleryman hears in a lifetime. And around them on
the grass are 100 cases of apparent epilepsy. Can you dig it? We just
let it happen, man.

Finally, at a certain point, the music stopped dead. Everything
stopped. There wasn't a sound, except for a little breeze in the
leaves, like in "Blow-Up." Then Lord Fairfax stepped out in front
of his tribe and walked forward, his bells jangling like spurs. It was
time for the two to do their thing. But first let me hip you to what
they looked like.

Marco? I can't describe it. He was too beautiful, man. Can you
dig a violet leather mini-sari with Traditional American Indian
fringework? He was wearing one, man. Chartreuse tights on his legs.
And shoes? Are you ready? Pilgrim Father Buckle Shoes! It was
beautiful. And ankhs? Godseyes? Yin-Yangs? Mandalas? Beads?
Talismans? Amulets? Charms? The cat could HARDLY MOVE,
man! I mean this was a very beautiful cat. And I haven't even
mentioned his buttons. "Let's Suck Toes" — "Undergo
Lysurgery" — "Down to Lunch" — you name it and he was
wearing it. Plus a complete set of Ron Boise Kama Sutra Sculpture
buttons, each position set against a background of I Ching hexa-
grams, astrological signs and Tarot symbols.

Now if Marco was beautiful, Lord Fairfax was just AS beautiful. It wasn't his clothes because he didn't have any on — except for
a Traditional Borneo Indian penis sheath, which was also long
enough to keep a stash in (You get them at The Yoni in Bell

Gardens). What he had on was groovy body paint. Like on his chest, in pale rose on an umber ground, it said "LOVE" — but in lettering so psychedelic — dig this — in lettering so psychedelic that the cat who did it *can't even read what he wrote*. And he won't be able to either until the next time he gets that high. At exactly 983 mikes you can read what the lettering says. One mike less and it's totally meaningless. Across Lord Fairfax's back was "BORN TO LOSE" in traditional Red, White and Blue with three eagles vert and, on a bend sable, five martlets or. And his buns, man. On his left was a really delicate watercolor of Bodhidharma regarding a plum blossom. And on his right was a silk-screened reproduction of a photo of Jerry ("Captain Trips") Garcia turning on with the Hopi. Between them, up his ass, was a lit stick of incense ("Nirvana" — which you can score at the Kazoo).

So there they are, baby — mano a mano. In front of one tribe is Lord Fairfax with his long wavy brown hair and beard, standing tall and dreamy like some kind of saint on a church wall in Borneo. And in front of the other tribe is Marco, a lot shorter, smiling, with flowers in his mouth and flowers twined in his blond beard, and with the eternal Atman gazing out through his trippy blue eyes.

The two cats stared at each other lovingly; they were beginning to do their thing. Neither one wavered or blinked or even got watery eyed. In fact, it was just the opposite. As time passed . . . ten minutes . . . fifteen minutes . . . a half hour . . . their thing got more intense and more loving. The ordinary cat couldn't have taken that kind of heavy trip. They would have loved him to death.

In fact, if you didn't have your head together, you couldn't even bear being in the vicinity. Like the narks. They couldn't take it. After 30 minutes of those good vibrations, the plainclothes cops completely blew their cool. No matter how freaky their threads were, or how much acid they had dropped, or how tight they were with the tribes, the narks just had to split. They were clutching their throats, man! The cats were SCREAMING! Aargh! Aargh! And they ran back to the squad cars parked on the road. It was like when Dracula sees the cross on the chick's neck, man. They just weren't ready for that kind of love.

I'm sure you can dig that there were some surprises that morning. Like four of Lord Fairfax's dancers ran off to the squad cars, gnawing on their badges. And Marco's wife? A nark! Can you believe it? Marco's WIFE, man! That morning at Crystal Springs was the moment of truth. If you were the heat, or even if you were just a weekend hippy, it was tough titty on you.

But dig. None of this even reached Marco and Lord Fairfax. I may have noticed the cops splitting. The tribes may have noticed them; in fact there were a great many rocks and bottles thrown (thrown, I should add, not in anger but in love). But Marco and Fairfax just kept up that love stare. Lord Fairfax's incense even burned down but he didn't seem to notice it. They went on for another half hour. Then Lord Fairfax spoke. He said:

"You're a beautiful cat."

I guess you could say that it was sort of Marco's move. But he didn't say anything. He stared up at Lord Fairfax for a long time, squinting his stoned blue eyes in the sun. Maybe another half hour went by. Then Marco asked:

"What did you say man?"

"I said you're beautiful."

"Oh." Marco didn't say anything else for another long time. Finally he took Lord Fairfax's hand and squeezed it and said slowly, "I can't tell you, man. It's too beautiful. You may not know it but you've just changed my life."

Now you would have thought that nobody could be laying down more love than Lord Fairfax. But Marco's gratitude. Marco's beautiful gratitude! It was too much. You had to cry, man. And meanwhile the play was kind of tossed back to Lord Fairfax.

But Fairfax was right in there playing heads-up ball. He reached out with his other hand, gently touching Marco's face, and he said, "Marco, it's the you in me that's changed the you in you."

What a trip! Lord Fairfax was all love and admiration and yet the kind of deep talk he was laying down left you wondering if maybe Marco was too lightweight intellectually to be a spiritual leader. And yet you felt that Lord Fairfax in his humility thought himself the lesser cat. It was too much.

Now metaphysics was never Marco's bag so no one was surprised when he didn't try to top Lord Fairfax in the "you-in-me" thing. But still, what Marco did say — "Teach me, man" — seemed unnecessarily weak. Like he was dwelling on what he should have been staying away from. And Marco's people started to look a little nervous. "Teach me" seemed like asking for trouble.

Even Lord Fairfax looked puzzled. But he smiled and said, "There is nothing to teach and nothing to learn."

Some people I've talked to say they felt at that point that Lord Fairfax was walking into a trap. But I don't think so. It wasn't that kind of thing. It was too beautiful.

Anyway, Marco said softly, "Nothing to teach and nothing to learn. What is there then?"

Lord Fairfax didn't answer right away. He walked back to where his tribe was and came back with a basket of tangerines. He handed them to Marco. "Love," he said.

Now there was something going down that Lord Fairfax couldn't have known because nobody knew except some of the kids in Marco's tribe. You see, Marco couldn't eat tangerines when he was stoned. They put him on a big nausea trip. But here he was all the same with a love gift of tangerines. The cat was in trouble. He looked at them for a minute. Then he started passing them out to his tribe. But after everyone had taken theirs, there were still some left over. So he bit into one. The kids who were hip to his tangerine problem came running up to stop him but he waved them away. "One swallow," he said with his mouth full, "doesn't make a bummer."

Marco might have looked a little green. But if he was nauseated, he maintained. He smiled up at Lord Fairfax and said, "You're right, man. Love IS what's happening. I love you. I give you my tribe."

Fantastic! Marco was really looking good in there! It was Lord Fairfax's move and, if you thought about it, you knew he only had one. It was like chess, man. There was only one answer he could make. He said, "Marco, I'm glad you gave me your tribe because now I can make you a gift of both tribes. You are a beautiful, loving cat. You are our spiritual leader."

Almost at once everyone there began to realize that Marco had blown it. Because if Marco's giving one tribe made him a beautiful, loving cat, then Lord Fairfax had come through as a twice-as-beautiful, twice-as-loving cat by giving two tribes. And what's more, Fairfax had made the ultimate move. Like you couldn't top it. Marco had set up his own checkmate. The cat was in real trouble now.

There was a silent wait. Everyone was trying to figure out what Marco could do and was feeling maybe a little sorry for him. But Marco looked very cool. And then he said, suddenly:

"Why thank you, I accept. Thank you very much. Very kind of

you." And he nodded quickly to The Warren Commission, which immediately went into a very freaky thing that had everybody dancing in seconds.

Everybody, that is, except Lord Fairfax, who was standing there looking at Marco. Marco kissed him and said, "My first action as spiritual leader of the combined tribes is to appoint you Tribe Metaphysician and Love Fountain."

But Lord Fairfax was on a weird trip. In fact, it was 15 or 20 minutes before he walked over to Marco, who was dancing, and asked:

"What did you say?"

Still dancing, Marco repeated, "I accept and I appoint you Metaphysician and Love Fountain."

"Oh. Groovy." Lord Fairfax nodded his head to the music. "Groovy," he said again. "Groovy." He walked away, still nodding his head, to get a tangerine. "That's groovy." He peeled it. "Yeah, that's pretty damn groovy all right." Meanwhile, everyone was dancing.

This past week there's been some grumbling among the people who had been in Lord Fairfax's tribe. A couple of them have said that maybe Marco copped out on the love thing. There's even been some talk about running a full-page put-down of Marco in the *Free Press*. But Marco meanwhile has consolidated his position very quickly. His new tribe has already received official recognition from such tribes as the L.A. Oracle and Hugh Romney's Hog Farm people. Marco is also working out a consular treaty with Vito's Fraternity of Man, and he has been laying a lot of canned goods on Plastic Man and the other diggers.

As for what people are now referring to as the "love duel," Marco doesn't say too much. But yesterday, when I was rapping with him about it, he opened up a little. He said that it was possible that Lord Fairfax had been a little straighter than him that day but that there was such a thing as being too straight.

"Too much dharma," Marco said, "spoils the karma." And he told me his private opinion of Lord Fairfax, which was that Fairfax was indeed a beautiful, loving cat but maybe a little too loving and too beautiful to be a good administrator.

Chapter 3

The Sturdy Oak:
A Manly Air of Toughness, Confidence, and Self-Reliance

From early childhood on, almost every little boy is exhorted to "be a man," but given few concrete ideas about how to achieve this goal. This dimension of the male role is more amorphous than the other three, since it comprises a variety of attributes. Avoiding anything feminine is relatively easy, once one knows what the society considers feminine; status and success are measurable achievements, with clear methods for their attainment; finally, one's aggression and violence are easily apparent.

The metaphor of the male as the "sturdy oak" and the female as the "clinging vine" has been a common one in America. Looking at an oak tree, one can see a solid trunk that will not bend with the wind, that will always be there, and that will give shelter to those who need it. These same attributes are also seen as an integral part of the role of the American man.

But since there are several diverse elements to the "sturdy oak" aspect, and there is not always unanimity on which aspects are most important in determining masculinity, this dimension of the male role takes on the character of role playing more than any of the others. American men are supposed to be tough, confident, self-reliant, strong, independent, cool, determined, and unflappable. Yet, a man is not always all of these simultaneously, and it is difficult, if not impossible, to assess whether someone who is being tough and confident is more or less manly than someone who is acting cool and independent.

This leads men in our society to have somewhat mixed notions about how to enact this element of the male role, with a major consequence being the chronic question, "Am I enough of a man?" As Fasteau illustrates, this was a prevailing concern of Lyndon Johnson in his unwillingness to halt the bombing in Vietnam. On all the other dimensions of the male role, Johnson received "top scores"; he had as much status as was possible; he did not show any signs of femininity; and he could be aggressive when necessary. Nevertheless, he was afraid of being seen as "less of a man" than Kennedy, if he gave in to the demands to halt the bombing. Had he defined being a "sturdy oak" in a different way, he might have stopped the bombing in the face of criticism, by stressing his independence and confidence.

Because there is no readily available measure of being a "sturdy oak," many men reach out to the most obvious ones—public personalities, especially popular entertainment figures—for guidance. This often leads men to try to incorporate the dramatized behavior of these glamorized men into their everyday lives. It is one thing for Hollywood to depict a man defending himself from armed robbery, for whatever the outcome, it has already been written into the script; it is another issue for someone to act in the same manner when actually confronted by the situation. Newspapers are filled with accounts of men who did just that, and who were killed in the process of trying to live up to their idea of how to act like a "real man." This is not meant to be an indictment of the entertainment industry, but merely an illustration of how, in groping for a way to be a "real man," with few concrete guidelines, the American male often confuses the fantasy with the reality.

The personality of men has, however, been shaped by this dimension of the male role, and in carrying out the other demands of the role, the requirement of being a "sturdy oak" becomes incorporated. It has almost become a comedy routine in films to see the lack of self-confidence of the violent male, who therefore is metamorphosed into a comical figure.

American men are faced with the problem of having to be "sturdy oaks" in all areas of their lives—at work, at home, in the society at large—with only a hazy idea of how best to go about it. It is not surprising that they constantly feel vulnerable to the charge of not being a "real man," and spend much time trying to ensure their invulnerability on this score.

IF

RUDYARD KIPLING

Rudyard Kipling's *If*, written around the turn of the century, epitomizes the male ideal of Kipling's time, and for the next half-century was memorized by every schoolboy. No longer do school children memorize this poem, but it still remains in the minds of many as the ideal of what a "real man" should be.

If you can keep your head when all about you
    Are losing theirs and blaming it on you,
If you can trust yourself when all men doubt you,
    But make allowance for their doubting too;
If you can wait and not be tired by waiting,
    Or being lied about, don't deal in lies,
Or being hated, don't give way to hating,
    And yet don't look too good, nor talk too wise:

If you can dream—and not make dreams your master;
    If you can think—and not make thoughts your aim;
If you can meet with Triumph and Disaster
    And treat those two impostors just the same;
If you can bear to hear the truth you've spoken
    Twisted by knaves to make a trap for fools,
Or watch the things you gave your life to, broken,
    And stoop and build 'em up with worn-out tools:

If you can make one heap of all your winnings
    And risk it on one turn of pitch-and-toss,
And lose, and start again at your beginnings
    And never breathe a word about your loss;
If you can force your heart and nerve and sinew
    To serve your turn long after they are gone,
And so hold on when there is nothing in you
    Except the Will which says to them: "Hold on!"

If you can talk with crowds and keep your virtue,
    Or walk with Kings—nor lose the common touch,
If neither foes nor loving friends can hurt you,
    If all men count with you, but none too much;
If you can fill the unforgiving minute
    With sixty seconds' worth of distance run,
Yours is the Earth and everything that's in it,
    And—which is more—you'll be a Man, my son!

THE SECRET LIFE OF WALTER MITTY

JAMES THURBER

The name of Walter Mitty has become a symbol for the meek man who becomes a hero in his fantasies. It is not the fantasy itself, but the content of such dreams that tells us a lot about American men—how the need to be tough, confident, and self-reliant becomes incorporated into one's "secret life" even (or especially?) if one is the exact opposite.

"We're going through!" The Commander's voice was like thin ice breaking. He wore his full-dress uniform, with the heavily braided white cap pulled down rakishly over one cold gray eye. "We can't make it, sir. It's spoiling for a hurricane, if you ask me." "I'm not asking you, Lieutenant Berg," said the Commander. "Throw on the power lights! Rev her up to 8,500! We're going through!" The pounding of the cylinders increased: ta-pocketa-pocketa-pocketa-*pocketa-pocketa*. The Commander stared at the ice forming on the pilot window. He walked over and twisted a row of complicated dials. "Switch on No. 8 auxiliary!" he shouted. "Switch on No. 8 auxiliary!" repeated Lieutenant Berg. "Full strength in No. 3 turret!" The crew, bending to their various tasks in the huge, hurtling eight-engined Navy hydroplane, looked at each other and grinned, "The Old Man'll get us through," they said to one another. "The Old Man ain't afraid of Hell!" . . .

"Not so fast!" You're driving too fast!" said Mrs. Mitty. "What are you driving so fast for?"

"Hmm?" said Walter Mitty. He looked at his wife, in the seat beside him, with shocked astonishment. She seemed grossly unfamiliar, like a strange woman who had yelled at him in a crowd. "You were up to fifty-five," she said. "You know I don't like to go more than forty. You were up to fifty-five." Walter Mitty drove on toward Waterbury in silence, the roaring of the SN202 through the worst storm in twenty years of Navy flying fading in the remote, intimate airways of his mind. "You're tensed up again," said Mrs. Mitty. "It's one of your days. I wish you'd let Dr. Renshaw look you over."

Walter Mitty stopped the car in front of the building where his wife went to have her hair done. "Remember to get those overshoes while I'm having my hair done," she said. "I don't need overshoes," said Mitty. She put her mirror back into her bag. "We've been all through that," she said, getting out of the car. "You're not a young man any longer." He raced the engine a little. "Why don't you wear your gloves? Have you lost your gloves?" Walter Mitty reached in a pocket and brought out the gloves. He put them on, but after she had turned and gone into the building and he had driven on to a red light, he took them off again. "Pick it up, brother!" snapped a cop as the light changed, and Mitty hastily pulled on his gloves and lurched ahead. He drove around the streets aimlessly for a time, and then he drove past the hospital on his way to the parking lot.

. . . "It's the millionaire banker, Wellington McMillan," said the pretty nurse. "Yes?" said Walter Mitty, removing his gloves slowly. "Who has the case?" "Dr. Renshaw and Dr. Benbow, but there are two specialists here, Dr. Remington from New York and Mr. Pritchard-Mitford from London. He flew over." A door opened down a long, cool corridor and Dr. Renshaw came out. He looked distraught and haggard. "Hello, Mitty," he said. "We're having the devil's own time with McMillan, the millionaire banker and close personal friend of Roosevelt. Obstreosis of the ductal tract. Tertiary. Wish you'd take a look at him." "Glad to," said Mitty.

In the operating room there were whispered introductions: "Dr. Remington, Dr. Mitty. Mr. Pritchard-Mitford, Dr. Mitty." "I've read your book on streptothricosis," said Pritchard-Mitford, shaking hands. "A brilliant performance, sir." "Thank you," said Walter Mitty. "Didn't know you were in the States, Mitty," grumbled Remington. "Coals to Newcastle, bringing Mitford and me up here for a tertiary." "You are very kind," said Mitty. A huge, complicated machine, connected to the operating table, with many tubes and wires, began at this moment to go pocketa-pocketa-pocketa. "The new anesthetizer is giving way!" shouted an interne. "There is no one in the East who knows how to fix it!" "Quiet, man!" said Mitty, in a low, cool voice. He sprang to the machine, which was now going pocketa-pocketa-queep-pocketa-queep. He began fingering delicately a row of glistening dials. "Give me a fountain pen!" he snapped. Someone handed him a fountain pen. He pulled a faulty piston out of the machine and inserted the pen in its place. "That will hold for ten minutes," he said. "Get on with the operation." A nurse hurried over and whispered to Renshaw, and Mitty saw the man turn pale. "Coreopsis has set in," said Renshaw nervously. "If you would take over, Mitty?" Mitty looked at him and at the craven figure of Benbow, who drank, and at the grave, uncertain faces of the two great specialists. "If you wish," he said. They slipped a white gown on him; he adjusted a mask and drew on thin gloves; nurses handed him shining . . .

"Back it up, Mac! Look out for that Buick!" Walter Mitty jammed on the brakes. "Wrong lane, Mac," said the parking-lot attendant, looking at Mitty closely. "Gee, Yeh," muttered Mitty. He began cautiously to back out of the lane marked "Exit Only." "Leave her sit there," said the attendant. "I'll put her away." Mitty got out of the car. "Hey, better leave the key." "Oh," said Mitty, handing the man the ignition key. The attendant vaulted into the car, backed it up with insolent skill, and put it where it belonged.

They're so damn cocky, thought Walter Mitty, walking along Main Street; they think they know everything. Once he had tried to take his chains off, outside New Milford, and he had got them wound around the axles. A man had had to come out in a wrecking car and unwind them, a young, grinning garageman. Since then Mrs. Mitty always made him drive to a garage to have the chains taken off. The next time, he thought, I'll wear my right arm in a sling; they won't grin at me them. I'll have my right arm in a sling and they'll see I couldn't possibly take the chains off myself. He kicked at the slush on the sidewalk. "Overshoes," he said to himself, and he began looking for a shoe store.

When he came out into the street again, with the overshoes in a box under his arm, Walter Mitty began to wonder what the other thing was his wife had told him to get. She had told him twice, before they set out from their house for Waterbury. In a way he hated these weekly trips to town—he was always getting something wrong. Kleenex, he thought, Squibb's, razor blades? No. Toothpaste, toothbrush, bicarbonate, carborundum, initiative and referendum? He gave it up. But she would remember it. "Where's the what's-its-name?" she would ask. "Don't tell me you forgot the what's-its-name." A newsboy went by shouting something about the Waterbury trial.

. . . "Perhaps this will refresh your memory." The District Attorney suddenly thrust a heavy automatic at the quiet figure on the witness stand. "Have you ever seen this before?" Walter Mitty took the gun and examined it expertly. "This is my Webley-Vickers 50.80," he said calmly. An excited buzz ran around the courtroom. The judge rapped for order. "You are a crack shot with any sort of firearms, I believe?" said the District Attorney, insinuatingly. "Objection!" shouted Mitty's attorney. "We have shown that the defendant could not have fired the shot. We have shown that he wore his right arm in a sling on the night of the fourteenth of July." Walter Mitty raised his hand briefly and the bickering attorneys were stilled. "With any known make of gun," he said evenly, "I could have killed Gregory Fitzhurst at three hundred feet *with my left hand*." Pandemonium broke loose in the courtroom. A woman's scream rose above the bedlam and suddenly a lovely, dark-haired girl was in Walter Mitty's arms. The District Attorney struck at her savagely. Without rising from his chair, Mitty let the man have it on the point of the chin. "You miserable cur!" . . .

"Puppy biscuit," said Walter Mitty. He stopped walking and the buildings of Waterbury rose up out of the misty courtroom and surrounded him again. A woman who was passing laughed. "He said 'Puppy biscuit,'" she said to her companion. "That man said 'Puppy biscuit' to himself." Walter Mitty hurried on. He went into an A. & P., not the first one he came to but a smaller one farther up the street. "I want some biscuit for small, young dogs," he said to the clerk. "Any special brand, sir?" The greatest pistol shot in the world thought a moment. "It says 'Puppies Bark for It' on the box," said Walter Mitty.

His wife would be through at the hairdresser's in fifteen minutes, Mitty saw in looking at his watch, unless they had trouble drying it; sometimes they had trouble drying it. She didn't like to get to the hotel first, she would want him to be there waiting for her as usual. He found a big leather chair in the lobby, facing a window, and he put the overshoes and the puppy biscuit on the floor beside it. He picked up an old copy of *Liberty* and sank down into the chair. "Can Germany Conquer the World Through the Air?" Walter Mitty looked at the pictures of bombing planes and of ruined streets.

. . . "The cannonading has got the wind up in young Raleigh, sir," said the sergeant. Captain Mitty looked up at him through tousled hair. "Get him to bed," he said wearily. "With the others. I'll fly alone." "But you can't, sir," said the sergeant anxiously. "It takes two men to handle that bomber and the Archies are pounding hell out of the air. Von Richtman's circus is between here and Saulier." "Somebody's got to get that ammunition dump," said Mitty. "I'm going over. Spot of brandy?" He poured a drink for the sergeant and one for himself. War thundered and whined around the dugout and battered at the door. There was a rending of wood and splinters flew through the room. "A bit of a near thing," said Captain Mitty carelessly. "The box barrage is closing in," said the sergeant. "We only live once, Sergeant," said Mitty, with his faint, fleeting smile. "Or do we?" He poured another brandy and tossed it off. "I never see a man could hold his brandy like you, sir," said the sergeant. "Begging your pardon, sir." Captain Mitty stood up and strapped on his huge Webley-Vickers automatic. "It's forty kilometers through hell, sir." said the sergeant. Mitty finished one last brandy. "After all," he said softly, "what isn't?" The pounding of the cannon increased; there was the rat-tat-tatting of machine guns, and from somewhere came the menacing pocketa-pocketa-pocketa of the new flamethrowers. Walter Mitty walked to the door of the dugout humming "Auprès de Ma Blonde." He turned and waved to the sergeant. "Cheerio!" he said. . . .

Something struck his shoulder. "I've been looking all over this hotel for you," said Mrs. Mitty. "Why do you have to hide in this old chair? How did you expect me to find you?" "Things close in," said Walter Mitty vaguely. "What?" Mrs. Mitty said. "Did you get the what's-its-name? The puppy biscuit? What's in that box?"

"Overshoes," said Mitty. "Couldn't you have put them on in the store?" "I was thinking," said Walter Mitty. "Does it ever occur to you that I am sometimes thinking?" She looked at him. "I'm going to take your temperature when I get you home," she said.

They went out through the revolving doors that made a faintly derisive whistling sound when you pushed them. It was two blocks to the parking lot. At the drugstore on the corner she said, "Wait here for me. I forgot something. I won't be a minute." She was more than a minute. Walter Mitty lighted a cigarette. It began to rain, rain with sleet in it. He stood up against the wall of the drugstore, smoking. . . . He put his shoulders back and his heels together. "To hell with the handkerchief," said Walter Mitty scornfully. He took one last drag on his cigarette and snapped it away. Then, with that faint, fleeting smile playing about his lips, he faced the firing squad; erect and motionless, proud and disdainful, Walter Mitty the Undefeated, inscrutable to the last.

PHYSICAL STRENGTH, ONCE OF SIGNIFICANCE

JOHN H. GAGNON

The economic value of physical strength is rapidly disappearing, if it is not gone already. Yet even in the age of computers and space travel, men seem reluctant to abandon their traditional admiration for strength and muscles. As Gagnon points out, this interest is not quite as irrational as it might seem, for especially in adolescence and social relationships, physical dominance is still an asset.

Any traveller by car crossing the United States—or virtually any country—will be inevitably stopped one or more times by road building or repair projects. During these enforced waits he may see huge machines gouging the earth, filling chasms, carrying giant loads of earth and stone from one place to another. The thoughtful traveller may reflect on the amount of work that these machines can do

Reprinted from *Impact of Science on Society*, **21**, no. 1, by permission of UNESCO. © UNESCO, 1971.

and, if he has a historical bent, will think about the masses of human labour that it took to perform similar tasks in the past.

Such thoughts usually subside when the halt is over, but the traveller has experienced one of the central disjunctures of modern life: that physical strength, a basic evolutionary attribute of the body that increased the survival capacity of man when he lived in the world as nature made it, has lost much of its centrality to human existence.

In the recent historical past of most modernized societies, physical strength, as represented in the large musculature of the body, was a reasonably important parameter for social differentiation. It arranged men in crude hierarchies in both the world of work and the world of warfare. It differentiated men from women and was in some ultimate sense the basis for family authority.

As is characteristic in human affairs, what began as an instrumental attribute that distinguished between persons ultimately became a moral attribute as well. Stronger men came to be thought to be better men and men were (and are) elected to political office because they have a 'strong' character (commonly recognized by an immobility of countenance). And temporary distinctions based on a transient capacity (for strength wanes) became hardened into what are thought to be just, true and beautiful social orders. . . .

Physical Strength in Work

It was with the movement from the land to the factory that characterized the Industrial Revolution that there occurred the major breaking point between a world where there was a relatively sure connexion between physical capacity and worldly rewards (though regulated by other status considerations) and a modern world where physical effort and consequent gain exist only in the most abstract relation. . . .

This is not to say that the workers of the earlier years of the Industrial Revolution did not work hard, nor that physical exhaustion did not accompany their daily lives. But the very character of the work had changed: the pre-industrial worker lived inside a world of universal natural constraints (when to plant, when to reap), while the post-industrial worker lived inside a world of particularized artificial constraints (the factory whistle, which machine to tend, which motion to make). Many broad sectors of the early and later periods of the industrial world still had requirements for great physical strength, but the declining significance of strength can be seen in the large-scale employment of children and women in factories doing the same operations as men. While the utilization of child and female labour was also present in agriculture and cottage industry, there was a division of labour according to sex and age, based on the levels of effort or skill required. . . .

With the latter-day entry into the automation phase of the Industrial Revolution, however, the impulse has been toward totally labour-saving devices. The interposition of a complex series of automatic or semi-automatic mechanisms between the worker and his output has completed the near elimination of the general requirement of physical strength that was begun by the early factory system. The 'controlled paying out of energy' noted by Thompson is now the characteristic of nearly all work. Work is not raw effort, but is rather co-ordination and synchronization, the interfacing of man and machine—with the man operating as a more complex decision-making instrument linking together mechanical processes.

In my road-building example, the large-muscled earth-mover driver seen beside his huge machine, perhaps with a tattoo on his arm, is only a symbolic harking back to an older work style. The earth-mover cab is air-conditioned, his control pedals and levers are power-assisted and his work is coordinated with that of the steam shovel and the dump truck, with so many loads of earth to be moved a day. His muscles are irrelevant, as irrelevant as are those of the white-collar worker who runs the computer which makes out his pay-check or the industrial manager who handles the stock portfolios of the corporation. Their hierarchical status is not determined by strength, but by the abstraction of income differentials, which is convertible into variations in life styles.

Physical Strength in War

It is at the breakdown of peaceful cultural process that the erosion of physical strength as a major variable in human affairs is most obvious.

In the earliest days of warfare, strategy and tactics certainly played a significant role, but perhaps as significant—and very easily forgotten by bloodless historians of warfare—was the ability to bash or hack another man to death with club, axe or sword. The possession of great physical strength was given a further advantage through the employment of blunt or sharp instruments, and, while the arrow and spear are marginal equalizers, Davids rarely defeated Goliaths. Skill in combat, even when organized in the phalanx or the legion, still required a strong arm and vigorous body.

The armoured knight was, perhaps, the culmination of the union of physical strength and the social hierarchies of prestige in the West. But the knight and his castle were levelled by the gun, a weapon that made nearly all men equal. The armed infantryman of Cromwell's New Style Army marked the end of chivalry and opened the way to mass armies whose basic tools of war are fire-power and cannon fodder. The religious ideology that fathered the disciplined factory system in the West was the basis of its disciplined military system as well.

Modern weaponry, even in limited warfare, has taken on an industrial character to which a wide latitude of physical capacities can be conscripted. Automatic weapons in the hands of a determined local peasantry level differences between colonized and colonizer, and any man can press the button to fire an intercontinental ballistic missile. Indeed, in the film *Dr. Strangelove* a cripple is used to exemplify the cerebral quality of modern warfare.

The hand-gun, which is perhaps the most significant symbol of the levelling effects of modern technology on violence, is the central element in the mythic version of the American West presented in films. Its role in the democratizing of violence requires that its use be shrouded in rules that are as formal and restrictive as those of chivalry. Indeed, the obligatory fist fight in which the hero of the American western engages is a reaction against the equalizing influence of the portable gun: morality requires that older 'man-to-man' codes of conduct be affirmed and older methods of creating hierarchy between men be retained. . . .

Physical Strength and Social Roles

This is a transitional period, and there are still many alive who have experienced the need for physical strength and who have been allocated social and economic positions based on whether they possessed it or not. Further, the socialization procedures of even advanced societies—those procedures that condition children to fit into their society—still operate on the basis of the conventional historical distinctions between men and men, men and women, and adults and children which are founded on this attribute. Thus today, as during all periods of transition, we have the coexistence of differing styles of socialization and the continued existence of adults who operate according to a relatively inappropriate set of values and beliefs.

In our present style of socialization most parents still exhort their male children to be strong, to test themselves in sports, and to compete physically with other children. In the child's world, physical strength still retains some of its historical significance even though parents, especially of the middle class, seek to minimize the role of fighting and promote negotiations in settling disputes. Boys whose worlds are made up of both disorganized games and organized sport learn that physical strength is one of the measures of manhood. They see themselves as stronger or weaker than other boys, more skillful or less skillful in physical pursuits.

In an important sense, the possession of physical prowess is given too much weight and tends to acquire characterological implications. Physical strength and physical courage become identified with moral strength and moral courage, and the willingness to fight other boys for one's rights is an emblem of manliness. The physically weak boy may be bullied or left out of group play while the stronger boy will be selected for leadership positions and in most games becomes the chooser of sides or the captain of the team.

There are obviously substantial social class differences in the significance of physical strength in the creating of social hierarchies among boys, with the physically stronger being more important in working- and lower-class communities than in the middle class. One must be cautious not to see the child's world as the war of all-against-all and to recognize that a considerable body of social skills is required in all social classes for positions of leadership. However, the less complex the social environment, the less these skills tend to dominate the situation.

Though the environments of many children have become symbolically dense through television or mechanical toys, the primary resource that the young male has is still his own body. What he can and cannot do in comparison with others of his own age, those younger, and those older is one of the ways in which he gains and loses in social acceptance, and also conditions his acceptance of himself. In this sense the child's world is close to the pre-industrial world, and for most boys physical capability continues to be a powerful source of the sense of self and the sense of social position.

If strength serves to differentiate male children from each other, it at the same time serves to distinguish them from females. There is very little evidence that little boys are, in fact, stronger than little girls and given the wide variation in physical developmental rates there are substantial numbers of females who are larger and stronger than males of the same age. However, what is crucial is the socialization differences that determine the legitimacy for each sex of the expression of physical strength or the use of violence.

While overt aggressive behaviour is inhibited in both genders (once again, especially in the middle class) there is considerable covert approbation given to young men for engaging in aggressive physical activities. Superiority in physical strength, even if only presumed, or in the ability to use physical strength, is one of the primary signs to the young man that he is a man and not a woman.

As children grow older the training tracks for the two genders diverge, with a steady insistence that young men should be strong and young women weak. As they progress through secondary education the earlier hierarchies among young males based on strength tend to dissolve, and cognitive and socio-emotional skills begin to predominate. Nonetheless, those important previous experiences do not disappear from a young man's mind: if he was weak as a child, he may remember it with some shame or anger; if strong, those skills that brought him rewards in the past may be perseverated in long after they lose their utility.

The awareness of strength as a differentiator between men and women continues to be retained, however. Perhaps, it is even strengthened as the young male grows to full height, weight, and strength and is encouraged in his physical development by sports and recreations from which girls are excluded. . . .

Sports as an Expression of Masculinity

The male spectator in the stands (or before the television set) who is watching an athletic contest can feel himself as one with his 'side', and 'his team' can represent for him the expression of aggression and physical skill. Vicarious feelings of success and failure are acted out through skilled surrogates who win (or lose) for him. At the same time, the fan feels a sense of solidarity with other males who are on his side as fans as well as solidarity with the members of the team. . . .

The increasing popularity of contact sports such as American football, as compared to the declining attendance, relative to population, at non-contact games such as baseball and cricket, suggests that there is an increased need among males for physical contact and at least the potentiality of violence. Indeed, the passionate identification with a team can sometimes lead to outbreaks of actual violence among the fans themselves. The outbreaks of 'barracking' at European football (soccer) matches in England and the violence of fans at soccer matches in Latin American countries are indicators of the fact that these are collective occasions for acting out masculinity feelings.

During early adulthood many young men continue in sporting activities of one sort or another. Some of these are expressive of male-male competition, such as the informal neighbourhood (American) football games that used to be common in working-class communities as described by James T. Farrell in his novel *Studs Lonigan*. Baseball teams of out-of-school young men are still relatively numerous in some regions of the United States, but their importance seems to be declining. Such participation in team sports is more characteristic of the working class than the white-collar class, despite the fact that young American males who go on to institutions of higher education have available to them a continuing sports programme. However, with the advent of television-linked large-scale professional spectator sports, fewer and fewer young men of any class today participate in the tradition of informal sports. . . .

Strength in Men-Women Relations

Other than sports it is probably the relation between men and women that most sustains the continuing sense of the role of physical strength in the maintenance of masculinity. Rarely is the belief on the part of men that they are stronger than women ever tested, since the patterns of deference are so well learned that females rarely compete physically with men.

Men lift packages, move furniture, open jars for women—all of these are man's work. Each such act, and there may be a dozen of them a day, reaffirms to the man that he as a male is stronger than a woman. The act of applying increased physical tension and the resultant successful release before a female audience emphasizes the difference between them. Other tasks, such as carrying children or groceries, may be equally difficult physically, but for many men they are woman's work and as such demeaning for a man. Frequently, it is not the difficulty of the task, but its social definition which is crucial as to whether a male will do it willingly.

Though there are many non-sexual activities in which men are allowed to display physical superiority to women, it is probably in the domain of sex that a confirmation of the expected differences in physical strength is most important. Sexual activity in both its physical and social aspects is highly stylized, with a relatively firmly prescribed set of roles and meanings. Generally, it is expected that the man will initiate the sexual contact and both socially and physically guide their sexual activities.

While the female, over the course of a long-term relationship, may well develop a greater degree of initiative, the male still expresses mastery in the sexual relationship. Premonitory signs of this pattern can be seen in the playful behaviour of young adolescents as they wrestle together. The boy holds the girl against her will and in this interaction the linking of erotic responses with mildly aggressive behaviour is further developed.

In nearly all areas of the sexual relationship it would be severely traumatic if a woman demonstrated that she is in fact stronger than the male. . . .

Reactions to the Waning Importance of Strength

It is very apparent that there are going to be few refuges in the future for a sense of masculinity that has at its core differences in physical strength. The emphasis on the symbolic and socio-emotional that is characteristic of modern advanced societies enters all areas of social life. As the explosive rhythms that Thompson noted in the Irish immigrant labourer have largely subsided in the world of work so are such rhythms and their value retreating in the worlds of sex and sport.

Man's body as the primary tool in shaping the world is nearly obsolete and the distinctions between men that were created on the basis of it have lost their validity. One can see this process rapidly invading and reorganizing all aspects of life. From the work-place to the bedroom new symbolic forms and adaptations today exist which do not depend on strength.

For some men this shift will be felt as a catastrophe: something that had organized their lives is now missing. Yet for the larger collectivity this change can only be seen as the culmination of a long process that began with the Industrial Revolution. . . .

For a long time to come societies and individuals in which strength remains an important organizing social attribute will continue to co-exist with societies and individuals in which it has become insignificant. In a relatively advanced country like Australia there is a very powerful all-male culture in which sport, drink, and other forms of male-male competition are the central organizing theme of social life. In the United States there still remains a large population of young men in the working class and lower economic classes for whom physical combativeness is a major source of an ongoing sense of manhood.

The rear-guard response   In those societies where the impact of technology is being most strongly felt there are three major groups of reactions to the declining importance of physical strength.

The first of these is the response of the cultural and social rear guard of the society to whom manliness and physical prowess are still intertwined. This generally comprises a large portion of the working- and lower economic-class male population who hold traditional views of gender roles: there are proper places for men and for women and hard physical labour characterizes the real man. They feel threatened by the abstract quality of social life, its verbal and symbolic focus, and both the adult males and their male children find today's long-haired, tradition-flouting youth offensive. The general response of this rear guard to all social change is to become more rigid and moralistic.

It is this group that is most interested in sports and provides the most ardent fans. Likewise, they wish to keep intact the conventional differences between men and women. Often the women of these men recognize the threat that their males feel, so they, too, cling to older and more conventional sex-role models. . . .

The cosmetic response   A second major response to the decline of strength as an instrumental attribute is to retain it as a cosmetic quality. Jogging, isometric exercises, certain individual sports, sunbathing—all are ways of maintaining youthfulness and physical attractiveness in order to retain a competitive position in the sexual market-place. Thus, the trim, lean body or the well-muscled body may occupy a bank clerk's chair where the actual physical strength required is extremely low. (The sudden efflorescence of colourful and variegated male clothing styles is also partially a manifestation of cosmetic sexual competitiveness between men—what we may call the 'peacock effect'.)

The point of all this is that the body then becomes an aesthetic object, an object of personal concern. And this means that the male body is coming to have the same cosmetic meaning for a man as the female body has for a woman. As in the case of women, attention to the body is given in order to attract the opposite sex, not because it will be more capable in sexual performance. Physical strength, as an aspect of physical beauty, thus becomes a secondary sex characteristic, retaining this significance without having any functional importance.

The response of failures The third response to the decline of strength as a primary sign of manhood is among those men who fail to achieve success in this symbol-using world. Psychologically, occupational failure can be experienced in many ways, but for a large number of men it is seen as reflection on their manliness. Given the importance of childhood training experiences in which success and failure were linked to differences in strength, it is possible for men to react to occupational failure with a sense of physical weakness or inferiority—and they sometimes even psychosomatically manifest physical weakness to justify their failure.

Such symbolic strategies for coping can also result in compensatory aggressive and violent behaviour towards women and children. Physical strength used to dominate the family compensates for the physical weakness implied when occupational failure looms.

MASCULINITY AND THE ROLE OF THE COMBAT SOLDIER

SAMUEL A. STOUFFER, *et al*.

In contemporary society, most men rarely have the opportunity to demonstrate their ability to be a "real man." Perhaps the only situation which allows them to express this aspect of their manhood is war. In the following excerpt from *The American Soldier*, Stouffer and his associates show how combat soldiers regard masculinity. Courage and "guts" under fire is the real test of manhood, as rear echelon soldiers were quickly informed when they encountered battle-tested troops.

The codes according to which a combat unit judged the behavior of its members, and in terms of which conformity was enforced, differed in their generality. Perhaps the most general was one drawn largely from civilian culture but given its special interpretation in the combat situation: Be a man. Conceptions of masculinity vary among different American groups, but there is a core which is common to most: courage, endurance and toughness, lack of squeamishness when confronted with shocking or distasteful stimuli, avoidance of display of weakness in general, reticence about emotional or idealistic matters, and sexual competency. The conditions in which the code is applied also vary. For example, it seems not to have been invoked in the same way in the recent war as in World War I. In World War II there was much less community pressure on the young men to get into the Army. There were few real counterparts to the white feather, painting homes yellow, use of the epithet "slacker." The general attitude was that everyone should do what he was assigned as well as he could, but it was *not* considered essential that the individual "stick his neck out." To oversimplify, it might be said that in World War I the test of social manhood began much farther from actual fighting than in World War II. In the First

Selections from *The American Soldier: Combat and its Aftermath*, Vol. 2 of *Studies in Social Psychology in World War II*, edited by Samuel A. Stouffer *et al.*, Social Science Research Council. Copyright © 1949 by Princeton University Press. Reprinted by permission of Princeton University Press.

World War, a man was more severely censured for failing to enter the armed services; this time, the test was more nearly whether he adequately filled his role once placed in the combat situation.

Combat posed a challenge for a man to prove himself to himself and others. Combat was a dare. One never knew for sure that he could take it until he had demonstrated that he could. Most soldiers facing the prospect of combat service had to deal with a heavy charge of anticipatory anxiety. The more they heard about how tough the fighting was, the greater the anxiety and the insecurity that came from doubt as to whether they could handle the anxiety. Thus, combat might actually come almost as a relief—it joined the issue and broke the strain of doubt and waiting.

A code as universal as "being a man" is very likely to have been deeply internalized. So the fear of failure in the role, as by showing cowardice in battle, could bring not only fear of social censure on this point as such, but also more central and strongly established fears related to sex-typing. To fail to measure up as a soldier in courage and endurance was to risk the charge of not being a man. ("Whatsa matter, bud—got lace on your drawers?" "Christ, he's acting like an old maid.") If one were not socially defined as a man, there was a strong likelihood of being branded a "woman," a dangerous threat to the contemporary male personality. The generally permissive attitude toward expression of fear . . . mitigated the fear of failure in manliness, but by no means obviated it. A man could show and admit fear without necessarily being branded a "weak sister," but only so long as it was clear that he had done his utmost.

The generalized code of masculinity serves as a context for various more specific codes that may be isolated more or less arbitrarily. The prescribed avoidance to claims of idealistic motivation will be considered later. The most direct application of the masculinity code was to the social role of the combat soldier. In fact, the code of the combat soldier can be summarized by saying that behavior in combat was recognized as a test of being a man. When this code was internalized, or enforced by playing on an internalized code of manliness, a man once in combat had to fight in order to keep his own self-respect: "Hell, I'm a soldier."

The ingredients of the veterans' conception of the good combat soldier appear vividly in Chart I. Veteran infantrymen of a division which had fought in North Africa and Sicily were asked to think of

CHART I
How Veteran Enlisted Infantrymen Characterized One of the
Best Combat Soldiers They Had Known

PERCENTAGE OF COMMENTS MENTIONING EACH CHARACTERISTIC, REGARDING

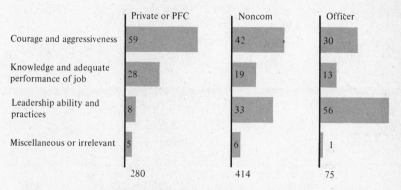

	Private or PFC	Noncom	Officer
Courage and aggressiveness	59	42	30
Knowledge and adequate performance of job	28	19	13
Leadership ability and practices	8	33	56
Miscellaneous or irrelevant	5	6	1
	280	414	75

The numbers at the bottom of the bars are the numbers of cases on which percentages are based.

one of the best combat soldiers they had known, and then to give his rank, and name some of the things they admired in him. As the chart shows, attributes characteristically ascribed to a good officer differed from those ascribed to a good private, while the pattern of attributes of the good noncom was intermediate between those of officer and private. Leadership ability and practices were most often mentioned in the case of officers, while courage and aggressiveness were most often mentioned for privates. "Knowledge and adequate performance of job"—a classification which did not include characteristics that could be grouped with leadership, and therefore tended to be descriptive of the good follower—was more often mentioned in regard to privates. Courage and aggressiveness ("guts"), which are central to the masculine ideal, thus were a prime ingredient of the combat man's notion of the good soldier. For privates and noncoms, characteristics in this category were mentioned more often than any others, while the category was second only to leadership qualities for officers.

A more concrete impression of some of the elements of masculinity involved in being a combat soldier may be seen in the following fragment of an interview with a wounded Infantry veteran of the North African campaign:

One time me and another guy were in a hole. The guy says "Let's get out of here." I talked to him (tried to calm him down) but he never was a soldier—did typewriting, ran errands for officers. He was a suck-ass for a colonel, not a real soldier. A real soldier is a guy—he'll drink and swear—but he relies on himself; a guy that can take care of himself.*

Here the combat soldier, the real soldier, is defined partly by contrast with someone who does not qualify as a man.

The man who lived up to the code of the combat soldier had proved his manhood; he could take pride in being a combat man and draw support in his role from this pride. Of this sort was the grim pride in being an "old beat-up Joe," who had suffered and endured and took a perverse satisfaction that things were working out for the worst, just as he had expected they would. A second aspect of this pride of the combat man appears in his typical resentment of the rear echelon. . . . This resentment, springing in part from envy of the favored circumstances at the rear, served one function of devaluing what was inaccessible and placing a higher moral value on what had to be put up with. The fact that rear-echelon soldiers accepted the lower status made the right to feel this invidious pride a real support to the combat man.

The pride in being a combat man may be illustrated by an account told to an interviewer at the front in Europe by a sergeant in a veteran Infantry battalion. He had been wounded and later returned to his outfit through the chain of replacement depots. His account of this revealed that he was indifferent to the physical conditions encountered, but like many combat men of similar experience he was very bitter about the treatment of combat veterans by the permanent personnel of the replacement depots. He complained that the cadre were indifferent to the welfare of replacements, "showed no respect for what the combat men had been through," tried to "shove people around," and so on through a long list. When asked for an example, he told of a corporal who was in charge of a group of veteran combat replacements:

He kept ordering us around and putting combat men on kitchen details. Finally I got fed up. I told him: "Look here, damn you—you stay out of here. There are men in here, and I don't want them contaminated."

---

* *Made in a United States hospital in spring of 1944.*

This was recounted with intensely explosive bitterness and contempt. Aside from its other complex aspects, the interview illustrates some of the strongest factors in the motivation of combat soldiers. The code of being a man is here explicit. The rear-echelon soldier is resented and despised because of his misuse of Army authority and his failure to share a community of experience and sentiment. And the final crushing comment which the combat soldier makes is to imply that the corporal is not a man—because he is not one of the fraternity of front-line fighters. The informant did not even feel it necessary to describe the corporal's reaction: the comment was conclusive, and no further argument had been deemed necessary. It is not difficult to imagine the tremendous sense of superiority which could be given by a social position which thus permitted having the last word.

VIETNAM AND THE CULT OF TOUGHNESS IN FOREIGN POLICY

MARC FEIGEN FASTEAU

This analysis of the impact of the male sex role on American foreign policy should be required reading for every politician, historian, and voter in the United States. We would be tempted to call it "Walter Mitty Wins the War in Vietnam," but the subject is far too serious for levity. Thousands of American men lie dead in Vietnam, and the male sex role may well have been the largest single factor in determining why they were ordered to go.

The Vietnam war has been for me, as it has been for many other Americans, a central influence in the evolution of my political beliefs and personal values. One of my most sustained intellectual endeavors has been the effort in the early years to decide whether the war made sense and then the longer and more difficult attempt, once it became clear to me that it was a pointless and futile undertaking, to understand what it was that kept the United States in the war. The process began in 1963, when I graduated from college and went to work as a member of Senator Mike Mansfield's staff, where my responsibilities led me to try to articulate and examine the underlying premises and rationale of our involvement. They did not stand up under scrutiny: Vietnam was not another Munich and there was no empirical or solid theoretical support for the "domino theory." In fact, the explanations were so clearly weak, that I could never quite understand how so many obviously intelligent men could believe them. Six years later, when everyone in his or her right mind knew the war was a disaster and still we couldn't get out, this nagging question connected up with an embryonic awareness of the masculine stereotype.

The precipitating event for me in making the connection was the publication of the Pentagon Papers. Here, at last, was the inside story—a good chunk of it at least—a twenty-year long view of the policymaking process, free of political if not bureaucratic posturing. I scoured the Papers eagerly for the analysis and motivation behind our involvement. But the most striking revelation of the Papers was not what they did say but what they did not say. Even at the highest and most private levels of our government, the rationale and supporting analysis for the American objective of winning in Vietnam had been incredibly flimsy. . . . The only lengthy and careful examinations of this question in the Papers were produced by Undersecretary of State George Ball and by the CIA in response to a question from President Johnson. The CIA concluded that

with the possible exception of Cambodia it is likely that no nation in the area would succumb to Communism as a result of the fall of Laos and South Vietnam. Furthermore, a continuation of the spread of Communism in the area would not be inexorable, and any spread which did occur would take time—time in which the total situation might change in a number of ways unfavorable to the Communist cause. [1]

Ball's memo examining the likely effect of U.S. withdrawal from Vietnam on a country-by-country, area-by-area basis concluded that only in Southeast Asia proper would there be an adverse effect and that this would be short-lived. [2] Both analyses were dismissed by the Administration without a response on their merits.

Why was there so little serious analysis or rethinking of United

States objectives in South Vietnam by the men holding power? Not because their achievement was thought to be cheap. Fairly early in the Johnson Administration, the President and his advisers were far more pessimistic in private than in public about the actual results of past war efforts and the forecasts about the results of each new escalation. CIA analyses consistently predicted the failure of escalation in the air and on the ground. . . .

In the spring of 1965 Johnson said privately to columnist James Wechsler, as he was to say to others: "I don't want to escalate this war, I want nothing more than to get our boys home. . . . But I can't run and pull a Chamberlain at Munich." This analogy was often drawn.[3] But it rested on a number of very doubtful assumptions: that Communist China created and controlled the Viet Cong in the South and could produce similar insurgencies elsewhere; or that North Vietnam itself had imperialist ambitions and the capacity to carry them out on a scale which would threaten the security interests of the United States; that a Communist regime would be worse for the people of South Vietnam than the government they had; that even if China did not create the insurgency in South Vietnam, the struggle there was still "a test case"—despite Vietnam's unique character as a divided country and a history which made the Communists the heirs of nationalist sentiment; that Indochina was strategically vital to U.S. security; that China would somehow be able to force national Communist regimes in Indochina into actions furthering Chinese ambitions but not their own; and, finally, that if the United States won in South Vietnam, Communist parties in other underdeveloped countries would roll over and die.

These propositions can be debated, although they do not stand up under careful review. The shocking fact, however, is that nowhere in the Papers do our policymakers even articulate any of these underlying propositions, much less examine them critically. . . .

This incredible lacuna suggests that the "domino theory" was primarily a rationale supporting a policy chosen for other, not fully conscious, motivations. Major decisions are not made on such a transparently thin basis unless another, unstated rationale and set of values are at work. No other reasons are spelled out in the Pentagon Papers, but the feeling that the United States must at all costs avoid "the humiliation of defeat" is the unarticulated major premise of nearly every document. For example, John McNaughton, Assistant

Secretary of Defense, McNamara's right-hand man and head of
International Security Affairs at the Pentagon, described United
States aims in South Vietnam, March 1965, as

*70%—to avoid a humiliating United States defeat (to our reputa-
tion as a guarantor). 20%—to keep South Vietnam (and the adjacent
territory) from Chinese hands. 10%—to permit the people of South
Vietnam to enjoy a better, freer way of life. . . .*[4]

It does matter sometimes whether a nation wins or loses, but
whether it matters depends on the particular circumstances and on
the specific consequences that flow from the defeat or victory.
Avoiding the "humiliation of defeat," per se, is not automatically an
important national objective. But for our Presidents and policymakers, being tough, or at least looking tough, has been a primary goal in
and of itself.

The connection between the war and the cult of toughness has
not been prominent in the flood of writings about Vietnam, but the
evidence is there, subtler in the Kennedy Administration and more
blatant under Johnson and Nixon.

There was the Kennedy emphasis on personal toughness. An
excessive desire to prove this quality had taken early root in John
Kennedy and showed itself first through wild recklessness in sports
that led to frequent injuries.[5] This need was demonstrated again in
the famous PT-boat incident during his Navy career. Kennedy's
bravery in rescuing a shipmate after his boat was rammed and
bringing the survivors to safety is well known. But during this
rescue, some of his actions appear to reveal the same straining after
heroics.

*Trying to signal American PT boats which patrolled a nearby chan-
nel at night, Kennedy swam alone into the dangerous passage and
was almost carried out to sea by the current. There was no need for
such foolishness, which endangered not only Jack but the rescue of
his crew. He had eight uninjured men with him, plus a plank,
lifejackets, and the island growth from which to make some sort of
float or raft (as recommended by Navy survival doctrine in the
South Pacific at that time) on which Kennedy and another man
could have put to sea.*[6]

Later, sharing his brother's values but being more outspoken, one of
the first things Robert Kennedy would want to know about someone

being considered as a Kennedy adviser or appointee was whether he was tough.[7] If he was—on to other questions; if not, he lost all credibility. . . .

Closely allied to the concern about toughness was the Kennedy drive to win at all costs. We have seen the efforts made by Joe, Sr. to drill this precept into the Kennedy sons. By all accounts he succeeded. Eunice Kennedy Shriver said of her brother:

Jack hates to lose. He learned how to play golf, and he hates to lose at that. He hates to lose at anything. That's the only thing Jack really gets emotional about—*when he loses. Sometimes, he even gets cross.*[8]

Throughout his adult life, Kennedy's affable and deceptively casual manner concealed, as a friendly biographer commented, a "keyed-up, almost compulsive, competitiveness."[9]

Kennedy's actions in Vietnam can be understood only against the background of these values, which he brought with him into the Presidency and which strongly colored the interpretation he placed on certain events that occurred early in his Administration: the Bay of Pigs fiasco, his Vienna meeting with Khrushchev, and, closely tied to the summit meeting, the confrontation with the Soviet Union over Berlin. . . .

Harriman, the American with the longest experience and demonstrably the best judgment in dealing with the Russians, an early dove on Vietnam, and a man long past concern with proving his own toughness, advised Kennedy not to view the meetings with Khrushchev as a personal confrontation. He told him,

Don't be too serious, have some fun, get to know him a little, don't let him rattle you, he'll try to rattle you and frighten you, but don't pay any attention to that. Turn him aside, gently. And don't try for too much. Remember that he's just as scared as you are. . . . Laugh about it, don't get into a fight. Rise above it. Have some fun.[10]

When Khrushchev, true to form, blustered and threatened in pursuit of his objectives, Kennedy disregarded Harriman's advice and retaliated in kind. After their last meeting, Kennedy met privately with James Reston of *The New York Times*. As reported by Halberstam, he told Reston of Khrushchev's attacks:

"I think he did it because of the Bay of Pigs, I think he thought that anyone who was so young and inexperienced as to get into that mess

could be taken, and anyone who got into it, and didn't see it through, had no guts. . . . So I've got a terrible problem. If he thinks I'm inexperienced and have no guts, until we remove those ideas we won't get anywhere with him. So we have to act." Then he told Reston that he would increase the military budget and send another division to Germany. He turned to Reston and said that the only place in the world where there was a real challenge was in Vietnam, and "now we have a problem in trying to make our power credible and Vietnam looks like the place." [11]

Shortly after his return to the United States, he requested 3.25 billion dollars more in defense funds, large increases in the armed forces, a doubling then tripling of the draft, authority to call up 150,000 reservists, and a vastly enlarged bomb-shelter program. Certainly a large measure of this apocalyptic response was based on a personal reaction to an unpleasant confrontation.

Khrushchev was not so stupid as to risk all-out nuclear war over Berlin. He had threatened several times before to sign a separate peace treaty with East Germany, but had never done so. [12] If he did, it was uncertain whether the East Germans would have tried to cut the access routes to West Berlin. And if they took such actions, there were, as in 1947, many gradations of diplomatic and economic pressure that could be applied before an overt military response was threatened. Nevertheless, Kennedy leaped to describe the problem in cataclysmic terms. "West Berlin," he told the American public in July 1961," . . .above all, has now become—as never before—the great testing place of Western courage and will, a focal point where our solemn commitments stretching back over the years to 1945, and Soviet ambitions now meet in basic confrontation. . . ." [13]

In October 1961, when it became clear that the Viet Cong were winning, Kennedy felt he had no choice. Vietnam was the place to prove his Administration's toughness. He sent two of his key advisers, Walt Rostow and General Maxwell Taylor, to Vietnam. Although the mission was said to be designed to give the President a first-hand, objective view of the facts, its composition reveals otherwise. Rostow and Taylor, as Kennedy well knew, were both hard-liners and leaders of the counterinsurgency movement. In particular, Rostow's eagerness to demonstrate the accuracy of his theories of guerrilla warfare was well known. [14] The mission included no one with countervailing views. The President had stacked the deck. No one would—and no one did, in the White House on their return—consider the option of doing nothing, or of removing the economic-aid mission then in place in South Vietnam. Although rejecting direct involvement of American troops (he had been burned once at the Bay of Pigs), Kennedy did accept the Rostow-Taylor recommendation to send combat support units, air-combat and helicopter teams, military advisers and instructors and Green Beret teams, an American involvement which had grown to more than 15,000 men by the end of 1963. The fact that a special national intelligence estimate prepared by U.S. agencies reported that "80–90 percent of the estimated 17,000 Viet Cong guerrillas had been locally recruited, and that there was little evidence that they relied on external supplies,"[15] thereby belying the "Communist monolith" theory of the war, was ignored by Kennedy (as Johnson would ignore, at great cost, other intelligence reports that pointed away from involvement). To "win the next one" Kennedy had taken the key step of committing American soldiers to the war, thereby giving the military a foot in the door and drawing press and national attention to the conflict and his Administration's commitment.

By the fall of 1963, when reports in the press that Viet Cong were doing very well against the South Vietnamese army and their American advisers could no longer be denied, Kennedy himself was unhappy with the commitment and—with Attorney General Robert Kennedy, his closest adviser—may have been looking for an opening to move away from it. . . .

But if there was at least a chance that the Kennedys were growing away from the view that they had to win in Vietnam, President Johnson and the advisers he inherited from Kennedy were not. McGeorge Bundy and Walt Rostow, academicians who became, under Johnson, the key White House advisers on Vietnam, were believers in the ultrarealism school of government. "Its proponents believed that they were tough, that they knew what the world was really like, and that force must be accepted as a basic element of diplomacy. . . Bundy would tell antiwar gadfly John Kenneth Galbraith with a certain element of disappointment, 'Ken, you always advise against the use of force—do you realize that?'". . . .[16]

Johnson's single most influential adviser on Vietnam, Secretary of Defense Robert McNamara, had shown that he could get things done before he got to Washington by serving as president of the

Ford Motor Company. . . . His chief passion was rationality, a quintessentially masculine and, finally, narrow rationality based on the premise that anything worth knowing can and ought to be reduced to numbers and statistics. . . .

This total distrust of feeling, of intuition, of nuance which can be conveyed only in personal contact was costly for McNamara. On his frequent early trips to South Vietnam, it led him to ignore the unquantifiable but real signs that the war was not going well, signs that, behind the body count and barrage of statistics about villages secured, the political structure of South Vietnam was falling apart. It led him to disregard the repeated warnings from the CIA that things were not what the numbers made them seem, that the bombing would not, in the phrase of the day, "break Hanoi's will to resist."

Most important, McNamara kept his professional life separate from the "unmasculine" values and impulses that would have led him to question the assumption that the United States had to win in Vietnam: compassion for our soldiers and the people of Vietnam; doubt about his mandate and ability to impose his view of the world on others; and the willingness to feel, through an act of empathy, what the other side is feeling and so understand that their "logic" might be different from his own. This schism made it impossible for him to challenge the objective of victory. Basic policy objectives, the starting point for strategic and tactical analysis, always grow out of underlying personal values. And values are closely linked to—in fact are the organized expression of—the emotions we consider legitimate and allow ourselves to express. . . .

McNamara's role was tragic. He had great drive, an incredibly organized intelligence, and a strong commitment to public service. And he had deeply humane and liberal impulses—and what goes with them, a strongly held ethical framework. But this side of his personality was compartmentalized, walled off from his professional life. In this tension, he exemplified the *best* in American public men and, in the end, the war tore him apart. He could not bring the humane side of himself to bear in thinking about the war. Instead, the cult of toughness went unchallenged as the unarticulated major premise of all the systems analysis, war gaming, and policymaking. For all his other sensitivities, he was as much a victim of it as the others. His spontaneous response in a hostile confrontation with a group of students after a speech at Harvard in November 1966 was to shout at them that he was tougher than they were—although that had nothing to do with the issue in dispute.

In Lyndon Johnson there was no foil, no wellspring of opposing values and perspectives that would have allowed him to understand the limitations of these men. He was more openly insecure about his masculinity than John Kennedy and often made explicit the connection between these doubts and his decisions of state. No one has captured this better than Halberstam in his discussion of Johnson's decision to begin the bombing of North Vietnam:

He had always been haunted by the idea that he would be judged as being insufficiently manly for the job, that he would lack courage at a crucial moment. More than a little insecure himself, he wanted very much to be seen as a man; it was a conscious thing. . . .[H]e wanted the respect of men who were tough, real men, and they would turn out to be the hawks. He had unconsciously divided people around him between men and boys. Men were activists, doers, who conquered business empires, who acted instead of talked, who made it in the world of other men and had the respect of other men. Boys were the talkers and the writers and the intellectuals, who sat around thinking and criticizing and doubting instead of doing. . . .

*   *   *

As Johnson weighed the advice he was getting on Vietnam, it was the boys who were most skeptical, and the men who were most sure and confident and hawkish and who had Johnson's respect. Hearing that one member of his Administration was becoming a dove on Vietnam, Johnson said, "Hell, he has to squat to piss." The men *had, after all, done things in their lifetimes, and they had the respect of other men. Doubt itself, he thought, was almost a feminine quality, doubts were for women; once, on another issue, when Lady Bird raised her doubts, Johnson had said of course she was doubtful, it was like a woman to be uncertain.*[17]

Others played on Johnson's fear of not being manly enough. In late 1964 and 1965, Joseph Alsop, a prowar Washington columnist, wrote a series of columns which suggested that the President might be too weak to take the necessary steps, weaker than his predecessor was during the Cuban missile crisis. The columns hit Johnson's rawest nerve. He was very angry about them, but not unaffected. Bill Moyers, one of his closest aides, recalled that the President told him, after a National Security Council meeting, of his fear that, if he got out of Vietnam, McNamara and the other ex-Kennedy men would think him "less of a man" than Kennedy, would call up Alsop and tell him so, and that Alsop would write it up in his column. In dealing with a man with these anxieties, the military always had the advantage. "In decision making," Halberstam put it, "they proposed the manhood positions, their opponents the softer, or sissy, positions."[18]

Johnson was more open than the other men in his Administration about the connection between his views about the war and his preoccupation with aggressive masculinity and sexuality. The day after ordering the bombing of North Vietnam PT-boat bases and oil depots, the first act of war against North Vietnam, Johnson buoyantly told a reporter, "I didn't just screw Ho Chi Minh. I cut his pecker off."[19] Speaking of Johnson's psychological stake in the war, Moyers has said,

It was as if there had been a transfer of personal interest and prestige to the war, and to our fortunes there. It was almost like a frontier test, as if he were saying, "By God, I'm not going to let those puny brown people push me around. . . ."

The cult of toughness has also biased the Vietnam policies of President Nixon and Henry Kissinger, his chief foreign-policy adviser, but in a subtler and, in some ways, purer form than in previous administrations. . . .

Kissinger became convinced in 1967–1968, as the result of his analysis of the political forces at work in Vietnam, that the United States could not win there in the sense of keeping a non-Communist government in power indefinitely.[20] And despite Nixon's public pronouncements, there is strong evidence that he shared this belief. Richard Whalen, a Nixon adviser and speechwriter during the 1968 campaign, quoted Nixon as saying in March of that year, "I've come to the conclusion that there's no way to win the war. But we can't say that, of course. In fact, we have to seem to say the opposite, just to keep some degree of bargaining leverage."[21] And at least privately, Kissinger explained that a genuine victory was not a vital United States objective. What he and Nixon did believe was critical—critical enough to justify four more years of war, ten thousand American casualties, countless Vietnamese killed, maimed, and homeless, endangerment of the Arms Limitation Agreement with the Soviet Union, and social and political upheaval at home—was that the United States avoid the *appearance* of losing. It was vital, in Kissinger's off-the-record words, that there be "a decent interval" between United States withdrawal and the collapse of the Saigon government, a period of time which would allow the Communist takeover of the South to appear to be the result of political forces within the country rather than the failure of United States assistance.[22] Again the rationale was that this was necessary to prevent a right-wing McCarthyite backlash at home as well as to preserve American "credibility"—a favorite Kissinger term— abroad. Kissinger wrote, in January 1969, that

the commitment of five hundred thousand Americans has settled the issue of the importance of Vietnam. For what is involved now is confidence in American promises. However fashionable it is to ridicule the terms "credibility" or "prestige," they are not empty phrases; other nations can gear their actions to ours only if they can count on our steadiness. . . . In many parts of the world—the Middle East, Europe, Latin America, even Japan—stability depends on confidence in American promises. Unilateral withdrawal or a settlement which, even unintentionally, amounts to it could therefore lead to the erosion of restraints and to an even more dangerous international situation. . . .[23]

So far so good; it is hard to argue with the premise that the United States has some responsibility for restraining the Soviet Union from efforts, however unlikely, to overrun Western Europe, from sending their own forces to fight in a "war of national liberation," or threatening Japan with nuclear weapons, or decisively shifting the military balance in the Middle East. Such actions are less likely if the Soviet Union, and this nation's friends, believe that the United States will respond, to the point of meeting force with force if necessary. But the other key premises of the Kissinger-Nixon foreign policy are more leaps of faith than applications of logic. "Credibility" is made into an absolute virtue, independent of the context in which it is demonstrated and the situations to which, like accumulated savings, it is later to be applied. Responding to a "challenge" where we have nothing at stake except credibility itself is considered just as important in maintaining this elusive virtue as

responding firmly where national security is directly and immediately threatened; maybe, in the Nixon-Kissinger calculus it is
even more important—if Americans are willing to fight over tiny,
remote South Vietnam, maybe the other side will believe that we are
ready to fight over anything. . . . This is a very high-risk strategy,
since it is based on the assumption that the Soviet Union will follow
a "weaker" policy of *not* turning every confrontation with the
United States into a test of its own credibility. In 1961, for example,
Kissinger wanted our forces to invade East Berlin and tear down the
Berlin Wall to maintain United States credibility, although he recognized the essentially nonaggressive motivation of the Soviet
Union.[24]

In short, the search for "peace with honor" in Vietnam, after
Kissinger's sophisticated intellectual gloss and skilled diplomatic
tactics are stripped away, was shaped and governed by the same
tired, dangerous, arbitrary, and "masculine" first principles: one
must never back away once a line is drawn in the dust; every battle
must be won; and, if one fails to observe the first two injunctions and
by some fluke the rest of the world doesn't care, the domestic
right—the "real men"—will get you for being too soft.

Kissinger is too subtle and private a person for these underlying
personal imperatives to be seen directly in what is known of his
character and work. But the same is not true of Nixon.

Nixon's particular variant of the cult of toughness is, in Garry
Wills' phrase, the "cult of crisis," the ultimate embodiment of the
self-made man, he is always remaking and testing himself, watching
from some disembodied vantage point to make sure his machinery is
working. And the test that counts, the action that separates the men
from the boys, that allows him to parade his efforts and virtue, and
to experience his worth in the marketplace of competition most
vividly, is the crisis. This can be seen in "his eagerness, always, to
be 'in the arena,' his praise of others for being cool under pressure,
for being 'tested in the fires.'"[25] The title and format of Nixon's
book, *Six Crises*, also reflects this preoccupation. Each chapter
describes a problem he faced, his efforts to deal with it, and the
lessons he learned, mainly about his own reactions to pressure.
Some of these lessons are quite revealing.

The most difficult part of any crisis, he wrote, "is the period of
indecision—*whether to fight or run away*."[26] But the choice, as he
poses it, is not a real choice at all. What self-respecting man, let

alone a President of the United States, can choose to "run away"? Even within the limited range of options he posits, he could have used other words—"walk away," "avoid the issue," for example—which encompass the possibility that retreat can be rational and dignified. "Run away" permits none of these overtones; it sounds just plain cowardly. More important, the *substance* of the issue, what is actually at stake (apart from honor and "credibility"), has dropped from sight. The emphasis is not on the problem at hand, not on trying to determine what objective is worth pursuing at what cost, but on *himself*—on his courage or lack thereof. . . .

During Nixon's 1958 tour through South America, he was told that violent anti-American demonstrations were likely at a planned visit to San Marcos University in Lima. There was real danger of physical injury. The decision: should be cancel the visit or go through with it? Here's how he saw it in *Six Crises:*

The purpose of my tour was to present a symbol of the United States as a free, democratic, and powerful friend of our South American neighbors. In this context, my decision became clear. If I chose not to go to San Marcos, I would have failed at least in Peru. But if I did go, I would have a chance to demonstrate that the United States does not shrink from its responsibilities or flee in the face of threats. . . .

* * *

But the case for not going was also compelling. I would be risking injury, not only to myself but to others. If someone was hurt, I would be blamed. And if I took the easier and safer course of canceling the visit to San Marcos and going to Catholic University I might well be able to put the blame on both the Peruvian officials and the Communists.

* * *

But my intuition, backed by considerable experience, was that I should go. . . . [If I did not go, it] would not be simply a case of Nixon being bluffed out by a group of students, but of the United States itself putting its tail between its legs and running away from a bunch of Communist thugs.[27]

Two things stand out: first his view of the challenge to him—which was, after all, only a small, transitory, and propagandistic piece of the mosaic of relations with Latin America—as affecting the long-

term realities of this country's fortunes; and, second, his tendency,
like Kennedy and Johnson, to sweep away all complexities in a
conflict and reduce the issue to the question of whether to stand up
to the schoolyard bully. (In Caracas, another stop, Nixon's car was
stoned by demonstrators and he was also physically threatened.
Every year Nixon celebrates the anniversary of that brush with
danger with a small party.). . .

Foreign affairs is an ideal area into which to project the need to
be tough and aggressive. There are fewer constraints in that sphere
than in domestic affairs. Domestic affairs are characterized by wide
dissemination of information and fast political response which tends
to check the transformation of psychological needs into policy.
Basic objectives in foreign affairs are necessarily stated in highly
abstract terms—"a world safe for diversity"—and are achievable, if
at all, only in the long term, making strategy and programs difficult
to evaluate. How, for example, could it be proven that progress
toward the objective of an economically strong, politically liberal
Latin America did or did not result from United States intervention
in the Dominican Republic in 1965? In foreign affairs, one can more
easily get away with labeling the other side in a confrontation as
thoroughly evil, a description which justifies complete victory and
makes a defeat less acceptable. There is less pressure to deal with
the enemy up close, as human beings rather than abstractions. And
only in foreign affairs can the President's advisers gather in the
White House communications center at three in the morning to read
freshly decoded cables describing battles in progress and use their
analytical skills to map out "scenarios" involving aircraft carriers,
generals and troops and real guns to "break the will of the enemy."
For the foreign-policy intellectuals of the Kennedy and Johnson
Administrations the Vietnam conflict was an opportunity to exercise
overt, direct power usually denied to scholars and foundation executives. It was their chance to play in the big leagues. . . .

It is fair to ask whether the need to dominate and win in every
confrontation situation isn't likely to be characteristic of anyone,
male or female, who climbs to the highest ranks of government in
our competitive society. The answer is a complicated no. Most
women are not as personally threatened as most men by the suggestion that they are not tough enough. As Daniel Ellsberg pointed out,
"In almost every case the wives of [the] major officials [directing the
United States' participation in the Vietnam war] *did* manage to see

both the impossibility of what their husbands were trying to achieve and the brutality of it and immorality of it."[28] The comprehensive Harris poll of American women's opinion conducted in 1970 supports Ellsberg's observation. Seven out of ten women and eight out of ten men are willing to go to war to defend the continental United States. But women are much less willing than men to go to war over actions that do not threaten the United States directly. . . . and significantly more women than men felt that the pace of Nixon's withdrawal of American forces from Vietnam was "too slow." Two out of three women but only 49% of men say they would become upset upon hearing "that a young draftee has been killed in Vietnam." . . .[29]

In the past women who did make it were able to do so only by adopting male values; it seems unlikely that these women would have done a better job on Vietnam, or the arms race. But, in the last five years under the influence of feminism, substantial numbers of women have broken away from the traditional female self-images and roles without adopting the compulsive toughness of the male stereotype. These women, and the smaller number of men who have begun to question the validity of the traditional male sex-stereotype, have the self-confidence to achieve positions of responsibility and power without feeling a personal need to respond to every challenge. Female or male, this kind of human being might well have kept us out of Vietnam.

References

1. CIA Memorandum, June 9, 1967, reprinted in *The Pentagon Papers, op. cit.,* p. 254.

2. The New York Times (ed.), *The Pentagon Papers* ([Quadrangle: 1971] Bantam ed.: 1971), pp. 449–454.

3. See the author's article, "Munich and Vietnam: A Valid Analogy?" *Bulletin of the Atomic Scientists* (September 1966), p. 22, for a full statement and critical discussion of this analogy.

4. *The Pentagon Papers, op. cit.,* p. 432.

5. Nancy Gager Clinch, *The Kennedy Neurosis* (Grosset & Dunlap: 1973), p. 100.

6. *Ibid.,* p. 114

7. David Halberstam, *The Best and the Brightest* (Random House: 1972), p. 273.

8. Clinch, *op. cit.*, p. 98 (emphasis added).

9. Joe McCarthy, *The Remarkable Kennedys* (Dial; 1960), p. 30, quoted in Clinch, *op. cit.*, p. 131.

10. Halberstam, *op. cit.*, p. 75.

11. *Ibid.*, p. 76.

12. Clinch, *op. cit.*, p. 194.

13. *Ibid.*, p. 195.

14. Halberstam, *op. cit.*, pp. 156–162.

15. *The Pentagon Papers, op. cit.*, p. 98.

16. Halberstam, *op. cit.*, p. 56.

17. *Ibid.*, pp. 531–532.

18. *Ibid.*, p. 178.

19. *Ibid.*, p. 414.

20. David Landau, *Kissinger: The Uses of Power* (Houghton Mifflin: 1972), pp. 155–158.

21. Richard Whalen, *Catch the Falling Flag: A Republican's Challenge to His Party* (Houghton Mifflin: 1972), p. 137.

22. Landau, *op. cit.*, pp. 158, 180–182.

23. Kissinger, *American Foreign Policy* (W. W. Norton: 1969), p. 112, quoted in Landau, *op. cit.*, pp. 186–187.

24. Landau, *op. cit.*, p. 71.

25. Garry Wills, *Nixon Agonistes* (Houghton Mifflin: 1970), p. 166.

26. Richard M. Nixon, *Six Crises* (Doubleday: 1962), p. xv.

27. Nixon, *op. cit.*, p. 199.

28. *New York Post*, June 22, 1971, p. 67.

29. Virginia Slims American Women's Opinion Poll, Louis Harris and Associates (1970), pp. 74–77.

Chapter 4

Give 'Em Hell:
The Aura of Aggression,
Violence, and Daring

Aggression (an offensive action or procedure) and violence (the exertion of any physical force to injure or abuse) comprise the fourth dimension of the male role in America. They stem, in part, from the need to win at any cost, this being the ultimate way of doing so. But the aura of aggression and violence also has an importance that transcends the need to be the victor: It increases one's masculinity to be *thought* of as being aggressive and violent, even if one never *actually* is so.

We further suggest that in the absence of receiving the conventional status rewards of the society, one way of maintaining a masculine image is by being considered aggressive and violent. Thus one sometimes encounters an otherwise unsuccessful man being acclaimed for his masculinity, simply because it is known that he will use force at the slightest excuse. In Latin countries, this ideal forms the basis of machismo, where violence maintains the position of the man as totally superior to that of woman.

In America, although machismo is not a part of the culture, the incipient threat of force is always present, as is its occasional use. An entire history of bloody labor–management relations testifies to this. Aggression toward women is frequent, with rape perhaps being the ultimate act of violence directed against females. Children, too, are the victims of violence, and increasing incidents of child abuse (by both men and women) are being brought to official attention. And these uses of violence are not disparate cases; it is increasingly apparent that they are all extensions of the prescriptive aspect of the male role which glorifies aggression and violence.

Men's violence toward one another can be seen in three major areas — criminal assault, sports, and war. Male-initiated assaults are considerably more frequent than female-initiated ones; many of the arguments in favor of gun-control legislation cite the high number of cases in which men have killed each other with "Saturday-night specials" after getting into a minor argument.

In sports, although they are defined as "good, clean fun," much of the game becomes a matter of aggressive and violent confrontations. It is no accident that the males in our culture who engage in the more combative athletics — football especially, but also basketball, baseball, hockey — are generally viewed as more masculine than the men who engage in the less combative sports, such as golf or swimming. In the latter case, the competition is between individuals, not teams, and the opportunities for violent confrontations are fewer.

War is not unlike the more violent athletic contests. Pitting one "team" against another, with ardent partisans for both, men proceed to try to win the contest. Indeed, in war, as in sports, it is not always clear what is the allowable level of violence; there are definite rules (the Geneva Convention, the rules for the particular sport), but these restrictions are not always adhered to. War also raises the problem of transfer of attitudes. Many soldiers returning from Vietnam (and other wars) have had difficulty adjusting to the fact that the level of violence acceptable to the American public at home was considerably lower than that acceptable — and engaged in — in a combat situation.

To some extent, the use of aggression and violence by American males is being questioned. The recent, more stringent rape laws, the increased vigilance in cases of child abuse, the proposed gun-control legislation, and the courts-martial for those committing excessive violence in Vietnam, all herald some changes in this dimension of the male role.

VIOLENCE AND THE MASCULINE MYSTIQUE

LUCY KOMISAR

Violence pervades most aspects of men's lives, and indeed is an integral part of the male role. Komisar reviews the different arenas in which men are allowed, and even encouraged, to express violent behavior in order to maintain their masculine image.

"We will not be humiliated," President Nixon declared in his speech to the country after the invasion of Cambodia. "It is not our power but our will and character that is being tested tonight." Agonizing over the specter of an America that acted like "a pitiful, helpless giant," he vowed that he would not see the nation become "a second-rate power" and "accept the first defeat in its proud 190-year history."

Nixon's resolve stiffens (masculine) and he sends troops into Cambodia so that we are not forced to submit (feminine) to a peace of humiliation. The big stick hasn't changed much since Teddy Roosevelt, only now it's a stockpile of missiles and bayonets on rifles and bombs that plow gracelessly into a womb that burns with napalm.

The United States of America is "the clear leader among modern, stable, democratic nations in its rates of homicide, assault, rape, and robbery, and it is at least among the highest in incidence of group violence and assassination," declared the National Commission on the Causes and Prevention of Violence. Most of those violent crimes are committed by males between the ages of 15 and 24; a majority of them are poor and a disproportionate percentage are black.

"Violence is actually often used to enable a young man to become a successful member of ghetto society," reported the Com-

From *Washington Monthly,* July 1970. Copyright © 1970 by Lucy Komisar. Reprinted by permission.

mission. "Proving masculinity may require frequent rehearsal of the toughness, the exploitation of women, and the quick aggressive responses that are characteristic of the lower-class adult male." The report called ghetto life a "subculture within dominant American middle-class culture in which aggressive violence tends to be accepted as normal in everyday life. . . . An altercation with overtones threatening a young man's masculinity, a misunderstanding between husband and wife, competition for a sexual partner, the need to get hold of a few dollars — these trivial events can readily elicit violent response."

The only thing wrong with that is the Commission's assumption that its observations apply only to the lower classes. What it has described, in fact, is the "masculine mystique," a conception of manhood so central to the politics and personality of America that it institutionalizes violence and male supremacy as measures of national pride. The masculine mystique is based on toughness and domination, qualities that once may have been necessary in a time when men felled trees and slew wild animals. Now they are archaic and destructive values that have no legitimate place in our world but continue to exist as idealized standards for some lofty state of "masculinity." The mystique has characterized many nations, but it is particularly dangerous in contemporary America because of our distinctively high levels of internal violence, our "Bonnie and Clyde" tendencies toward its glorification, our enormous capacities for mechanized warfare, and our virtual obsession with being Number One.

A quote from a man I know: "When I was a little boy and had come home crying after a beating from some local bully, my mother would push me out and lock the door, demanding that I go back to give as good as I had gotten. She said boys who didn't fight back were sissies."

Little boys learn the connection between violence and manhood very early in life. Fathers indulge in mock prize fights and wrestling matches with eight-year-olds. Boys play cowboys and Indians with guns and bows and arrows proffered by their elders. They are gangsters or soldiers interchangeably — the lack of difference between the two is more evident to them than to their parents. They are encouraged to "fight back," and bloodied noses and black eyes become trophies of their pint-sized virility.

Little Men

The differences between boys and girls are defined in terms of violence. Boys are encouraged to rough-house; girls are taught to be gentle ("ladylike"). Boys are expected to get into fights, but admonished not to hit girls. (It is not "manly" to assault females — except, of course, sexually, but that comes later.) Boys who run away from fights are "sissies," with the implication that they are queer. As little boys become big boys, their education in violence continues. The leadership in this country today consists of such little boys who attained "manhood" in the approved and heroic violence of World War II. They returned to a society in which street and motorcycle gangs, fast cars, and fraternity hazing confirmed the lessons of war — one must be tough and ready to inflict pain in order to get ahead.

The phallic/power symbol of our age is, of course, the automobile. The World Health Organization says that traffic accidents are the most common cause of death among young males in highly motorized countries. Often cars are stolen not to keep or sell, but for the joy of the ride and the sense of power and controlled violence it offers. Madison Avenue contributes its influence by selling cars as if they were magical potency potions. Chivalry's knight on horseback has become man on "horse-power" — even modern terminology substantiates the metaphor.

A young philosophy instructor at a Catholic men's college in New Jersey, who leads a "consciousness-raising" group for some of his students, says most of them have grown up with the same conception of what it takes to prove one's manhood: "You have a car and 'make' as many girls as possible. It's very important to have an impressive car; the freshmen all believe the ads that if you've got a Dodge Charger, you're going to get laid more." The system militates against tenderness, he says. "No physical display between men is acceptable except to fight, and the *only* acceptable response when someone questions your manhood is to fight. Most freshmen think there's something faggoty about being a draft dodger."

He adds, "Some guys are so obsessed with their manhood and masculinity that they can't make love: they feel it's effeminate to be sensitive or affectionate."

Boys are introduced into "manhood" through innocent pastimes like boxing, brawling, and football. And not-so-innocent pastimes like war. Consider phrases like "The manly art of self defense," "Join the army, be a man" (variation: "The army will make
a man out of him"). Gene Tunney's autobiography is called simply
A Man Must Fight. Men who have been brought up in this tradition,
and whose memories of war, real or imagined, have bolstered their
self-respect during years of bringing home the bacon, are
traumatized by the young men (students and peace marchers) who
refuse to accept pain, mutilation, and death as initiation rites into
manhood.

Even at a time when the protest leader is beginning to replace
the football star as campus hero, football remains a passion with a
large number of American men. The game, with its crashing, smash-
ing bodies and carefully controlled violence, deserves a closer
scrutiny to see how it reflects the quest for manhood.

The Great Touchdown of Virility

For the past half dozen years, I have observed the phenomenon of
the masculine mystique operating on a group of newspapermen who
frequent a bar in my neighborhood. They drink heavily, rhapsodize
about prize fighters and men who earn their living by physical labor,
share football afternoons watching the barroom television, and treat
women mostly as "dumb broads" to be taken in bed and ignored in
serious conversation. There are some exceptions.

Several of them urged me to read Frederick Exley's *A Fan's
Notes*, an autobiographical novel which had been nominated for the
National Book Award. I read it and realized how it must have been a
mirror for many of them — yet neither they nor Exley appear to
have understood the significance and the logic of his story.

The book's Fred Exley is an impotent writer (impotent in his
work and, in one episode, impotent in bed) who seeks fame and
recognition and whose hero is Giant's football player Frank Gifford.
Exley's father was a tough, athletic, working-class man whose
drinking often ended in violence. The son longs for "some sunnier
past" when men could prove their virility with the muscles in their
arms. His book never indicates any recognition of the fact that his
idolatry of football and of the hard-drinking laborer — and his

exploitation of women — mask the fear that he is "unmanly," that he is "womanish" — the epithet he uses to describe a despised Hollywood publicist. His anguished search is futile, for he reaches out for a definition of manhood that can no longer exist for most men, except through the shallow medium of television. Exley's own words offer a vivid picture of the masculine mystique. First the football hero as symbol of the time when manhood was easily defined and won by power and dominance:

Why did football bring me so to life? I can't say precisely. Part of it was my feeling that football was an island of directness in a world of circumspection. In football a man was asked to do a difficult and brutal job, and he either did it or got out. There was nothing rhetorical or vague about it; I chose to believe that it was not unlike the jobs which all men, in some sunnier past, had been called upon to do. It smacked of something old, something traditional, something unclouded by legerdemain and subterfuge. It had that kind of power over me, drawing me back with the force of something known, scarcely remembered, elusive as integrity — perhaps it was no more than the force of a forgotten childhood. Whatever it was, I gave myself up to the Giants utterly. The recompense I gained was the feeling of being alive.

Then Exley's image of his father as the symbol of the virility he seeks to attain:

. . . my father was "tough" . . . . He supported his family by climbing telephone poles for the Niagara Mohawk (until he was fired for fighting); and when I think of him now, I think of rough-cotton work shirts open at the collar, a broad masculine face made ruddy by exposure and a Camel cigarette dangling from the corner of his pensive mouth. There was nothing about him that did not suggest his complete awareness that he got his bread by the sweat of his brow and the power of his back. He seemed like almost the prototype of the plebian. Yet my father had more refined dreams. Like most athletes he lived amidst the large deeds and ephemeral glories of the past, recalling a time when it must have seemed more Elevated . . . . Moreover, in an attempt to more vividly recreate that past, my father drank — I was about to say too much, which would not be entirely accurate. My father could not, or so my mother

recalls, drink even the most limited amounts of beer without becoming moody, argumentative, and even violent; and on one occasion he beat a man so badly that the man had to have pulled what few teeth my father left him.

Lastly, Exley's certainty that he had failed the test of masculinity in the eyes of his father. He was a small boy being introduced to Steve Owen, the coach of the Giants:

> *"Are you tough?" Owen asked.*
> *"Pardon, sir?"*
> "Are you tough?"
> *"I don't know, sir."*
> *Owen looked at my father. "Is he tough, Mr. Exley?"*
> *Though more than anything I wanted my father to say that I was, I was not surprised at his answer.*
> *"It's too soon to tell."*

Hunting, bullfighting, cockfighting. Is it a more "humane" sport to shoot an animal for the pure joy of watching it fall or more "virile" to torture it slowly under the guise of letting it fight back and subjecting the killer to the threat of death himself? What thrilling, "macho" feeling overcomes spectators at the gruesome sight of two male chickens with metal spurs attached to their feet fiercely hacking each other to bits? Ernest Hemingway went to his own violent death without making all that perfectly clear.

How far is it from the glorification of man killing animals to what amounted to national admiration for the killers of the Prohibition era and the men who terrorized the country with gangland power? After all, Dutch Schultz and Al Capone were only following in the heroic, virile tradition of Billy the Kid and the James brothers. And like Hemingway's bullfighters, they did everything with flamboyant style. In 1872, a Kansas City newspaper, reporting a robbery in which a little girl was shot in the leg, called it "so diabolically daring and so utterly in contempt of fear that we are bound to admire it and revere its perpetrators." Still dripping with nobility a few days later, it said that the robbers had carried out their crime "with the halo of medieval chivalry upon their garments." The criminals were thought to be Frank and Jesse James.

If manhood is equivalent to strength and power, those attributes must be constantly tested and proven to new challengers. "I knew a guy who was very short," a friend of mine recalls. "He told me that he used to fantasize that he was Audie Murphy. He would go into a working-class bar where nobody knew him and he'd do this act. He'd sit at the bar, maybe for a half hour and growl at the bartender. After a while, someone would come over and maybe say something or poke him on the shoulder, and he'd spin around and hit the guy over the head with a beer bottle. He was always sitting there waiting for someone to provoke him, and he always had the bottle ready."

Some people say men fight in bars because they get drunk, but that has nothing to do with it. Men fight in bars because that's the only place where it's allowed. (That is probably the reason why Exley's father got into fights after only a few beers.) Society instills feelings in men that they ought to fight and then makes it illegal — except in war. Working-class bars are "masculine" places — the football on TV, the absence of women, and the fights are all part of the effort to recapture that lost ideal.

Postscript: On May 29, a short item buried in the back pages of *The New York Times* reported that actor Audie Murphy, America's most decorated soldier in World War II, had been booked for assault with intent to commit murder after a gun went off during a fight he had with a dog trainer.

In the old West ("where men were men and women were women") gunfighters were often called on to prove themselves in duels with younger men who wagered their lives against the chance to be known as "the man who shot the fastest gun in . . . , etc." Today's shoot-em-ups in defense of manhood unfortunately tend to involve more than the principals.

The Soft Battlefield

The ultimate proof of manhood, however, is in sexual violence. Even the language of sex is a lexicon that describes the power of men over women. Men are "aggressive" as they "take" or "make" women, showing their potency ("power") in the "conquest." Women, on the other hand, "submit" and "surrender," allowing themselves to be "violated" and "possessed." Havelock Ellis declares the basic sado-masochism of such a concept to be "certainly normal." He says: "In men it is possible to trace a tendency to inflict pain on the women they love. It is still easier to trace in women a delight in experiencing physical pain when it is inflicted by a lover and an eagerness to accept subjection to his will."

Sadism *cum* virility is offered the fans who flock to James Bond films to see their hero play out their fantasies alternately in sensual embraces with women and bloody combat with men. In "Goldfinger," for instance, Bond has his arms around a chorus girl when he sees the reflection of an assassin in her eye. He wards off the blow with her body, a consummation which seems as satisfying to his manhood as the one he originally had in mind. There is as little tenderness and as much brutality in the sexual encounters as in the fight scenes. If homosexuality were in fashion, it is likely that James Bond could make love to the men and beat up the women without changing his sentiments toward either.

Chivalry was an early example of the worship of masculine violence tied in with sexual dominance. Then and later, duels were fought to protect the honor of women and wars waged to uphold the honor of states. In the latter endeavor, the women were raped instead of honored. Both traditions have been proudly continued, and in both the women have been objects to conquer and to parade as the validation of someone's manhood: *they have no honor of their own.*

Rape on foreign battlefields has always been met on the home-front with shrugs about men having certain "needs" and the "tensions" that build up in wartime. So soldiers get penicillin along with their K-rations, and they express their "manhood" by forcing women to submit to them. Those that lie with prostitutes are participating in rape in just as real a sense — they are enjoying the bitter fruits of the rape of a country that forces its citizens to choose between death and degradation.

In 1966, an American patrol held a 19-year-old Vietnamese girl captive for several days, taking turns raping her and finally murdering her. The sergeant planned the crime in advance, telling the soldiers during the mission's briefing that the girl would improve their "morale." When one soldier refused to take part in the rape, the sergeant called him "queer" and "chicken"; another testified later that he joined in the assault to avoid such insults. When one *country* ravages another to avoid being called "chicken," how unusual is it that soldiers follow suit? Both in the name of that elusive "manhood."

According to Seymour Hersh, some of the GIs who conducted the My Lai massacre raped women before they shot them. The day after that "mission," an entire platoon raped a woman caught fleeing a burning hut. And a couple of days later a helicopter door gunner spotted the body of a woman in a field. She was spread-eagled, with an Eleventh Brigade patch between her legs. Like a "badge of honor," reported the gunner. "It was obviously there so people would know the Eleventh Brigade had been there."

Machismo and the Don Juan cult, modern versions of chivalry, are brushed off as Latin oddities. Spaniards and Italians defend their honor with "passion killings" — and everyone winks. But they are not the only men who regard women as trophies in rape or seduction or who think wife-beating is a joke (literally, as in "When did you stop beating your wife?"). How different are those passion killings from Southern lynchings conducted in the name of white womanhood and against the imagined sexual onslaughts of black men? It is not a coincidence that white supremacy in the South organized the "Knights" of the Ku Klux Klan. That was an assertion of masculinity in the face of humiliation by other men; it was as much male supremacy as white supremacy.

The writing of Eldridge Cleaver epitomizes the way in which many black men, too, hold violence equivalent to masculinity, fully in the American tradition. "The boxing ring is the ultimate focus of masculinity in America," says Cleaver in *Soul on Ice;* "the two-fisted testing ground of manhood, and the heavyweight champion, as a symbol, is the real Mr. America." Cleaver recognizes the historical significance of violence in our culture:

Whether we quench our thirst from the sight of a bleeding Jesus on the Cross, from the ritualized sacrifice in the elevation of the Host and the consecration of the Blood of the Son, or from bullfighting, cockfighting, dogfighting, wrestling or boxing, spiced with our Occidental memory and heritage of the gladiators of Rome and the mass spectator sport of the time of feeding Christians and other enemies of society to the lions in the Coliseum — whatever the mask assumed by the impulse, the persistent beat of the drum over the years intones the chant.

However, his own cry is not a protest against that definition of masculinity but anguish that black men cannot live up to it:

In back rooms, in dark stinking corners of the ghettos, self-conscious black men curse their own cowardice and stare at their rifles and pistols and shotguns laid out on tables before them, trembling as they wish for a manly impulse to course through their bodies and send them screaming mad into the streets shooting from the hip. Black women look at their men as if they are bugs. . . .

Hemingway and Mailer: The Bulls of Literature

Alan Sillitoe, author of "Saturday Night and Sunday Morning," writes: "An intellectual obsession with violence is a sign of fear. A physical obsession with it is a sign of sexual impotence." Interesting, then, that Ernest Hemingway, who composed hosannas to manly brutality, took his own life with a gun and that Norman Mailer, one of America's most self-conscious "machos," once stabbed his wife and has been in more than one barroom and cocktail party brawl.

In 1927, Hemingway published *Men Without Women*, a collection of stories which I expect reflect his conception of ultimate manhood. The stories are variously written about a bullfighter, a boxer, several soldiers, some hired gunmen, etc. Women are represented as unwelcomely pregnant (in a story pointedly titled "White Elephants"); as prostitutes, as deceivers, or as fools. Ultimately, Hemingway's answer is to eschew women for more "masculine" pastimes — fishing, for example:

I lay in the dark with my eyes open and thought of all the girls I had ever known and what kind of wives they would make. It was a very interesting thing to think about and for a while it killed off trout-fishing and interfered with my prayers. Finally, though, I went back to trout-fishing, because I found that I could remember all the streams and there was always something new about them while the girls, after I had thought about them a few times, blurred and I could not call them into my mind and finally they all blurred and all became rather the same and I gave up thinking about them almost altogether. ("Now I Lay Me")

Critic Leslie Fiedler thinks Hemingway's concern with violence reflects a pathological inability to deal with adult sexuality. If, as Sillitoe says, obsession with violence is a sign of impotence, trading women for fish is one way to avoid that embarrassing confrontation.

Mailer is more extravagant than Hemingway in his exaltation of violence: "Men who have lived a great deal with violence are usually gentler and more tolerant than men who abhor violence," he says. "Boxers, bullfighters, a lot of combat soldiers, Hemingway heroes, in short, are almost always gentle men."

What romantic drivel! My Lai, cauliflower ears and broken noses, slit throats, cement blocks splashing into Mafia cemeteries, guts spilling out of gored intestines — do the actors in such violent dramas radiate the compassion and understanding Mailer attributes to them? Not to mention the Chicago police Mailer himself has had occasion to describe without recourse to adjectives like "gentle" or "tolerant."

If Mailer's ideal man of the world is described in such incredible terms, what about his man in bed? Sex is conquest, a contest, an opportunity for domination. Mailer compares the "event" in bed to the bullfight. Sometimes he sees himself as the matador, sometimes as the bull. He calls his penis "the avenger" (For what "crime" or "insult" does he avenge himself against women?) and he recalls how he "threw her a fuck the equivalent of a 15-round fight."

In *Sexual Politics,* feminist Kate Millett devotes an entire chapter to an analysis of Mailer's obsession with violence, showing how his equation of violence and masculinity masks an overriding fear of homosexuality as well as a contempt for women. Beginning with *The Naked and the Dead*, Mailer could barely speak either of sex or violence in terms that did not include the other. Millett cites a speech by Sergeant Croft:

All the deep dark urges of man, the sacrifices on the hilltop, the churning lusts of night and sleep, weren't all of them contained in the shattering, screaming burst of a shell . . . the phallus-shell that rides through a shining vagina of steel . . . the curve of sexual excitement and discharge, which is after all the physical core of life.

Mailer equates the opposite of violence — pacifism — with the opposites of maleness — femaleness and homosexuality — both of which arouse his contempt. The logical outcome of this ideology, says Millett, is war and violence, the only protection against the pacifism he labels "unmanly." And the violence that Mailer venerates is the logical extension and proof of the aggressiveness this society considers an innate part of the truly masculine personality. "Men are aggressive, women are passive," says the conventional wisdom. "Men are dominant and venturesome; women are yielding and receptive." The dictionary definition of passive is "inactive, but acted upon; offering no resistance, submissive; taking no part, inert." That sounds more like a vegetable than a human being of *any* sex.

The truth of the matter is that neither men nor women are born "aggressive" or "passive"; the values of masculinity and femininity (as this society sees them) are drummed into them by parents, teachers, the media, and other agents of social education. The California Gender Identity Center, for one, has discovered that it is easier to use surgery to change the sex of an adolescent male who has been erroniously brought up as a female than to undo the cultural conditioning that has made him act like a woman. The report of the Center concludes that masculine and feminine roles are determined by *social forces*, not by the nature of a person's genitals.

In other words, this society has inculcated values of aggression and dominance in males and those values have led logically to violence and destruction in the name of good old, unadulterated manhood. Behavioral scientists back up this assertion with their own investigations and analyses. Sometimes teenage delinquents play the same games adults do — they hope to preserve their honor through "cold wars" without resorting to actual battle. Anthropologist Walter Miller, who studied gangs in the 1950's, observed a number of groups in full-scale war preparations 15 times; only once did they escalate into conflict. "A major objective of the gang members was to put themselves in the position of fighting without actually having to fight." They often avoided warfare by tipping off the police or "reluctantly" accepting mediation from social workers.

The similarity between saber-rattling by teenage delinquents and modern nation-states is obvious. "Gang members fight to secure and defend their honor as males; to secure and defend the reputation of their local areas and the honor of their women; to show that an affront to their pride and dignity demands retaliation," says Miller, adding almost unnecessarily that "great nations engage in national wars for almost identical reasons." (The "theatre of war" is a fit appellation for the locus of this kind of masculine play-acting.) Miller concludes that teenage violence and international warfare stem from the same pathological root.

An End to the Game

Violence and male supremacy have been companions in the course of civilization. The domination of women by men has been the prototype of the control men have tried to exercise over other men — in slavery, in war, and in the marketplace. Bernard Clark, professor of government at the London School of Economics, speaks glowingly of "the fierce masculine joy of striving for possession according to some more or less acknowledged rules of a game." That is the game that President Nixon plays, the game that wins acclaim from Hemingway and Mailer, the game that enshrined Jesse James as a national hero, and the game that spills buckets of human blood and guts on battlefields at home and abroad.

That game says that to be a man one must possess, control, dominate — and that domination must be assured by force and violence. Masculinity is interpreted to *demand* male supremacy. Ironically, now in the black community, men are calling on women to step back so that they can "assert their manhood." The "masculinity game" can't have a winner unless it also has a loser. The rules of the game require that the losers be reduced to humiliation and powerlessness — to the classic status of women. Such was the "emasculation" of black men under slavery and segregation. And consequently, they know that the reassertion of that kind of "manhood" requires the suppression of their women.

John Wayne is the quintessential player in The Game. His role in "The Green Berets" would be an embarrassing parody if patriotic zeal were not immune to wit. Wayne is tough-fisted, hard-talking, and never walks away from a fight; thanks to providence, righteousness, and his rugged, muscular frame, he never loses. But it never happens in real life like in the movies. They probably wouldn't like the metaphor, but the "hard hats" constitute a Greek chorus to masculinity — they extol it through physical labor, vulgar comments at passing women, and patriotic fervor for "our brave fighting men in Vietnam." Sometimes the defense of their manhood, otherwise largely expressed through applauding someone else's violence, forces them to beat up people who disagree with them.

The enemies of national "virility" are called "effete," a word that means "sterile, spent, worn-out" and conjures up the picture of an effeminate pantywaist — the inveterate 90-pound weakling who is

always getting sand kicked in his face, probably by a burly construction worker. More to the point, effete comes from "out" plus
"fetus" — exhausted by bearing.

Perhaps we *are* "exhausted by bearing" — tired to death of
bearing up under the super-masculine mystique that is a national
neurosis and that sets a country to counting bodies the way it counts
touchdowns — and cataloguing both as a measure of its manhood.

Is it only coincidental that in the early morning hours of the last
demonstration of outrage at the invasion of Cambodia and the deaths
of American college students, President Nixon was compelled to
talk about football — or that he repeated that theme in May at a Billy
Graham rally in Knoxville, Tennessee?

"As one who warmed the bench for four years, it's finally good
to get out on the football field here at Volunteer Stadium," he said.
"And even if we're on the 20-yard line, we're going to be over that
goal line before we're through." Nixon talks about "our-brave-
fighting-men-in-Vietnam" as if they were Fred Exley's Giants — the
essence of manhood wrapped up in hard hats and shoulder pads. All
America has to suffer because young Richard Nixon never made the
team.

Ironically, the "he-men" who occupy the ringside seats at prize
fights, football games, and wars don't recognize the significant difference between their "masculinity" and that of the athlete and
frontiersman they adulate. They generally enjoy their violence
vicariously; there is no call for personal courage. Richard Nixon is
still warming the bench, and sending others to shoot Vietnamese
villagers or scorch them with napalm is hardly an exercise in bravery.

The President is the symbol of a country with a castration
complex — a nation that feels its manhood already wilted by the
refusal of the Viet Cong to spread its legs for the gang-bang we have
organized.

The beginning of a challenge to the masculine mystique of
violence and domination comes now from those who were its first
victims: women. Today women are demanding new definitions of
masculine and feminine that do not require the dominance of one sex
over the other. We have rejected all the myths about masculine
aggression and feminine passivity and we seek to replace them with
values that encourage human relations based on equality, compassion, and respect.

Today the masculine mystique is no longer just a matter of concern for the women who have suffered its ill effects most universally. The caveman mentality outlived its usefulness when technology made the hunter obsolete, and its extension into national and international politics now threatens to destroy everything men *and women* have built since then.

Today men need a kind of courage that is only exhibited by those who have no doubts at all about their *manhood* — and that is the courage to assert their *humanity*.

WHY WE OPPOSE VOTES FOR MEN

ALICE DUER MILLER

Alice Duer Miller's amusing but effective rejoinder to those who would exclude women from public affairs has a contemporary ring, yet was written in 1915. She clearly perceived, as did few of her (or our) contemporaries, that men's penchant for violence was at least as dangerous to society as any trait ascribed to women.

1. Because man's place is in the army.
2. Because no really manly man wants to settle any question otherwise than by fighting about it.
3. Because if men should adopt peaceable methods women will no longer look up to them.
4. Because men will lose their charm if they step out of their natural sphere and interest themselves in other matters than feats of arms, uniforms and drums.
5. Because men are too emotional to vote. Their conduct at baseball games and political conventions shows this, while their innate tendency to appeal to force renders them particularly unfit for the task of government.

SUPER BOWL

WARREN FARRELL

Sports are good, clean fun — or are they? In this incisive analysis of professional football, Farrell considers the deliberately violent and dehumanizing strains beneath the facade of sportsmanship, teamwork, and healthy competition.

There might be something suspect in football being held in such priority that sixty-five million people can arrange their day to allow a three-hour bloc of time for one event — the annual Super Bowl.[1] Sixty-five million persons is between one third and one quarter of the American population, the very great majority of whom are men[2] — doubtless more than half the men and boys who are old enough to watch TV in the United States. . . .

Football, like war, is a scientific and brutal game; even the vocabulary of football is similar to that of war. A "bomb" is something thrown which destroys the opposite side. To bomb effectively is to "score." There is always an us and a them. There are commands to take the offensive and to prepare one's defenses. Both football and war feature spying and scouting, and special units for extra degrees of violence. (When the vocabulary is not interchangeable with that of war, it is with that of sex: "getting into the hole," "thrusting," and the announcer's admiration for each man successful at "deep penetration.")

The special team employed during every kickoff or punt is called the suicide squad. The comparison to war is made by Rich Saul, a lineman for the Los Angeles Rams who is notorious for his play on suicide squads. "If you compare football to war, then the special teams are the marines or the infantry. We're the first ones to get into the game, we initiate the hitting, we determine where the battle is going to be fought and on whose grounds."[3] Saul, who says he enjoys his job, "slams into ball carriers with such intensity that he mangled five steel face masks on the front of his helmet."[4] John Bramlett, a thirty-year-old veteran, says, "I just think about hurting the other person because every time you get kicked senseless, you can count on knocking two or three other people senseless. That's a pretty good feeling."[5] Fans made a legend out of Gil Mains of Detroit almost ten years ago. His fame was based on his willingness to launch himself feet first at the heart of an offensive wedge (a group of about four especially tough and quick men who block for the ball carrier). His attacking position is commonly called a "head-hunter" (his primary aim is to get the ball-carrier's head). On the special teams the injury rate is eight times greater than for any other position.[6]

The dependence on approval is so great that players continue to play with injuries no matter how painful they are. The men entering the suicide squads are tough men who use their strength as a way of compensating for their insecurity about making it on the club in any other way. These men are "mostly tough rookies and second year men" who "realize that their survival on the club — and the road to a starting job — is directly related to their ferocity and fearlessness."[7]

On the field a series of rituals are taking place which are designed to reinforce and provoke the utmost aggressiveness of which each man is capable. The pep talk is one ritual. The boy is manipulated by a number of reinforcing loyalties — the loyalty to his school, the coach, his team and team pride, and his own personal pride. In the game itself the loyalty to family and neighbors is added. Prior to the game the team captain yells, "Okay, let's go get them!" and the team screams, "Yeah!" repeatedly. A third ritual, described by Dave Meggyesy, formerly of the St. Louis Cardinals, as part of his high school team's preparation, is a special church service by a minister (a former college athlete), who gives an inspirational talk.[8] Almost every type of tactic is permitted when the boys go all out for victory. The side with which one identifies is seen as all good and the other as all bad.

If the effect of professional football is not clear by the end of the first half of the game, it becomes clear at half time. The first event is the introduction of young male children who will competitively vie with each other for honors such as the best passer. Seven-year-old boys test their strength before sixty-five million people, and the young boy at home sees already that he is not quite the man some of his peers are. . . . No sooner do the boys clear off the field than women (called "girls") come onto the field. They are scantily clad, swinging their hips in unison, with outfits cut to reveal their buttocks and bosoms. As the cameras zero in on the former their legs slowly withdraw in a coy but obvious "see if you can get me. . . ."

The armchair viewers of the Super Bowl meanwhile have been treated to a spectacle which the crowd at the stadium has missed — the commercials. The theme of all but two of the commercials was muscle, strength, power and speed (no different from the football game). The first of the two exceptions featured five women in sexy outfits attempting to gain the favor of one man by being chosen to serve him a Dutch Masters cigar. The man, literally on a throne, acts unaffected and cooly discriminating as the five women move their bodies caressingly toward him in repeated attempts to be recognized. The smoke from the cigars creates a fantasy atmosphere of clouds as the commercial ends, along with the fantasy of millions of men. . . .

A beer advertisement first prepares us for the introduction of the beer. We see a rowing team of all men. The camera focuses on their muscles — the strength and power of the men become clear, but they all take directions perfectly from their leader. The importance of strict obedience is coupled with victory, and victory coupled with being a man. The beer is introduced as the well-earned reward, with the concluding comment, "It's sort of good to be with men who won't settle for second best."

The razor-blade ad follows a similar pattern. The blades are tungsten, but they are not introduced until they are associated with a powerful steelworker drilling through tough tungsten steel. His shirt sleeve is cut short (and ragged) to reveal his muscles. Sparks bounce off his helmet. He balances himself above the city drilling the steel that makes the city (a far cry from "softer hands with Dove"). Now the tungsten blades can be introduced. They are blades "as tough as steel, for men with tough beards. . . ."

The game draws to a close. The winning coach is Tom Landry, "the man they say is unemotional." The winning team is the Dallas Cowboys, "the team they say is unemotional." But the victory is tremendous, a clear-cut triumph: 24 to 3. The cameras pick the victorious coach out of the crowd. He barely cracks a smile. The time for emotions is certainly here, and a few of the football players do express happiness, but the game ends on a note of patriotism, not

emotionalism. The *National* Football League champions are repeatedly referred to as the *world* champions. There are no bound-
aries to male power and no limits on male fantasies — except
emotional limits.

References

1. *The New York Times*, January 15, 1972, estimated this number of
   Americans as the number watching the Super Bowl on January 15,
   1972.
2. *Ibid.*
3. *The New York Times*, March 4, 1972.
4. *Ibid.*
5. "The Wedge Meets the Headhunters," *Life*, December 3, 1971, p. 34.
6. *Ibid.*, p. 39.
7. *Ibid.*, p. 34.
8. Dave Meggyesy, *Out of Their League* (Berkeley, Calif.: Ramparts
   Press, 1970), p. 24.

SEX, WAR, AND VIOLENCE IN THE NOVELS OF NORMAN MAILER

KATE MILLETT

The deeper ramifications of sex with force and violence in
the minds of adult males probably are illuminated more
clearly in the writing of Norman Mailer than in any other
source in the English language. Millett sees a deep and
inevitable link in Mailer's work between sexuality, and
savage, destructive violence, and demonstrates this clearly
with selections from his writings.

When a novelist is obsessed with certain traits of behavior, his
characters tend to repeat themselves from one book to the next.

There is a character in Mailer's fiction who continues to appear under different guises, and according to the author's ambivalent response, may be villain or hero, or more likely villain as hero. The first such figure is Sergeant Croft of *The Naked and The Dead,* where the portrait seems to be as unfriendly as it is incisive. Like D.J., the prodigy ("there's blood on my dick") of *Why Are We in Vietnam?,*[1] Croft began as a hunter. Like Sergius O'Shaugnessy of *The Deer Park,* Croft has "the cruelty to be a man."[2]

The larger part of Croft's existence is passed in homicidal rage. His first murder, the cold-blooded execution of a striker whom he dismisses as a "dog," left him with a memorable "excitement."[3] It is an exhilaration he spends the rest of his life recapturing, both in sexuality ("You're all a bunch of fuggin whores . . . all a bunch of dogs . . . You're all deer to track"),[4] and in the organized slaughter of warfare: ("I hate the bastards . . . I'm gonna really get me a Jap)."[5] *The Naked and The Dead* describes the American campaign on "Anopopei" in the Philippines. Since the Japanese who hold the island are without supplies and close to starvation, the invasion ends as a "Jap hunt," a Croftian holiday. Preparing to shoot a prisoner, Croft anticipates "the quick lurching spasms of the body when the bullets would crash into it,"[6] and the *frisson* which awaits him is the exact counterpart to what he knows of sexual experience.

Mailer regards Croft as the megalomaniac ambition of the frontier with no further room to exercise itself. "His ancestors pushed and labored and strained, drove their oxen, sweated their women, and moved a thousand miles." But in Croft this force has turned into an exclusively destructive energy:[7] "He pushed and labored inside himself and smoldered with an endless hatred," his "main cast of mind" a "superior contempt."[8] "He hated weakness and loved practically nothing."[9] Croft's most withering insult is to castigate his subordinates as "a pack of goddam women."[10] While a youth learning to track his first game (game whom he conceives to be female, because prey), he cursed himself with the same fury when his gun wavered before firing — "Jus' a little old woman."[11]

Another factor has contributed to Croft's maniacal anger — his wife's adultery: "It ended with him going to town alone, and taking a whore when he was drunk, beating her sometimes with a wordless choler."[12] Mailer suggests that it is the impetus of this sexual rage which has brought Croft to the Army and halfway round the world to vent his spleen on strangers.

If Croft stands for run of the mill fascism in the novel, General Cummings, the refined sadist at the pinnacle of the class structure which Army hierarchy represents so saliently, is the higher totalitarianism. He too considers killing sexual, and sexuality murderous. First a sample of Cummings the lover:

He must subdue her, absorb her, rip her apart and consume her . . . [thinking] "I'll take you apart, I'll eat you, oh, I'll make you mine, you bitch." [13]

Next the general:

the deep dark urges of man, the sacrifice on the hilltop, the churning lusts of night and sleep, weren't all of them contained in the shattering, screaming burst of a shell . . . the phallus-shell that rides through a shining vagina of steel . . . the curve of sexual excitement and discharge, which is after all the physical core of life. [14]

As sex is war, war is sexual. Can one deny "the physical core of life"? The connection between sex and violence appears not only as metaphor, but seems to express a conviction about the nature of both phenomena.

A superficial reading might convince one that Mailer's brilliant anatomy of these two cancerous personalities is rendered without any traces of admiring or positive identification. But in the last chapters of the book a subtle shift takes place in the treatment of Croft; a curious effort is made to persuade the reader that he is not mad but heroic. The novel goes GI and spoils itself in cheap patriotism. [15] Years later Mailer not only admitted that his ideas about violence had "changed 180 degrees" since his first work, but even confided that "beneath the ideology of *The Naked and The Dead* was an obsession with violence. The characters for whom I had the most secret admiration, like Croft," he remarks nonchalantly "were violent people." [16]

The ambiguity intrudes again in *Barbary Shore,* the quasi-political novel that followed, in which an undercurrent hostility continues to connect, even equate combat and cruelty with sexuality. In a book whose overt message is a shocked protest against the extermination camps of Nazi and Soviet, the brutality of our century, the hero and the novel's moral arbiter recalls with gratification how, as a soldier in enemy territory, he "made love from the hip":

I never saw the girl. Above my head in magnification of myself the barrel of the machine gun pointed toward the trees . . . I went back to the hay and stretched out in a nervous half-sleep which consisted of love with artillery shells and sex of polished steel. . . .[17]

In *The Naked and The Dead* Mailer had presented Croft with a foil named Lieutenant Hearne. A weak liberal, a university man, Hearne is engaged in a forlorn struggle against both the insidious enticements of the Cummings' way of life among the rich and powerful, whose heir apparent his class origins destine him to be, and the brutality of Croft whose officer and fighting equal he is finally so anxious to become — the last a folly which permits Croft to have him shot. But in Steven Rojack, hero of *An American Dream,* the intellectual Hearne does at last manage to become a Croft of civilian life whose most precious memory is the night his platoon cheered their young lieutenant's histrionic victory over a nest of German soldiers. Rojack has ever since been possessed of a rage which only murder can quell, and he manages to bring about the deaths of two white women and a black man all in the novel's thirty-two hours. Mrs. Rojack is snuffed out by a blow for male supremacy, Cherry by her lover's sentimentality, and Shago Martin so that the white man may keep a corner on "his woman" in the face of black encroachment. The novelist assures us meanwhile that "murder offers the promise of vast relief. It is never unsexual."[18] In the sex war Mailer conducts throughout *An American Dream,* divorce is a "retreat," separation a species of cold war, sexual intercourse a "bang," or more explosively, a "bangeroo," male comrades are fellow "swords" and victory is announced in a froth-at-the-mouth Croftism:

gentle, I had not plumbed the hatred . . . I had an impulse to go up to her and kick her ribs, grind my heel on her nose, drive the point of my shoe into her temple and kill her again, kill her good this time, kill her right. I stood there shuddering from the power of this desire. . . .[19]

"Desire" is a happy verbal choice, for in the fantasy of virility which Mailer is so adept both at analyzing and at the same time identifying with in such a curious fashion, sexuality and violence are so inextricably mixed that the "desire to kill" is a phrase truly aphrodisiac. Nor is it very surprising that Rojack's victims should be women and blacks, or, with the exception of Rojack's service, the victims of Mailer's soldiers for three wars, Orientals: such are the white male's subjects, the objects of his dominant wrath.

Mailer's latest study of the Wasp male psychosis, *Why Are We in Vietnam?*, is perhaps his most interesting. It is carried out through the imagination of an eighteen-year-old pondering the implications of his recent rite of passage into the murderous order of his peers. Hollingsworth, the evil genius of *Barbary Shore*, had first introduced the notion of sexuality as butchery:

. . . he named various parts of her body and described what he would do to them, how he would tear this and squeeze that, eat here and spit there, butcher rough and slice fine, slash, macerate, pillage, all in an unrecognizable voice which must have issued between clenched teeth, until his appetite satisfied, I could see him squatting beside the carcass, his mouth wiped carefully with the back of his hand. With that, he sighed, as much as to say, "A good piece of ass, by God." [20]

Now the beguiling youth D. J. Jethroe, is introduced to tell us of the Alaskan bear hunt which has introduced him to "animal murder . . . and murder of the soldierest sort," [21] describing his initiation into the company of men in a Hip-Pop diction whose metaphor is sexual-military: "Now remember!" he instructs the reader before the killing begins, "Think of cunt and ass — so it's all clear." [22] To convince us that sex and violence are inextricable in the culture into which he is being welcomed as an adult, D.J. offers us the evidence of his senses: "ever notice how blood smells like cunt and ass all mix in one?" [23] Already perfectly at ease among the "sexual peculiarities of red-blooded men," at home with the hero "who can't come unless he's squinting down a gunsight," D.J. renders the intercourse of his parents in terms of an explosion. Using a "dynamite stick for a phallus," Big Daddy himself ("he don't come, he explodes, he's a geyser of love, . . . he's Texas will power.") . . . Just as D.J. fancies his penis a gun to "those Dallas debutantes and just plain common fucks who are lucky to get drilled by him," [24] he first gives in to the fever of the hunt when he catches sight of a great wounded bear splattering her death's blood into the forest. The transition from hunting and sex to war itself is Mailer's interest in the novel. . . .

Mailer is at pains to convince us that the violence endemic in his novels and essays is in fact endemic in humanity, or at least that portion of it which merits his attention, since children, queers, and women fail to qualify and pacifists are "unmanly."[25] It follows that by definition the male is violent and for those blessed with this higher condition, "the message in the labyrinth of the genes would insist that violence was locked with creativity"[26] since it is "ineradicable," one stifles it "at one's peril" for it gives the holder "sufficient stature to claim he is a man."[27]

Moreover, the world of nature which D.J. and his still more manic pal Tex encounter in Alaska, the very "force of the North," with its sage "don't bullshit" air of reality, the essential environment of life itself, is one long lesson in violence where great prey upon small, male upon female. . . .[28] Even with a smirk on his face, D.J. fulfills the requirements of his test, joining the ranks of the Hemingway cult. Most important of all, he has avoided the traps of homosexuality, compassion, and effeminacy, and emerges from the cold white summit with the very "power"[29] of the mountain Croft was unworthy to climb. . . .

For all his elaborate cynicism, and pompous alienation, D.J., like Rojack, is a caricature who ends by vindicating American virility. Yet because Mailer has insisted so often that the violence which masculinity presupposes, even requires, cannot be denied, we must conclude that the reason "why we are in Vietnam" is only because "we" must be.[30] Such is the nature of things. Sitting at their farewell dinner, Tex and D.J. happily anticipate going off to see "the wizard in Vietnam."[31] A considerable practitioner of psychoanalysis himself, Mailer protests he is against the trade because it would kill the mystery and spontaneity of human motivation, but one is reminded here of the popular Freudian formula: observe, codify, sanction, and prescribe. "Vietnam, hot damn."[32]

References

1. Norman Mailer, *Why Are We in Vietnam?* (New York: Putnam, 1967), p. 7.

2. Norman Mailer, *The Deer Park* (novel) (New York: Putnam, 1955), Berkeley reprint, p. 198.

3. Norman Mailer, *The Naked and The Dead* (New York: Holt, Rinehart and Winston, 1948), Signet reprint, p. 127.

4. *Ibid.*, p. 130.

5. *Ibid.*, p. 123.

6. *Ibid.*, p. 153.

7. *Ibid.*, p. 130.

8. *Ibid.*, p. 124.

9. *Ibid.*

10. *Ibid.*, p. 405.

11. *Ibid.*, p. 125.

12. *Ibid.*, p. 129.

13. *Ibid.*, pp. 325–326.

14. *Ibid.*, pp. 440–443.

15. It is heartbreaking the way Mailer throws the book away on the last page by failing to stop at the proper moment, e.g., when the last Japanese is butchered. Instead he adds a final page of cute dugout humor which reduces the novel to a movie script.

16. Norman Mailer, *The Presidential Papers* (New York: Putnam, 1963), p. 136.

17. Norman Mailer, *Barbary Shore* (New York: Holt, Rinehart and Winston, 1951), Signet reprint, pp. 114–115.

18. Norman Mailer, *An American Dream* (New York: Dial, 1965), p. 8.

19. *Ibid.*, p. 50.

20. *Barbary Shore,* p. 146.

21. *Why Are We in Vietnam?,* p. 7.

22. *Ibid.*, p. 9.

23. *Ibid.*

24. *Ibid.*, p. 42.

25. *The Presidential Papers,* p. 128.

26. *Ibid.*, p. 40.

27. *Ibid.*, pp. 21, 22, 23.

28. *Why Are We in Vietnam?,* p. 57.

29. *Ibid.*, p. 157.

30. Mailer saw the years of the cold war as years of national disease, intimating any number of times that "an insipid sickness demands a violent far-reaching purgative." (*The Presidential Papers,* p. 134.) For some ten years he was literally crying out for war — the question is — which one?

31. *Why Are We in Vietnam?,* p. 208.

32. *Ibid.*

MY LAI 4

SEYMOUR HERSH

The record of American intervention in Vietnam holds
many stories of tragedy, yet none seems more terrible than
what happened on March 16, 1968. This Pulitzer-Prize-
winning report by Seymour Hersh is strong reading, but
My Lai 4 really happened. It could happen again. The
young men of Charlie Company grew up in the same
America as we did. In their behavior, unusual though their
situation may have been, we see the outcome of the potential for violence which is solidly rooted in the male sex role.

The hamlet itself had a population of about 700 people, living either
in flimsy thatch-covered huts— "hootches," as the GIs called them
— or in solidly made red-brick homes, many with small porches in
front. There was an east-west footpath just south of the main cluster
of homes; a few yards further south was a loose surface road that
marked a hamlet boundary. . . .

The first two platoons of Charlie Company, still unfired upon,
entered the hamlet. Behind them, still in the rice paddy, were the
third platoon and Captain Medina's command post. Calley and some
of his men walked into the plaza area in the southern part of the
hamlet. None of the people was running away; they knew that U.S.
soldiers would assume that anyone running was a Viet Cong and
would shoot to kill. There was no immediate sense of panic. . . .

Some of Calley's men thought it was breakfast time as they
walked in; a few families were gathered in front of their homes
cooking rice over a small fire. Without a direct order, the first
platoon also began rounding up the villagers. There still was no
sniper fire, no sign of a large enemy unit. Sledge remembered thinking that "if there were VC around, they had plenty of time to leave
before we came in. We didn't tiptoe in there."

The killings began without warning. Harry Stanley told the
C.I.D. that one young member of Calley's platoon took a civilian

into custody and then "pushed the man up to where we were standing and then stabbed the man in the back with his bayonet . . . The man fell to the ground and was gasping for breath." The GI then "killed him with another bayonet thrust or by shooting him with a rifle . . . There was so many people killed that day it is hard for me to recall exactly how some of the people died." The youth next "turned to where some soldiers were holding another forty- or fifty-year-old man in custody." He "picked this man up and threw him down a well. Then [he] pulled the pin from a M26 grenade and threw it in after the man." Moments later Stanley saw "some old women and some little children — fifteen or twenty of them — in a group around a temple where some incense was burning. They were kneeling and crying and praying, and various soldiers . . . walked by and executed these women and children by shooting them in the head with their rifles. The soldiers killed all fifteen or twenty of them . . ."

There were few physical protests from the people; about eighty of them were taken quietly from their homes and herded together in the plaza area. A few hollered out, "No VC. No VC." But that was hardly unexpected. Calley left Meadlo, Boyce and a few others with the responsibility of guarding the group. "You know what I want you to do with them," he told Meadlo. Ten minutes later — about 8:15 A.M. — he returned and asked, "Haven't you got rid of them yet? I want them dead." Radioman Sledge, who was trailing Calley, heard the officer tell Meadlo to "waste them." Meadlo followed orders: "We stood about ten to fifteen feet away from them and then he [Calley] started shooting them. Then he told me to start shooting them. I started to shoot them. So we went ahead and killed them. I used more than a whole clip — used four or five clips." There are seventeen M16 bullets in each clip. Boyce slipped away, to the northern side of the hamlet, glad he hadn't been asked to shoot. Women were huddled against their children, vainly trying to save them. Some continued to chant, "No VC." Others simply said, "No. No. No. . . ."

By this time, there was shooting everywhere. Dennis I. Conti, a GI from Providence, Rhode Island, later explained to C.I.D. investigators what he thought had happened: "We were all psyched up, and as a result, when we got there the shooting started, almost as a chain reaction. The majority of us had expected to meet VC combat troops, but this did not turn out to be so. First we saw a few men running . . . and the next thing I knew we were shooting at every-thing. Everybody was just firing. After they got in the village, I guess you could say that the men were out of control.''

Brooks and his men in the second platoon to the north had begun to systematically ransack the hamlet and slaughter the people, kill the livestock and destroy the crops. Men poured rifle and machine-gun fire into huts without knowing — or seemingly caring — who was inside. . . .

Roberts and Haeberle also moved in just behind the third pla-toon. Haeberle watched a group of ten to fifteen GIs methodically pump bullets into a cow until it keeled over. A women then poked her head out from behind some brush; she may have been hiding in a bunker. The GIs turned their fire from the cow to the woman. "They just kept shooting at her. You could see the bones flying in the air chip by chip." No one had attempted to question her; GIs inside the hamlet also were asking no questions. Before moving on, the photographer took a picture of the dead woman. Haeberle took many more pictures that day; he saw about thirty GIs kill at least a hundred Vietnamese civilians.

When the two correspondents entered My Lai 4, they saw dead animals, dead people, burning huts and houses. A few GIs were going through victims' clothing, looking for piasters. Another GI was chasing a duck with a knife; others stood around watching a GI slaughter a cow with a bayonet.

Haeberle noticed a man and two small children walking toward a group of GIs: "They just kept walking toward us . . . you could hear the little girl saying, 'No, no . . .' All of a sudden the GIs opened up and cut them down." Later he watched a machine gunner suddenly open fire on a group of civilians — women, children and babies — who had been collected in a big circle: "They were trying to run. I don't know how many got out." He saw a GI with an M16 rifle fire at two young boys walking along a road. The older of the two — about seven or eight years old — fell over the first to protect him. The GI kept on firing until both were dead. . . .

Now it was nearly nine o'clock and all of Charlie Company was in My Lai 4. Most families were being shot inside their homes, or just outside the doorways. Those who had tried to flee were crammed by GIs into the many bunkers built throughout the hamlet for protection — once the bunkers became filled, hand grenades were lobbed in. Everything became a target. Gary Garfolo borrowed

someone's M79 grenade launcher and fired it point-blank at a water
buffalo: "I hit that sucker right in the head; went down like a shot.
You don't get to shoot water buffalo with an M79 every day."
Others fired the weapon into the bunkers full of people. . . .

Carter recalled that some GIs were shouting and yelling during
the massacre: "The boys enjoyed it. When someone laughs and
jokes about what they're doing, they have to be enjoying it." A GI
said, "Hey, I got me another one." Another said, "Chalk up one for
me." Even Captain Medina was having a good time, Carter thought:
"You can tell when someone enjoys their work." Few members of
Charlie Company protested that day. For the most part, those who
didn't like what was going on kept their thoughts to themselves.

Herbert Carter also remembered seeing Medina inside the hamlet well after the third platoon began its advance: "I saw all those
dead people laying there. Medina came right behind me." At one
point in the morning one of the members of Medina's CP joined in
the shooting. "A woman came out of a hut with a baby in her arms
and she was crying," Carter told the C.I.D. "She was crying because her little boy had been in front of their hut and . . . someone
had killed the child by shooting it." When the mother came into
view, one of Medina's men "shot her with an M16 and she fell.
When she fell, she dropped the baby." The Gi next "opened up on
the baby with his M16." The infant was also killed. Carter also saw
an officer grab a woman by the hair and shoot her with a .45-caliber
pistol: "He held her by the hair for a minute and then let go and she
fell to the ground. Some enlisted man standing there said, 'Well,
she'll be in the big rice paddy in the sky. . . .' "

There were some small acts of mercy. A GI placed a blanket
over the body of a mutilated child. An elderly woman was spared
when some GIs hollered at a soldier just as he was about to shoot
her. Grzesik remembered watching a GI seem to wrestle with his
conscience while holding a bayonet over a wounded old man. "He
wants to stab somebody with a bayonet," Grzesik thought. The GI
hesitated . . . and finally passed on, leaving the old man to die.

Some GIs, however, didn't hesitate to use their bayonets.
Nineteen-year-old Nguyen Thi Ngoc Tuyet watched a baby trying to
open her slain mother's blouse to nurse. A soldier shot the infant
while it was struggling with the blouse, and then slashed at it with his
bayonet. Tuyet also said she saw another baby hacked to death by
GIs wielding their bayonets.

Le Tong, a twenty-eight-year-old rice farmer, reported seeing one woman raped after GIs killed her children. Nguyen Khoa, a thirty-seven-year-old peasant, told of a thirteen-year-old girl who was raped before being killed. GIs then attacked Khoa's wife, tearing off her clothes. Before they could rape her, however, Khoa said, their six-year-old son, riddled with bullets, fell and saturated her with blood. The GIs left her alone.

There were "degrees" of murder that day. Some were conducted out of sympathy. Michael Terry, the Mormon who was a squad leader in the third platoon, had ordered his men to take their lunch break by the bloody ditch in the rear of the hamlet. He noticed that there were no men in the ditch, only women and children. He had watched Calley and the others shoot into that ditch. Calley seemed just like a kid, Terry thought. He also remembered thinking it was "just like a Nazi-type thing." When one soldier couldn't fire any more and threw down his weapon, "Calley picked it up." Later, during lunch, Terry and his men saw that some of the victims were still breathing. "They were pretty badly shot up. They weren't going to get any medical help, and so we shot them. Shot maybe five of them."

James Bergthold saw an old man who had been shot in both legs: "He was going to die anyway, so I figured I might as well kill him." He took his .45-caliber pistol (as a machine-gun ammunition carrier, he was entitled to one), carefully placed the barrel against the upper part of the old man's forehead and blew off the top of his head. Carter had watched the scene and remembered thinking that Bergthold had done the old man a favor. "If me and you were together and you got wounded bad," Carter later told an interviewer, "and I couldn't get you to a doctor, I'd shoot you, too."

Part II

Learning the Role

Chapter 5

Socialization:
Learning How to be a Man

In the preceding section of this book we examined the basic dimensions of the male role, but we left unanswered the question, "How does a boy learn to be a man?" The obvious answer, "by socialization," begs the question, for one must then ask, "What elements of the socialization process are unique to boys in our society, and prepare them to be men when they reach adulthood?"

Everyone can list the more obvious ones. "Little boys don't cry," is often heard, but no one proclaims "Little girls don't cry." The command, "Don't let Johnny bully you," has no counterpart for females. While both girls and boys are asked, "What do you want to be when you grow up?" the expected answers are vastly different. A little boy is supposed to list an occupation (and preferably one with a fair degree of status), whereas a little girl is supposed to respond, "A wife and mommy."

These elements of the male role begin being learned early in the socialization process. Often the young boy doesn't know exactly what he *is* supposed to do, for the learning frequently consists of hearing what he *is not* supposed to do. "Don't be a sissy," "Don't be a scaredy cat," and above all, "Don't act like a girl." It is no wonder that many boys in our society have trouble trying to figure out just what it is they should be, when the only positive command they receive is, "Act like a man," with little idea of what a man actually is.

Since father is away at work most of the day, and the only

adults they are likely to encounter are women, many boys begin to feel that being a male is being whatever females aren't. This is coupled with the proscriptions of what not to do, rather than of what to do, so that little boys often develop an image of a *male role,* rather than an idea of what real flesh-and-blood *men* are like. Virtually all males in our society have been through this same process, and the peer group tends to reinforce the somewhat stereotyped ideas boys have about masculinity, instead of correcting any misconceptions. Thus, as they are growing up, American boys have few opportunities to experience a wide range of behavior that might theoretically be possible for persons learning the male role.

By the time adolescence is reached, American youth clearly understand the prescriptive aspects of their role — be a success, win at any cost, be tough and strong, be aggressive, be a man. These demands of the male role reach their apogee in high school athletics, where the diverse elements of this role are intertwined. One can easily be a visible success by being on the winning team and especially by being the team's high scorer; athletics demand the much-valued strength and toughness and many sports have heavy overtones of aggression and violence. By meeting these role demands successfully, success in another crucial area can be realized — one is desirable to women.

Toward the end of adolescence, the importance of women in men's lives becomes a major focus, for this is a concern which will permeate the rest of men's lives, and the "rules" about relationships with women now have to be learned. And learned they are, by much trial and error, and often with a great deal of pain. The insecurities about women which are felt by many men are accentuated by the locker-room bragging about sexual conquests, most of which is false, but readily believed by the insecure listeners. Little is expressed about deeper feelings — the problems, the fears, the tender emotions — since men have learned that such communications are prohibited, so talk proceeds on a superficial level, both with other men and with the women themselves. American men thus reach adulthood readily equipped to play the male role as the society expects it should be played, with little room for individual preferences to be expressed.

SEX-ROLE PRESSURES AND THE SOCIALIZATION OF THE MALE CHILD

RUTH E. HARTLEY

Hartley's classic article on male socialization, written at a time when masculinity seldom was studied critically, pinpoints a major dilemma in the early years of men's lives. Boys learn what they must not be before they gain much knowledge of what it is they are supposed to be. The consequences of this process can be painful and long lasting, often leading to a life-long aversion to any quality thought to be "feminine" and a constant striving for the ways in which to be "masculine."

First of all, demands that boys conform to social notions of what is manly come much earlier and are enforced with much more vigor than similar attitudes with respect to girls. Several research studies, using preschool children as their Ss, indicate that boys are aware of what is expected of them because they are boys and restrict their interests and activities to what is suitably "masculine" in the kindergarten (2, 4, 11, 14, 32), while girls amble gradually in the direction of "feminine" patterns for five more years (2, 4). In other words, more stringent demands are made on boys than on girls and at an early age, when they are least able to understand either the reasons for or the nature of the demands. Moreover, these demands are frequently enforced harshly, impressing the small boy with the danger of deviating from them, while he does not quite understand what they are. To make matters more difficult, the desired behavior is rarely defined positively as something the child *should* do, but rather, undesirable behavior is indicated negatively as something he should *not* do or be — anything, that is, that the parent or other people regard as "sissy." Thus, very early in life the boy must either stumble on the right path or bear repeated punishment without warning when he accidentally enters into the wrong ones. This situation gives us practically a perfect combination for inducing

From *Psychological Reports*, 1959, **5**, pp. 457–468. Reprinted with permission of author and publisher.

anxiety — the demand that the child do something which is not clearly defined to him, based on reasons he cannot possibly appreciate, and enforced with threats, punishments, and anger by those who are close to him. Indeed, a great many boys do give evidence of anxiety centered in the whole area of sex-connected role behaviors, an anxiety which frequently expresses itself in overstraining to be masculine, in virtual panic at being caught doing anything traditionally defined as feminine, and in hostility toward anything even hinting at "femininity," including females themselves. This kind of overreaction is reminiscent of the quality of all strong emotion precipitated early in life before judgment and control have had a chance to develop.

This, however, is only one source of difficulty. Another related one comes from the simple fact that fathers are not at home nearly as much as mothers are. This means that the major psychodynamic process by which sex-roles are learned — the process of identification — is available only minimally to boys since their natural identification objects, their fathers, are simply not around much of the time to serve as models (6, 28). Illustrative of the children's awareness of this state of affairs, many Ss expressed themselves in the following vein: "My father . . . I don't see him very often." "It's harder to know about boys (than about girls) . . . Father hardly has time to talk to me." "Men are harder to tell about . . . to tell the truth, my father isn't around much."

The absence of fathers means, again, that much of male behavior has to be learned by trial and error and indirection. One outcome of this state of affairs is the fact that boys, as a group, tend to resemble their fathers in personality and attitudes much less than girls resemble their mothers. This has been impressively documented by the results of a number of research studies conducted by different workers using different Ss and collecting data by different methods (1, 18, 21, 33, 35).

In addition to the effect of the relative absence of fathers from boys' experience, we also have evidence that the relations between boys and their fathers tend to be less good than those between girls and their mothers or fathers (23, 24, 27). Since identification is affected by the quality of relationships existing between the child and the identification model (25, 37), this diminishes still further the boy's chance to define his sex-roles easily and naturally by using his male parent as a model (5, 26). Boys having trouble in sex-roles, for example, often report their fathers as the punishing agents, their mothers as protectors. Fathers in general seem to be perceived as punishing or controlling agents (9, 10).

Where, then, we might ask, *do* boys find meaningful, positive guides for the specifics of their behavior as males? The answer seems to point largely to their peer groups and somewhat older youths. For a boy, then, contact with, and acceptance by, his peers is tremendously important, because he has to look to them to fill in the gaps in his information about his role as a male, and he has to depend on them to give him practice in it. Unfortunately, both the information and the practice he gets are distorted. Since his peers have no better sources of information than he has, all they can do is to pool the impressions and anxieties they derived from their early training. Thus, the picture they draw is at once oversimplified and overemphasized. It is a picture drawn in black and white, with little or no modulation, and it is incomplete, including only a few of the many elements that go to make up the role of the mature male. Thus, we find overemphasis on physical strength and athletic skills (12, 31, 39), with almost a complete omission of tender feelings or acceptance of responsibility toward those who are weaker. It is, after all, a picture drawn by children and it is not enough. Unfortunately, it is almost all that many boys have to go by, and its power to induce anxiety is amply attested (15, 17, 22, 34, 39).

And now we come to what is perhaps the source of greatest difficulty for the growing boy — the conflict in role demands that our social structure imposes on him. On the one hand, we have insisted that he eschew all "womanly" things almost from the cradle, and enforced these demands in a way that makes whatever is female a threat to him — for that is what he must not be. Ordinarily, one responds to threat by trying to escape from it or by trying to destroy the threatening object. But this the boy cannot do, for society puts him directly under the jurisdiction of women, without relief, for most of his waking day. On the one hand, he is told that he is supposed to be rugged, independent, able to take care of himself, and to disdain "sissies." On the other, he is forced into close contact with the epitome of all sissy-things — women — for most of his day and he is commanded to obey and learn from them. In other words, he is compelled to knuckle under to that which he has been taught to despise. Need we wonder that he tends to rebel at times or has trouble making a smooth adjustment?

Moreover, the demeanor of the women with whom he is forced
to associate is often such that the boy feels that women just don't
like boys. We found many indications to this belief in our Ss'
responses to a hypothetical adoption story that they were asked to
complete. Almost invariably mothers were assumed to prefer girls to
boys. The reasons given for this were drawn from the boys' own
experience with their mothers: "She says boys are rough." "A girl
wouldn't be so wild — she would not run so much and play rough
. . . a girl is more kind." If a mother is assumed to want a boy, it is
for a nefarious purpose, as in the following: "She'd want a boy so
she can give him to the Indians . . . girls are always good."

Admittedly, the pressures of male-oriented socialization are not
exerted on all equally. Some suffer more than others, notably those
with physical endowments or special abilities which are not con-
gruent with the common cultural definition of the male role, and
those who have even poorer opportunities than usual for forming
sex-appropriate identifications. Thus, the small boy, the weak boy,
the boy whose physical coordination is poor — these are especially
penalized. But the lad with better-than-average endowments also
suffers if these endowments happen to be in areas not included in the
culture's definition of what is "masculine" — music, for example, or
art. It takes an unusually rugged physique to offset the disadvantage
of a creative talent.

To illustrate what we mean by the "demands" of the male role,
let me quote from the boys themselves. This is what they tell us boys
have to know to be able to do — their view of masculine role at their
own age level (8 and 11 years): they have to be able to fight in case a
bully comes along; they have to be athletic; they have to be able to
run fast; they must be able to play rough games; they need to know
how to play many games — curb-ball, baseball, basket-ball, football;
they need to be smart; they need to be able to take care of themselves; they should know what girls don't know — how to climb,
how to make a fire, how to carry things; they should have more
ability than girls; they need to know how to stay out of trouble; they
need to know arithmetic and spelling more than girls do. (The last
point is probably the greatest blow of all for an 8-year-old.)

We learn a little more when we ask, "What is expected of
boys?" We find that they believe grown-ups expect them to be
noisy; to get dirty; to mess up the house; to be naughty; to be
"outside" more than girls are; not to be crybabies; not to be "sof-

ties"; not to be "behind" like girls are; and to get into trouble more than girls do. Moreover, boys are not allowed to do the kind of things that girls usually do, but girls may do the kind of things that boys do.

Going beyond the immediate present, this is what the boy sees as his future, described in terms of the things men need to know and be able to do: they need to be strong; they have to be ready to make decisions; they must be able to protect women and children in emergencies; they have to have more manual strength than women; they should know how to carry heavy things; they are the ones to do the hard labor, the rough work, the dirty work, and the unpleasant work; they must be able to fix things; they must get money to support their families; they need "a good business head." In addition to their being the adventurers and protectors, the burden bearers, and the laborers, they also need to know how to take good care of children, how to get along with their wives, and how to teach their children right from wrong.

We are also told that, in contrast to women, men are usually in charge of things; they work very hard and they get tired a lot; they mostly do things for other people; they are supposed to be bolder and more restless, and have more courage than women. Like boys, they, too, mess up the house.

On the positive side, men mostly do what they want to do and are very important. In the family, they are the boss; they have authority in relation to the disposal of monies and they get first choice in the use of the most comfortable chair in the house and the daily paper. They seem to get mad a lot, but are able to make children feel good; they laugh and make jokes more than women do. Compared with mothers, fathers are more fun to be with; they are exciting to have around; they have the best ideas.

One wonders, looking over these items, whether the compensations are enough to balance the weight of the burdens that boys see themselves as assuming in order to fulfill the male role adequately. Looked at from this point of view, the question is not why boys have difficulty with this role, but why they try as hard as they do to fulfill it. Perhaps a glance at the characteristics of the female role from the boys' eye view can give us the answer.

Concerning girls, boys tell us: they have to stay close to the house; they are expected to play quietly and be gentler than boys; they are often afraid; they must not be rough; they have to keep

clean; they cry when they are scared or hurt; they are afraid to go to
rough places like rooftops and empty lots; their activities consist of
"fopperies" like playing with dolls, fussing over babies, and sitting
and talking about dresses; they need to know how to cook, sew, and
take care of children, but spelling and arithmetic are not as important for them as for boys. Though reeking of limitations and re-
straint, this picture is not very full. Not until we ask about adult
women do we get any sort of depth or reflection of the affective
aspects of the female role.

Concerning adult women we are told: they are indecisive; they
are afraid of many things; they make a fuss over things; they get
tired a lot; they very often need someone to help them; they stay
home most of the time; they are not as strong as men; they don't like
adventure; they are squeamish about seeing blood; they don't know
what to do in an emergency; they cannot do dangerous things; they
are more easily damaged than men; and they die more easily than
men. Moreover, they are "lofty" about dirty jobs; they feel themselves above manual work; they are scared of getting wet or getting
an electric shock; they cannot do things men do because they have a
way of doing things the wrong way; they are not very intelligent;
they can only scream in an emergency where a man would take
charge. Women are the ones who have to keep things neat and tidy
and clean up household messes; they feel sad more often than men.
Although they make children feel good, they also make boys carry
heavy loads; haul heavy shopping carts uphill; keep them from going
out when they want to go, or demand that they stay out when they
want to come in. They take the pep out of things and are fussy about
children's grades. They very easily become jealous and envy their
husbands.

Concerning women's traditional household activities, we get
the following reflections: "They are always at those crazy household duties and don't have time for anything else." "Their work is
just regular drudging." "Women do things like cooking and washing
and sewing because that's all they can do." "If women were to try
to do men's jobs the whole thing would fall apart with the women
doing it." "Women haven't enough strength in the head or in the
body to do most jobs." "In going to adventurous places women are
pests — just a lot of bother. They die easily and they are always
worried about their petticoats." "I don't know how women would
get along without men doing the work." Natural exploiters, women

are good people to stay away from because, as one boy told us, "If I play with my mother, I'll end up doing the dishes and she'll be playing with my father."

When he sees women as weak, easily damaged, lacking strength in mind and in body, able to perform only the tasks which take the least strength and are of least importance, what boy in his right senses would not give his all to escape this alternative to the male role? For many, unfortunately, the scramble to escape takes on all the aspects of panic, and the outward semblance of non-femininity is achieved at a tremendous cost of anxiety and self-alienation. From our data, we would infer that the degree of anxiety experienced has a direct relationship to the degree of pressure to be "manly" exerted on the boy, the rigidity of the pattern to which he is pressed to conform, the availability of a good model, and the apparent degree of success which his efforts achieve.

Variations in degree of anxiety and in modes of handling it are reflected in the observable range of boys' responses to the socialization pressures put on them. In our sample of Ss, we have identified four major configurations* thus far: (a) overstriving, with explicit hostility expressed against the opposite sex and with marked rigidity concerning the differentiation between the role activities assigned to men and those assigned to women; (b) over-striving with less hostility, but with marked rigidity; (c) a tendency to give up the struggle, accompanied by protest against social expectations; and (d) a successful, well-balanced implementation of the role, which is positive in approach, showing clear differentiation between concepts of male and of female roles, but with an understanding of the complementary relationships between the roles, and marked flexibility in relation to the activities assignable to them.

Summary

From the interviews of 41 8- and 11-year old males, four adjustment patterns to the male sex role are apparent. Sources of conflict experienced by these young children are lack of adequate models,

---

* The author identified these configurations by inspection of the protocols and checked her judgment with Dr. Frank Hardesty, who, as Research Associate on the Project, has been intimately involved in planning the collection of data, and who had collected data from at least a third of the Ss.

extensive supervision by women, conflicting nature of multiple role demands, lack of clear, positive definition of the male sex role in socialization practices, and rigidity of role demands.

References

1. Beier, E. G., & Ratzeburg, F. The parental identification of male and female college students. *J. abnorm. soc. Phychol.*, 1953, **48**, pp. 569–572.

2. Brown, D. G. Sex-role preference in young children. *Psychol. Monogr.*, 1956, **70**, No. 14 (Whole No. 421).

3. Brown, D. G. Inversion and homosexuality. *Amer. J. Orthopsychiat.*, 1958, **28**, pp. 424–429.

4. Brown, D. G. Sex-role development in a changing culture. *Psychol. Bull.*, 1958, **54**, pp. 232–242.

5. Cava, E. I., & Raush, H. L. Identification and the adolescent boy's perception of his father. *J. abnorm. soc. Psychol.*, 1952, **47**, pp. 855–856.

6. Cottreli, L. The adjustment of the individual to his age and sex roles. *Amer. sociol. Rev.*, 1942, **7**, pp. 617–620.

7. *Department of Mental Hygiene, State of California: Statistical report, year ending June 30, 1955.* Sacramento, Calif.: Dept. of Mental Hygiene, 1955.

8. *Department of Mental Hygiene, State of New York: 1956 annual report.* Albany, N.Y.: Dept. of Mental Hygiene, 1957.

9. Emmerich, W. Young children's discriminations of family roles. Paper read at the Society for Research in Child Development, Bethesda, Md., March, 1959.

10. Emmerich, W. Parental identification in young children. *Genet. Psychol. Monogr.*, in press.

11. Fauls, L. B., & Smith, W. D. Sex-role learning of five-year-olds. *J. genet. Psychol.*, 1956, **89**, pp. 105–117.

12. Feinberg, M. R., Smith, M., & Schmidt, R. An analysis of expressions used by adolescents at varying economic levels to describe accepted and rejected peers. *J. genet. Psychol.*, 1958, **93**, pp. 133–148.

13. Frank, L. K. Study of changing sex-roles. Paper read at symposium, Psychological Implications of Changing Sex-Roles. Amer. Psychol. Ass., New York, Sept., 1958.

14. Gilbert, G. M. A survey of "referral problems" in metropolitan child guidance centers. *J. clin. Psychol.*, 1957, **13**, pp. 37–40.

15. Goodenough, E. W. Interest in persons as an aspect of sex difference in the early years. *Genet. Psychol. Monogr.,* 1957, **55,** pp. 287–323.

16. Gowan, J. C. The underachieving gifted child, a problem for everyone. *Except. Child,* 1955, **21,** pp. 247–249; 270–271.

17. Gray, S. W. Masculinity-femininity in relation to anxiety and social acceptance. *Child Developm.,* 1957, **28,** pp. 204–214.

18. Gray, S. W., & Klaus, R. The assessment of parental identification. *Genet. Psychol. Monogr.,* 1956, **54,** pp. 87–109.

19. Hacker, H. M. The new burdens of masculinity. *Marriage Fam. Living,* 1957, **19,** pp. 227–233.

20. Hamburger, C. The desire for change of sex as shown by personal letters from 465 men and women. *Acta Endocrinologica,* 1953, **14,** pp. 361–375.

21. Lazowick, L. M. On the nature of identification. *J. abnorm. soc. Psychol.,* 1955, **51,** pp. 175–183.

22. MacDonald, M. W. Criminally aggressive behavior in passive effeminate boys. *Amer. J. Orthopsychiat.,* 1938, **8,** pp. 70–78.

23. Meltzer, H. Sex differences in parental preference patterns. *Char. & Pers.,* 1941, **10,** pp. 114–128.

24. Meltzer, H. Sex Differences in children's attitudes to parents. *J. genet. Psychol.,* 1943, **62,** pp. 311–326.

25. Mowrer, O. H. *Learning theory and personality dynamics.* New York: Ronald, 1950.

26. Mussen, P. H. & Payne, D. E. Parent-child relations and father identification among adolescent boys. *J. abnorm. Soc. Psychol.,* 1956, **52,** pp. 358–362.

27. Nimkoff, M. F. The child's preference for father or mother. *Amer. sociol. Rev.,* 1942, **7,** pp. 517–524.

28. Parsons, T. Age and sex in the social structure of the United States. *Amer. sociol. Rev.,* 1942, **7,** pp. 604–616.

29. *Patients in mental institutions, 1955:* Part II. *Public hospitals for the mentally ill.* Public Health Service Publication No. 574. Washington, D.C.: U.S. Gov't Printing Office, 1956.

30. *Patients in mental institutions, 1955:* Part III. *Private hospitals for the mentally ill and general hospitals with psychiatric facilities.* Public Health Service Publication No. 574. Washington, D.C.: U.S. Gov't Printing Office, 1956.

31. Pope, B. Socio-economic contrasts in children's peer culture prestige values. *Genet. Psychol. Monogr.,* 1953, **48,** pp. 157–220.

32. Rabban, M. Sex-role identification in young children in two diverse social groups. *Genet. Psychol. Monogr.*, 1950, **42,** pp. 81–158.

33. Roff, M. Intra-family resemblances in personality characteristics. *J. Psychol.*, 1950, **30,** pp. 199–227.

34. Ronge, P. H. The feminine protest. *Amer. J. indiv. Psychol.*, 1956, **2,** pp. 112–115.

35. Schoeppe, A. Sex differences in adolescent socialization. *J. soc. Psychol.*, 1953, **38,** pp. 175–185.

36. Schwartz, E. F. Statistics of juvenile delinquency in the United States. *Ann. Amer. Acad. polit. soc. Sci.*, January, 1949.

37. Symonds, P. M. *The dynamics of human adjustment.* New York: Appleton-Century-Crofts, 1946.

38. Tuddenham, R. D. Studies in reputation: III. Correlates of popularity among elementary-school children. *J. educ. Psychol.*, 1951, **42,** pp. 257–276.

39. Tuddenham, R. D. Studies in reputation: I. Sex and grade differences in school children's evaluation of their peers. II. The diagnosis of social adjustment. *Psychol. Monogr.*, 1952, **66,** No. 1 (Whole No. 333).

40. Ullman, C. A. *Identification of maladjusted school children.* Public Health Monograph No. 7. Washington, D. C.: U.S. Gov't Printing Office, 1957.

WHAT GHETTO MALES ARE LIKE: ANOTHER LOOK[1]

ULF HANNERZ

This selection by Hannerz illustrates an area of controversy: the socialization of young black males in the urban ghetto. While not denying certain differences in this process, Hannerz points to many factors, such as the peer group, which play a vital and similar role in the growth of both black males and white males.

Ever since the beginnings of the study of black people in the Americas investigators have commented on the ways in which black men and women — in particular some men and women — differ in their behavior from their white counterparts. . . [2]

Much has been made of the notion that young boys in the ghetto, growing up in matrifocal households, are somehow deficient in masculinity, or uncertain about masculinity, because their fathers are absent or peripheral in household affairs.[3] It is said that they lack the role models necessary for learning male behavior, the kind of information about the nature of masculinity which a father would transmit unintentionally merely by going about his life at home is missing. The boys therefore supposedly experience a great deal of sex role anxiety, as a result of this cultural vacuum. . . . It is possible that such a view contains more than a grain of truth in the case of some quite isolated female-headed households. Evidence from studies of such households in other social contexts point in this direction. In the ghetto situation, however, there may be less to this than meets the eye.[4] First of all, a female-headed household without an adult male in residence but where young children are growing up — and where it is thus likely that the mother is still rather young — is seldom one where adult males are forever absent. More or less steady boyfriends (sometimes including the separated father, on visits which may or may not result in a marital reunion) pass in and out. Even if these men do not assume a central household role, the boys can obviously use them as source material for identifying male behavior. To be sure, this male role model is not a mainstream role model, but it still shows what males are like.

Furthermore, not only males can teach males about masculinity. Although role-modeling is probably essential, other social processes can contribute to identity formation. Mothers, grandmothers, aunts, and sisters who have observed men at close range have adopted expectations about the typical behavior of men which they express and which influence the boys in the household. The boys will come to share in the imagery of the women concerning men as they are exposed to women's conversations, and often they will find that men who are not regarded as good household partners (that is, in the mainstream male role) are still held to be attractive social companions. Thus the view is easily imparted that the hard men, good talkers, clothes-horses and all, are not altogether unsuccessful as males. The women also act more directly toward the boys in these terms — they have expectations of what men will do, and whether they wish the boys to follow in these steps or not, they instruct them in the model. Boys are advised not to "mess with" girls, which is at the same time emphasized as the natural thing which they will otherwise go out and do — and when the boys start their early adventures with the other sex, the older women may scold them but at the same time point out, not without satisfaction, that "boys will be boys." This kind of maternal (or at least adult female) instruction of young males is obviously a kind of altercasting, or more exactly, socialization to an alter role — that is, women cast boys in the role complementary to their own according to their experience of man-woman relationships. One single mother of three boys and two girls put it this way:

You know, you just got to act a little bit tougher with boys than with girls, 'cause they just ain't the same. Girls do what you tell them to do and don't get into no trouble, but you just can't be sure about the boys. I mean, you think they're OK and next thing you find out they're playing hookey and drinking wine and maybe stealing things from cars and what not. There's just something bad about boys here, you know. But what can you say when many of them are just like their daddies? That's the man in them coming out. You can't really fight it, you know that's the way it is. They know, too. But you just got to be tougher.

This is some ways an antagonistic socialization, but is built upon an expectation that it would be unnatural for men not to turn out to be in some ways bad — that is fighters, drinkers, lady killers, and so forth. There is one thing which is worse than a no-good man — the sissy, who is his opposite. A boy who seems weak is ofter repri-manded and ridiculed not only by peers but also by adults, including his mother and older sisters. The combination of role-modeling by peripheral fathers or temporary boyfriends with altercasting by adult women certainly provides for a measure of male role socialization within the family.

However, when I said that the view of the lack of models in the family was too narrow, I did not refer to the lack of insight into social processes in many matrifocal ghetto families so much as to the emphasis on the family as *the* information storage unit of a commu-nity's culture.[5] I believe it is an ethnocentrism on the part of the middle class commentators to take it for granted that if information about sex roles is not transmitted from father to son within the family, it is not transmitted from generation to generation at all. There exists in American sociology, as well as in the popular mind what has [been] termed a "sentimental model" for family life, according to which the family is an inward-turning isolate, meeting most of the needs of its members, and certainly the needs of sociability. The "sentimental model" is hardly ever realistic even as far as mainstream American families are concerned, and it has even less relevance for black ghetto life. Ghetto children live and learn out on the streets just about as much as within the confines of the home. Even if mothers, aunts, and sisters would not have streetcorner men as partners, there is an ample supply of them on the front staircase or down at the corner. Many of them have such a regular attendance record as to become quite familiar to children and are frequently very friendly with them. Thus again, there is no lack of adult men showing what adult men are like. It seems rather unlikely that one can deny all the role-modeling effect of these men on their young neighbors. Some of these men may be missing in the U.S. census records, but they are not missing in the ghetto community.

Much of the information gained about sex roles outside the family comes not from adult to child, however, but from persons in the same age bracket or only slightly higher. The idea of culture stored in lower age grades must be taken seriously. Many ghetto children start participating in the peer groups of the neighborhood at an early age, often under the watchful eye of an elder sibling. In this way they are initiated into the culture of the peer group by interacting with children — predominantly of the same sex — who are only a little older than they are. And in the peer group culture of the boys, expressions of the male sex role are a highly salient feature . . . .

Most ghetto boys can hardly avoid getting into peer groups, and once they are in them they are efficiently socialized into a high degree of concern with their sex role. Much of the joking, the verbal contests, and more or less obscene singing among small ghetto boys — obligatory forms of interaction among them — serve to alienate them from dependence on mother figures and train them to the exploitative, somewhat antagonistic attitude toward women which is typical of streetcorner men. This is not to say the cultural situation is always very neat and clear-cut, and this is particularly obvious in the case of the kind of insult contest called "playing the dozens," "sounding," or in Washington, D.C., "joning," a form of ritualized

interaction which is particularly common among boys in their early
teens . . . . When one boy says something unfavorable about
another's mother, the other boy is expected either to answer in kind
or fight, in a kind of defense of his honor (on which apparently that
of his mother reflects). But the lasting impression is that there is
something wrong about mothers — they are not as good as they
ought to be . . . .

The other point of significance is that the criteria of judgment
about what a good woman should be like are apparently
mainstream-like. She should not be promiscuous, and she should
stick to the mainstream-like female role and not be too dominant.
The boys, then, are learning and strengthening a cultural ambivalence involving contradictions between ideal and reality in female
behavior. We will return to a discussion of such cultural ambivalence later. But the point remains that even this game involves
continuous learning and strengthening of a cultural definition of what
women are like which is in some ways complementary to the definition of what men are like. And much of the songs, the talk, and
action — fighting, sneaking away with girls into a park or an alley, or
drinking out of half empty wine bottles stolen from or given away by
adult men — are quite clearly preparations for the streetcorner male
role. If boys and men show anxiety about their masculinity, one may
suspect that this is induced as much by existing cultural standards as
by the alleged nonexistence of models.[6]

This socialization within the male peer group is a continuing
process; the talk that goes on, continuously or intermittently, in the
social sessions of adult men at the street corner or on the front steps
may deal occasionally with a football game or a human-interest story
from the afternoon newspaper, but more often there are tales from
personal experience about drinking adventures (often involving the
police), about women won and lost, about feminine fickleness and
the masculine guile which sometimes triumphs over it, about clothing or there may simply be comments on the women passing down
the street: "Hi ugly . . . don't try to swing what you ain't got."

This sociability within the male peer group, then, like much
other sociability seems to be a culture-building process. Shared
definitions of reality are created out of the selected experiences of
the participants. Women are nagging and hypocritical; you can't
expect a union with one of them to last forever. Men are dogs; they
have to run after many women. There is something between men

and liquor; liquor makes hair grow on your chest. The regularity with which the same topics appear in peer group sociable conversation indicates that they have been established as the expected and appropriate subjects in this situation, to the exclusion of other topics. . . .

Let me tell you fellows, I've been arrested for drunkenness more than two hundred times over the last few years, and I've used every name in the book. I remember once I told them I was Jasper Gonzales, and then I forgot what I had told them, you know. So I was sitting there waiting, and they came in and called Jasper Gonzales, and nobody answered. I had forgotten that's what I said, and to tell you the truth, I didn't know how to spell it. So anyway, nobody answered, and there they were calling, "Jasper Gonzales! Jasper Gonzales!" So I thought that must be me, so I answered. But they had been calling a lot of times before that. So the judge said, "Mr. Gonzales, are you of Spanish descent?" And I said, "Yes, your honor, I came to this country thirty-four years ago." And of course I was only thirty-five, but you see I had this beard then, and I looked pretty bad, dirty and everything, you know, so I looked like sixty. And so he said, "We don't have a record on you. This is the first time you have been arrested?" So I said, "Yes, your honor, nothing like this happened to me before. But my wife was sick, and then I lost my job you know, and I felt kind of bad. But it's the first time I ever got drunk." So he said, "Well, Mr. Gonzales, I'll let you go, 'cause you are not like the rest of them here. But let this be a warning to you." So I said, "Yes, your honor." And then I went out, and so I said to myself "I'll have to celebrate this." So I went across the street from the court, and you know there are four liquor stores there, and I got a pint of wine and next thing I was drunk as a pig.

Were you here that time a couple of weeks ago when these three chicks from North Carolina were up here visiting Miss Gladys? They were really gorgeous, about 30-35. So Charlie says why don't we stop by the house and he and Jimmy and Deekay can go out and buy them a drink. So they say they have to go and see this cousin first, but then they'll be back. But then Brenda [Charlie's wife] comes back before they do, and so these girls walk back and forth in front of the house, and Charlie can't do a thing about it, except hope they won't knock on his door. And then Jimmy and Deekay come

*and pick them up, and Fats is also there, and the three of them go
off with these chicks, and there is Charlie looking through his
window, and there is Brenda looking at them too, and asking Charlie does he know who the chicks are.*

Peer groups thus give some stability and social sanction to the
meaning which streetcorner men attach to their experiences —
meanings which may themselves have been learned in the same or
preceding peer groups. They, probably more than families, are information storage units for the ghetto-specific male role. At the same
time, they are self-perpetuating because they provide the most satisfactory contexts of legitimizing the realities involved. In other
words, they suggest a program for maleness, but they also offer a
haven of understanding for those who follow that program and are
criticized for it or feel doubts about it — and of course, all streetcorner males are more or less constantly exposed to the definitions
and values of the mainstream cultural apparatus, so some cultural
ambivalence can hardly be avoided. So if a man is a dog for running
after women . . . he wants to talk about it with other dogs who
appreciate that this is a fact of life. If it is natural for men to drink, let
it happen among other people who understand the nature of masculinity. Thus the group maintains constructions of reality, and life
according to this reality maintains the group. . . .[7]
  Streetcorner men certainly are aware of the ideal of mainstream
male role performance — providing well for one's family, remaining
faithful to one's spouse, staying out of trouble, and so on — and now
and then everyone of them states it as his own ideal. What we find
here, then, may be seen as a bi-cultural situation. Mainstream culture and ghetto-specific culture provide different models for living,
models familiar to everyone in the ghetto. Actual behavior may lean
more toward one model or more toward the other, or it may be some
kind of mixture, at one point or over time. The ghetto-specific
culture, including the streetcorner male role, is adapted to the situation and the experience of the ghetto dweller; it tends to involve
relatively little idealization but offers shared expectations concerning self, others, and the environment. The mainstream culture, from
the ghetto dweller's point of view, often involves idealization, but
there is less real expectation that life will actually follow the paths
suggested by it. This is not to say that the ghetto-specific culture
offers no values at all of its own, or that nothing of mainstream

culture ever appears realistic in the ghetto; but in those areas of life where the two cultures exist side by side as alternative guides to action (for naturally, the ghetto-specific culture, as distinct from mainstream culture, is not a "complete" culture covering all areas of life),[8] the ghetto-specific culture is often taken to forecast what one can actually expect from life, while the mainstream norms are held up as perhaps ultimately more valid but less attainable under the given situational constraints. "Sure it would be good to have a good job and a good home and your kids in college and all that, but you got to be yourself and do what you know." Of course, this often makes the ghetto-specific-culture expectations into self-fulfilling prophecies, as ghetto dwellers try to attain what they believe they can attain. . . .

A man whose concerns in the peer group milieu are drinking and philandering will try to be "good" in the company of his mother or his wife and children, even if a complete switch is hard to bring about. There also are peer groups, of course, which are more mainstream-oriented than others, although even the members of these groups are affected by streetcorner definitions of maleness. To some extent, then, the varying allegiance of different peer groups to the two cultures is largely a difference of degree, as the following statement by a young man implies.

These fellows down at the corner there just keep drinking and drinking. You know, I think it's pretty natural for a man to drink, but they don't try to do nothing about it, they just drink every hour of the day, every day of the week. My crowd, we drink during the weekend, but we can be on our jobs again when Monday comes.

Contextual culture change on the part of a man can then also be brought about by a change of peers — and there are men who move from one group to another with concomitant changes of be-havior. . . . Ghetto men may spend more time with the family, or more time with the peer group, and the extent to which they choose one or the other, and make a concomitant cultural selection, still appears to depend considerably on personal attachment to roles, and to changes in it. . . .[9]

The question of whether streetcorner males have mainstream culture or a specific-ghetto culture, then, is best answered by saying that they have both, in different ways.

Notes

1. This paper is based on fieldwork in a black low-income neighborhood in Washington, D.C., between 1966 and 1968. The study was made possible by a grant from the Carnegie Corporation and the Urban Language Study of the Center of Applied Linguistics. An earlier version was presented at the 66th annual meeting of the American Anthropological Association, Washington, D.C., December 3, 1967. The subject of ghetto sex roles will be dealt with more extensively in the author's forthcoming book, *Soulside: Inquiries into Ghetto Culture and Community*.

   Those portions which are quotations of ghetto dwellers derive from notes made as soon as possible after the statements were made. They are probably quite accurate in terms of content and vocabulary but should not be taken to give any indication of the phonology and the syntax of the actual speech.

2. The term "black" will generally be used here for ethnic identification, in line with the current trend of preference among at least younger and more politically aware Negroes in the U.S.

3. Matrifocality is defined here in behavioral rather than compositional terms — if the household affairs are female-dominated, it is a matrifocal household even if a marginal husband-father resides in it. Viewed this way, of course, matrifocality becomes a matter of degree.

4. Another aspect of the impact of matrifocality on children in a black community was discussed from an anthropological vantage point by Powdermaker (1939:197), where she also pointed to the difficulties with cross-cultural psychological inferences: "There is little if any indication that the fatherless household among these Negroes tends to result in the kind of psychological complications which clinical workers have come to associate with middle-class white households where there is no father. The economic situation is one guard against this. The Negro mother usually works out during the day, or, if she is home, she is extremely busy doing her own work or the washing she takes in from outside. She lacks time, opportunity and energy to lavish on her children the over-protection which leads to those emotional difficulties characteristic of certain fatherless white families. Equally important is the circumstance that most mothers, even in households which lack a man, do not want for sexual outlet, and therefore are not impelled to seek from their children some substitute for the satisfaction normally derived from a mate."

5. The notion of social groupings as information storage units of culture has been introduced and explored by Roberts (1964).

6. This means that even if peer groups and their culture meet a need for some anxious males, as is generally suggested, they are a part of the ghetto scene which demands adjustment to its standards also by males without such prior anxiety, as a price of a membership which may be difficult to avoid. Whether fathers are present or not, the peer group sets its own model of masculinity for members. Some writers, such as Rohrer and Edmonson (1960), seem to be on the verge of recognizing the peer group as a reality *sui generis* in the socialization of boys, but they are still reluctant to admit that sexual identity anxiety is not necessarily the first-order determinant. In their picture, peer group life seems forever invented anew as an answer to this psychological need. Yet the rituals of this life show that there is a lively cultural tradition.

7. A relevant statement on conversation as an instrument for the maintenance of social reality is that by Berger and Luckmann (1966:140 ff.).

8. One may, of course, prefer to speak of the ghetto-specific sub-culture. The amount of analytical sharpening which the sub-culture concept has brought to sociology and anthropology has not been impressive, however, so using it consistently here may not have balanced the clumsiness of expression which it would have added. It should be clear, however, that ghetto-specific culture consists only of a relatively small number of cultural items and complexes compared to the amount of general American culture which ghetto dwellers and others share.

9. In adherence to Goffman's definitions (1961:88–9), *commitment* to a role refers here to impersonal structural arrangements which force an individual to certain lines of action, which *attachment* refers to a person's being "affectively and cognitively enamored, desiring and expecting to see himself in terms of the enactment of the role and the self-identification emerging from this enactment."

MY MALE SEX ROLE — AND OURS

JOSEPH PLECK

Joseph Pleck has been a pioneer in the study of masculinity. In this candid and powerful essay, he tells a story of fragile individuality versus a cultural role, which, except for the details, could be the story of Everyman.

From *WIN*, April 11, 1974. Reprinted by permission.

When Jimmy was 10, he made his second try to get into a Detroit area Little League, and was turned down. His father, who had been a college football star, was so disappointed that he refused to talk to Jimmy all evening. Later that night, Jimmy swallowed some pills from his parents' medicine cabinet. . .

—Dolores Katz, "Why children attempt suicide."
Detroit Free Press, February 3, 1974, p. 1-A.

For some of us the most untrustworthy people in our lives were males of our own age. We've learned, therefore, to be most guarded about ourselves when we're with men our age. . . . Being male has meant being devoured by other males, the way animals are thought to, but really don't. . . .

—Unbecoming Men, pp. 59–60.

*I know why you fear strong women,
Hate gentle men. . .*

—Robin Morgan, Monster

I

My first encounter with the male sex role started with sports in grade school. I had very positive anticipations about physical education when I started to go to school. I thought it would be a wonderful thing to learn about my body, and to learn how to do things that I had seen others do, just as I was excited about learning how to read and write, which I had been looking forward to for a long time. But "physical education" was very different from what I expected. At the end of one class, early in first grade, the teacher told us to take our shoes off and to put them in a pile in the center of the gym. Then he mixed all the shoes around, and told us we had to get our shoes back. The catch was that the last person to get his shoes back on would have to do ten pushups. A mad scramble ensued, and I was the last. I don't remember whether I did the ten pushups or not, but I doubt it. Thus began my career in "phys ed."

There was a dodgeball game we played regularly, which had two forms. In the first form, there were two teams, and the idea was to throw the ball at people on the other team. If you hit them, they were out, but if they caught the ball you threw at them, then you were out — the game going on until everyone on one team was out.

In the second form, sometimes called "bombardment," or "German" dodgeball, the principle was the same, except that there were no teams, only individuals. With several balls going in a class of 30, the energy level could get quite high. I was never much good at throwing the ball with any force or accuracy, but I got to be very good at dodging, so my basic strategy was to avoid being hit. But the problem was that I often ended up as one of the last two people in the game. Then the other person would keep throwing the ball at me until I was so worn down and exhausted that I would finally be hit, with the whole class watching this gladitorial contest. This got to be extremely painful, both because I always lost and also because it showed everyone else that I couldn't really throw the ball. I soon learned to let myself get hit about halfway through the game. I learned several things in this game: I learned to be hyper-alert to attacks from other men, and good at dodging them; I also learned that it is extremely important to avoid being conspicuous in the male war of all-against-all.

When I was in the cub scouts in the fifth grade, the big event of the year was a boxing tournament. In my match all I could do was try to defend myself against the other boy hitting me. He hit me a lot, and in spite of the lesson I had learned from dodgeball, I stubbornly refused to be knocked down (perhaps because my parents were there), so mostly I was standing there being hit in the face. Finally the match was over, and the other boy was declared the winner. It was noted approvingly how "tough" I had been in not being knocked down by the blows I received. I don't remember my father saying anything, although he may have.

The most dreadful aspect of sports in school was the daily choosing up of sides for whatever the game was during the lunch period. Whatever it was, I was always picked last. I remember noticing that another boy, who also wasn't very good, had worked it out that he would always be the umpire or referee in these games, and thinking to myself what a brilliant solution this was. The umpire role is one of the few *bona fide* ways to participate in sports without any physical competence. The problem, however, was that there was room for only one umpire. I remember being mad at myself that I hadn't thought of it first. However, in a lot of other situations involving competition with men, I have learned to take safe, non-competitive "umpire" roles whenever possible.

When I went to high school, things were a little better because there were no longer any lunchtime sports, but I now had physical education every day instead of twice a week. I remember most of all a father-and-son picnic and softball game in my homeroom when I was a freshman. I knew this wouldn't be a good experience, but I was not strong enough to refuse to participate in it, as several other people in the homeroom did. After my father and I arrived, things got right down to business with the softball game. I was the only person on both teams, the fathers and the sons, not to get a hit; I struck out every time. I don't think I have ever felt so ashamed of myself as I felt then, or felt that anyone else was so ashamed of me as my father was then. In the picnic which followed, my father and I avoided each other completely. Driving home with him was excruciating. I didn't attempt anything even remotely athletic on my own initiative for about five years after that experience.

What seems so sad about it now is that my father and I shared in other ways that were important and meaningful. I remember particularly how he liked to walk around the back yard while I played the piano, hearing the sound come through the back porch windows. But none of this mattered during this archetypal Testing of the Sons' Strength before the Fathers of the Tribe. I had failed the test. No matter how else we related to each other, my father and I had to go through a male sex role ordeal that would leave us feeling horrible about each other and ourselves. Why?

At a weekend men's liberation conference last year, we decided to have a volleyball game. The group of us had some decisions about whether we wanted to keep score, and we came up with some interesting ideas about scoring systems that would reward cooperation and sharing instead of competition, both within each team and between the two teams. To my surprise many men seemed threatened and defensive about criticism of competition in sports. The game started up without a clear decision about the scoring system, and it turned out after a while that our side thought we were playing under a cooperative scoring system, while the other side thought we had decided to use the traditional competitive system. In a way, I felt like this had been happening to me all my life. So many times with other men, I thought we were playing cooperatively, and they thought we were playing competitively, and I got hurt sometimes, not so much by what the other men did to me objectively as by their ridicule that I could be so naive as to think that we could really be cooperating.

The other thing that happened during the game was that one man was accidentally hit in the face with the ball, breaking his glasses and shaking him up. This brought back a lot of memories, for it somehow seemed that in every game, someone got hurt like this. What followed was a confusing sequence in which the man was limping off the field trying to make light of how badly he was shaken up, trying to appear strong. At the same time, the other men wanted to reach out to him to help him, but hesitated, partly because the man who was hurt seemed to push it away, but also because they seemed scared of those caring feelings in themselves. Finally the game just started up again.

I've had many discussions with men about competition in sports. Many men say that competition is good because it makes people play harder and better. Though it has a certain plausibility, this argument mystifies what is going on in competition. Competition doesn't "improve" sports; sports provides a vehicle for teaching and reinforcing competition in males. That's why society makes sports a central feature of male upbringing, and that's what males learn from it. Some men say that sports "wouldn't be the same" without competition. They are right.

My experience with sports in school left me hating and feeling distant from my body, something I have really regretted. I always felt like it wasn't *me* who couldn't catch the ball, it was *my body*. Although my body has changed, my experience of it is in many ways much the way it was in grade school. And that experience was not based on any real exploration of my body, any real encounter with its full range of capacities to be strong, or to be coordinated, or to move, let alone to feel, or to give pleasure to myself or others, or to be beautiful. No, that experience of my body was based strictly on how well my body performed certain highly specialized acts of coordination when competing with other men.

More importantly, these experiences left me with a sense of myself as a marginal person, someone who doesn't share the things that are most important to everybody else. I didn't have sports as the major psychological reference point in my life, as nearly every other boy in grade school did, and I did not subscribe to the dominant system of values, images, and symbols it entailed. I saw the world differently from other boys. I identified sports as a major aspect of what I was supposed to be like as a male, which oppressed me because I could not do it, no matter how hard I tried. Sports expressed values about competition and aggression that I knew were awful. And I knew that these perceptions themselves, perhaps even more than my failure at sports itself, made me different from other people.

Recently a women friend told me she thought I would have been happier as a woman, considering the interests and qualities I have. After my initial shock, I asked her whether she hadn't really wanted to be a man at one time or another in her life, because of the relative privilege men have. She said no, she knew all that, but she just didn't think she could stand going through male gym class, no matter what other advantages there were to being a man. After a while, I could see her point.

II

In response to the tremendous pressure I felt from other boys in grade school, by third grade I realized that although I didn't have physical skills, the intellectual skills which I did have would be very important later in life. With them, I thought, I would come out far ahead of the people who were making me so unhappy now. I believe that I came up with this idea all by myself, and I had to believe it in order to survive. It always struck me as unfair that those who weren't any good in school got to say that school was dumb and useless, and that so many other boys would agree with them, while people like me never got to say the same thing about sports.

Though I knew in a general way that education was essential to "making it," I couldn't see any connection between the kinds of things people did in school and the jobs adult males had. I recall thinking during the sixth grade that I had about 11 more years, counting college, in which my life would proceed smoothly because I did so well in school. But then how would I get a job? What was there that I could do after all those years of school that anyone would pay me for?

After a Catholic grade school, I went to a public school which was extremely competitive intellectually. Sports were important in high school, but intellectual performance was also heavily stressed (in the service of the community's status ambitions), so that one could work out a respectable identity by doing well in school. I felt pretty inferior to those who had been in public grade school and junior high system in my area, which was extremely good, much better than the Catholic school I had gone to, and I was anxious about how well I would do. I was placed in a superelitist accelerated program, which flattered me, but also scared me.

In the school's intellectual group, it was important to be creative and artistic as well as intelligent. Because of my intellectual performance, I was able to make a place for myself as a hanger-on of the intellectual-artistic group, but never felt I belonged. I understand now that I was accepted on the condition that I constantly build up the egos of the other people and devalue myself for being so unartistic and for coming from a background that was culturally and intellectually deprived by the standards prevalent in this group. Several people in fact set out to give me "culture," which was no doubt well-intentioned, but which I see in retrospect was extremely patronizing and oppressive.

Anyway, I did well academically in high school, and got some satisfaction from the work I did. In spite of my putting myself down for not being a sculptor or whatever, I felt better about myself than I had felt anywhere before. But the intellectual competition made me anxious, especially as college admission time approached. In some sense, I had turned to intellectual work as a compensation for being terrible at sports, and saw intellectual work as a refuge from the masculine competition and aggression that I knew and hated so much in athletics. But intellectual work became just another arena from that aggression and competition. Although I did well, that competition led to constant, nagging feelings of inadequacy, and distorted my relationship with others.

But my feelings of inadequacy were different from what I had felt earlier in sports. First, I couldn't assume any distance from my feelings of intellectual inadequacy, as I could in sports. I couldn't criticize the system of intellectual competition that made me so anxious (as was so easy for me to do in athletic competition, even if only to myself), because I *believed* in intellectual work. *This* is what I was supposed to be good at, wasn't it? Profoundly as I had been wounded by my failure in sports, at the deepest level I never believed it to be important in the same way that I believed intellectuality to be important.

Second, I had the feelings of inadequacy of someone who was relatively successful, not those of someone who is a complete failure. I was getting enough positive rewards from what I was doing that most of the time I not only repressed or blamed myself for my nagging sense of inadequacy, I also was unaware that those who were not doing well in school hated themselves and deeply resented people like me — just as the boys I felt so inferior to in grade school had been totally unaware of how I felt. In escaping from sports, I had been drawn into a system in which I was relatively successful, in which it was now other people who were made to feel rotten about themselves. In going from grade school to high school, I had graduated from being a total failure as a male to being a member of the great "normal" majority who do relatively well, while hating themselves and oppressing others. I had been transformed from a self-despising "failed" male to one who simply had normal male self-hatred and feelings of inadequacy.

III

I hope it's clear that my complaint is not with sports. I know many other men who were good at sports and terrible in school, and I can see how deeply they were wounded by it, especially if their parents were middle class. (Relating to women is another very important area of competition among males, which I don't deal with here.) I've come to know my body much better in the last few years, and I've particularly enjoyed regular running. In a post-revolutionary society, there will certainly be a place for sports — and for intellectual work, too — though neither will be socially structured the way they are now.

My own personal story, though, does happen to be with sports, and my experiences with it suggest two larger points to me, the first having to do with self-hatred, and the second with violence. In talks I've had with other men, I've been struck by how often men will say they enjoyed sports, and never felt critical of them, or hurt by them, and yet tell of experiences which tell a quite different story. Sometimes they describe how anxious they felt before games, or how glad they were to be injured so they wouldn't have to play in particularly crucial ones; or sometimes they tell about how bad they felt about certain sports they weren't good in. Yet they do not connect these experiences to their larger feelings about sports.

All this seemed less odd to me when I thought more about my experience in schools. I would certainly tell most people that I have always enjoyed school. Yet I can remember the insomnia and anxiety attacks I had so often, up to and including finishing my doctoral dissertation; how in high school and college I was close to having an ulcer, or how, when teachers would criticize classes I was in for not working hard enough, I was sure the teacher was talking about me. Other men, too, have described college as a wonderful intellectual experience for them, and then described times when they were horribly wounded by tactless and glib criticisms of their work.

These examples illustrate how people can continue to believe in particular social values in spite of the fact that they are failures according to these values. The social values in our culture — for masculinity, femininity, beauty, success, normality, and whatever — are so idealized that all but the tiniest minority of people are failures, to greater or lesser measure. Yet the majority who are relative failures do not challenge the legitimacy of the values that adjudge them to be of so little worth. Most people learn a "false consciousness," an alienation from their own experience, in which they repress the resentment they would otherwise feel. It is in fact seen as a sign of maturity *not* to be angry or critical of such social values, instead accepting them along with one's own failure. How people continue to believe so fervently in values and norms according to which they can only be failures is an awe-inspiring phenomenon, and surely must be one of the most puzzling questions in understanding individuals' relationships with society.

The major side effect of this phenomenon is the personal self-hatred which is prevalent to so startling a degree in our society. In their book, *The Adjusted American: Normal Neurosis in American Society,* Gail and Snell Putney point out how each society perceives some social problems as solvable, but others as inevitable and part of the human condition. In some primitive societies, it is thought to be inevitable that the majority of children will die before they reach three or four years of age. Our society would see such a state of affairs shocking, and take immediate action. However, our society believes that it is an inevitable aspect of the human condition that most people have low self-esteem, and are emotionally crippled by feelings of inadequacy. In my own case, what pains me most about my experience, both early and more recent, is that while I now know that I was and am basically alright, I was so rarely allowed to experience myself as alright — in sports because I was a complete failure, and in intellectual work, because though I performed well, I could never be perfect and live up to my perception of what I was supposed to be.

The basic fact of social organization is that the losers, the people at the bottom of any social system, experience the world very differently than everybody else. The world of the boy who is always picked last in sports is very different from the world of other boys, just as is the world of the boy who is the "dumbest" in his class. It is a terrifying subterranean netherworld, full of hatred and violence which is expressed mostly against the self. If other people really knew and felt what those at the bottom were feeling, it would devastate them.

For the first time, many groups today are challenging the value systems that have oppressed them, and proposing alternate values. "Black is beautiful," "sisterhood is powerful," and "gay is good" are countervalues which are extremely threatening to mainstream society. These counter-values deal directly with a major problem which members of these groups have faced — the problem of believing in, at some level, a white male heterosexual value system in which they are by definition losers and failures. Adherence to these values has generated self-hatred in these groups. Challenging mainstream values, and bringing into awareness this self-hatred and repressed anger, is an extremely painful process, but also a joyful one. The energy of those who stop hating themselves is the most powerful social force that can be unleashed in any society.

Besides self-hatred, the second major theme in my experience with other men is the theme of violence. Male culture is a hostile, devouring culture in which men must adopt an aggressive stance toward the world in order to survive — in spite of all its romanticization by Lionel Tiger and others. As in my grade school dodgeball game, the great secret is to learn how to turn other men's attacks on you to your own advantage. The competitive questions, hostile joking, and clever put-downs of male culture are everyday interpersonal atrocities which are so routinized that we are hardly aware of them, or of how deeply violent they are. To be a man with other men means to always fear being attacked, victimized, exploited, and in an ultimate sense, murdered by other men.

My fear of this violence has been the most paralyzing inhibiter of my relationships with other men. Other men must hate the parts of me that do not conform to the male ideal, the parts of me that show me to be a traitor to my sex. I have had to make myself inconspicuous, and conceal my perception of the world, and especially my perceptions of maleness. However, there have been times when I have been with men who have also been alienated from this culture of male violence. Some of those times, I have felt safe and realized that I could drop my defensive stance, I have literally cried with relief.

IV

We live in a patriarchal, male-dominated culture. The feminist analysis of the effect of patriarchal society on woman is becoming more advanced and sophisticated. But there has been no systematic examination of the implications of patriarchal culture for men, and especially on relationships among men. We need a "sexual politics" of men's relationships with other men, because patriarchy is a *dual* system both in which men oppress women, and in which men oppress themselves and other men.

The dominant theme in men's relationships with other men in our society can be termed "patriarchal competition." This patriarchal competition is not tied to any particular areas of activity, like sports or the military, but in fact pervades nearly every context of encounter among men. Some areas may reveal this competition more explicitly than others, but no area provides a refuge from it. The major effect of competition among men according to patriarchal values is self-hatred, because no man can live up to the ideals he has been socialized to hold for himself about his performance relative to other men. His failure to meet these oppressive standards is experienced as reflecting on the deepest core of his sexual being. Men's need to control and reduce this self-hatred is an extremely powerful motivational force in male behavior. This self-hatred is the mediating link between individual male psychology and the larger sexual politics of masculinity. Patriarchal competition also generates a constant undercurrent of violence among men, physical and psychological, extraordinary and routinized, which men must learn to defend themselves against and to manipulate to their own advantage. In a culture of patriarchal competition among men, which depends so much on hatred toward the self and violence toward others, loving oneself and loving other men are indeed revolutionary acts. . . .

Today, men's liberation exists — not as a movement, exactly, but as an idea. Men's liberation means undoing the effects of patriarchal competition among men and finding out what we can be with each other. I know that one thing I share in common with all

other males in our society is that each of us has faced an overwhelming cultural demand to be "a man" in competition with other men —
however different have been the arenas in which we have struggled,
however successfully or unsuccessfully we have responded to this
demand with our unique resources, and most importantly, however
much we have been pitted against each other by this very demand.
Because of this shared experience, I also have in common with all
other men the vision and prospect of men's liberation, a liberation
that will at last make it possible for us to be brothers together.

ATHLETICS IN HIGH SCHOOL

JAMES S. COLEMAN

> In the crucial years of high school, when adolescents are
> displaying and refining their sex role attitudes and be-
> havior, the importance of athletic skill for men is remark-
> ably disproportionate to its role in adult life. In examining
> this phenomenon, Coleman notes the processes which tend
> to perpetuate the dominance of athletics among American
> high school students.

The amount of attention devoted to athletics would be most striking
to an innocent visitor to a high school. A visitor entering a school
would likely be confronted, first of all, with a trophy case. His
examination of the trophies would reveal a curious fact: The gold
and silver cups, with rare exception, symbolize victory in athletic
contests, not scholastic ones. The figures adorning these trophies
represent men passing footballs, shooting basketballs, holding out
batons; they are not replicas of "The Thinker." The concrete symbols of victory are old footballs, basketballs, and baseballs, not
works of art or first editions of books won as literary prizes. Altogether, the trophy case would suggest to the innocent visitor that
he was entering an athletic club, not an educational institution.

  Walking further, this visitor would encounter teen-agers burst-

From *The Annals of the American Academy of Political and Social Science*, **338**,
November 1961. Reprinted by permission.

ing from classrooms. Listening to their conversations, he would hear both casual and serious discussions of the Friday football game, confirming his initial impression. Attending a school assembly that morning, he would probably find a large segment of the program devoted to a practice of school yells for the athletic game and the announcement of a pep rally before the game. At lunch hour, he would be likely to find more boys shooting baskets in the gymnasium than reading in the library. Browsing through a school yearbook, he would be impressed, in his innocence, with the number of pages devoted to athletics.

Altogether, this visitor would find, wherever he turned, a great deal of attention devoted to athletics. As an impressionable stranger, this visitor might well suppose that more attention is paid to athletics by teen-agers, both as athletes and as spectators, than to scholastic matters. He might even conclude, with good reason, that the school was essentially organized around athletic contests and that scholastic matters were of lesser importance to all involved. . . .

Considering his impressions, such a visitor to American high schools might ask himself two questions: First of all, why is it this way? He had assumed, naively, that schools were for learning, yet his impressions led to a different conclusion. He had talked with educators about curriculum, new academic programs, and scholastic standards. Yet, upon visiting the schools, he found the adolescents' attention on athletics, and all the excitement and enthusiasm he found was focused around athletic contests. Why the discrepancy. . . ?

Impact on freshmen

The attention focused upon athletics in high schools directly affects the impact of the schools upon their incoming freshmen. Football, which is played in the fall as school begins, is especially important. A major element in the impact of athletics is the visibility of athletic stars. A boy who achieves something, however creditable his achievement, can be a model to emulate only if that achievement is made visible by the structure of activities in the school.

Some idea of the relative visibility of scholastic achievement and athletic achievement can be gained through a finding from the survey of the ten schools. About six weeks after school opened in the fall, each boy in every school was asked to name the boy whom he saw as the best student in his grade and the boy who was the best athlete. This can be a difficult task for freshmen, but it is less difficult in those areas for which school activities focus attention on achievement. Thus, a comparison of the proportions of boys able to answer the questions provides some guide to the relative visibility of scholastic and athletic achievements in each of the four years of school.

Table 1 shows this comparison. The data indicate, in general, that the best athletes are more visible than the best scholars. The difference is greatest for the freshmen — the best athlete is known 10 percent more often than the best scholar in the small schools and 14 percent more often in the large schools. Only in the junior and senior years does the visibility of the best scholars catch up with that of the best athletes. Thus, for the impressionable freshmen, the achievements that stand out most are those of the athlete, not those of the scholar.[1]

Table 1

Comparative Visibility of Best Athletes and Best Scholars to Their Classmates

	Freshmen	*Sophomores*	*Juniors*	*Seniors*
Small Schools				
Percent naming best athlete	68%	75%	88%	85%
Percent naming best scholar	58%	66%	83%	88%
Number of cases	317	292	214	205
Large Schools				
Percent naming best athlete	54%	56%	48%	72%
Percent naming best scholar	40%	47%	57%	68%
Number of cases	635	1,049	749	557

Note: Percentages are based on the nine public schools.

Assuming adolescents desire to be successful, known, and recognized, one consequence of the visibility of achievement in athletics or scholarship would be the desire to achieve in these particular areas. Does the environment and climate of opinion in the school affect these desires? Boys were asked, in the fall shortly after school had started and again in the spring toward the end of the school year, how they would most like to be remembered at school — as a brilliant student, an athletic star, or most popular. One would suppose, if schools focus attention on scholastic endeavors, that the effect of the school year would be to increase the strength of the brilliant-student image relative to that of the athletic-star image. Yet, for the freshmen and sophomores of the schools surveys, matters are quite different. Of all those responding either "brilliant student" or "athletic star," 44 percent in each grade responded "brilliant student" in the fall and only 37 percent gave this response in the spring.[2] Rather than increasing in strength over the school year, the brilliant-student image declined in strength relative to that of the athlete. It appears, then, that the very functioning of the school itself tends to reduce the initial interest of the adolescent in being seen as a brilliant student, or tends differentially to increase his interest in being seen as an athletic star.

Another effect of athletics upon the incoming freshmen concerns the "leading crowd" in school. Most high schools, other than the very smallest, have a leading crowd in each grade, though schools larger than about 2,000 in enrollment may have more than one. This crowd is recognized by other students and by its own members, and most students can name members of the leading crowd in their grade. . . .

Among the freshmen in each of the four schools studied for leading cliques, the one attribute shared by every boy in every leading clique — twenty-three boys in all — was being out for either football or basketball. Most of the twenty-three were out for both. No other attribute — in background, activities, or attitudes — so sharply distinguished the leading cliques. In the later years of school, the leading cliques were found to be less uniformly athletic, but, among freshmen, they were found to be totally so. . . .

Athletics in the status system

One of the most important aspects of any social system is its distribution of status: the way status attaches to different persons and to different activities. The importance of the distribution of status lies partly in its effect as a motivating device, for it motivates people toward those activities which confer status upon them. To the extent that adolescents are concerned with status among their peers — and every indication suggests that the great majority of them are so motivated — their motivations and aspirations in various activities are shaped by the distribution of status.

It is important, then, in assessing the consequences of the attention to athletics in high schools, to examine the position of athletics in the adolescent status system. In the present research, this was done by several means.

Each boy was asked to assess what was required in his school to be a member of the leading crowd, and he was asked to rank various attributes for making a boy popular.

In response to the first question, the two attributes most often mentioned were personality — mentioned by 23 percent of the boys — and a good reputation — mentioned by 17 percent. Next in order, however, was athletic ability — mentioned by 16 percent. This was followed by good looks and success with girls — mentioned by 14 percent — and good grades or "brains" — mentioned by 12 percent.

In ranking attributes for their effect in making a boy popular, six attributes were available to be ranked from first to sixth. These attributes, with their average rank in all schools, were the following.[3]

Being an athletic star	2.2
Being in the leading crowd	2.6
Leader in activities	2.9
High grades, honor roll	3.5
Having a nice car	3.9
Coming from the right family	4.5

These answers show the great value that boys attribute to athletic achievement in gaining popularity. It is ranked considerably above any other item and far above good grades, which is fourth among the six. . . .

Other studies

Other research shows that these facts are not limited to the ten schools surveyed nor even to high schools in the Middle West.

In a large, predominantly Jewish, middle class high school in New York City, Abraham Tannenbaum studied evaluations of stereotyped, fictitious students.[4] These fictitious students were distinguished in short descriptive statements on the bases of intelligence, athletic ability, and studiousness. Juniors in the high school were then asked to ascribe traits— some desirable, some undesirable — to each of the eight fictitious characters. Tannenbaum devised a mean acceptability rating from the ascribed traits, and the fictitious students fell in the following order of acceptability, from high to low:

1. Brilliant nonstudious athlete
2. Average nonstudious athlete
3. Average studious athlete
4. Brilliant studious athlete
5. Brilliant nonstudious nonathlete
6. Average nonstudious nonathlete
7. Average studious nonathlete
8. Brilliant studious nonathlete

As the order shows, all athletes had higher acceptability ratings than any nonathlete. Brilliance apparently had little effect in increasing acceptability, and studiousness reduced acceptability. Thus, in a school in which, because of its location and student body, one would expect to find brilliance or studiousness outdistancing athletics, the results are otherwise — and consistent with the results in the ten midwestern high schools.

Notes

1. Other areas of achievement were included in the questionnaire, for example, knowing about cars and being most attractive to the girls. The visibility for both of these was far below that for athletes or scholars.
2. The number of cases was over 800 in each grade, so the difference reported is significant beyond the .001 level.
3. The ranks average to 3.3 rather than 3.5 as they should, because not every boy assigned all ranks.
4. Abraham J. Tannenbaum, "Adolescents' Attitudes Toward Academic Brilliance" (unpublished Ph.D. dissertation, New York University, 1960).

BEING A BOY

JULIUS LESTER

In the sometimes grim testing period of adolescence, many men remember social relations with the opposite sex as the greatest test of all. Lester, a teacher of Afro-American studies, remembers the anxieties of his teenage years with unusual insight and humor.

As boys go, I wasn't much. I mean, I tried to be a boy and spent many childhood hours pummeling my hardly formed ego with failure at cowboys and Indians, baseball, football, lying, and sneaking out of the house. When our neighborhood gang raided a neighbor's pear tree, I was the only one who got sick from the purloined fruit. I also failed at setting fire to our garage, an art at which any five-year-old boy should be adept. I was, however, the neighborhood champion at getting beat up. "That Julius can take it, man," the boys used to say, almost in admiration, after I emerged from another battle, tears brimming in my eyes but refusing to fall.

My efforts at being a boy earned me a pair of scarred knees that are a record of a childhood spent falling from bicycles, trees, the tops of fences, and porch steps; of tripping as I ran (generally from a fight), walked, or simply tried to remain upright on windy days.

I tried to believe my parents when they told me I was a boy, but I could find no objective proof for such an assertion. Each morning during the summer, as I cuddled up in the quiet of a corner with a book, my mother would push me out the back door and into the yard. And throughout the day as my blood was let as if I were a patient of 17th-century medicine, I thought of the girls sitting in the shade of porches, playing with their dolls, toy refrigerators and stoves.

There was the life, I thought! No constant pressure to prove oneself. No necessity always to be competing. While I humiliated myself on football and baseball fields, the girls stood on the sidelines laughing at me, because they didn't have to do anything except be

---

From *Ms.* **1,** no. 11, July 1973. Reprinted by permission.

girls. The rising of each sun brought me to the starting line of yet another day's Olympic decathlon, with no hope of ever winning even a bronze medal.

Through no fault of my own I reached adolescence. While the pressure to prove myself on the athletic field lessened, the overall situation got worse — because now I had to prove myself with girls. Just how I was supposed to go about doing this was beyond me, especially because, at the age of 14, I was four foot nine and weighed 78 pounds. (I think there may have been one 10-year-old-girl in the neighborhood smaller than I.) Nonetheless, duty called, and with my ninth-grade gym-class jockstrap flapping between my legs, off I went.

To get a girlfriend, though, a boy had to have some asset beyond the fact that he was alive. I wasn't handsome like Bill McCord, who had girls after him like a cop-killer has policemen. I wasn't ugly like Romeo Jones, but at least the girls noticed him: "That ol' ugly boy better stay 'way from me!" I was just there, like a vase your grandmother gives you at Christmas that you don't like or dislike, can't get rid of, and don't know what to do with. More than ever I wished I were a girl. Boys were the ones who had to take the initiative and all the responsibility. (I hate responsibility, so much that if my heart didn't beat of itself, I would now be a dim memory.)

It was the boy who had to ask the girl for a date, a frightening enough prospect until it occurred to me that she might say no! That meant risking my ego, which was about as substantial as a toilet-paper raincoat in the African rainy season. But I had to thrust that ego forward to be judged, accepted, or rejected by some girl. It wasn't fair! Who was she to sit back like a queen with the power to create joy by her consent or destruction by her denial? It wasn't fair — but that's the way it was.

But if (God forbid!) she should say Yes, then my problem would begin in earnest, because I was the one who said where we would go (and waited in terror for her approval of my choice). I was the one who picked her up at her house where I was inspected by her parents as if I were a possible carrier of syphilis (which I didn't think one could get from masturbating, but then again, Jesus was born of a virgin, so what did I know?). Once we were on our way, it was I who had to pay the bus fare, the price of the movie tickets, and whatever she decided to stuff her stomach with afterward. (And the smallest girls are all stomach). Finally, the girl was taken home where once again I was inspected (the father looking covertly at my fly and the mother examining the girl's hair). The evening was over and the girl had done nothing except honor me with her presence. All the work had been mine.

Imagining this procedure over and over was more than enough: I was a sophomore in college before I had my first date.

I wasn't a total failure in high school, though, for occasionally I would go to a party, determined to salvage my self-esteem. The parties usually took place in somebody's darkened basement. There was generally a surreptitious wine bottle or two being passed furtively among the boys, and a record player with an insatiable appetite for Johnny Mathis records. Boys gathered on one side of the room and girls on the other. There were always a few boys and girls who'd come to the party for the sole purpose of grinding away their sexual frustrations to Johnny Mathis's falsetto, and they would begin dancing to their own music before the record player was plugged in. It took a little longer for others to get started, but no one matched my talent for standing by the punch bowl. For hours, I would try to make my legs do what they had been doing without effort since I was nine months old, but for some reason they would show all the symptoms of paralysis on those evenings.

After several hours of wondering whether I was going to die ("Julius Lester, a sixteen-year-old, died at a party last night, a half-eaten Ritz cracker in one hand and a potato chip dipped in pimiento-cheese spread in the other. Cause of death: failure to be a boy"), I would push my way to the other side of the room where the girls sat like a hanging jury. I would pass by the girl I wanted to dance with. If I was going to be refused, let it be by someone I didn't particularly like. Unfortunately, there weren't many in that category. I had more crushes than I had pimples.

Finally, through what surely could only have been the direct intervention of the Almighty, I would find myself on the dance floor with a girl. And none of my prior agony could compare to the thought of actually dancing. But there I was and I had to dance with her. Social custom decreed that I was supposed to lead, because I was the boy. Why? I'd wonder. Let her lead. Girls were better dancers anyway. It didn't matter. She stood there waiting for me to take charge. She wouldn't have been worse off if she'd waited for me to turn white.

But, reciting "Invictus" to myself, I placed my arms around

her, being careful to keep my armpits closed because, somehow, I had managed to overwhelm a half jar of deodorant and a good-size bottle of cologne. With sweaty armpits, "Invictus," and legs afflicted again with polio, I took her in my arms, careful not to hold her so far away that she would think I didn't like her, but equally careful not to hold her so close that she could feel the catastrophe which had befallen me the instant I touched her hand. My penis, totally disobeying the lecture I'd given it before we left home, was as rigid as Governor Wallace's jaw would be if I asked for his daughter's hand in marriage.

God, how I envied girls at that moment. Wherever *it* was on them, it didn't dangle between their legs like an elephant's trunk. No wonder boys talked about nothing but sex. That thing was always there. Every time we went to the john, there *it* was, twitching around like a fat little worm on a fishing hook. When we took baths, it floated in the water like a lazy fish and God forbid we should touch it! It sprang to life like lightning leaping from a cloud. I wished I could cut it off, or at least keep it tucked between my legs, as if it were a tail that had been mistakenly attached to the wrong end. But I was helpless. It was there, with a life and mind of its own, having no other function than to embarrass me.

Fortunately, the girls I danced with were discreet and pretended that they felt nothing unusual rubbing against them as we danced. But I was always convinced that the next day they were all calling up all their friends to exclaim: "Guess what, girl? Julius Lester got one! I ain't lyin'!"

Now, of course, I know that it was as difficult being a girl as it was a boy, if not more so. While I stood paralyzed at one end of a dance floor trying to find the courage to ask a girl for a dance, most of the girls waited in terror at the other, afraid that no one, not even I, would ask them. And while I resented having to ask a girl for a date, wasn't it horrible to be the one who waited for the phone to ring? And how many of those girls who laughed at me making a fool of myself on the baseball diamond would have gladly given up their places on the sidelines for mine on the field?

No, it wasn't easy for any of us, girls and boys, as we forced our beautiful, free-flowing child-selves into those narrow, constricting cubicles labeled *female* and *male*. I tried, but I wasn't good at being a boy. Now, I'm glad, knowing that a man is nothing but the figment of a penis's imagination, and any man should want to be something more than that.

Part III

Changing the Role

Chapter 6

Challenges to the Male Sex Role

The traditional expectations of behavior for American men have generally been unquestioned, but now some of the assumptions of the male role are being scrutinized.

Some men, especially those involved in the counter-culture, are beginning to see the quest for status and success as unimportant. Among those involved in communal living, competition frequently becomes minimal. The tough image was recently challenged on a large-scale basis by the thousands of young men who refused to fight in the Vietnam War. So too, the "killer" image is questioned by the courts-martial of those involved in excessive violence in Vietnam. And finally, some men are beginning to show their "softer" emotions in public — an act aided by the increasing prominence of the Gay Liberation Movement, and their belief that one can still be a man even though one does not conform to all the existing role demands.*

Furthermore some of these very issues have been raised by the Women's Liberation Movement. In their drive to gain equality for both women and men, feminists see that the factors which oppress women are also those which oppress men. But their first priority is women's rights, and many men, becoming afraid of the possibility of women "taking over," have therefore espoused traditional roles more strongly than ever. But the idea that if women "win," men will

---

* For some men, however, the growth of Gay Liberation may lead them to accentuate their hard-core masculinity, for fear of being identified as homosexual.

"lose," does not really address the issue as to what changes men themselves might like to see in their role.

To this end the Men's Liberation Movement was created. Similar in many ways to the women's movement — most notably as regards consciousness-raising groups — this embryonic movement appears to be growing, especially in urban areas. Here the focus is on men — what changes they want in their lives and how best to effect these changes.

Changing the male role creates different problems, however, from changing the female role. Women, always the subordinate sex, are demanding more. Men, on other other hand, have always been the superordinate sex with the power, and it is infinitely more difficult for those in power to give up some of it than it is for those with no power to acquire some. Since this might mean taking on some of the characteristics of the lower status group, and thereby losing some of the status they value so highly, many men are reluctant to alter any aspect of their role. Even when men are the victims of sex discrimination, they often find it difficult to seek redress — after all, they are the stronger sex and the role demands that they be strong even if they suffer.

Both men and women will ultimately benefit from eliminating sex role playing, and although a society without sex roles is difficult to imagine, it is only in such a society that men will be able to realize their full potential as human beings, without the artificial constraints that the male role imposes on them.

WOMEN'S LIBERATION AS MEN'S LIBERATION: TWENTY-ONE EXAMPLES

WARREN FARRELL

Many men are threatened by women's liberation because they fear that if women "win" men will "lose." Some aspects of the male role may change when women achieve equality, but such change does not necessarily mean losing. It can even benefit men, as Farrell demonstrates in the next selection.

From *The Liberated Man,* by Warren Farrell. Copyright © 1974 by Warren Farrell. Reprinted by permission of Random House, Inc.

Two women who were at opposite poles on the subject of women's liberation were shocked to find themselves suddenly agreeing on one point: *Women's liberation is a threat to men.* Men fear losing their masculinity, losing top jobs to women, losing status and power.

It is inevitable that *many* men will *feel* threatened. But I challenge the assumption that men *must necessarily be* threatened by defining twenty-one specific areas in which men can benefit from what is now called women's liberation. (All of these benefits must be seen in the context of the accompanying responsibilities, particularly the sharing by men of the responsibility for child care and housework.)

1. *If a woman has her own life and destiny to control, she will not be as likely to feel the need to control her husband.* Men who complain, "My wife has too much power already — she controls the whole house," often forget that an independent woman does not have so much at stake in what he does because she has her own stakes. She can approach him as an equal — someone with power, rather than as a vassal needing to manipulate the power which he alone possesses. Men call this vicarious controlling coy and cute when they do not object to it, devious, cunning, and underhanded when they do. They incorrectly worry about the aggressive female dominating them. As Marya Mannes points out, "The real aggressors are the female killer sharks in the guise of submissive females. These women use guerilla tactics to ambush and conquer the male." [1]

2. *The basis for any marriage or living arrangement can be more genuine.* The man does not have to pretend to love his attaché to cover his guilt feelings of "leaving her with nothing" when she has "given her best years to him." When a woman has diverse interests or a career her "best years" are redefined as all those years in which she makes the most of herself mentally and as a total person. She is thus not a physical mannequin subject to a deterioration process from the twenties onward, nor is she hanging on to the man because she has no other means of financial security, or because she knows so little of the outside world she is afraid to enter it without her husband's protection. If the man and woman do not get along and the children are perceived as a responsibility of *both* of them, they can make a decision together as to whether a divorce is appropriate. . . .

3. *Sexual interest heightens in an unstereotyped relationship.*

Many men wonder privately why sex has become so boring with the same woman with whom it was an undying preoccupation before marriage.[2] One man in his late twenties amplified this: "It isn't that I lost my sexual interest in her as soon as I made her (we made love for over a year before we got married), but my interest seemed to decrease pretty soon after the honeymoon. . . ."

A conventional marriage often becomes sexually one-sided. Her sexual interest in him increases because his availability is uncertain, just as hers was uncertain before marriage, when his sexual interest was high. His sexual interest in her decreases because she is always there waiting for him. His mind, if not his body, begins to wander. Meanwhile, she is expected to sleep faithfully at his side. . . .

One aspect of women's liberation is the demand not to be considered a sexual possession. In a real way this demand is likely to re-create the sexual interest many husbands have lost in their wives. . . .

4. *The man becomes psychologically free from the woman's view of him as a security object – a view which governs his choice of goals.* The role-playing, "submissive" female often brags as much about the quality of a guy's school or job ("I went out with this guy last night. He is an engineer from MIT . . .") as he brags about the quality of her body. The man becomes a security object because when the woman lives vicariously the only goal of his from which she benefits is security — and this goal becomes his goal. He becomes so enslaved to the money he's making that he loses his emotional ties to the person for whom he thinks he is slaving. By contrast, a man who lives with a liberated woman can think through his own goals. . . .

5. *Sharing of the breadwinning role by a woman frees a man from a great deal of the pressure that the corporation can presently exert on a man afraid to lose his position because he is the sole support of the family.* Many a radical man suddenly turns moderate when he realizes that "I now have a wife and children to take care of." He knows that if he objects to his company's investments in South Africa or even to his boss's petty political preferences, he may lose his job. *The sole-breadwinner status gives the corporation a subtle leverage over its employees.* It stymies creativity and basic questioning. It makes his job a "job" and not an employment opportunity. It defines his manhood as his breadwinning status and makes him sacrifice leaves of absence or more interesting jobs for

the raising of his status. It is only when that responsibility for breadwinning is shared that he can afford to take risks on his job which may result in his being fired — since he then knows he is not leaving the family in the poorhouse if he is fired.

6. *A man can devote more time to his children, in a more positive atmosphere*. Tensions which develop between the mother and children during the day are placed in the lap of the father at night. The father who is relieved of the role of "arbiter of accumulated tensions" ("Wait until daddy gets home") finds less strain in the relations between him and his wife and himself and the children. He is free to develop a closer relationship with the children due to his increased responsibility for them which he can handle because of the decreased pressure from other roles. . . .

7. *When his living friend* has economic self-sufficiency the man has greater leeway to choose an interesting low-paying position rather than an unfulfilling higher-paying position*. For example, a man who loves teaching is often pressured into administration because of money and status. If his living friend is less educated or skilled he assumes he must make the sacrifice of taking the less fulfilling job rather than making the sacrifices which will enable his living friend to develop her own economic independence. His freedom to take the lesser paying position will be particularly valued once men do not consider themselves a failure if their attachés make more money than they do. The concept that one person should feel better if another person does not do as well is more than absurd — it is destructive.

8. *In poverty homes, if both parents work, the additional money gives the man and his family the basic freedom to keep food on the table and the option of holding the family together*. In other families it offers the resources to travel, take advantage of the high cost of culture or afford better-quality education for the children. It allows middle-income parents to fly to a long weekend vacation spot and to afford a baby-sitter when they want complete privacy.

9. *The advent of women into the market of "men's jobs" can be seen not as competition, but as the lessening of the need to compete*. For example, the man whose living friend has economic independence can take off a year or two to obtain the education and

---

* A person with whom one is living; used when one does not wish to categorize the relationship as deeply emotional.

training necessary for a better position — or just to pursue a dream. Many men may still reject this analysis by saying "in the long run men will not benefit because business will not be able to absorb all these women, there won't be enough jobs to go around and we will all be working harder to share the same pie." Intellectual and liberal/radical men add that women working is just another asset to middle-class families which will help neither the working class or men.

First, if the reason for bringing up the myth of women's place in the home during peacetime and forgetting the myth during wartime is to prevent women from competing, nothing could be a more cynical channeling of human potential on so artificial a basis. Secondly, middle-class women working hurts neither men or working-class women, but creates a broad demand for services and therefore jobs which these women are now doing for free. . . .

10. *The man in the poverty bracket whose family presently receives welfare only if he* leaves *the family can benefit from "homemaker payment."* "Homemaker payment" is paying the man or woman who is doing the housework or caring for children half of the other person's check, which is sent directly to tir* by the employer. This legitimate income will tend to make housework and child care more respectable. Then the man whose living friend is able to earn a better living outside the home will feel free to take care of children inside the home. The benefit to the children of having a father around the home who is legitimately earning an income is invaluable.

11. *The responsibilities of the man within the home, while in some situations becoming greater, will in other situations be lessened.* Women are socialized not to perceive of themselves as assuming many of the responsibilities they might otherwise assume. For example, in a Parker Pen advertisement, the voice-over says, "You might as well give her a gorgeous pen to keep her checkbook *un*balanced with. A sleek and shining pen will make her feel prettier. Which is more important to any girl than solving mathematical mysteries."[3] It is inconceivable this would be said about a man, and if it were said of a black person the company would have a suit on its hands. The point here, though, is the increased responsibilities this image implicity shifts to a man within the home.

---

* Him or her.

Other chores within the home now become the man's by the same narrowness of role definition. These are: painting rooms, painting the house itself, repairing cabinets, mowing the lawn and weeding the garden, shoveling snow, putting up fences, refinishing playrooms and sometimes building entire rooms or occasionally even the house. Some of these chores, such as building, are more creative, while mowing the lawn or shoveling the snow, like dusting, are part of a never-ending routine. The release of men from automatically having to do these chores will appeal to some men. Others will be attracted to the idea of *doing* many of these chores together. Living friends washing dishes together, preparing a meal together, putting up shelves in the study or painting a room together can share an experience which will draw them closer together rather than farther apart. The fact that a man and woman should be able to do things together does not mean they should always do things together. The ability, though, gives them the choice.

12. *Role definitions limit men in responsibilities they might otherwise enjoy pursuing around the home*. During one of my interviews one man named Bill said his wife did not care much for sewing but said that he had wanted to sew some holders on which to hang his tools. He asked his wife for some thread. Her reaction was defensive and threatened. Although she did not like to sew and would have agreed in theory that he could do it "any time he wanted," when faced with the situation she was threatened with a loss of identity and purpose (despite the fact that she has all her credits toward a Ph.D.). Bill explained that he eventually did sew the holders and showed them to one of his neighbors who was with him in his tool shed. A few days later a second neighbor mocked, "Billy, my wife would like you to join the girls at the sewing circle next week." The pressures and kidding which result from any attempt to deviate make one recognize how emotionally attached most of us are to even the simplest of role definitions.

13. *Women's liberation frees a man from being the sole source of his attaché's happiness*. In the interviews one policeman mentioned he didn't discuss his real fears on the beat with his wife because she would "be worried sick" about them all day. If the man feels he must be the only reinforcement his wife has, he not only burdens himself but degrades his wife, since she must then be in the position of jumping around like a puppy dog always looking for a crumb of affection. This degradation in turn becomes one of the

thousands of elements contributing to some men's subliminal hostility toward women. The present cycle, then, does her an injustice, and confines him in his masculine tendency to suppress fear and not to ask for help.

14. *The liberated woman can allow a man more autonomy in his personal life.* Since she has not been waiting for him all day she is much less likely to mind if he wishes to have a drink before coming home, stop off at the gym, go bowling or go out with the boys. The very fact the man needs to go out with the boys after working all day says something about his relationship with his attaché. This point is cyclical. If his attaché is interesting when he does come home, his preference for "the boys" will decrease accordingly. As society encourages a pattern of independently fulfilled women, the need to get away from what the man perceives as a nagging wife will lessen. What men often want to escape now is the woman who is uninterested in his world and who often has nothing in common with him but the same home and children. . . .

15. *The reduction of anxiety about one's sex role.* Many men say, "If I don't teach my boy to be a boy, he'll lose his identity. I'll make him insecure." In fact, the opposite is often true. Stereotyped sex roles create lifelong *anxieties* over whether the child is deviating from or living up to the sex-role standards. . . .[4]

16. *Anxiety about homosexuality decreases as artificial standards of masculinity decrease.* Perhaps Kagan, an important psychologist, best summarizes this point in saying, "The occurrence of homosexual behavior or fear of being a homosexual is often related to anxiety over not attaining the masculine ideal." An adolescent male who is ignored by girls, is slight of build, and has nonmasculine interests often begins to believe he might be homosexual. The anxiety resulting leads him to avoid women to save himself from rejection. He interprets his apathy and avoidance as an indication that he is a homosexual. Kagan explains that this leads to panic and still less initiation of contact with women.[5] The benefit implied here is obviously not the reduction of homosexuality per se, but its reduction as a course taken out of negative reasons such as fear (just as heterosexuality is often developed out of negative reasons such as a compulsive need to adjust to the stereotype of masculinity). When men fear their own homosexuality less they will repress it less and not stigmatize others who are so inclined for more

positive reasons. The reduction in anxiety benefits both homosexuals and heterosexuals.

17. *The man can develop a balanced ego as a result of sexual relationships with women which do not always force him to risk refusal.* A man's ego is the second most fragile instrument he possesses. Why? Even in a "liberated' relationship men are still expected to risk the first sexual contact — before the relationship is secure enough to be certain "the pass" will be accepted. (Seldom does a woman touch a man's genitals for the first time — before he has ever touched hers.) The man is the one who must risk refusal. No wonder his ego becomes sensitive. His physical response to rejection may be to "try harder," but the physical response belies the underlying emotional hurt. He objectifies women rather than risk the increased damage entailed by rejection after emotional involvement. Conversely, a relationship with women balanced by being asked rather than always having to do the asking creates a balanced sense of ego and an ability to be emotionally involved.

18. *Men who learn to listen to women rather than making presentations acquire a new set of values that accompanies true listening.* When I listened at women's liberation meetings rather than "solving a problem," I was at first surprised to find that I learned considerably more than when I was preparing my question/ speech and blocking out what others were saying. The fact that the women generally arrived at better solutions to a problem became a contributing factor to my increasing respect for women over the past few years. I believe a number of men will find that developing the ability to really listen will completely alter their perspective on a number of presently assumed values.

19. *Intellectual achievement is a benefit to the boy not caught up in striving to reach artificial masculine standards.* The more intelligent the boy the less likely he is to need to be traditionally masculine, while the boy who has overcome the fear of being called "sissy" for achieving becomes free to use his intelligence in nonstereotyped ways. This intellectual achievement also occurs among girls who are brought up to be more active or "male" than is traditionally considered appropriate.

20. *Men become free of many of the legal burdens which discriminate against them.* Legal changes in the automatic responsibility of men for alimony,[6] jury duty,[7] and even their later retirement

age under Social Security,[8] serve to benefit men. In some universities such as Temple, men are not admitted to daytime continuing-education courses. Their freedom to take off during the day to pursue their education is limited. The legal barriers to obtaining paternity leave also limit their ability to participate equally in child care.

Most of these freedoms are closely linked to women's present dependency on men. The women's liberation groups' agreement with the phase-out of the husband's almost automatic alimony payment is predicated on the assumption that the woman's role will change to one of financial independence.

21. *Upon retirement, men's lives will not be as empty as those of men whose loss of position means loss of self-identity.* At present the man who retires often senses a vacuum in his life. Often the vacuum contributes to his death;[9] occasionally he seizes the cooking and household responsibilities as a way to fill it. Ironically, this can effectively kill the woman not only by creating a vacuum in her life, but also by making her brutally aware that those specialties to which she devoted her entire life and on which her husband was presumably dependent, he is now perfecting with reckless abandon. If a couple shares responsibility and halves the burden during their entire life together, however, they would continue to do so easily when retired, and in addition would have an equal amount of leisure time to pursue outside activities.

Notes

1. Marya Mannes, "Women's Lib: Can Men Gain?", Sunday Newark *Star-Ledger*, December 13, 1970, Section 3, p. 1.

2. The use of "marriage" and "husband and wife" is done for the sake of brevity, but application of all these points applies to any man and woman living together, and usually under most alternate life styles as well.

3. Reprinted in *The Militant*, August 7, 1970, as an example of women's advertising image. The underlining ("*un*balanced") is mine.

4. Kagan, Jerome, "Acquisition and Significance of Sex Typing and Sex Role Identity," in Martin L. Hoffman and Lois Wladis Hoffman, eds. *Review of Child Development Research*. New York: Russell Sage Foundation, 1964, p. 163.

5. *Ibid.*, p. 161.

6. The Family Law Act which went into effect in 1970 in California, for example, provides for 50–50 division of community family property and alimony payments based to such an extent on need rather than sex that is called "spousal support."

7. As late as 1961, eighteen states permitted women to be automatically exempted from service on jury duty. In 1970, in the state of New York, the decision for the case of *Leighton v. Goodman,* upheld the exemption. However, it did note that "the times may very well be ripe" for a change in the statutes. See John D. Johnson, Jr., and Charles L. Knapp, "Sex Discrimination by Law: a Study in Judicial Perspective," *New York University Law Review,* Vol. 46, No. 4 (October 1971), pp. 717–719.

8. The 1972 amendment to H.R. 1 provides for the equalization of these benefits as of 1975.

9. Dr. Effie Ellis, Special Assistant to the Vice President, American Medical Association.

ON MALE LIBERATION

JACK SAWYER

In one of the first public statements heralding a "men's liberation movement" in the United States, Sawyer gives a clear statement of what is now wrong and the human ideals toward which we should begin to move.

Male liberation calls for men to free themselves of the sex role stereotypes that limit their ability to be human. Sex role stereotypes say that men should be dominant; achieving and enacting a dominant role in relations with others is often taken as an indicator of success. 'Success,' for a man, often involves influence over the lives of other persons. But success in achieving positions of dominance and influence is necessarily not open to every man, as dominance is relative and hence scarce by definition. Most men in fact fail to achieve the positions of dominance that sex role stereotypes ideally call for.

From *Liberation,* August, September, October 1970, **15,** nos. 6, 7, 8. Reprinted by permission.

Stereotypes tend to identify such men as greater or lesser failures, and in extreme cases, men who fail to be dominant are the object of jokes, scorn, and sympathy from wives, peers, and society generally.

One avenue of dominance is potentially open to any man, however — dominance over a woman. As society generally teaches men they should dominate, it teaches women they should be submissive, and so men have the opportunity to dominate women. More and more, women, however, are reacting against the ill effects of being dominated. But the battle of women to be free need not be a battle against men as oppressors. The choice about whether men are the enemy is up to men themselves.

Male liberation seeks to aid in destroying the sex role stereotypes that regard 'being a man' and 'being a woman' as statuses that must be achieved through proper behavior. People need not take on restrictive roles to establish their sexual identity.

A major male sex role restriction occurs through the acceptance of a stereotypic view of men's sexual relation to women. Whether or not men consciously admire the Playboy image, they are still influenced by the implicit sex role demands to be thoroughly competent and self-assured — in short, to be 'manly.' But since self-assurance is part of the stereotype, men who believe they fall short don't admit it, and each can think he is the only one. Stereotypes limit men's perception of women as well as of themselves. Men learn to be highly aware of a woman's body, face, clothes — and this interferes with their ability to relate to her as a whole person. Advertising and consumer orientations are among the societal forces that both reflect and encourage these sex stereotypes. Women spend to make themselves more 'feminine,' and men are exhorted to buy cigarettes, clothes, and cars to show their manliness.

The popular image of a successful man combines dominance both over women, in social relations, and over other men, in the occupational world. But being a master has its burdens. It is not really possible for two persons to have a free relation when one holds the balance of power over the other. The more powerful person can never be sure of full candor from the other, though he may receive the kind of respect that comes from dependence. Moreover, people who have been dependent are coming to recognize more clearly the potentialities of freedom, and it is becoming harder for those who have enjoyed dominance to maintain this position. Persons bent on maintaining dominance are inhibited from developing themselves. Part of the price most men pay for being dominant in one situation is subscribing to a system in which they themselves are subordinated in another situation. The alternative is a system where men share, among themselves, and with women, rather than strive for a dominant role.

In addition to the dehumanization of being (or trying to be) a master, there is another severe, if less noticed, restriction from conventional male sex roles in the area of affect, play, and expressivity. Essentially, men are forbidden to play and show affect. This restriction is often not even recognized as a limitation, because affective behavior is so far outside the usual range of male activity.

Men are breadwinners, and are defined first and foremost by their performance in this area. This is a serious business and results in an end product — bringing home the bacon. The process area of life — activities that are enjoyed for the immediate satisfaction they bring — are not part of the central definition of men's role. Yet the failure of men to be aware of this potential part of their lives leads them to be alienated from themselves and from others. Because men are not permitted to play freely, or show affect, they are prevented from really coming in touch with their own emotions.

If men cannot play freely, neither can they freely cry, be gentle, nor show weakness — because these are 'feminine,' not 'masculine.' But a fuller concept of humanity recognizes that all men and women are potentially both strong and weak, both active and passive, and that these and other human characteristics are not the province of one sex.

The acceptance of sex role stereotypes not only limits the individual but has bad effects on society generally. The apparent attractions of a male sex role are strong, and many males are necessarily caught up with this image. Education from early years calls upon boys to be brave, not to cry, and to fight for what is theirs. The day when these were virtues, if it ever existed, is long past. The main effect now is to help sustain a system in which private 'virtues' become public vices. Competitiveness helps promote exploitation of people all over the world, as men strive to achieve 'success.' If success requires competitive achievement, then an unlimited drive to acquire money, possessions, power, and prestige, is only seeking to be successful.

The affairs of the world have always been run nearly exclusively by men, at all levels. It is not accidental that the ways that elements of society have related to each other has been disastrously competitive, to the point of oppressing large segments of the world's population. Most societies operate on authoritarian bases — in government, industry, education, religion, the family, and other institutions. It has been generally assumed that these are the only bases on which to operate, because those who have run the world have been reared to know no other. But women, being deprived of power, have also been more free of the role of dominator and oppressor; women have been denied the opportunity to become as competitive and ruthless as men.

In the increasing recognition of the right of women to participate equally in the affairs of the world, then, there is both a danger and a promise. The danger is that women might end up simply with an equal share of the action in the competitive, dehumanizing, exploitative system that men have created. The promise is that women and men might work together to create a system that provides equality to all and dominates no one. The women's liberation movement has stressed that women are looking for a better model for human behavior than has so far been created. Women are trying to become human, and men can do the same. This implies that sex should not be limited by role stereotypes that define 'appropriate' behavior. The present models of neither men nor women furnish adequate opportunities for human development. That one half of the human race should be dominant and the other half submissive is incompatible with a notion of freedom. Freedom requires that there not be dominance and submission, but that all individuals be free to determine their own lives as equals.

SAYING GOODBYE TO SUPERMAN

BARBARA J. KATZ

Men's liberation is a small but growing movement in America, and one of which most people know very little. This article discusses the aims and goals of the movement and offers some concrete examples of how men are being affected by it.

The word "brother" is taking on a new meaning.
—MEN AGAINST COOL, *a Chicago group.*

The men are on the march. But it's a quiet, decidedly uncoordinated march, so hidden from view that one must listen very carefully to hear its stirrings. It's the first, faltering footsteps of men's liberation movement.

Men's liberation? That's right. In cities, suburbs, and small towns as diverse as Fresno, Calif., Lawrence, Kan., and Fort Lee, N.J., an estimated 300 men's groups now meet regularly to explore the ways in which sex-role stereotypes limit and inhibit them. In heart-of-the-country places like Oberlin, Ohio; Lansing, Mich.; and Iowa City, Iowa, conferences on such topics as "the new masculine consciousness" attract hundreds of participants. And once in a while, in sophisticated urban centers like New York City and Chicago, small groups of men demonstrate against the "crippling sex-role training" found in children's books and the "exploitation of the insecurities of men" practiced by Playboy king Hugh Hefner.

Some men put their new views into print in publications like Brother: A Forum for Men against Sexism, published in Berkeley, Calif. Some are writing books: At least five books on men's liberation are now in the works. Others form organizations, like Boston's Fathers for Equal Justice, to try to dispel what they regard as a widespread view of men — particularly divorced men — as bystanders unconcerned with the rearing of their children. Others act as

individuals, like the teacher from New York City who has successfully challenged a school policy denying men the right to take child-
care leaves.

An Introspective Lot

Generally, though, the men taking part in this new movement —
mostly white, middle-class, and in their mid-20's to mid-50s — are
more introspective than political. Most have become involved in
response to the women's movement: At first defensive under female
questioning of accepted sex roles, they soon came to question these
roles themselves.

Unlike the members of the women's movement, however, they
have not yet formulated a widely accepted set of social and political
goals, nor produced a highly visible structure to fight for these goals.
Some would even deny they are members of a "movement." Es-
chewing rhetoric, they explore their concerns about the traditional
male sex role on an intensely personal level, usually within groups of
from 6 to 10 members.

*In a brightly lit, comfortable living room in North Arlington,
Va., four men, one of them with his 3-month-old son on his knee, are
"rapping." Jean, a 37-year-old sandy-haired, craggy-faced lawyer,
is talking:*

*"I was brought up in a family where traditionally the males
keep everything to themselves. You grin and bear it and never
recognize that there are any problems. Or if there is a problem, you
just take a deep breath, throw back your shoulders, and say, 'I'm a
big guy and I'm just gonna live through it and override it.'*

*"Competitive pressures are something else I've always felt
strongly — 'Get in there and compete and work your 10-hour days
and work every week end.' I've always done a lot of that, sort of
following the road map that others have laid out, neglecting my
family and my personal desires in the process. I'm trying to get out
of both these binds now, but it's not that easy to change the rules
after playing the game the old way for so long."*

"'Getting ahead' and 'staying cool' — these have been the two
main prescriptions of the male role in our society," says Joseph
Pleck, a psychology instructor at the University of Michigan and a
frequent speaker at men's conferences. "But it's becoming clear to

many of us that many of our most important inner needs cannot be met by acting in the ways we have been expected to act as men."

Dr. Robert Gould, a psychiatrist at New York's Metropolitan General Hospital and speaker at a recent men's conference at Oberlin College, agrees: "It's more difficult to appreciate men's distress, since they have the dominant role in society, but their role is just as rigidly defined and stereotyped."

The 'John Wayne Image'

The idealized male-sex role, Gould explains, is to be tough, competitive, unfeeling, emotionally inexpressive, and masterful — "to come as close as possible to satisfying the John Wayne image." But trying to play that role exacts its price. Says Gould: "By striving to fulfil the role society sets forth for them, men repress many of their most basic human traits. They thus cut off about half their potential for living."

Men's consciousness-raising, or "rap," groups are one tool for increasing that potential. In these groups, men simply try to talk honestly about their lives to other men — a new experience for many — and to raise the questions that have begun to bother them.

Why, the men ask, aren't men supposed to express emotions? Why must men never reveal weakness? Why can't men be more than "buddies" with one another, sharing their feelings, not just their views on sports, women, and work? Why can't men touch one another, the way women do, without being thought homosexual?

Why must men be the sole or major breadwinner? Why must they always assume the dominant role with women? Why must they prove their "manliness" by "putting down" or "beating out" the next guy? Why must men always strive to "get ahead" instead of just enjoying their work? Why aren't men supposed to have too much to do with children, even their own?

Forming New Groups

Warren Farrell, who teaches the sociology of sex roles at Brooklyn College and heads the National Organization for Women's task force on the "male mystique," believes that men's groups are "the basic instrument of the men's liberation movement." Farrell, whose book, *The Liberated Man* was published recently, travels around

the country lecturing on men's liberation and after each talk invites
members of the audience to become the nucleus of a new group. "So
far we've formed at least 50 groups this way," he says. So great is
the demand for men's groups, he says, that he and other concerned
men are now planning a national conference to train group
"facilitators."

Why this sudden concern for men's liberation? Most men in the
movement today credit the growing strength of the women's liberation movement. For every woman rethinking *her* role, they say,
there's probably a man somewhere rethinking *his*.

*In a small, pleasant living room in Berwyn, Ill., a Chicago
suburb, eight men, one with a 7-month-old daughter, and four cats
of mixed descent sit in the overstuffed furniture and sprawl on the
floor. Bowls of turkey soup — made by one of the men — and jugs of
wine and apple juice are passed around. George, a tall, gangly,
47-year-old Unitarian minister, is talking:*

*"When my wife got involved in the women's movement several
years ago, her thinking and questioning about her role started
having an effect on both our lives. I saw I had to start dealing with
some of the issues she was raising.*

*"When I first joined a group, about four years ago, we did some
'guilt-tripping' at first — flagellating ourselves for the ways we were
oppressing women — but we soon moved on to sharing other problems. We soon came to see that it wasn't just the women in our lives
who were having problems and that we were having problems relating to, but we also had problems within ourselves, and problems
relating to each other. We discovered that in some way we had been
dehumanized, and we came to want to find out what it means to be a
male human being."*

But is the move toward greater awareness only a process of
raising questions? No, reply the men who've stayed with it. There
are answers and gains.

For some men, it's meant their first close male friendships. For
others, it's meant a lessening of competitive pressure and a greater
recognition of the importance of personal and family desires.

For Jean, the Virginia lawyer trying to emerge from his double
bind, it's meant "being able to show more emotion with our little
daughter" and a willingness to take "an enormous amount of time

off of work" — even at the risk of cutting his salary — to help his wife through a difficult pregnancy.

For George, the Chicago minister, it's meant a "net energy gain" from the support provided by "people I really dig." It's meant being able to share the most personal of concerns with peers who understand and share his concerns — even his emotional struggle over the "finality" of the vasectomy he's considering.

For Mark, a 40-year-old burglar-alarm specialist in Chicago, it's meant being able to view his wife "more as an equal partner, a whole person, a friend. Before I saw her primarily as a mother and house-keeper, and I was always playing the big protector, the big man around the house. That's really a pretty crummy role, and besides, you can't have a really open relationship with a servant. It's been a lot nicer lately."

'A Crummy Role'

And for Jeff, a 26-year-old advertising executive in Deale, Md., it's meant the discovery that "vulnerability isn't necessarily a bad thing," and that "crying is a tremendous release." It's also enabled him to face the fact that, although successful at his job, he doesn't like what he's doing. "It's so easy to get caught up in simply doing what you're trained to do, what you're expected to do, even if you know it's not what you really want," he says. Jeff is planning to switch to an entirely different field — ecological architecture.

Liberation, these men say, does not mean that men will be "liberated" from the need to work or to share family respon-sibilities. It does mean becoming aware of what they see as the subtle ways they are forced into doing things because they must satisfy society's expectations of "what it takes to be a man."

Unlearning Expectations

Those who have given some thought to men's liberation say there are two major obstacles to overcome if one is to "unlearn" those expectations: The first is recognizing and unlearning the underlying contempt they say most men feel for women: the second is question-ing the male "hierarchy of values."

"Men learn from the time they're boys that the worst possible

thing is to be considered feminine — a 'sissy,' " says Warren Farrell. "The male's fear that he might be thought of as a female — with
all the negative implications that carries — has been the central basis
of his need to prove himself 'masculine.' A more positive image of
women frees a man to come in contact with the so-called feminine
parts of his personality and allows him to start displaying human
emotions without fear of being called feminine."

'Hierarchy of Values'

The male "hierarchy of values," with its emphasis on competition
and "success," is so ingrained in our society that "it takes a revolution in one's thinking to see what it's about," says psychiatrist
Robert Gould. "In American society, success has nothing to do with
how you live your life," he says, "but with whether you satisfy
American values of what success is — wealth, power, and status.
One learns very early that if you're bigger and stronger and louder,
you'll win all the marbles. One seldom questions whether what is
given up in the process of winning the marbles — meaningful relationships with people, enjoyment of work for its own sake — is
worth it."

The men taking part in the men's movement *are* doing that
questioning. But their movement is small and, while growing, not yet
at the pace of the women's movement. Some, like Jim, a 33-year-old
reporter in Washington, D.C., believe "the real guts of this is in the
children we bring up."

"Surely our impact, for good or ill, is going to have an impact
on them," he says. "We're not going to find exact answers to all our
questions immediately, but certainly we're setting a different example from what we had."

LEGAL CHALLENGES TO DISCRIMINATION AGAINST MEN

ANDREA S. HAYMAN

Men have always controlled the legal system, and laws discriminating on the basis of sex are generally acknowledged to favor men. In an article specially edited for this book, Hayman discusses areas in which discrimination *against men* is being recognized and challenged, and outlines some implications and consequences of change in these areas.

Introduction

The past few years have witnessed increasing debate concerning the women's liberation movement. Essentially a social phenomenon, women's liberation has also led to an awareness and development of women's legal rights. Far less attention has been given to the complementary concepts of men's liberation and possibilities for change in men's legal rights. Most people tend to equate the quest for sexual equality with women's equality, and while this is usually the case, there are many instances in the federal and state laws of discrimination against men, based on sex-role stereotypes.

Men's rights advocates have challenged several of these discriminatory laws, thus far without much success, although a few major men's rights victories have been won. But the limited emergence of men's rights has had less societal impact than women's rights. Perhaps this is because most or many men probably don't want to be "liberated." It is, on balance, a man's world, and men who have been socialized with the idea of the superiority of masculine values are not likely to opt for feminization of their roles or a decrease in the relative power of the sexes. In fact, thus far most changes in men's rights have been due to changes in women's rights and roles. For example, men are saddled with having to pay alimony less often because more women work or are capable of supporting themselves. However, as men's legal rights change, albeit slowly, men's attitudes will be influenced.

Women's liberation and women's rights alone would cause some changes in men's rights, but major changes probably will not take place without some special emphasis on men's rights, as such. Men have most of the legislative and judicial power and can prevent dramatic change. Even men who are not opposed outright to sexual equality tend to perceive the issue as a *women's* problem, and, thus far, the route to equality has not been modification of both male and female sex roles, but alteration of women's values to conform to the masculine model. However, the relationship between women's liberation and men's liberation must be recognized. Women will not be able to fully alter their life styles unless men alter theirs too.

Men's liberation may mean that men must give up some power, but at the same time men will be giving up some of their burdens. A broadening of men's rights will benefit men insofar as each man has more options open to him. Sexual equality should not be confused with sexual sameness. Men's and women's liberation need not necessarily lead to the same androgynous behavior by men and women. Rather, all persons can develop individually without the limitations of a sex stereotype.

In this article I will discuss some of the ways in which laws discriminate against men, and some of the challenges to such laws which have been brought in recent years.[1] It is designed to give the lay reader a preliminary idea of how sex discrimination affects men, what changes may occur in the future,[2] and how this will in turn affect their roles and those of women.

A brief history In early sex discrimination cases brought by women the courts almost always upheld the discriminatory laws as rationally based on the "natural order" or "divine ordinance." It was presumed that women's primary functions were to be good wives and mothers, that women were innocent and weak and should be sheltered in the protection of their homes as much as possible, and that women lacked the intelligence and capacity for logical thinking found in men. On the other hand, men were presumed to be the natural family providers, to be emotionally and physically strong, to be chivalrous, and to be more intelligent, rational, worldly, aggressive, competitive, and possibly dangerous than women. When statutes embodying such stereotypes were challenged, the courts assumed the veracity of such "facts" and thus found they had a reasonable basis and were constitutional. The lack of judicial response to claims of sex discrimination continued almost uniformly until the 1960s.

The inclusion of sex in Title VII of the Civil Rights Act of 1964 [hereinafter, Title VII] began as a joke but in subsequent years was given real vitality, and extensive administrative guidelines for enforcement of the Act were promulgated. Executive Orders extending protection from sex discrimination were issued. Several states also passed legislation prohibiting sex discrimination in employment. Sex discrimination, at least in the employment context, was finally being treated as the real problem it was (although it has by no means been eliminated). In this changing climate concerning sex discrimination it was hoped that the courts would be more willing to hold sex-based classifications unconstitutional on equal-protection grounds. A few federal district and state courts did just this. Then, in 1971, the Supreme Court decided *Reed* v. *Reed.*

Reed involved a challenge to an Idaho statute which provided that between persons equally entitled to administer a decedent's estate, males must be preferred to females. The court held the statute unconstitutional under the Fourteenth Amendment. Implicit in the Court's holding that the sex-based classification was arbitrary is a repudiation of the "divine ordinance" type of reasoning.

In 1973 the Supreme Court decided *Frontiero* v. *Richardson.* The Court held statutes under which a serviceman could automatically claim his wife as a dependent to collect certain benefits, while a servicewoman had to prove her husband was in fact dependent to obtain the same benefits, violated due process of law.[3] The statutes were based on the presumption that men work and women do not work, and the stated legislative purpose of "administrative convenience" was held an insufficient governmental interest to justify the dissimilar treatment of men and women.

In 1974 the Court, in deciding *Kahn* v. *Shevin,* upheld the constitutionality of a Florida statute under which widows, but not widowers, are entitled to a certain property tax exemption. The stated governmental purpose in *Kahn* was to equalize the disparity in the economic position of men and women. The appellant widower presented statistics indicating that a large number of women work and support their families, but the Court accepted as valid the underlying presumption of the statute: that men work and women do not work. *Frontiero* would seem to have precluded such a tacit assumption about sex roles, but the Court distinguished the classification in *Frontiero* as based *solely* on administrative convenience, as opposed to Florida's remedial policy.

These are just a few of the sex discrimination cases the Supreme Court has considered in recent years. However, familiarity with them is necessary to an understanding of many of the cases discussed below. It should be noted that at the present time it is not entirely clear what is the standard of judicial review to apply in sex discrimination/equal protection cases. Ordinarily a statute must be found to have a reasonable and just relationship to a permissible state objective to be upheld against a challenge on equal protection grounds. *Reed* hinted that the Court would insist on more than minimum rationality as justification. Four justices in *Frontiero* declared that sex discrimination, like race discrimination, is inherently suspect and subject to "strict judicial scrutiny." The standard of review is significant because the result in a case may depend on the standard of review applied. Thus the reader might bear in mind that the outcome of some of the cases discussed below might be different depending on the degree of scrutiny applied by the Court.

Finally, one ought to bear in mind the question of how adoption of the Equal Rights Amendment [hereinafter, ERA] would affect male victims of sex discrimination. Theoretically the courts could interpret the Fifth and Fourteenth Amendments in a way which would afford the same guarantee as the ERA. However, one of the reasons for the intense lobbying by ERA proponents has been the refusal of the courts to do this. Even if a majority of the Supreme Court holds that classifications based on sex are inherently suspect, the courts still have some leeway in finding that the classifications are justified by compelling state interests. While few of the challenged classifications discussed below were subjected to strict scrutiny, clearly some of them would be upheld even under that standard but not under the ERA. The ERA would prohibit almost all classifications based on sex, except those taking into account physical characteristics unique to one sex. The impact of the ERA on men's rights is already important because several states have adopted amendments to their state constitutions similar in wording to the proposed federal ERA.

Domestic Relations

The domestic-relations law of most states reflects the traditional division of labor between husband and wife. While the domestic-relations law contains many disabilities for women, at the same time it is probably the area of greatest discrimination against men. Men are assigned certain burdens, based on the common-law notion that husbands have a duty to support their families, and wives have the reciprocal duty to take care of husband, children, and house. State statutes provide that husbands have the primary duty to support their wives and children. Wives are usually secondarily responsible for their children's support and may be liable for supporting their husbands if the latter are incapable of supporting themselves. The wife's secondary liability is not designed to help the husband with his burden but rather to prevent additions to the public assistance rolls. Failure of a husband to support his wife is in many states a criminal offense, as is failure of a parent to support a child.

Within the family, the mother is supposed to be the best — if not the only — person qualified to care for her children. Even wives who work full time are expected to shoulder the responsibilities of housekeeping and child care, including making the arrangements for alternative child care. When the father helps with child care, he is not seen as expanding his role, but rather as helping the mother with her work.

The embodiment of these sex roles into the domestic-relations law may have made sense in the earlier part of this century, but changes in the status of women and changes in patterns of marriage and divorce compel certain revisions in the law. One-sided support laws were legislated at a time when a couple had a much better chance of staying married until "death do us part." If the marriage ended in divorce or separation, the husband's duty of support became his one-sided duty to pay alimony. Few women were capable of being self-supporting, and even today feminists will concede that support and alimony laws are necessary for the protection of many women. However, if these laws are somewhat anachronistic when so many women are self-supporting, they may operate even more unfairly given the current divorce rate.

It is well known that the percentage of marriages ending in divorce is rising. Far less stigma attaches to divorced persons, and even divorce laws have changed to make getting a divorce easier. A divorced person who remarried was once the exception; today it is the rule. Also, divorces today tend to occur much earlier in the marriage and the average length of a marriage ending in divorce is shorter.[4] Thus, more people are reentering the marriage market, and it is very common for a person to be married more than once. For a man wishing to marry a second (or third) time, lifelong financial obligations to a former wife (or wives) can be insurmountable obstacles. While the law should attach serious financial responsibilities to the act of marriage, financial obligations which are not necessary for the protection of the wife probably should not be imposed on the husband *pro forma,* or as a penalty. In general the domestic-relations law has been moving toward equalization of rights between men and women, or toward allocation of responsibilities on an individual basis, but, as will be discussed below, certain changes have yet to be made.

Wife support and alimony   The man's duty to support his wife is carried over to the alimony laws. Support and alimony laws serve two purposes — they keep persons off public assistance and they provide a monetary basis of the marriage contract. The basic contractual element is seen by the fact that a wife can lose her right to support or alimony through her failure to perform her marital duties or through her improper conduct. Because alimony laws are also premised on the concept of reciprocal duties of husband and wife, many state statutes permit the courts to award alimony to wives only, and a court has no discretion to award it to a needy husband in the absence of statutory authorization. Men challenging one-sided support and alimony laws have had little success.

Most of such challenges have been brought under the equal protection clause. The courts have sustained the constitutionality of these statutes, holding that they have a rational basis in that most husbands work and most wives are their dependents. This result has been reached even in cases where the husband earned less money than his wife. If the courts were more strict in their examination of these statutes, searching for more justification than minimum rationality, this form of discrimination might not be upheld.[5] It seems clear that these laws could not stand under the ERA,[6] and at least one state with its own ERA has already given some indication of this. However, even under the ERA, support obligations would not change in most instances.

If, as under the ERA, a support or alimony law was required to be neutral on its face, the obligations could be determined by various factors, including financial resources, earning capacity, and service to the family unit. In fact, at the present time, most husbands would still owe a duty of support to their wives when these factors are weighed. But if both spouses have similar earnings and undertake domestic work equally, the husband would not have to support the wife from his earnings.

However, at present, even where an alimony statute is written in sex-neutral terms, an award to a husband is considered extraordinary. Although theoretically the wife would have to demonstrate her need in order to receive alimony, wives who are not needy frequently are awarded alimony from wealthy husbands in order that they be "supported in the manner to which they are accustomed," whereas with few exceptions, only truly needy husbands are awarded alimony. This is probably because even under a neutral statute some judges tacitly assume the wife is *more* entitled to alimony, perhaps because after divorce she is in a damaged position on the marriage market, or to "compensate" her for past services.

On the other hand, courts have become increasingly reluctant to grant any alimony or substantial alimony to a wife who is, or has the capacity to be, self-supporting. Alimony awards are also more frequently made for a limited period, until children in the wife's custody have reached their majority, or until the wives have acquired training enabling them to be self-supporting. And some judges simply refuse alimony to young women without children.

Curiously, at the same time that the women's liberation movement has brought about a greater awareness of the injustices in the alimony laws, it has also led some judges to uphold alimony awards, on the basis of the new respect that women have demanded be accorded to domestic work. Thus, in upholding a high award of alimony to a wife who had never worked outside the home, the judge in one matrimonial action realized that the man would not have advanced so far in his career without the aid of his wife, and noted the financial worth of the many services the wife provided.

Child support Upon dissolution of the marriage, the duty to support the children remains with the husband, even if the mother is awarded custody. Again, the mother usually has a secondary duty of support, and in fashioning child-support orders the court is to consider the best interests of the child. As with alimony, in most circumstances the husband will be charged with the financial obligation, but in taking into account the best interests of the child, it seems more likely that a court will order a woman to contribute to the child's support than that it would order her to pay alimony.

Criminal nonsupport laws sometimes penalize either parent who fails in his or her duty toward the child, but the father has the primary duty. A father challenged the Colorado felony nonsupport statute which applies only to men, and although that state has adopted an ERA, the Colorado Supreme Court upheld the statute as applied to that father whose failure to support his child occurred before the ERA went into effect.

Most advocates of equality for the sexes do not propose to eliminate alimony and child support laws entirely. To the extent that they reflect the current reality that more men than women are employed, and that men earn more than women, such laws may be seen as affording necessary protection to many individuals who were never prepared to be self-supporting, and who are unable to become self-supporting for a period of time after the marriage breaks up. Judges may have unrealistic expectations of what a woman who has never worked before can earn, and there is no reason why neutral alimony statutes could not be drafted so as to protect a spouse who has been out of the work force or who has a young child in her care. The objections are that most of the current laws, and the construction put on all these laws by the courts, encourage women to remain outside the labor force, and unfairly close off options to men who can't afford to terminate a marriage.

Even if alimony and child support are awarded without a presumption in favor of women, as would probably be required under the ERA, at least for the near future men will bear more of the burden because of their stronger economic position. As with spousal support, the ERA would prohibit a state from imposing greater obligations for child support on a husband than on a wife solely because of his sex. If one spouse takes care of domestic work and the other spouse contributes to the family financially, the latter spouse could be held primarily responsible for child support.

Marriage age   The primary liability of the husband for support of his family has also been a reason for the maintenance of different ages at which men and women may marry. Several states have laws which establish different ages at which a person can marry without parental consent, typically 18 for women, and 21 for men. Historically, the basis for the difference in minimum marriage ages was related to the presumed difference in the age at which men and women were physically mature and could reproduce. The common-law age of consent was 14 for males, 12 for females. Since minimum marriage age without parental consent is well above the normal age of puberty, this rationale can no longer support the difference in law. A sociologist studying the family states that since "one youngster may be forbidden to marry because of parental refusal, and another of the same age may marry with parental consent, it is clear that Western laws concerning minimum ages at marriage were aimed at maintaining the power of the parent, not at enforcing a 'right age at marriage.' "[7] However, the justifications advanced by courts upholding such differentials are that women mature more quickly than men, and that men should use this extra time to prepare to earn a living since they will have to support families.

Under the ERA, different ages of consent for men and women could not be sustained. Maturity is difficult to measure, and it could not be proved that women mature emotionally more quickly than men. Given today's economic realities, the law should give women equal encouragement to prepare to earn a living. In reality women often have to support themselves and/or their families even though they have not been prepared to do so, and even under support and alimony laws favoring women. Women remain single, husbands die or become incapacitated, or women may be deserted — in all these instances and more a woman might suddenly find she must earn a living. Cases upholding the age differentials have ignored these realities. In light of the discussion of the increasing divorce rate and the courts' growing reluctance to grant alimony, the rationale of such cases has even less vitality.

Custody Although at common law the father had all rights to custody of children, today upon dissolution of marriage the mother is almost always awarded custody of minor children, unless she is deemed morally unfit. Many states used to have a statutory presumption that the mother is best fit to care for young children, or a judicially created presumption to that effect. Today only Utah has this statutory presumption, and it was recently in effect upheld by the Utah Supreme Court.

In all other states, the standard for awarding custody is to do what is in the best interests of the child. Although a number of states expressly provide that sex of the parent shall not be relevant in determining custody, and some other states provide criteria for determining the child's best interest and do not include sex of the parent, a presumption in favor of mothers is still very much alive. This presumption is applied judicially either expressly or as a silent factor in a judge's decision. However, it seems that use of such a presumption is incongruous with making a determination in the best interests of the child. In fact, the judicial use of this presumption may deprive the child of due process of law. The presumption has also been criticized because it does not project the family into the post-divorce situation where both the mother's and father's roles must be assumed by the woman. Even if the mother conformed to the court's notion of the "ideal mother," that does not mean she will continue to do so after a divorce, particularly if she must go to work.

Courts have awarded custody to fathers in several cases, but generally not where all things were equal between mother and father. In one case a court indicated that custody should be awarded to the parent who best fulfills the mothering function. The court found that the father was more nurturant, and awarded him custody as well as child-support payments from the mother.

Unwed fathers   All that has been said above was with respect to children born in wedlock. However, a natural father has had fewer rights in his children when he is unwed. The mother is deemed the natural guardian of an illegitimate child. Although an unwed father can be made to pay for child support if paternity is proved, he has few, if any, rights with respect to the child unless the mother marries him. Generally, the mother can consent to have the child adopted by a third person and the father's consent is not required, and the father need not even be given notice of the proceedings. The consitutionality of permitting adoption contingent solely on the mother's consent is certainly questionable in light of the Supreme Court's decision in 1972 in *Stanley vs. Illinois*. The Court struck down a statute which provided that children of unwed fathers become wards of the state upon the death of the mother. The Court rejected the presumption that unwed fathers are unfit to raise their children, and held that Stanley was entitled to a hearing on the question of fitness. The Court stated that under due process of law, all parents are entitled to a fitness hearing before their children are removed from their custody. Denying the hearing to unmarried men while granting it to all married men and all women, denies unmarried men equal protection of the law. Since the Stanley decision there has been a greater judicial and legislative recognition of the rights of a natural father in various contexts.

Abortion   Finally, men may feel they are the victims of sex discrimination because they cannot prevent the women they have impregnated from having abortions. The Supreme Court in *Roe* v. *Wade* specifically found it unnecessary to consider the father's right, if any, since none had been asserted. In the first post-*Roe* case raising this issue, an unwed father, who wanted to marry the mother, sought an injunction preventing the abortion. The court refused to issue the injunction, relying heavily on the fact that it was still the first trimester of the pregnancy, the period in which the mother's right of privacy is paramount under *Roe*. In a subsequent case a court invalidated a statute which required written consent of a married woman's husband for an abortion, because his consent could be withheld even during the first trimester. However, the court suggested that a narrower statute, granting the husband some rights regarding the fetus, might be constitutionally permissible.

Recently, another state court has considered the issue of the husband's rights. While conceding that the husband has a legitimate interest in the abortion decision, the court in *Doe* v. *Doe* held that the husband had no right to restrain his wife from procuring an abortion on the basis of *Roe* v. *Wade* and *Doe* v. *Bolton*. However, the dissenting judges claimed that the husband's rights to the birth and raising of children are fundamental, and that the husband has a judicially cognizable interest which the court would have to balance against the wife's right of privacy. Thus, if the case reaches the Supreme Court, two questions must be answered. What rights, if any, does the father have in the fetus? Second, what is the relationship between these rights and the woman's right to privacy?

Employment and Employment Benefits

The traditional sex role for men requires that men work, and there are few occupations which men have not entered. Women, on the other hand, have yet to penetrate many occupations or to achieve equal treatment on the job, and accordingly most of the commentary on employment discrimination focuses on the problem from a woman's perspective. Many laws and regulations concerning employment are based on the sex stereotypes of men as their families' supporters and women as their husbands' dependents. Such laws often have a discriminatory impact on both men and women.

Job opportunities   The civil rights and women's rights movements have brought about passage of several federal and state statutes designed to prevent discrimination in employment. The protection afforded by these acts is in most respects far greater than that afforded by the equal protection clause. These acts pertain to public and private employers, whereas the coverage of the equal protection clause is limited to state action. The prohibitions of these acts refer to discrimination based on sex, and that includes discrimination against men. The most important statute is Title VII of the Civil Rights Act of 1964, the key provision of which states:

It shall be an unlawful employment practice for an employer (1) to fail or refuse to hire or to discharge any individual, or otherwise to discriminate against any individual with respect to his compensation, terms, conditions, or privileges of employment, because of such individual's race, color, religion, sex or national origin.

The Act makes an exception in the case of a bona fide occupational qualification (BFOQ) reasonably necessary to the normal operation of the particular business.

In *Diaz* v. *Pan American World Airways* a man who wanted to be an airline steward challenged Pan American's practice of hiring only stewardesses. Pan American claimed that generally females were better for the aspect of the job relating to calming passengers, and that from an administrative point of view it was easier to hire only women. The court, however, followed the Equal Employment Opportunity Commission (EEOC) Guidelines that require the BFOQ exception to be read narrowly, and concluded that the customers' preference for females did not amount to a BFOQ for the job. Also, the court found that the convenience of hiring only females did not amount to a business necessity.

While *Diaz* makes it clear that customer preference is no excuse for job discrimination, situations where considerations of privacy come into play may compel a different result. Thus, for example, a man may be denied a job as an attendant in a women's restroom, although, strictly speaking, he can perform the job. There are few genuine BFOQs, where the job literally can't be performed by the opposite sex, such as wet-nurse, model, escort, semen donor and possibly actress, stripper, and topless waitress. And, although some jobs could be performed by either sex, conditions might give rise to a BFOQ nonetheless, as in the case of a restroom or lockeroom attendant.

Grooming regulations   A great number of cases have been brought raising the question of whether employers' grooming codes, which limit the length of male employees' hair, discriminate on the basis of sex in violation of Title VII. Male employees who failed to conform to such codes challenged their dismissal or restriction to non-public-contact positions. The courts have responded to such claims differently, and two lines of cases have emerged. One group of cases holds that grooming codes regulating men's hair length constitute sex discrimination and are not a business necessity amounting to a BFOQ. The other line takes the view that reasonable grooming codes are permissible even though they differ for men and women. Recently, this second view has become more widely followed in the federal courts. However, a grooming code which applies only to men might not be sustainable even under the second line of cases, if female employees are allowed to look unkempt or offbeat.

But long hair on men says little about *sex* stereotypes. The employer does not fire a man because he is less manly but because of the non-sex-based characteristics which might be attributed to him, such as a non-conventional or radical life style. If a woman wears long hair, she does not trigger the same prejudiced responses in others, as a man with long hair might. One problem with holding that grooming codes must treat both sexes identically is that it may be a denial of equal protection or due process to treat persons with different characteristics equally.

Assuming for the sake of argument that grooming codes do constitute discrimination based on sex, is the BFOQ exception a defense? The cases which have upheld the BFOQ defense have involved individuals in contact with the public. Maintaining a good public image has been held "reasonably necessary" to the normal operation of the business, although the employer has the burden of proving a business loss to justify the BFOQ defense.

Protective legislation   An area of law where both sexes may claim discrimination concerns protective labor legislation and statutes which confer a "benefit" on women. In 1908, the Supreme Court decided *Muller* v. *Oregon,* upholding the constitutionality of a statute restricting the number of hours a woman could work in a factory or laundry. The Court had earlier held a statute limiting the number of hours male and female bakery employees could work unconstitutional, but the Court distinguished *Muller* on the ground that women are the weaker and childbearing sex who require special protection which the state may require employers to provide. *Muller* gave states the license to enact a broad range of laws regulating the employment of women in several respects. While *Muller* has not been overruled, the courts have held that Title VII supersedes conflicting state protective employment laws by virtue of the supremacy clause of the United States Constitution. Since the passage of Title VII several states have repealed or modified their statutory restrictions on women's employment. However, some regulations still exist which may be challenged as unlawful discrimination under Title VII.

For example, one type of restrictive law establishes maximum hours that a woman may work. It discriminates against women who are denied the opportunity to work for additional income, and may disadvantage men who would like to be able to refuse overtime work without jeopardizing their jobs. Yet other states confer benefits, such as those providing that women must be paid time-and-a-half for overtime, and men who receive only regular wages for overtime work are discriminated against. On the other hand, such statutes have the effect of discouraging employers from hiring women so that they can avoid paying the higher rate. When such laws have been challenged, the reasoning of the courts has depended in part on the sex of the complainant.

Most of the lawsuits challenging protective laws have been brought by women. This is somewhat ironic, since *Muller* sought to secure equality of opportunity for women by safeguarding their competitive position. However, the issue of sex discrimination against men has been raised in the context of suits brought by the employer as well as in suits brought by men. Thus courts have held that an employer who is required to pay female employees time-and-a-half for overtime must also pay male employees the same premium. In another case, where an employer was required to provide rest periods for women only, the court invalidated the regulatory law because it conflicted with Title VII. It is important to note this difference in judicial remedy. In some cases of discrimination the "benefit" is extended to the other sex, while in some bases the benefit is removed altogether. While the decision to extend or invalidate the benefit depends in part on the circumstances of the case, the state courts have not been uniform in their choice, even in virtually identical cases.

Under the ERA, prohibitive and restrictive laws would be invalidated. The ERA does not permit classifications based on sex except those dealing with physical characteristics unique to one sex, and thus operates something like the BFOQ exception under a very narrow interpretation.

Fringe benefits   Differentials in fringe benefits, including retirement benefits, based on sex are also prohibited under Title VII. Thus in several cases courts have struck down, as violations of Title VII, schemes whereby women could retire on full pensions earlier, with fewer years of service, than men.

The EEOC Guidelines provide that "It shall be an unlawful employment practice for an employer to make available benefits for the wives and families of male employees where the same benefits are not made available for the husbands and families of female employees." Employers' and union health insurance plans covering spouses of male employees only have been held unlawful, as have payments of death benefits to surviving spouses of male employees only. Also it has been held unlawful to allow widowers of female employees to collect death benefits only if incapable of self-support, while all widows of male employees collect the benefit automatically. However, in an earlier case, a state court had held that the state's workman's compensation law, which provided compensation for all widows but for widowers only if they were dependent on the covered employee for support, was a reasonable classification based on the disparate earning power of men and women. As noted earlier, both sexes can claim discrimination in this type of case: the women who receive fewer benefits for their work, and the male survivors who do not collect the benefit.

Social Security   An employment-related problem is that both men and women are subject to discrimination under the Social Security Act, which was originally fashioned according to sex stereotypes. The Act was designed to provide protection to male breadwinners and their dependents. Although it is still true that in most families men are the primary earners, today many are headed by women. Some discriminatory provisions are currently being challenged, and some have been amended by Congress. For example, one section of the Act provided a different method for computing benefits for men and women at age sixty-two, resulting in greater benefits for women. It was upheld as reasonable on the ground that it was designed to reduce the disparity between the economic and physical capabilities of men and women. This section was again challenged in the aftermath of *Reed* and *Frontiero*. However, the court likened this case to *Kahn* and upheld the differential on the same remedial purpose ground. Congress voted to extend the beneficial method of computation to men.

In March, 1975 the Supreme Court decided *Weinberger* v. *Wiesenfeld*. In that case a widower with a young child sought social security benefits under another section of the Act, which provides benefits for a widowed parent who has a child of the insured worker in "her" care. His wife had been the primary wage earner for the few years prior to her death.

The decision was based entirely on the denial of equal protection to women such as Mrs. Wiesenfeld, rather than on the basis of the surviving man's rights. The Court likened the challenged section to the classification struck down in *Frontiero,* finding them based on the "identical 'archaic and overbroad' generalization" that "male workers' earnings are vital to the support of their families, while the earnings of female wage earners do not significantly contribute to their families' support." This section of the Social Security Act was found to be even more pernicious than the classification in *Frontiero* because Mr. Wiesenfeld was not given the opportunity to prove his dependency, and because Mrs. Wiesenfeld was deprived of part of her own earnings even though she was unable to obtain full coverage for her family. The court further rejected the argument of the Government that the classification was justified because it was designed to help remedy the economic difficulties of women who have to support themselves and their families.

Husbands, widowers, and children of working women, who were not originally covered by the Social Security Act, have been covered since 1950. However, to date, they must demonstrate that one-half of their support was provided by the covered female employee. (Wives of covered male workers are presumed dependent.) Divorced and surviving divorced wives, but not husbands, who were married to the covered spouse for more than 20 years are entitled to benefits. Both of these classifications have been challenged recently in federal district courts, and in light of *Wiesenfeld* have a good chance of being struck down.

It seems clear that the ERA would require elimination of all sex-based classifications in the Social Security Act. This would not necessarily result in vastly greater benefits being distributed under all sections of the Act. The primary earner would still receive the worker's benefits, and the spouse, regardless of sex, would receive the derivative benefits.

Reverse discrimination   One final possibility of discrimination against men in the employment area concerns reverse discrimination due to affirmative action programs and maximum majority ("benign") quotas for certain jobs. The extent to which such programs are constitutionally permissible is not clear. In *De Funis* v. *Odegaard,* the Supreme Court declined to consider the merits of a claim that a state school's admissions policy which gave preferential treatments to members of certain minority groups was unconstitutional, and held the case moot. Although the issue of reverse discrimination has usually arisen in the context of racial discrimination, men could challenge affirmative action programs benefiting women, just as whites have challenged such programs favoring racial minority group members.

A few cases similar to *De Funis* have already been brought in state courts. While both involve admission to educational institutions, similar principles would apply to job opportunities. One state court has held that a university's medical college's special admissions program for racial minorities discriminated against a white applicant in violation of the equal protection clause. The university intends to appeal the decision, and it is very likely that in this or another case the Supreme Court will be confronted with the substantive issue of *De Funis* within the next year or two. In the meantime it appears that affirmative action benefiting women will be upheld. However, the courts will probably, but not necessarily, come to the same conclusions regarding sexual, as opposed to racial, discrimination on this issue.

Under the ERA, affirmative action and benign quotas favoring women could not be sustained. While reverse racial discrimination may be justified by compelling state interests, the ERA may not be qualified in this manner. Nonetheless, the authors of a leading article on the ERA conclude that the courts could grant affirmative relief in particular cases to remedy the effects of past discrimination, and remedial measures could be the proper subject of legislative action.[8]

Criminal Law

Age   Age of majority is a factor in defining criminal conduct, and as with the age of marriage differentials discussed earlier, age/sex differentials in the criminal law have been challenged. Thus, an Oklahoma statute providing that, for purposes of the criminal law, a child was any male under 16 and any female under 18 was held unconstitutional because the purpose of such a disparity had not been demonstrated. However, the court did not say that age differentials could not be upheld if the state purpose was more specific.

Penalties   Occasionally men have been subject to stiffer penalties than women once they are involved in the criminal process. In a case in Maine, a man who was sentenced for his escape from a maximum security prison sought release from custody on the ground that a female escapee from the women's reformatory, serving an identical sentence for the same original offense, would have been punished by a much shorter sentence. The court ruled that the classification was neither arbitrary nor unreasonable. The court stated that it was reasonable for the legislature to conclude that because of their greater aggressiveness and tendency towards violence, male escapees presented more of a danger to the prison personnel and public than did women, and a stronger deterrent to escape was warranted.

Definition by sex   Some laws make activity criminal when performed by the male sex only. Frequently such laws relate to conduct of a sexual nature and reflect the stereotypic ideal of the chaste woman who needs to be sheltered. For example, in some states it is a crime for a man to have sexual intercourse with a chaste woman. Also, it may be a crime to impugn the chastity of a virtuous woman, or to use obscene language in the presence of a woman, and the courts have noted that the primary purpose of the Mann Act, which prohibits men from transporting women across state lines for immoral purposes, is to protect "women who are weak from men who are bad."

In some states an unmarried man may be punished for adultery if he has relations with a married woman, but an unmarried woman commits no offense if she has relations with a married man. In a few states sodomy is made criminal only if performed by men. This reflects the fact that historically male homosexuals have been targets of the criminal process to a greater extent than female homosexuals. Where a sodomy statute covers both male and female homosexuals but almost only men are prosecuted, a male defendant might challenge the constitutionality of the law on the grounds of selective enforcement.

Perhaps the most well recognized laws that are sometimes claimed to be discriminatory concern statutory rape and rape. It is a crime for an adult male to have sexual intercourse with a female below a certain age of consent, in spite of her actual consent or the male's lack of knowledge of her true age. In some jurisdictions there may be an analogous offense of corrupting the morals of a minor if the adult involved is female. However, this offense is not taken, prosecuted, or punished as seriously as statutory rape.

Forcible rape statutes make it a felony for a man to force a woman to engage in sexual intercourse. Such statutes are arguably discriminatory in two ways. One argument is that such statutes are unlawful insofar as they only refer to rape committed by men. A woman could sexually abuse a man short of raping him, but such acts usually constitute the same offense as where a man abuses a woman sexually, which is a less serious crime than rape. A second argument is that rape statutes are discriminatory because they do not cover homosexual rape. Homosexual rape is usually covered by forcible sodomy statutes, but these do not always carry as strong a penalty as rape statutes. Massachusetts recently amended its rape statute to refer to "persons" committing rape, in order to include homosexual rape.

Forcible rape statutes which limit liability to men could survive the ERA, to the extent that they are narrowly drawn as based on unique physical characteristics of men as the perpetrators, or of women as the victims.

Education

Sex discrimination by educational institutions is prohibited by federal law. However, exempted from coverage are religious institutions and military schools, public and private elementary and secondary schools, private undergraduate institutions, and public undergraduate institutions that have admitted only one sex since their founding. In one case decided prior to the passage of this law, male plaintiffs sought to enjoin the enforcement of a state statute which limits admission to one of the several state-supported colleges to "girls." The federal district court noted that there were other state schools the men could attend (including one that was all male), that historically the curriculum at the women's college was female oriented, and that pedagogical opinion on the wisdom of maintaining single-sex schools was divided. The court concluded that "[u]nder these circumstances this court cannot declare as a matter of law that a legislative classification premised as it is on respectable pedagogical opinion, is without any rational justification and violative of the Equal Protection Clause." The result in this case is not changed by the federal law because the college never admitted male students.

Women are similarly discriminated against when they are kept out of men's schools. But two lay authors have stated that they "do not find the arguments against women's colleges as persuasive as the arguments against men's colleges. This is a wholly contextual judgment. If America were now a matriarchy . . . we would regard women's colleges as a menace and men's colleges as a possibly justified defense."[9]

An analogous problem concerns sex-based curricula in a coeducational institution. Women have brought several suits seeking admission to traditionally male shop courses. A few suits have also been brought by male students seeking admission to home economics courses. A final issue is that men may also claim that they are the victims of reverse discrimination with respect to sexually integrated schools' benign quotas or affirmative action admission policies, as discussed above in the employment context.

Military

In the history of our country men have always had the burden of national defense. Only men have been subject to conscription, and even though the draft has been abolished in favor of an all-volunteer service, still only men must register with their draft boards. During the years of the Vietnam War several challenges to the draft were brought on the ground that the Selective Service Act denied men equal protection. The courts have upheld the Act as reasonable, remarking for example: "Congress followed the teachings of history that if a nation is to survive, men must provide the first line of defense while women keep the home fires burning." "For the most part physical strength is a male characteristic."

It would seem that such comments relate more to historical reasons for restricting women from combat and sea duty, than from noncombatant military service. However, combat soldiers represent only a small percentage of all military personnel. Many jobs classified as combat jobs, such as that of airplane pilot, do not require excessive strength, but are simply thought of as male activities. Thus the argument concerning physical strength really does not justify drafting only men. Even if women were drafted for noncombat jobs only, fewer men would have to be drafted. Moreover, many women probably are physically capable of combat duty. Thus under the draft men are further discriminated against insofar as fewer men would be needed for combat duty if some of the women who are capable of it were forced to serve in that manner.

Whether or not in the future men and women will be admitted to the armed forces on the same basis, questions may be raised concerning the disparate treatment they receive once they become servicepersons. Although the more frequent claim is that servicewomen are the victims of discrimination, in 1975 the Supreme Court decided *Schlesinger* v. *Ballard* in which a serviceman complained of discrimination. A discharged naval officer challenged on due process grounds the provisions under which male officers passed over twice for promotion are subject to a mandatory discharge, while female officers are guaranteed a minimum of thirteen years service. The Court stated that Congress could have rationally concluded that giving women the longer period was fair because women have less opportunity for promotion due to restrictions on combat and sea duty (which were not challenged). The dissenting justices cited substantial evidence indicating that in fact, Congress intended that male and female officers have equal tenures. Further, they noted there is no compelling legislative purpose for the different tenures since women officers are compared to other women officers for promotion.

Much debate on the ERA concerned the question of whether women would be subject to the draft if men were, and the conclusion seems clear that they would be. And, the ERA would require that once in the service, men and women be treated equally in all other respects. Exceptions to this rule would be those based on privacy, such as maintaining separate barracks, and those based on unique physical characteristics, such as exemptions from certain jobs while pregnant. Also, equalization measures which would substantially impair morale, in effect depriving Congress of its ability to maintain combat forces, might not be required.

Taxation

The traditional role of man as the breadwinner is sometimes reflected in disparate treatment of the sexes under the tax law. Sometimes the purpose of the disparate treatment is claimed to be the narrowing of the gap between men's and women's economic positions, as in *Kahn*. The decision in *Kahn* may be viewed as a particular setback in this area in light of a previous decision by a federal court of appeals in *Moritz* v. *Commissioner of Internal Revenue*. *Moritz* concerned a challenge to the Internal Revenue Code provision allowing a dependent-care deduction to women, widowers, divorcées, and husbands under certain circumstances, but denying it to single men. The court held that Moritz was entitled to a deduction for the care of his incapacitated mother, finding that the statute "is not one having a fair and substantial relation to the object of the legislation dealing with the amelioration of burdens on the taxpayer."

Jury Duty

Men have traditionally had the privilege and the duty of serving on juries. Jury duty may also be viewed as a burden because it can interfere with one's routine and result in a loss of income. Today no state completely excludes women from serving on juries, but several states have automatic exemptions for women. A few states used to have a system whereby a woman's name was not put on the jury rolls unless she actually requested it, and such a system was upheld by the Supreme Court in *Hoyt* v. *Florida* in 1961.

New challenges were mounted in light of the more recent judicial attitudes toward sex discrimination. In *Healy* vs. *Edwards,* both male and female plaintiffs challenged an exemption similar to the one upheld in *Hoyt*. While the male plaintiffs claimed that the exemption put an extra burden on the men, the court did not consider this point. Rather they found that one group of women, who were litigants in other suits and claimed that the exemption worked to deprive them of a jury of their peers, had standing to sue. Noting the changes wrought by *Reed* and *Frontiero,* the court found that *Hoyt* was no longer binding, and held the selection system unconstitutional because it denies all litigants due process of law, and female litigants of equal protection of the laws.

In *Taylor* v. *Louisiana,* a male felon challenged his conviction on the ground that he had been deprived of the right to an impartial trial under the same jury selection system involved in *Healy*. While the Court stated "it is no longer tenable to hold that women as a class may be excluded or given automatic exemptions based solely on sex if the consequence is that criminal jury venires are almost totally male," it did say that the states could provide reasonable exemptions.

No court has yet ruled that men are unduly burdened because of the exemption for women. To the extent that *Taylor* could be interpreted to prohibit an automatic exemption for women jurors exercisable upon being called for duty, it will have the effect of lessening that burden. Although the Court in *Taylor* did not specifically pass on this form of exemption, it would seem prohibited as a method of criminal jury selection if not pegged to actual child-care responsibilities. Even an exemption for women based on child-care needs could be challenged on equal protection grounds by similarly circumstanced men who are not given the benefit of the exemption.

Conclusion

The law discriminates against men in a variety of contexts, based on stereotypical assumptions about men's social and economic roles. Thus far many of the victories for men have been decided on the theoretical basis of women's rights. If a majority of the Supreme Court holds that sex is a suspect classification, and male plaintiffs are afforded the benefit of this standard, many discriminatory laws would be struck down. However, even under strict scrutiny the Supreme Court would probably uphold sex-specific remedial legislation although it results in discrimination against men. Adoption of the ERA would equalize men's and women's rights in almost all instances.

Most of the problems discussed in this essay directly affect only a few men, in a statistical or percentage sense, since most men conform to the traditional male role. Even if certain statutes are drawn in sex-neutral terms, there will still be a disparity in their effect because of the reality of the difference in the current roles of most men and women. Laws based on sex stereotypes help perpetuate limitations on both men and women. But if one accepts the premise that it is still, on balance, a man's world, fewer men than women will be motivated to utilize newly won rights. This does not diminish the importance of the legal challenges in the area of men's rights, because a change in judicial and legislative opinion does have an effect on individuals' opinions and social roles, which in turn affect legal opinion, and the process works in a full circle. The Equal Rights Amendment, if adopted, will figure very heavily in this circular process.

Notes

1. The cases are not grouped according to analytic similarities, but rather by substantive areas of law. Thus cases brought under the equal protection clause, the due process clause, federal and state legislation, and state constitutions are considered together. Also, Supreme Court opinions are grouped with lower federal and state court cases. Thus, the reader is cautioned that particular cases discussed may not be of equal weight or may not even be persuasive in a given jurisdiction. For complete citations and fuller discussion of the cases mentioned herein see Hayman, *Discrimination Against Men* (Columbia University Law Library).

2. Two caveats should be noted. The law is constantly changing, especially as it is altered by judicial opinions, and in that this is a relatively new topic of law altogether. Thus any particular point of law stated herein may no longer be accurate at the time of reading this article. Second, while many of the cases discussed are inconsistent with each other, part of the seeming inconsistency could be explained by a more detailed legal analysis which I have tried to avoid here. Similarly, some seemingly consistent results might not really be consistent on a certain point of law.

3. The Fourteenth Amendment guarantee of equal protection applies to state laws and action. The Fifth Amendment due process clause implicitly gives the same guarantee concerning the federal government. Federal laws under the Fifth Amendment are reviewed the same way as state laws under the Fourteenth Amendment.

4. For the statistics on divorce see W. Goode, *World Revolutions and Family Patterns,* p. 85 and pp. 81–86 passim, (1963).

5. But see, Husband M. v. Wife M., 321 A.2d 115 (Sup. Ct. Del. 1974).

6. For an extensive discussion of how the ERA will affect current laws see Brown, Emerson, Falk, and Freedman, *The Equal Rights Amendment: A Constitutional Basis for Equal Rights for Women,* 80 Yale L.J., 871 (1971).

7. W. Goode, *op. cit.*, p. 41 (1963).

8. Brown, Emerson, Falk, and Freedman, *op. cit.*, p. 904.

9. C. Jencks and D. Reisman, *The Academic Revolution,* p. 298 (1968).

X: A FABULOUS CHILD'S STORY

LOIS GOULD

A society without sex roles — what would life be like then?
Gould's story shows what happens to one young child who
is reared without the traditional sex role stereotypes; but
imagine if *everyone* was raised that way . . .

Once upon a time, a baby named X was born. This was was named
X so that nobody could tell whether it was a boy or a girl. Its parents
could tell, of course, but they couldn't tell anybody else. They
couldn't even tell Baby X, at first.

You see, it was all part of a very important Secret Scientific
Xperiment, known officially as Project Baby X. The smartest scientists had set up this Xperiment at a cost of Xactly 23 billion dollars
and 72 cents, which might seem like a lot for just one baby, even a
very important Xperimental baby. But when you remember the
prices of things like strained carrots and stuffed bunnies, and pop-
corn for the movies and booster shots for camp, let alone 28 shiny
quarters from the tooth fairy, you begin to see how it adds up.

Also, long before Baby X was born, all those scientists had to be
paid to work out the details of the Xperiment, and to write the
Official Instruction Manual for Baby X's parents and, most important of all, to find the right set of parents to bring up Baby X. These
parents had to be selected very carefully. Thousands of volunteers
had to take thousands of tests and answer thousands of tricky questions. Almost everybody failed because, it turned out, almost everybody really wanted either a baby boy or a baby girl, and not Baby X
at all. Also, almost everybody was afraid that a Baby X would be a
lot more trouble than a boy or a girl. (They were probably right, the

scientists admitted, but Baby X needed parents who wouldn't *mind* the Xtra trouble.)

There were families with grandparents named Milton and Agatha, who didn't see why the baby couldn't be named Milton or Agatha instead of X, even if it *was* an X. There were families with aunts who insisted on knitting tiny dresses and uncles who insisted on sending tiny baseball mitts. Worst of all, there were families that already had other children who couldn't be trusted to keep the secret. Certainly not if they knew the secret was worth 23 billion dollars and 72 cents — and all you had to do was take one little peek at Baby X in the bathtub to know if it was a boy or a girl.

But, finally, the scientists found the Joneses, who really wanted to raise an X more than any other kind of baby — no matter how much trouble it would be. Ms. and Mr. Jones had to promise they would take equal turns caring for X, and feeding it, and singing it lullabies. And they had to promise never to hire any baby-sitters. The government scientists knew perfectly well that a baby-sitter would probably peek at X in the bathtub, too.

The day the Joneses brought their baby home, lots of friends and relatives came over to see it. None of them knew about the secret Xperiment, though. So the first thing they asked was what kind of a baby X was. When the Joneses smiled and said, "It's an X!" nobody knew what to say. They couldn't say, "Look at her cute little dimples!" And they couldn't say, "Look at his husky little biceps!" And they couldn't even say just plain "kitchy-coo." In fact, they all thought the Joneses were playing some kind of rude joke.

But, of course, the Joneses were not joking. "It's an X" was absolutely all they would say. And that made the friends and relatives very angry. The relatives all felt embarrassed about having an X in the family. "People will think there's something wrong with it!" some of them whispered. "There *is* something wrong with it!" others whispered back.

"Nonsense!" the Joneses told them all cheerfully. "What could possibly be wrong with this perfectly adorable X?"

Nobody could answer that, except Baby X, who had just finished its bottle. Baby X's answer was a loud, satisfied burp.

Clearly, nothing at all was wrong. Nevertheless, none of the relatives felt comfortable about buying a present for a Baby X. The cousins who sent the baby a tiny football helmet would not come and visit any more. And the neighbors who sent a pink-flowered romper suit pulled their shades down when the Joneses passed their house.

The *Official Instruction Manual* had warned the new parents that this would happen, so they didn't fret about it. Besides, they were too busy with Baby X and the hundreds of different Xercises for treating it properly.

Ms. and Mr. Jones had to be Xtra careful about how they played with little X. They knew if they kept bouncing it up in the air and saying how *strong* and *active* it was, they'd be treating it more like a boy than an X. But if all they did was cuddle it and kiss it and tell it how *sweet* and *dainty* it was, they'd be treating it more like a girl than an X.

On page 1,654 of the *Official Instruction Manual,* the scientists prescribed: "plenty of bouncing and plenty of cuddling, *both.* X ought to be strong and sweet and active. Forget about *dainty* altogether."

Meanwhile, the Joneses were worrying about other problems. Toys, for instance. And clothes. On his first shopping trip, Mr. Jones told the store clerk, "I need some clothes and toys for my new baby." The clerk smiled and said, "Well, now, is it a boy or a girl?" "It's an X," Mr. Jones said, smiling back. But the clerk got all red in the face and said huffily, "In *that* case, I'm afraid I can't help you, sir." So Mr. Jones wandered helplessly up and down the aisles trying to find what X needed. But everything in the store was piled up in sections marked "Boys" or "Girls." There were "Boys' Pajamas" and "Girls' Underwear" and "Boys' Fire Engines" and "Girls Housekeeping Sets." Mr. Jones went home without buying anything for X. That night he and Ms. Jones consulted page 2,326 of the *Official Instruction Manual.* "Buy plenty of everything!" it said firmly.

So they bought plenty of sturdy blue pajamas in the Boys' Department and cheerful flowered underwear in the Girls' Department. And they bought all kinds of toys. A boy doll that made pee-pee and cried, "Pa-pa." And a girl doll that talked in three languages and said, "I am the Pres-i-dent of Gen-er-al Mo-tors." They also bought a storybook about a brave princess who rescued a handsome prince from his ivory tower, and another one about a sister and brother who grew up to be a baseball star and a ballet star, and you had to guess which was which.

The head scientists of Project Baby X checked all their purchases and told them to keep up the good work. They also reminded the Joneses to see page 4,629 of the *Manual,* where it said, "Never make Baby X feel *embarrassed* or *ashamed* about what it wants to play with. And if X gets dirty climbing rocks, never say 'Nice little Xes don't get dirty climbing rocks.' "

Likewise, it said, "If X falls down and cries, never say 'Brave little Xes don't cry.' Because, of course, nice little Xes *do* get dirty, and brave little Xes *do* cry. No matter how dirty X gets, or how hard it cries, don't worry. It's all part of the Xperiment."

Whenever the Joneses pushed Baby X's stroller in the park, smiling strangers would come over and coo: "Is that a boy or a girl?" The Joneses would smile back and say, "It's an X." The strangers would stop smiling then, and often snarl something nasty — as if the Joneses had snarled at *them.*

By the time X grew big enough to play with other children, the Joneses' troubles had grown bigger, too. Once a little girl grabbed X's shovel in the sandbox, and zonked X on the head with it. "Now, now, Tracy," the little girl's mother began to scold, "little girls mustn't hit little . . ." and she turned to ask X, "Are you a little boy or a little girl, dear?"

Mr. Jones who was sitting near the sandbox, held his breath and crossed his fingers.

X smiled politely at the lady, even though X's head had never been zonked so hard in its life. "I'm a little X," X replied.

"You're a *what*?" the lady exclaimed angrily. "You're a little b-r-a-t, you mean!"

"But little girls mustn't hit little Xes, either!" said X, retrieving the shovel with another polite smile. "What good does hitting do, anyway?"

X's father, who was still holding his breath, finally let it out, uncrossed his fingers, and grinned back at X.

And at their next secret Project Baby X meeting, the scientists grinned, too. Baby X was doing fine.

But then it was time for X to start school. The Joneses were really worried about this, because school was even more full of rules for boys and girls, and there were no rules for Xes. The teacher would tell boys to form one line, and girls to form another line. There would be boys' games and girls' games, and boys' secrets and girls' secrets. The school library would have a list of recommended books for girls, and a different list of recommended books for boys.

There would even be a bathroom marked BOYS and another one marked GIRLS. Pretty soon boys and girls would hardly talk to each other. What would happen to poor little X?

The Joneses spent weeks consulting their *Instruction Manual* (there were 249½ pages of advice under "First Day of School"), and attending urgent special conferences with the smart scientists of Project Baby X.

The scientists had to make sure that X's mother had taught X how to throw and catch a ball properly, and that X's father had been sure to teach X what to serve at a doll's tea party. X had to know how to shoot marbles and how to jump rope and, most of all, what to say when the Other Children asked whether X was a Boy or a Girl.

Finally, X was ready. The Joneses helped X button on a nice new pair of red-and-white checked overalls, and sharpened six pencils for X's nice new pencilbox, and marked X's name clearly on all the books in its nice new bookbag. X brushed its teeth and combed its hair, which just about covered its ears, and remembered to put a napkin in its lunchbox.

The Joneses had asked X's teacher if the class could line up alphabetically, instead of forming separate lines for boys and girls. And they had asked if X could use the principal's bathroom, because it wasn't marked anything except BATHROOM. X's teacher promised to take care of all those problems. But nobody could help X with the biggest problem of all — Other Children.

Nobody in X's class had ever known an X before. What would they think? How would X make friends?

You couldn't tell what X was by studying its clothes — overalls don't even button right-to-left, like girls' clothes, or left-to-right, like boys' clothes. And you couldn't guess whether X had a girl's short haircut or a boy's long haircut. And it was very hard to tell by the games X liked to play. Either X played ball very well for a girl, or else X played house very well for a boy.

Some of the children tried to find out by asking X tricky questions, like "Who's your favorite sports star?" That was easy. X had two favorite sports stars: a girl jockey named Robyn Smith and a boy archery champion named Robin Hood. Then they asked, "What's your favorite TV program?" And that was even easier. X's favorite TV program was "Lassie," which stars a girl dog played by a boy dog.

When X said that its favorite toy was a doll, everyone decided that X must be a girl. But then X said that the doll was really a robot, and that X had computerized it, and that it was programmed to bake fudge brownies and then clean up the kitchen. After X told them that, the other children gave up guessing what X was. All they knew was they'd sure like to see X's doll.

After school, X wanted to play with the other children. "How about shooting some baskets in the gym?" X asked the girls. But all they did was make faces and giggle behind X's back.

"How about weaving some baskets in the arts and crafts room?" X asked the boys. But they all made faces and giggled behind X's back too.

That night, Ms. and Mr. Jones asked X how things had gone at school. X told them sadly that the lessons were okay, but otherwise school was a terrible place for an X. It seemed as if Other Children would never want an X for a friend.

Once more, the Joneses reached for their *Instruction Manual*. Under "Other Children," they found the following message: "What did you Xpect? *Other Children* have to obey all the silly boy-girl rules, because their parents taught them to. Lucky X — you don't have to stick to the rules at all! All you have to do is be yourself. P.S. We're not saying it'll be easy."

X liked being itself. But X cried a lot that night, partly because it felt afraid. So X's father held X tight, and cuddled it, and couldn't help crying a little, too. And X's mother cheered them both up by reading an Xciting story about an enchanted prince called Sleeping Handsome, who woke up when Princess Charming kissed him.

The next morning, they all felt much better, and little X went back to school with a brave smile and a clean pair of red-and-white checked overalls.

There was a seven-letter-word spelling bee in class that day. And a seven-lap boys' relay race in the gym. And a seven-layer-cake baking contest in the girls' kitchen corner. X won the spelling bee. X also won the relay race. And X almost won the baking contest, except it forgot to light the oven. Which only proves that nobody's perfect.

One of the Other Children noticed something else, too. He said: "Winning or losing doesn't seem to count to X. X seems to have fun being good at boys' skills *and* girls' skills."

"Come to think of it," said another one of the Other Children, "maybe X is having twice as much fun as we are!"

So after school that day, the girl who beat X at the baking contest gave X a big slice of her prizewinning cake. And the boy X beat in the relay race asked X to race him home.

From then on, some really funny things began to happen. Susie, who sat next to X in class, suddenly refused to wear pink dresses to school any more. She insisted on wearing red-and-white checked overalls — just like X's. Overalls, she told her parents, were much better for climbing monkey bars.

Then Jim, the class football nut, started wheeling his little sister's doll carriage around the football field. He'd put on his entire football uniform, except for the helmet. Then he'd put the helmet *in* the carriage, lovingly tucked under an old set of shoulder pads. Then he'd start jogging around the field, pushing the carriage and singing "Rock-abye Baby" to his football helmet. He told his family that X did the same thing, so it must be okay. After all X was now the team's star quarterback.

Susie's parents were horrified by her behavior, and Jim's parents were worried sick about his. But the worst came when the twins, Joe and Peggy, decided to share everything with each other. Peggy used Joe's hockey skates, and his microscope, and took half his newspaper route. Joe used Peggy's needlepoint kit, and her cookbooks, and took two of her three baby-sitting jobs. Peggy started running the lawn mower, and Joe started running the vacuum cleaner.

Their parents weren't one bit pleased with Peggy's wonderful biology experiments, or with Joe's terrific needlepoint pillows. They didn't care that Peggy mowed the lawn better, and that Joe vacuummed the carpet better. In fact, they were furious. It's all that little X's fault, they agreed. Just because X doesn't know what it is, or what it's supposed to be, it wants to get everybody *else* mixed up, too!

Peggy and Joe were forbidden to play with X any more. So was Susie, and then Jim, and then *all* the Other Children. But it was too late; the Other Children stayed mixed up and happy and free, and refused to go back to the way they'd been before X.

Finally, Joe and Peggy's parents decided to call an emergency meeting of the school's Parents' Association, to discuss "The X Problem." They sent a report to the principal stating that X was a "disruptive influence." They demanded immediate action. The Joneses, they said, should be *forced* to tell whether X was a boy or a girl. And then X should be *forced* to behave like whichever it was. If the Joneses refused to tell, the Parents' Association said, then X must taken an Xamination. The school psychiatrist must Xamine it physically and mentally, and issue a full report. If X's test showed it was a boy, it would have to obey all the boys' rules. If it proved to be a girl, X would have to obey all the girls' rules.

And if X turned out to be some kind of mixed-up misfit, then X should be Xpelled from the school. Immediately!

The principal was very upset. Disruptive influence? Mixed-up misfit? But X was an Xcellent student. All the teachers said it was a delight to have X in their classes. X was president of the student council. X had won first prize in the talent show, and second prize in the art show, and honorable mention in the science fair, and six athletic events on field day, including the potato race.

Nevertheless, insisted the Parents' Association, X is a Problem Child. X is the Biggest Problem Child we have ever seen!

So the principal reluctantly notified X's parents that numerous complaints about X's behavior had come to the school's attention. And that after the psychiatrist's Xamination, the school would decide what to do about X.

The Joneses reported this at once to the scientists, who referred them to page 85,759 of the *Instruction Manual.* "Sooner or later," it said, "X will have to be Xamined by a psychiatrist. This may be the only way any of us will know for sure whether X is mixed up — or whether everyone else is."

The night before X was to be Xamined, the Joneses tried not to let X see how worried they were. "What if . . .?" Mr. Jones would say. And Ms. Jones would reply, "No use worrying." Then a few minutes later, Ms. Jones would say, "What if . . .?" and Mr. Jones would reply, "No use worrying."

X just smiled at them both, and hugged them hard and didn't say much of anything. X was thinking. What if . . .? And then X thought: No use worrying.

At Xactly 9 o'clock the next day, X reported to the school psychiatrist's office. The principal, along with a committee from the Parents' Association, X's teacher, X's classmates, and Ms. and Mr. Jones, waited in the hall outside. Nobody knew the details of the tests X was to be given, but everybody knew they'd be *very* hard, and that they'd reveal Xactly what everyone wanted to know about X, but were afraid to ask.

It was terribly quiet in the hall. Almost spooky. Once in a while, they would hear a strange noise inside the room. There were buzzes. And a beep or two. And several bells. An occasional light would flash under the door. The Joneses thought it was a white light, but the principal thought it was blue. Two or three children swore it was either yellow or green. And the Parents' Committee missed it completely.

Through it all, you could hear the psychiatrist's low voice, asking hundreds of questions, and X's higher voice, answering hundreds of answers.

The whole thing took so long that everyone knew it must be the most complete Xamination anyone had ever had to take. Poor X, the Joneses thought. Serves X right, the Parents' Committee thought. I wouldn't like to be in X's overalls right now, the children thought.

At last, the door opened. Everyone crowded around to hear the results. X didn't look any different; in fact, X was smiling. But the psychiatrist looked terrible. He look as if he was crying! "What happened?" everyone began shouting. Had X done something disgraceful? "I wouldn't be a bit surprised!" muttered Peggy and Joe's parents. "Did X flunk the *whole* test?" cried Susie's parents. "Or just the most important part?" yelled Jim's parents.

"Oh, dear," sighed Mr. Jones.

"Oh, dear," sighed Ms. Jones.

"*Sssh*," ssshed the principal. "The psychiatrist is trying to speak."

Wiping his eyes and clearing his throat, the psychiatrist began, in a hoarse whisper. "In my opinion," he whispered — you could tell he must be very upset — "in my opinion, young X here . . ."

"Yes? Yes?" shouted a parent impatiently.

"*Sssh!*" ssshed the principal.

"Young *Sssh* here, I mean young X," said the doctor, frowning, "is just about . . ."

"Just about *what*? Let's have it!" shouted another parent.

" . . . just about the *least* mixed-up child I've ever Xamined!" said the psychiatrist.

"Yay for X!" yelled one of the children. And then the others began yelling, too. Clapping and cheering and jumping up and down.

"*SSSH!*" SSShed the principal, but nobody did.

The Parents' Committee was angry and bewildered. How *could* X have passed the whole Xamination? Didn't X have an *identity* problem? Wasn't X mixed up at *all*? Wasn't X *any* kind of a misfit? How could it *not* be, when it didn't even *know* what it was? And why was the psychiatrist crying?

Actually, he had stopped crying and was smiling politely through his tears. "Don't you see?" he said. "I'm crying because it's wonderful! X has absolutely no identity problem! X isn't one bit mixed up! As for being a misfit — ridiculous! X knows perfectly well what it is! Don't you, X?" The doctor winked, X winked back.

"But what *is* X?" shrieked Peggy and Joe's parents. *"We* still want to know what it is!"

"Ah, yes," said the doctor, winking again. "Well, don't worry. You'll all know one of these days. And you won't need me to tell you."

"What? What does he mean?" some of the parents grumbled suspiciously.

Susie and Peggy and Joe all answered at once. "He means that by the time X's sex matters, it won't be a secret any more!"

With that, the doctor began to push through the crowd toward X's parents. "How do you do," he said, somewhat stiffly. And then he reached out to hug them both. "If I ever have an X of my own," he whispered, "I sure hope you'll lend me your instruction manual."

Needless to say, the Joneses were very happy. The Project Baby X scientists were rather pleased, too. So were Susie, Jim, Peggy, Joe, and all the Other Children. The Parents' Association wasn't, but they had promised to accept the psychiatrist's report, and not make any more trouble. They even invited Ms. and Mr. Jones to become honorary members, which they did.

Later that day, all X's friends put on their red-and-white checked overalls and went over to see X. They found X in the back yard, playing with a very tiny baby that none of them had ever seen before. The baby was wearing very tiny red-and-white checked overalls.

"How do you like our new baby?" X asked the Other Children proudly.

"It's got cute dimples," said Jim.

"It's got husky biceps, too," said Susie.

"What kind of baby is it?" asked Joe and Peggy.

X frowned at them. "Can't you tell?" Then X broke into a big, mischievous grin. *"It's a Y!"*

Additional References

General Books

Bednarik, Karl, *The Male in Crisis* (New York: Knopf, 1970).

Benson, Leonard, *Fatherhood: A Sociological Perspective* (New York: Random House, 1968).

Brenton, Myron, *The American Male* (New York: Fawcett Premier Paperback, 1966).

Farrell, Warren, *The Liberated Man* (New York: Random House, 1974).

Fasteau, Marc, *The Male Machine* (New York: McGraw-Hill, 1974).

Komisar, Lucy, *The Machismo Factor* (New York: Macmillan, 1976).

Korda, Michael, *Male Chauvinism: How it Works* (New York: Random House, 1973).

Marine, Gene, *A Male Guide to Women's Liberation* (New York: Avon Books, 1972).

Pleck, Joseph, and Jack Sawyer, *Men and Masculinity* (Englewood Cliffs, N.J.: Prentice-Hall, 1974).

Steinmann, Anne, and David Fox, *The Male Dilemma* (New York: Jason Aronson, 1973).

No Sissy Stuff

Bartholome, Fernando, "Executives as Human Beings," *Harvard Business Review,* **50**(6), Nov.–Dec. 1972.

Clark, Don, "Homosexual Encounter in All-Male Groups," in L. Solomon and B. Berzon (eds.), *New Perspectives on Encounter Groups* (San Francisco: Jossey-Bass, 1972).

Jourard, Sidney, "Some Lethal Aspects of the Male Sex Role," in Jourard, *The Transparent Self* (New York: Van Nostrand, 1964).

Julty, Sam, "A Case of 'Sexual Dysfunction,' " *Ms.* 1(9), April 1973.

Komarovsky, Mirra, "Patterns of Self-Disclosure of Male Undergraduates," *Journal of Marriage and the Family,* 36(4), Nov. 1974.

Levy, Charles, "ARVN as Faggots: Inverted Warfare in Vietnam," *Transaction,* 18(12), Oct. 1971.

Manville, W. H., "The Locker-Room Boys," *Cosmopolitan,* Nov. 1969.

Plumb, J. H., "A Return to Manliness," *Horizon,* 9(1), Winter 1967.

Weinberg, George, *Society and the Healthy Homosexual* (New York: Doubleday Anchor Book, 1973).

The Big Wheel

Bass, Bernard, "Male Managers' Attitudes Toward Working Women," *American Behavioral Scientist* 15, 1971.

Della Fave, L. Richard, "Success Values: Are they Universal or Class-differentiated?" *American Journal of Sociology* 80(1), 1974.

Gronseth, Erik, "The Breadwinner Trap," in L. Howe (ed.), *The Future of the Family* (New York: Simon & Schuster, 1972).

Korda, Michael, "Office Power — You are Where you Sit," *New York,* Jan. 13, 1975.

Maccoby, Michael, " 'Winning' and 'Losing' at Work," *IEEE Spectrum,* July 1973.

Polatnick, Margaret, "Why Men Don't Rear Children: A Power Analysis," *Berkeley Journal of Sociology* 18, 1973–74.

Shepard, Harold, "Discontented Blue Collar Workers — A Case Study," *Monthly Labor Review* 94, April 1971.

Shostak, Arthur, "Middle-aged Working Class Americans at Home: Changing Definitions of Manhood," *Occupational Mental Health* 2(3), 1972.

Silverstein, Michael, "Power and Sex Roles in Academia," *Journal of Applied Behavioral* Science 8(5), 1972.

Turner, Ralph, "The Male Occupational Role," in Turner, *Family Interaction* (New York: John Wiley, 1970).

The Sturdy Oak

Chass, Murray, "A Gut Issue: Who Shapes Up Best, Athletes or Dancers?" *The New York Times,* Aug. 18, 1974.

Henley, Nancy, "Power, Sex and Non-verbal Communication," *Berkeley Journal of Sociology* **18**, 1973–74.

Levinson, Daniel, "The Male Mid-Life Decade," in David Ricks (ed.), *Life History Research in Psychopathology*, Vol. 3, (Minneapolis: University of Minnesota Press, 1974).

Ramey, Estelle, "Men's Cycles," *Ms.* Spring 1972.

Stone, I. F., "Machismo in Washington," *New York Review of Books*, May 18, 1972.

Give 'Em Hell

Blumenthal, M., R. Kahn, F. Andrews, and K. Head, *Justifying Violence. Attitudes of American Men* (Ann Arbor: Institute for Social Research, 1972).

Feshbach, Seymour, "Aggression," in P. Mussen (ed.), *Carmichael's Manual of Child Psychology* (New York: John Wiley, 1970).

Kirkpatrick, Clifford, and Eugene Kanin, "Male Sex Aggression on a University Campus," *American Sociological Review* **22**(1), 1957.

Parsons, Talcott, "Certain Primary Sources and Patterns of Aggression in the Social Structure of the Western World," in Parsons, *Essays in Sociological Theory* (New York: The Free Press, 1954).

Pogrebin, Letty, "Do Women Make Men Violent?" *Ms.* **3**(5), Nov. 1974.

Steinem, Gloria, "The Myth of the Masculine Mystique," International Education **1**, 1972.

Toby, Jackson, "Violence and the Masculine Ideal: Some Qualitative Data," *Annals of the American Academy of Political and Social Science* **36**, March 1966.

Socialization

Biller, H., and D. Liebman, "Body Build, Sex-role Preference, and Sex Role Adoption in Junior High School Boys," *Journal of Genetic Psychology* **118**, 1971.

Knox, William, and Harriet Kupferer, "A Discontinuity in the Socialization of Males in the United States," *Merrill-Palmer Quarterly* **17**, July 1971.

Komarovsky, Mirra, "Cultural Contradictions and Sex Roles: The Masculine Case," *American Journal of Sociology* **78**(4), 1973.

Mussen, Paul, "Long-term Consequences of Masculinity of Interests in Adolescence," *Journal of Consulting Psychology* **26**, 1962.

Simpson, Tony, "Real Men, Short Hair." *Intellectual Digest* **3**, Nov., 1973.

Challenges

Farrell, Warren, "Guidelines for Consciousness Raising," *Ms.* **7**, Feb. 1973.

Miller, S. M., "The Making of a Confused Middle-Class Husband," *Social Policy* **2**(2), July–August 1971.

Pleck, Joseph, "Is Brotherhood Possible?" in N. Glazer-Malbin (ed.), *Old Family/New Family: Interpersonal Relationships* (New York: Van Nostrand Reinhold, 1975).

Sawyer, Jack, "On the Politics of Male Liberation," *WIN,* Sept. 1, 1971.

Steinem, Gloria, "What it Would be Like if Women Win," *Time* **96**(9), Aug. 31, 1970.

About the Authors

Jack O. Balswick is Associate Professor of Sociology at the University of Georgia, Athens, Georgia. His teaching and research interests include the sociology of sex roles, personality formation and change, and the sociology of religion. He is currently engaged in a research project sponsored by the National Institute of Mental Health on the factors contributing to male inexpressiveness and its effect upon family relationships.

Robert Brannon, Assistant Professor of Psychology at Brooklyn College, CUNY, has been conducting research on masculinity and men's reactions to women's liberation. He is preparing a survey project on masculinity for *Psychology Today,* speaks in behalf of Men's Liberation and organizes men's consciousness-raising groups. He is one of a small number of male psychologists active in The Association For Women In Psychology, and has served that group as Membership Chairperson, Treasurer, and Coordinator of the Feminist Research Committee. He received his undergraduate education at Harvard University and his graduate training at The University of Michigan.

Myron Brenton, a freelance, has authored six books and hundreds of magazine articles, most in the category of human behavior. His latest book, *Friendship,* analyzes a relationship that has received relatively little attention from social scientists.

James S. Coleman is Professor of Sociology at the University of Chicago. He is the author of books on adolescent peer groups, mathematical sociology, collective decisions, and educational sociology. He is principal author of the 1966 study *Equality of Educational Opportunity,* which surveyed the effects of school characteristics on student academic achievement and which is often referred to as "The Coleman Report."

Deborah S. David, Assistant Professor of Sociology, Brooklyn College, CUNY, received her doctorate from Columbia University, with a dissertation comparing career patterns of male and female scientists and engineers. She has written papers on several aspects of sex roles, and has also published work on criminal victimization. She is currently Treasurer of Sociologists for Women in Society, having also served as Annual Program Chairperson.

Jerry Farber is the author of two collections of essays, *The Student As Nigger* and *The University of Tomorrowland*. He is an Associate Professor of Comparative Literature at San Diego State Univeristy.

Warren Farrell is Adjunct Assistant Professor of Sociology at Brooklyn College, CUNY, and is active in organizing men's consciousness-raising groups.

Marc Feigen Fasteau practices law in New York in partnership with his wife, feminist attorney Brenda Feigen Fasteau.

John H. Gagnon is Professor of Sociology and Psychology at the State University of New York, Stony Brook, and has published extensively in the area of human sexuality.

Lois Gould is an author working in New York.

Robert Gould, M.D., is the Director of Out-Patient Psychiatry, Metropolitan Hospital, New York.

Ulf Hannerz is Associate Professor of Social Anthropology at Stockholm, Sweden, and is currently engaged in urban anthropological research in Kanfanchan, Nigeria. He is the author of *Soulside: Inquiries into Ghetto Culture and Community* and *Caymanian Politics: Structure and Style in a Changing Island Society*.

Ruth E. Hartley is currently Visiting Professorial Fellow of Human Development in the School of Social Inquiry at Murdoch University in West Australia. With Eugene L. Hartley, she is engaged in developing a program in human development and psychological studies at undergraduate and graduate levels.

Andrea S. Hayman is an attorney specializing in constitutional law.

Seymour M. Hersh is a reporter for *The New York Times* in its Washington bureau.

Barbara J. Katz is a reporter for *The National Observer*, based in Washington, D.C. Her major avocation is the feminist movement, which she believes holds hope for men as well as for women.

Rudyard Kipling, the late English poet, journalist, and novelist, was known for his works on life in India and his children's books.

Lucy Komisar's book *The Machismo Factor* is in preparation. She is the author of *The New Feminism* and *Down and Out in the U.S.A.* (a history of American welfare) and has written for *The Saturday Review, New York Magazine, The New York Times* and other publications. She also lectures.

Michael Korda was born in London, England, in 1933, and educated at Le Rosey in Switzerland, and at Magdalen College, Oxford. He served in the Royal Air Force, and moved to the U.S. in 1958. He is Vice President and Editor in Chief of Simon & Schuster, Inc., and is the author of *Male Chauvinism!* and *Power!*

Gregory K. Lehne is an Assistant Professor at Antioch College, The Human Ecology Center, Columbia, Maryland. He is interested in human development and education, and sexuality education and counseling.

Julius Lester is the author of numerous books and presently teaches at the University of Massachusetts in Amherst.

Alice Duer Miller was an American poet and novelist.

Kate Millett is also the author of *The Prostitution Papers* and *Flying*. She is a sculptor and filmmaker who lives in New York City.

Donn Pearce is now working as a detective in Florida.

Charles W. Peek is an Assistant Professor of Sociology at the University of Georgia. In addition to his interest in sex roles, he is currently pursuing research on drunken driving as a type of deviance.

Joseph H. Pleck is a psychologist affiliated with the Institute for Social Research and the Residential College, both at the University of Michigan. With Jack Sawyer he coedited *Men and Masculinity.*

F. Reif is Professor of Physics and Chairman of the Group in Science and Mathematics Education at the University of California, Berkeley.

Jack Sawyer is 44 and lives in Berkeley, California, on past earnings as a psychology professor. He works on relating mind, body, spirit, society, and his own life. He is affiliated with the Wright Institute, a social-clinical psychology graduate school. With Joseph Pleck, he coedited *Men and Masculinity.*

James F. Short, Jr., is Director of the Social Research Center and Professor of Sociology at Washington State University. He served as Director of Research for the National Commission on the Causes and Prevention of Violence, in 1968 and 1969. He was a Fellow at the Center For Advanced Study in the Behavioral Sciences and has been visiting professor at the Universities of Chicago and Hawaii, and at Stanford University.

Arthur B. Shostak is presently studying blue-collar lifestyles on an Office of Education grant in preparation for a new book (1976) on the subject. Special attention will be paid to problem-solving skills, and mental health issues in the working class.

Samuel A. Stouffer was noted for his pioneering use of research methodology in the study of social problems.

Fred L. Strodtbeck is Professor of Social Psychology in the Sociology and Behavioral Science Departments, and Director of the Social Psychology Laboratory at The University of Chicago. He is currently engaged in cross-cultural studies of sex roles and with continuing work on the interaction of families.

James Thurber, the late humorist, was the author of many books, essays, and stories, many of which deal with the "war between the sexes."

Pierre L. van den Berghe is Professor of Sociology at the University of Washington in Seattle. He specializes in stratification, race and ethnic relations, and age and gender differentiation. His research has taken him to South Africa, Kenya, Nigeria, Mexico, Guatemala and Peru.

Thorstein Veblen, the late economist, wrote *The Theory of the Leisure Class,* and other works on American industry.

Robin M. Williams, Jr., is Henry Scarborough Professor of Social Science at Cornell University, where he has been a member of the faculty since 1946. During 1974–75 he was on leave at the Center for Creative Leadership in Greensboro, North Carolina. He serves as an adviser to several scientific and professional agencies.